NE능률 영어교과서

대한민국 고등학생 **10**명 중 **4.7**명이 보는 교과서

영어 고등 교과서 점유율 1위

(7차, 2007 개정, 2009 개정, 2015 개정)

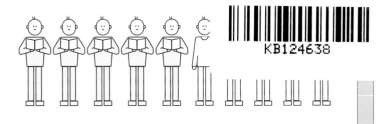

KB124638

리딩튜터

그동안 판매된
리딩튜터 1,900만 부
차곡차곡 쌓으면 19만 미터

에베레스트 21배 높이

190,000m

에베레스트 8,848m

능률보카

그동안 판매된
능률VOCA 1,100만 부

대한민국 박스오피스
**천만명을 넘은 영화
단 28개**

VO CA

그래머존

그동안 판매된 450만 부의 그래머존을 바닥에 쭉 ~ 깔면

1000km 서울 - 부산 왕복가능

서울

부산

교재 검토에 도움을 주신 선생님들

강건창 광주 살레시오중학교
강수정 인천 석정중학교
구영애 파주 금촌중학교
김민정 순천 엘린 영어교습소
김민정 파주 삼광중학교
김선미 천안 천안서여자중학교
김수연 서울 잉글리시아이 고덕캠퍼스
김수영 광주 숭일중학교
김연숙 서울 휘문중학교
김영현 광주 수피아여자중학교
김유빈(Annie) 동탄 애니원잉글리쉬
김현정 천안 광풍중학교
김혜원 인천 갈산중학교
나은진 서울 화곡중학교
노수정 서울 빌드업 영어교습소
문혜옥 시흥 은행중학교
민세원 광명 소하중학교
박인화 서울 일성여자중고등학교

박창현 광주 고려중학교
박혜숙 서울 경원중학교
반지혜 서울 대원국제중학교
방선영 광명 소하중학교
배영주 부산 이사벨중학교
배정현 서울 대명중학교
변재선 부천 부천중학교
서은조 서울 방배중학교
성수정 부산 주례여자중학교
신주희 서울 광성중학교
신희수 서울 이수중학교
안인숙 울산 현대중학교
양윤정 시흥 능곡고등학교
오영숙 서울 양강중학교
오하연 부산 인지중학교
오형기 서울 배문중학교
윤선경 서울 영국이엠학원
이수경 춘천 강원중학교

이임주 인천 만수북중학교
이정순 서울 일성여자중고등학교
이정재 파주 광탄중학교
이정희 천안 봉서중학교
이진영 울산 신정중학교
이효정 서울 신사중학교
장영진 광주 서강중학교
정찬희 광명 소하중학교
조혜진 성남 동광중학교
최문희 인천 삼산중학교
최수근(Claire) 광교 RISE 어학원
최은주 서울 등명중학교
최지예 대전 삼천중학교
최현우 창원 용원중학교
홍준기 광주 동신중학교
황나리 대전 덕명중학교

1316
LISTENING LEVEL 2

지은이	NE능률 영어교육연구소
영문교열	Curtis Thompson, Keeran Murphy, Angela Lan
디자인	닷츠
내지 일러스트	박응식, 윤병철
맥편집	김재민

Copyright©2024 by NE Neungyule, Inc.

All rights reserved. No part of this publication may be reproduced, stored in a retrieval system, or transmitted in any form or by any means, electronic, mechanical, photocopying, recording, or otherwise, without the prior permission of the copyright owner.

✖ 본 교재의 독창적인 내용에 대한 일체의 무단 전재 · 모방은 법률로 금지되어 있습니다.
✚ 파본은 구매처에서 교환 가능합니다.

Let's grow together

NE능률이
미래를
창조합니다.

건강한 배움의 고객가치를 제공하겠다는 꿈을 실현하기 위해
40년이 넘는 시간 동안 열심히 달려왔습니다.

앞으로도 끊임없는 연구와 노력을 통해
당연한 것을 멈추지 않고

고객, 기업, 직원 모두가 함께 성장하는 NE능률이 되겠습니다.

NE능률의 모든 교재가 한 곳에 - 엔이 북스

NE_Books

www.nebooks.co.kr ▼

NE능률의 유초등 교재부터 중고생 참고서,
토익·토플 수험서와 일반 영어까지!
PC는 물론 태블릿 PC, 스마트폰으로 언제 어디서나
NE능률의 교재와 다양한 학습 자료를 만나보세요.

✓ 필요한 부가 학습 자료 바로 찾기
✓ 주요 인기 교재들을 한눈에 확인
✓ 나에게 딱 맞는 교재를 찾아주는 스마트 검색
✓ 함께 보면 좋은 교재와 다음 단계 교재 추천
✓ 회원 가입, 교재 후기 작성 등 사이트 활동 시 NE Point 적립

건강한
배움의 즐거움

영어교과서 리딩튜터 능률보카 빠른독해 바른독해 수능만만 월등한 개념 수학 유형더블
NE_Build & Grow   NE_Times   NE_Kids(굿잡, 상상수프)   NE_능률 주니어랩   아이챌린지

기초부터 실전까지 중학 듣기 완성

1316

1316 LISTENING

LEVEL 2

STRUCTURE & FEATURES

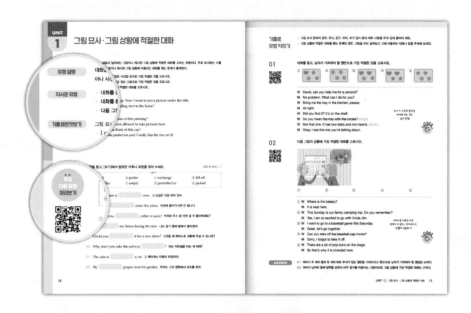

기출로 유형 익히기

기출 문제를 들어보면서 최신 출제 경향을 알 수 있습니다. 내용 파악에 도움이 되는 듣기 전략, 정답의 결정적인 근거가 되는 '정답 단서'와 오답을 유도하는 '오답 함정'을 통해 해당 유형에 대한 적응력을 키울 수 있습니다.

유형 설명 & 지시문 유형 & 기출 표현 맛보기

해당 기출 문제 유형의 전반적인 특징과 대표 지시문을 확인할 수 있습니다.
유형별 실제 기출 문장을 제시하여 해당 문제의 정답과 직결된 표현을 익힐 수 있습니다.

주요 어휘·표현 미리보기

본격적인 문제 풀이에 앞서 해당 단원에 등장할 중요한 어휘와 표현을 미리 학습할 수 있습니다.

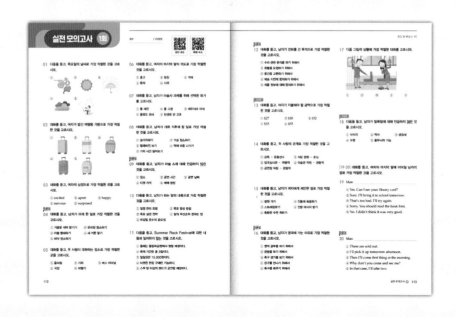

실전 모의고사

실제 중학 영어듣기 능력평가 유형을 충실히 반영한 실전 모의고사 6회분으로 문제 풀이 능력을 향상할 수 있습니다.

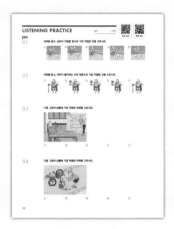

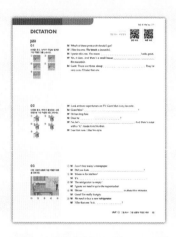

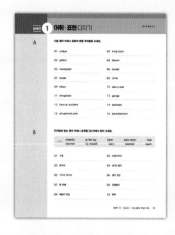

LISTENING PRACTICE

다양한 소재와 상황으로 구성된 대화 및 담화를 통해 해당 유형을 집중적으로 훈련할 수 있습니다. 단원마다 고난도 문제와 영국식 발음으로 녹음한 문제가 포함되어 있어 실전에 대한 자신감을 키울 수 있습니다.

DICTATION

주요 표현을 받아쓰면서 시험에 자주 나오는 구문을 익힐 수 있습니다. 또한, '정답 단서'와 '오답 함정'을 참고하여 학습한 내용을 확실히 점검할 수 있습니다.

어휘·표현 다지기

듣기에 등장한 어휘와 표현을 정리하고 복습할 수 있습니다.

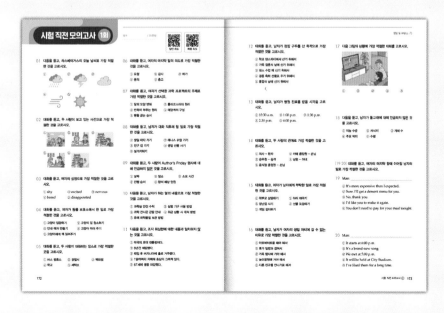

시험 직전 모의고사

실제 시험 형식으로 구성된 2회분의 모의고사로, 중학 영어듣기 능력평가 직전에 활용할 수 있습니다. 듣기 MP3 파일, Dictation, 어휘·표현 테스트지는 www.nebooks.co.kr에서 내려받을 수 있습니다.

CONTENTS

SECTION

2

실전 모의고사 &
시험 직전 모의고사

1316 LISTENING

LEVEL 2

중2 기출 문제 유형 분석

	유형	형태	단어 수 (words)	페어 수 (pairs)	2020 2회	2021 1회	2021 2회	2022 1회	2022 2회	2023 1회	계
1	그림 묘사	대화	55~79	3~4.5	1	1	1	1	1	1	6
2	심정	대화	62~67	3~4		1	1	1	1	1	5
3	특정 정보	담화	45~54		1	1	1	1	1	1	6
		대화	66~78	3.5~4	1	1	1	1	1	1	6
4	대화 장소	대화	62~79	3.5~4.5	1	1	1	1	1	1	6
5	의도	대화	57~76	3~4	1	1	1	1	1	1	6
6	한 일 · 할 일	대화	62~77	3.5~5	2	2	2	2	2	2	12
7	언급하지 않은 내용	대화	64~82	3~4	1	1	2	1	1	1	7
		담화	57~63		1	1		1	1	1	5
8	주제 · 화제	담화	54~64		1	1	1	1	1	1	6
9	내용 불일치	대화	72~77	3~4.5	2	1	1	1	1	1	7
10	목적	대화	68~78	3.5~4.5	1	1	1	1	1	1	6
11	숫자 정보	대화	65~76	4~4.5	1	1	1	1	1	1	6
12	화자 간 관계	대화	63~79	3.5~4	1	1	1	1	1	1	6
13	부탁 · 제안한 일	대화	65~80	3.5~4.5	1	1	1	1	1	1	6
14	이유	대화	67~78	4~4.5	1	1	1	1	1	1	6
15	그림 상황에 적절한 대화	대화			1	1	1	1	1	1	6
16	마지막 말에 대한 응답	대화	65~72	3.5~4.5	2	2	2	2	2	2	12
	계				20	20	20	20	20	20	

Section

1

유형 설명
UNIT 1-12

그림 묘사·그림 상황에 적절한 대화

유형 설명

대화를 듣고, 내용과 일치하는 그림이나 제시된 그림 상황에 적합한 대화를 고르는 유형이다. 주로 묘사하는 사물이나 사진, 그림을 찾거나 제시된 그림 상황에 어울리는 대화를 찾는 문제가 출제된다.

지시문 유형

· 대화를 듣고, 여자가 만든 사진첩 표지로 가장 적절한 것을 고르시오.
· 대화를 듣고, 남자가 보고 있는 그림으로 가장 적절한 것을 고르시오.
· 다음 그림의 상황에 가장 적절한 대화를 고르시오.

기출 표현 맛보기

그림 묘사

· I put the title at the top. Now I want to put a picture under the title.
· Who is this man standing next to the horse?

그림 상황에 적절한 대화

· **M** Can I take pictures of this painting?
  W Sorry. You are not allowed to take pictures here.
· **M** What do you think of this cap?
  W It just looks perfect on you! I really like the star on it!

주요 어휘·표현 미리보기

다음을 듣고, [보기]에서 알맞은 어휘나 표현을 찾아 쓰세요.   정답 및 해설 p. 2

| 보기 |
| ⓐ instead | ⓑ prefer | ⓒ exchange | ⓓ fell off |
| ⓔ shaped like | ⓕ empty | ⓖ permitted to | ⓗ picked |

01 The classroom is ＿＿＿＿＿＿ now. 그 교실은 지금 비어 있어.

02 You are not ＿＿＿＿＿＿ enter this place. 이곳에 들어가시면 안 됩니다.

03 Which do you ＿＿＿＿＿＿, coffee or juice? 커피와 주스 중 어떤 걸 더 좋아하세요?

04 I ＿＿＿＿＿＿ my horse during the race. 나는 경기 중에 말에서 떨어졌어.

05 Could you ＿＿＿＿＿＿ it for a new dress? 그것을 새 원피스로 교환해 주실 수 있나요?

06 Why don't you take the subway ＿＿＿＿＿＿? 대신 지하철을 타는 게 어때?

07 The cake is ＿＿＿＿＿＿ a car. 그 케이크는 자동차 모양이야.

08 We ＿＿＿＿＿＿ grapes from his garden. 우리는 그의 정원에서 포도를 땄어.

· 그림 묘사 문제의 경우, 무늬, 문구, 위치, 추가 장식 등의 세부 사항을 주의 깊게 들어야 해요.
· 그림 상황에 적절한 대화를 묻는 문제의 경우, 그림을 미리 살펴보고 그에 어울리는 대화나 말을 추측해 보세요.

01

대화를 듣고, 남자가 가져와야 할 쟁반으로 가장 적절한 것을 고르시오.

①  ②  ③  ④  ⑤

W David, can you help me for a second?
M No problem. What can I do for you?
W Bring me the tray in the kitchen, please.
M All right.
W Did you find it? It's on the shelf.
M Do you mean the tray with the circles? 오답 함정
W Not that one. It has two stars and two hearts. 정답 단서
M Okay, I see the one you're talking about.

남자가 언급한 함정을
제거해 보는 것도
좋은 방법!

02

다음 그림의 상황에 가장 적절한 대화를 고르시오.

① ② ③ ④ ⑤

① **W** Where is the bakery?
　M It is near here.
② **W** This Sunday is our family camping trip. Do you remember?
　M Yes, I am so excited to go with Uncle Jim.
③ **W** I want to go to a baseball game this Saturday.
　M Great, let's go together.
④ **W** Can you take off the baseball cap inside?
　M Sorry. I forgot to take it off.
⑤ **W** There are a lot of pop stars on the stage.
　M So that's why it is crowded now.

키워드를 이용한 오답
선택지가 있으니 단어보다는
상황에 집중하자!

ANSWER

01 여자가 두 개의 별과 두 개의 하트 무늬가 있는 쟁반을 가져오라고 했으므로 남자가 가져와야 할 쟁반은 ④이다.
02 여자가 남자와 함께 달력을 보면서 야구 경기를 떠올리는 그림이므로 그림 상황에 가장 적절한 대화는 ③이다.

LISTENING PRACTICE

일반 속도   빠른 속도

01 대화를 듣고, 남자가 구입할 엽서로 가장 적절한 것을 고르시오.

①    ②    ③    ④   ⑤

02 대화를 듣고, 여자가 좋아하는 슈퍼 영웅으로 가장 적절한 것을 고르시오.

①   ②   ③   ④   ⑤

03 다음 그림의 상황에 가장 적절한 대화를 고르시오.

①   ②   ③   ④   ⑤

04 다음 그림의 상황에 가장 적절한 대화를 고르시오.

①   ②   ③   ④   ⑤

05

대화를 듣고, 남자가 사는 집의 현관문으로 가장 적절한 것을 고르시오.

①   ②   ③   ④   ⑤

고난도

06

대화를 듣고, 두 사람이 보고 있는 광고로 가장 적절한 것을 고르시오.

①   ②   ③   ④   ⑤

07

다음 그림의 상황에 가장 적절한 대화를 고르시오.

①   ②   ③   ④   ⑤

08

다음 그림의 상황에 가장 적절한 대화를 고르시오.

①   ②   ③   ④   ⑤

09 대화를 듣고, 남자의 책상으로 가장 적절한 것을 고르시오.

① ② ③ ④ ⑤

10 대화를 듣고, 여자가 만든 케이크로 가장 적절한 것을 고르시오.

① ② ③ ④ ⑤

고난도

11 다음 그림의 상황에 가장 적절한 대화를 고르시오.

① ② ③ ④ ⑤

12 다음 그림의 상황에 가장 적절한 대화를 고르시오.

① ② ③ ④ ⑤

DICTATION

정답 단서 오답 함정

 일반 속도   빠른 속도

01

대화를 듣고, 남자가 구입할 엽서로
가장 적절한 것을 고르시오.

① ②

③ ④

⑤

M Which of these postcards should I get?

W I like this one. The beach is beautiful.

M I prefer this one. The moon _____ _____ _____ looks great.

W Yes, it does. And there's a small house _____ _____ _____ the mountain.

M Look! There are three sheep _____ _____ _____. They're very cute. I'll take that one.

02

대화를 듣고, 여자가 좋아하는 슈퍼
영웅으로 가장 적절한 것을 고르시오.

W Look at those superheroes on TV. Giant Man is my favorite.

M Giant Man? _____ _____ _____ _____?

W He has long hair.

M Does he _____ _____ _____?

W No, he's _____ _____ _____ _____. And there's a star with a "G" inside it on his shirt.

M I see him now. I like his style.

03

다음 그림의 상황에 가장 적절한 대화
를 고르시오.

① ② ③ ④ ⑤

① **W** I can't find today's newspaper.

  M Did you look _____ _____ _____ _____?

② **W** Where is the kitchen?

  M It's _____ _____ _____ _____ _____.

③ **W** The refrigerator is empty!

  M I guess we need to go to the supermarket.

④ **W** Dinner _____ _____ _____ in about five minutes.

  M Great! I'm really hungry.

⑤ **W** We need to buy a new refrigerator.

  M I like that one. Is it _____ _____?

04

다음 그림의 상황에 가장 적절한 대화를 고르시오.

① ② ③ ④ ⑤

① **M** Can I borrow your bicycle?

    W Sure. It's _____ _____ _____.

② **M** The doctor is ready to see you.

    W Finally! I've been waiting too long.

③ **M** What happened to your elbow?

    W I _____ _____ _____ yesterday.

④ **M** Did you _____ _____ _____ _____?

    W Yes, and I hurt my knee.

⑤ **M** Sorry, I can't go bike riding with you.

    W Okay, I'll _____ _____ _____.

05

대화를 듣고, 남자가 사는 집의 현관문으로 가장 적절한 것을 고르시오.

①   ②

③   ④

⑤

M This is my apartment. Do you want to come inside?

W Sure. I really like your front door. It _____ _____.

M Yes, it is. My favorite part is _____ _____ _____ _____ _____.

W Yes. It's _____ _____ _____ _____ _____ _____. And your apartment number is right below it.

M That's right. And my brother put a sun-shaped sticker _____ _____ _____.

W It looks really cheerful!

06

대화를 듣고, 두 사람이 보고 있는 광고로 가장 적절한 것을 고르시오.

①   ②

③   ④

⑤

W Look at this advertisement. It's for an amusement park.

M Is that the name of the amusement park _____ _____ _____ _____?

W Yes, Fantasy Planet. And that's the park's mascot standing in front of a castle.

M It looks like a big rabbit _____ _____ _____.

W Yes! Her name is Wendy Rabbit. Look at the two little kids standing next to her.

M They're _____ _____ _____ and smiling.

W They look so happy. We should go there someday!

M Sure! It looks like a fun place.

07

다음 그림의 상황에 가장 적절한 대화를 고르시오.

① ② ③ ④ ⑤

① **W** What do you think about this painting?
   M I think it's unique.
② **W** You can't _____ _____ _____ in the gallery.
   M Oh. I'm sorry.
③ **W** _____ _____, little boy. Where did you see your mother last?
   M I was with her in the lobby.
④ **W** You _____ _____ _____ _____ take pictures in the gallery. The flash will harm the paintings.
   M Then can I take a picture _____ _____ _____?
⑤ **W** It is so beautiful! Do you know who painted this one?
   M I have no idea.

08

다음 그림의 상황에 가장 적절한 대화를 고르시오.

① ② ③ ④ ⑤

① **W** I climbed this tree, but I can't _____ _____ _____.
   M I'll come up and help you.
② **W** Do we have any more apples?
   M Sorry, but I think we ate them all already.
③ **W** I want to _____ _____ _____, but I can't reach it.
   M Wait here! I'll go get a ladder.
④ **W** Eating fruit and vegetables is good for your health.
   M I know, but I _____ _____ _____ fast food.
⑤ **W** Good morning! What can I get for you today?
   M I'd like some milk and _____ _____ _____ _____ _____, please.

09

대화를 듣고, 남자의 책상으로 가장 적절한 것을 고르시오.

① ② ③ ④ ⑤

M Come in my room _____ _____ _____. What do you think of my new desk?
W I like it. There are _____ _____ _____.
M Yes. There are three _____ _____ _____. And I put my computer on it.
W I see. But why didn't you put a desk lamp on it too?
M I don't think I really need one.

10

대화를 듣고, 여자가 만든 케이크로
가장 적절한 것을 고르시오.

①   ②

③   ④

⑤

W Happy birthday, Arthur! This is for you.

M Thanks! Wow, this cake looks great.

W I _____ _____ _____. Do you like it? I know you love blueberries.

M I sure do! This _____ _____ _____ _____ is so cute.

W I wanted to write "Happy Birthday" at first, but it was _____ _____ _____ _____. So I drew that instead.

M Well, the cake looks delicious. Can I taste it now?

W Sure. Go ahead.

M Hmm… *[pause]* This is amazing! I never knew you were _____ _____ _____ _____.

11

다음 그림의 상황에 가장 적절한 대화
를 고르시오.

① ② ③ ④ ⑤

① **M** Oh no. There is _____ _____ _____ _____ _____.

W Oh, you should go to the customer service center.

② **M** I got you a shirt. Do you like it?

W Oh, I love it. Thank you!

③ **M** I need to _____ _____ _____ for another one.

W Do you want me to come with you?

④ **M** I'd like to _____ _____ _____. There is a hole in it.

W Sure. Could you show me the receipt?

⑤ **M** I don't think _____ _____ _____ _____.

W All right. How about this blue shirt?

12

다음 그림의 상황에 가장 적절한 대화
를 고르시오.

① ② ③ ④ ⑤

① **W** How can I _____ _____ _____ _____ _____?

M Go straight and turn right at the corner.

② **W** The road is packed with cars. What should we do?

M We'd better _____ _____ _____, or we'll be late.

③ **W** I'm sorry. There was a lot of traffic.

M That's okay. Please take a seat.

④ **W** Do you want me to _____ _____ _____ _____ _____?

M No thanks. I'll take a taxi.

⑤ **W** Where should we _____ _____ _____?

M I don't know. There aren't any parking spots here.

A

다음 영어 어휘나 표현의 뜻을 우리말로 쓰세요.

01 unique

02 living room

03 gallery

04 drawer

05 newspaper

06 receipt

07 ladder

08 climb

09 elbow

10 take a seat

11 refrigerator

12 garage

13 have an accident

14 postcard

15 amusement park

16 advertisement

B

우리말에 맞는 영어 어휘나 표현을 [보기]에서 찾아 쓰세요.

	보기	cheerful	at the top	harm	calm down	hole
		hammer	by oneself	carry	talented	reach

01 구멍

02 손상시키다

03 혼자서

04 (손이) 닿다

05 가지고 다니다

06 생기 있는

07 맨 위에

08 진정하다

09 재능이 있는

10 망치

심정·의도

대화를 듣고, 화자가 느끼는 심정이나 말하는 의도를 파악하는 유형이다. 대화 상황을 고려하여 화자의 전반적인 심정이나 마지막 말에 담긴 의도를 고르는 문제가 출제된다.

지시문 유형

· 대화를 듣고, 여자의 심정으로 가장 적절한 것을 고르시오.
· 대화를 듣고, 남자의 마지막 말의 의도로 가장 적절한 것을 고르시오.

기출 표현 맛보기

심정
· It's the first snow this year. I've waited so long for this. (excited)
· I hope it's nothing serious. (worried)

의도
· I'm sure you'll get on the team next time. Cheer up! (격려)
· You should not give our snacks to animals. (충고)

주요
어휘·표현
미리보기

다음을 듣고, [보기]에서 알맞은 어휘나 표현을 찾아 쓰세요.   정답 및 해설 p. 5

───────	보기	───────
ⓐ the peak season	ⓑ stayed up late	ⓒ pay off	ⓓ vote for
ⓔ turn down	ⓕ bothering	ⓖ the rest	ⓗ unforgettable

01 When is _____ for visiting Spain? 스페인을 방문하는 성수기는 언제야?

02 I'm sorry for _____ you. 신경 쓰이게 해서 미안해.

03 We will _____ a new president soon. 우리는 곧 새 대통령에게 투표할 거야.

04 Please _____ the volume. 음량 좀 낮춰 주세요.

05 He lost _____ of the money there. 그는 그 돈의 나머지를 거기서 잃어버렸어.

06 They _____ yesterday. 그들은 어제 늦게까지 깨어 있었어.

07 Your effort will _____. 네 노력은 결실을 맺을 거야.

08 I received an _____ gift from my friend. 나는 친구로부터 잊지 못할 선물을 받았어.

- 심정을 추론하는 문제의 경우, 먼저 지시문을 읽고 누구의 심정을 골라야 하는지 파악하세요.
- 심정을 나타내는 선택지가 영어로 출제되므로 관련 어휘를 미리 익혀 두는 것이 좋아요.
- 기쁨, 슬픔, 놀람, 긴장, 분노 등 감정을 나타내는 어구나 감탄사, 화자의 어조에 유의하며 들어보세요.
- 의도를 파악하는 문제의 경우, 대체로 대화의 마지막 부분에 단서가 드러나므로 후반부를 들을 때 더욱 집중하세요!

01

대화를 듣고, 남자의 심정으로 가장 적절한 것을 고르시오.

① bored　　　　② happy　　　　③ nervous
④ proud　　　　⑤ satisfied

W　Hi, Junho. You don't look well. What's the matter?
M　Well... I have an English speaking contest tomorrow.
W　Don't worry! You practiced a lot. 오답 함정
M　Yeah... But I get afraid when I speak in front of many people. 정답 단서
W　You should take a deep breath before you start. You can do it.
M　I will try my best, but this contest makes me uncomfortable.

영어 말하기 대회를 하루 앞둔 남자가 여자와 대화를 나누고 있네.

02

대화를 듣고, 여자의 마지막 말의 의도로 가장 적절한 것을 고르시오.

① 사과　　　② 충고　　　③ 비난　　　④ 동의　　　⑤ 감사

M　Hey, Sujin. I'm excited about our field trip to Star Amusement Park tomorrow. Why don't we go together?
W　Sure, Ryan. Do you want to meet in front of the school at 8?
M　Okay. How are we going to get there from school?
W　I'm thinking of going there by bus. The 111 bus goes there.
M　How about taking the subway? There might be heavy traffic in the morning. Taking the subway will be faster than the bus.
W　You're right. I agree with you.

남자가 교통 체증을 우려해 버스 대신 지하철을 탈 것을 제안하고 있어.

ANSWER

01 남자가 많은 사람들 앞에서 말하는 것이 두렵고 대회 때문에 마음이 편치 않다고 말하고 있으므로, 남자의 심정으로 ③이 알맞다.

02 지하철을 타는 것이 버스보다 빠를 것이라는 남자의 말에 여자가 동의하고 있으므로 여자의 마지막 말의 의도로 ④가 알맞다.

01 대화를 듣고, 남자의 심정으로 가장 적절한 것을 고르시오.

① relaxed   ② nervous   ③ satisfied
④ angry   ⑤ proud

02 대화를 듣고, 여자의 심정으로 가장 적절한 것을 고르시오.

① curious   ② satisfied   ③ worried
④ disappointed   ⑤ surprised

03 대화를 듣고, 여자의 심정으로 가장 적절한 것을 고르시오.

① happy   ② shy   ③ worried
④ calm   ⑤ bored

04 대화를 듣고, 여자의 마지막 말의 의도로 가장 적절한 것을 고르시오.

① 격려   ② 충고   ③ 사과
④ 비난   ⑤ 축하

05 대화를 듣고, 남자의 마지막 말의 의도로 가장 적절한 것을 고르시오.

① 허가   ② 비난   ③ 거절
④ 충고   ⑤ 요청

고난도

06 대화를 듣고, 남자의 심정으로 가장 적절한 것을 고르시오.

① thankful　　　② excited　　　③ regretful
④ nervous　　　⑤ surprised

07 대화를 듣고, 여자의 심정으로 가장 적절한 것을 고르시오.

① relieved　　　② joyful　　　③ jealous
④ angry　　　⑤ worried

08 대화를 듣고, 남자의 심정으로 가장 적절한 것을 고르시오.

① nervous　　　② excited　　　③ bored
④ surprised　　　⑤ scared

고난도

09 대화를 듣고, 여자의 마지막 말의 의도로 가장 적절한 것을 고르시오.

① 설득　　　② 격려　　　③ 동의
④ 허가　　　⑤ 충고

10 대화를 듣고, 남자의 마지막 말의 의도로 가장 적절한 것을 고르시오.

① 제안　　　② 사과　　　③ 위로
④ 승낙　　　⑤ 충고

DICTATION

정답 단서 오답 함정

일반 속도

빠른 속도

01

대화를 듣고, 남자의 심정으로 가장 적절한 것을 고르시오.
① relaxed ② nervous
③ satisfied ④ angry
⑤ proud

[Telephone rings.]

W Hello, Mama's Pizza. May I help you?

M Yes. I ordered a pizza about an hour ago, but it _____ _____ _____ yet.

W Let me check. Can I _____ _____ _____?

M It's 365 Royal Street.

W Unfortunately, it looks like we _____ _____ _____ and forgot about your order.

M You're kidding. My whole family is waiting.

W I'm terribly sorry. We'll deliver it _____ _____ _____ _____.

02

대화를 듣고, 여자의 심정으로 가장 적절한 것을 고르시오.
① curious ② satisfied
③ worried ④ disappointed
⑤ surprised

M How was your vacation? You wanted to go to Italy, didn't you?

W Yes, I really wanted to. But I couldn't go.

M Why not?

W Summer is _____ _____ _____ in Italy, so flights were too expensive.

M I'm sorry to hear that.

W No, it was okay. I went to China instead. And _____ _____ _____!

M Really?

W Yes! I _____ _____ _____ _____ _____, and the Great Wall was terrific.

03

대화를 듣고, 여자의 심정으로 가장 적절한 것을 고르시오.
① happy ② shy
③ worried ④ calm
⑤ bored

M Why are you smiling, Gina? Do you have good news?

W I _____ _____ _____ _____ my mom.

M What did she say?

W She said that she finally _____ _____! She has been waiting for this for a long time.

M That's wonderful! I'm glad her _____ _____ _____ _____ _____.

W Me too. She and I are going out to dinner tonight to celebrate.

04

대화를 듣고, 여자의 마지막 말의 의
도로 가장 적절한 것을 고르시오.

① 격려　　　② 충고
③ 사과　　　④ 비난
⑤ 축하

W Hi, Mike. What are you carrying?

M They're posters. They say "Vote for Mike for School President!"

W That's great. Are you _____ _____ _____?

M No, I'm taking them down. I can't _____ _____ _____.

W Why do you say that?

M Because Briana is also running for president. She's more popular than me.

W That doesn't mean you can't win. You still _____ _____ _____!

05

대화를 듣고, 남자의 마지막 말의 의
도로 가장 적절한 것을 고르시오.

① 허가　　　② 비난
③ 거절　　　④ 충고
⑤ 요청

M Jenny, why don't you _____ _____ _____ _____?

W Sorry, I couldn't hear you. What did you say?

M I asked you to turn down the volume.

W Why? I'm using my earphones. You can't hear the music.

M Actually, I can hear it. That means it _____ _____ _____ _____.

W Sorry, I didn't know _____ _____ _____ _____.

M It's not. I'm just _____ _____ _____ _____. Loud music can damage them.

06

대화를 듣고, 남자의 심정으로 가장
적절한 것을 고르시오.

① thankful　② excited
③ regretful　④ nervous
⑤ surprised

W How was your class today?

M Actually, it didn't _____ _____ _____.

W Why? What happened?

M I overslept, so I was late.

W Oh no! What did you do last night?

M I stayed up late playing computer games. I couldn't stop!

W That was a big mistake.

M I know. What's worse, I _____ _____ _____ _____. I shouldn't have stayed up late.

W Well, just make sure you don't do it again.

M I won't. I have definitely _____ _____ _____.

07

대화를 듣고, 여자의 심정으로 가장
적절한 것을 고르시오.

① relieved　② joyful
③ jealous　④ angry
⑤ worried

M Hey, Anne. What are you doing?

W I'm just thinking about _____ _____ _____.

M Really? What would you like to be?

W I'd like to be a French teacher, but my French isn't good enough.

M _____ _____ _____. It will improve.

W I hope so. I really like French.

M Don't give up. You'll _____ _____ _____ in no time.

W I don't know. I still have a long way to go.

대화를 듣고, 남자의 심정으로 가장
적절한 것을 고르시오.

① nervous   ② excited
③ bored   ④ surprised
⑤ scared

W Hi, Max. Why aren't you at school today?

M It's the anniversary of my school's founding, so all the students and teachers
_____ _____ _____ _____.

W Oh, that's nice. What are you going to do?

M I have _____ _____ _____. First, I'm going to watch my
favorite horror movies. Then I'll go to a baseball game with John this evening.

W Sounds fun! I wish _____ _____ _____ _____.

고난도

09

대화를 듣고, 여자의 마지막 말의 의
도로 가장 적절한 것을 고르시오.

① 설득   ② 격려
③ 동의   ④ 허가
⑤ 충고

W Did you go to the school's soccer game yesterday?

M Yes! It was so exciting. Were you there?

W Yes, I was. I didn't expect our school to win. The other team was _____
_____ _____ _____!

M I know. Everyone was really upset.

W Yes. Our team _____ _____ _____ _____. I hate to see
them lose.

M Fortunately, they didn't!

W That's right! Our team _____ _____ _____ at the end of the
game.

M It was so exciting when they scored the winning goal. It was _____
_____ _____.

W You can say that again!

10

대화를 듣고, 남자의 마지막 말의 의
도로 가장 적절한 것을 고르시오.

① 제안   ② 사과
③ 위로   ④ 승낙
⑤ 충고

M Thanks for helping me with my homework, Hanna.

W No problem. So, do you _____ _____ _____ for the rest of
the day?

M I'm going to meet Sam and Erica at a café.

W Oh! That sounds like _____ _____ _____ _____.

M How about you? What are you going to do?

W Nothing. I'll probably just go home and watch TV.

M Why don't you _____ _____ _____ _____?

A

다음 영어 어휘나 표현의 뜻을 우리말로 쓰세요.

01 join

02 whole

03 expect

04 terribly

05 improve

06 terrific

07 election

08 give up

09 career

10 president

11 damage

12 lose

13 relaxed

14 oversleep

15 expert

16 satisfied

B

우리말에 맞는 영어 어휘나 표현을 [보기]에서 찾아 쓰세요.

| 보기 | run for | lead | make sure | go well | make a mistake |
| | get promoted | score | what's worse | in no time | as soon as possible |

01 승진하다

02 반드시 (~하도록) 하다

03 잘 되어가다

04 곧

05 실수하다

06 설상가상으로

07 득점하다

08 앞서다

09 가능한 한 빨리

10 ~에 출마하다

유형 설명

대화를 듣고, 화자가 과거에 한 일이나 앞으로 할 일을 파악하는 유형이다. 주로 특정 시점에 한 일이나 대화 직후에 할 일을 묻는 문제가 출제된다.

지시문 유형

- 대화를 듣고, 여자가 아트센터에서 한 일로 가장 적절한 것을 고르시오.
- 대화를 듣고, 여자가 점심시간에 한 일로 가장 적절한 것을 고르시오.
- 대화를 듣고, 남자가 대화 직후에 할 일로 가장 적절한 것을 고르시오.
- 대화를 듣고, 두 사람이 대화 직후에 할 일로 가장 적절한 것을 고르시오.

기출표현맛보기

한 일

- I drew a scene from my favorite book on a cup.
- I went to the class farm to water the tomatoes.

할 일

- Let's go to the teachers' office now.
- We have kimchi, but no eggs at home. You should go and buy some.

주요 어휘·표현 미리보기

다음을 듣고, [보기]에서 알맞은 어휘나 표현을 찾아 쓰세요.   정답 및 해설 p. 8

| 보기 |
| ⓐ had a picnic | ⓑ come over to | ⓒ hard work | ⓓ answer |
| ⓔ hurts | ⓕ a part-time job | ⓖ stick to | ⓗ made a reservation |

01 We'll _____ the plan. 우리는 계획을 고수할 거야.

02 I have a headache. It really _____. 나 두통이 있어. 정말 아파.

03 My family _____ last Sunday. 우리 가족은 지난 일요일에 소풍을 갔어.

04 I'm looking for _____. 나는 아르바이트를 구하고 있어.

05 Building houses is _____. 집을 짓는 것은 힘든 일이야.

06 I couldn't _____ the question. 나는 질문에 답할 수가 없었어.

07 We _____ online. 우리는 온라인으로 예약했어.

08 Will you _____ my house before the concert? 콘서트 가기 전에 우리 집에 들를래?

28

기출로 유형 익히기

- 먼저 지시문을 읽고 누가 언제 한 일인지, 혹은 누가 언제 할 일인지 확인한 후 들으세요.
- 지시문과 다른 시점의 일, 상대방이 한 일이나 할 일이 함정으로 등장하므로 주의하세요!

01

대화를 듣고, 여자가 과학의 날에 한 일로 가장 적절한 것을 고르시오.

① 3D 영화 보기   ② 물 폭탄 만들기   ③ 자석 원리 실험하기
④ 에너지 절약 포스터 그리기   ⑤ 나무젓가락 비행기 만들기

W   That was a great science day! Did you have fun?

M   Of course. I made water bombs. 오답 함정

W   Nice. I wanted to watch a 3D movie but I couldn't.

M   That's too bad. What did you do then?

W   I built airplanes out of wooden chopsticks instead. 정답 단서

M   Did you like it?

W   Yeah, it was really fun.

M   Great! I'd like to make chopstick airplanes next year.

두 사람이 과학의 날에 한 일과 하고 싶었던 일에 대해 말하고 있어.

02

대화를 듣고, 남자가 대화 직후에 할 일로 가장 적절한 것을 고르시오.

① 식탁 닦기   ② 설거지하기   ③ 접시 꺼내기
④ 딸기잼 가져오기   ⑤ 팬케이크 만들기

M   Good morning, Mom. It smells so good. What are you making?

W   Good morning, Sean. I am making some pancakes for breakfast.

M   Wow, they look so great. You know pancakes are my favorite food for breakfast. I just want some strawberry jam on them.

W   It's already on the table. Can you take out some dishes?

M   All right. I'll get them right away.

요리 중인 여자가 남자에게 뭔가를 부탁하는 내용이야. 여자가 하고 있는 일과 남자가 할 일을 혼동하지 말자.

ANSWER

01 여자는 3D 영화를 보는 대신 나무젓가락 비행기를 만들었다고 했으므로 여자가 과학의 날에 한 일로 ⑤가 알맞다.

02 여자가 남자에게 접시를 꺼내 달라고 부탁했으므로 남자가 대화 직후에 할 일로 ③이 알맞다.

LISTENING PRACTICE

일반 속도

빠른 속도

01

대화를 듣고, 남자가 지난 주말에 한 일로 가장 적절한 것을 고르시오.

① 놀이공원 가기　　　② 병문안 가기　　　③ 패러글라이딩하기
④ 소풍 가기　　　　　⑤ 올림픽 경기 보기

02

대화를 듣고, 여자가 어제 한 일로 가장 적절한 것을 고르시오.

① 친구 만나기　　　　② 수학 숙제하기　　　③ 정원일 돕기
④ 휴대전화 새로 구입하기　　⑤ 할머니 병문안 가기

03

대화를 듣고, 남자가 점심시간에 한 일로 가장 적절한 것을 고르시오.

① 휴대전화 수리받기　　② 스파게티 요리하기　　③ 새 롤러스케이트 사기
④ 롤러스케이트 타기　　⑤ 친구 만나기

04

대화를 듣고, 두 사람이 대화 직후에 할 일로 가장 적절한 것을 고르시오.

① 낚시 가기　　　　　② 준비물 목록 작성하기　　③ 캠핑용품 구입하기
④ 등산 가기　　　　　⑤ 여행 일정 짜기

고난도
05

대화를 듣고, 남자가 대화 직후에 할 일로 가장 적절한 것을 고르시오.

① 강연 참석하기　　　② 영화 보러 가기　　　③ 친구 집 방문하기
④ 아르바이트하러 가기　　⑤ 영화표 예매하기

06

대화를 듣고, 여자가 어제 한 일로 가장 적절한 것을 고르시오.

① 태권도 수업 듣기   ② 우체국 봉사활동하기   ③ 댄스 수업 듣기
④ 미술학원 등록하기   ⑤ 친구와 운동하기

고난도
07

대화를 듣고, 남자가 오전에 한 일로 가장 적절한 것을 고르시오.

① 수영하기   ② 페인트칠하기   ③ 축구하기
④ 친구 집 가기   ⑤ 그림 그리기

08

대화를 듣고, 여자가 대화 직후에 할 일로 가장 적절한 것을 고르시오.

① 설거지하기   ② 숙제하기   ③ 컴퓨터 게임하기
④ 엄마 마중 나가기   ⑤ 분리수거 돕기

09

대화를 듣고, 남자가 대화 직후에 할 일로 가장 적절한 것을 고르시오.

① 기타 수업 가기   ② 새 유니폼 구입하기   ③ 경기 일정 변경하기
④ 축구 유니폼 세탁하기   ⑤ 축구 경기장 가기

10

대화를 듣고, 여자가 대화 직후에 할 일로 가장 적절한 것을 고르시오.

① 저녁 준비하기   ② 약속 시각 변경하기   ③ 치과 예약하기
④ 칫솔 구입하기   ⑤ 식당 예약 취소하기

DICTATION

정답 단서 오답 함정

일반 속도

빠른 속도

01

대화를 듣고, 남자가 지난 주말에 한 일로 가장 적절한 것을 고르시오.

① 놀이공원 가기
② 병문안 가기
③ 패러글라이딩하기
④ 소풍 가기
⑤ 올림픽 경기 보기

M Hey, Ann. Did you _____ _____ _____ at Olympic Park last weekend?
W Well, I wanted to, but I couldn't.
M Why not? The weather was perfect!
W David _____ _____ _____, so we decided to go next weekend instead. What did you do last weekend?
M I went paragliding in Danyang.
W Wow! That sounds amazing! _____ _____ _____?
M Not at all. I love extreme sports. You should come with me next time.

02

대화를 듣고, 여자가 어제 한 일로 가장 적절한 것을 고르시오.

① 친구 만나기
② 수학 숙제하기
③ 정원일 돕기
④ 휴대전화 새로 구입하기
⑤ 할머니 병문안 가기

M I called you yesterday, but _____ _____ _____.
W Did you? I didn't have my phone with me. Why did you call?
M I _____ _____ _____ about our math homework.
W Oh, sorry! I was helping my grandmother in her garden.
M That's okay. Mike _____ _____ _____ _____.
W I'm glad to hear that. Mike always knows the answers!

03

대화를 듣고, 남자가 점심시간에 한 일로 가장 적절한 것을 고르시오.

① 휴대전화 수리받기
② 스파게티 요리하기
③ 새 롤러스케이트 사기
④ 롤러스케이트 타기
⑤ 친구 만나기

M I'm so hungry!
W Didn't you have lunch?
M No, I didn't _____ _____ _____. I broke my phone yesterday while I was roller-skating.
W That's too bad. So did you _____ _____ _____ during your lunch break?
M Yes, I did. Did you eat?
W Yes, I went to an Italian restaurant with Brian.
M I see. I think I'll _____ _____ _____ _____.

04

대화를 듣고, 두 사람이 대화 직후에 할 일로 가장 적절한 것을 고르시오.

① 낚시 가기
② 준비물 목록 작성하기
③ 캠핑용품 구입하기
④ 등산 가기
⑤ 여행 일정 짜기

W Do you _____ _____ _____ for this weekend?
M Not really. How about you?
W My sister and I are _____ _____. I can't wait!
M That's great!
W Yes. We'll go hiking and fishing. And we'll have barbecues at night.
M Wow! That sounds fun. But _____ _____ _____ _____ _____ that you need to bring.
W Yes. A tent, a flashlight… I think I need to make a list.
M I'll help you make one. Give me a pen!

05

대화를 듣고, 남자가 대화 직후에 할
일로 가장 적절한 것을 고르시오.

① 강연 참석하기
② 영화 보러 가기
③ 친구 집 방문하기
④ 아르바이트하러 가기
⑤ 영화표 예매하기

W My friends and I are going to a science lecture this afternoon. Why don't you join us?

M I'm afraid I can't. I have to _____ _____ _____ _____ _____ now.

W That's too bad. Do you work tomorrow, too?

M No, I don't. I _____ _____ _____ _____.

W Really? Then why don't we all _____ _____ _____ _____ tomorrow?

M That sounds good.

W Let's meet at my apartment and then go to the cinema together.

M Sure.

06

대화를 듣고, 여자가 어제 한 일로 가
장 적절한 것을 고르시오.

① 태권도 수업 듣기
② 우체국 봉사활동하기
③ 댄스 수업 듣기
④ 미술학원 등록하기
⑤ 친구와 운동하기

W Are you still studying taekwondo, Matt?

M Yes, I am. How about you?

W No, I quit last week. I decided to _____ _____ _____ instead.

M Really? _____ _____ _____ _____?

W Yes, the first lesson was last night. I enjoyed it a lot.

M Where are the lessons held?

W In a studio above the post office. Do you want to join me?

M No thanks! I'll _____ _____ taekwondo.

07

대화를 듣고, 남자가 오전에 한 일로
가장 적절한 것을 고르시오.

① 수영하기 ② 페인트칠하기
③ 축구하기 ④ 친구 집 가기
⑤ 그림 그리기

[Cell phone rings.]

M Hello?

W Hello, Henry. This is Amy. Do you want to _____ _____ _____ _____ _____ with me?

M No thanks. I'm too tired.

W Why? Did you play soccer before lunch?

M No, I was home all morning.

W If you rested all morning, _____ _____ _____ _____ _____?

M I didn't rest. I painted my room.

W Oh! _____ _____ _____ _____ _____.

M Yes, it was. But my room looks really good!

W Great! You can show me when I come over to your house.

08

대화를 듣고, 여자가 대화 직후에 할
일로 가장 적절한 것을 고르시오.

① 설거지하기
② 숙제하기
③ 컴퓨터 게임하기
④ 엄마 마중 나가기
⑤ 분리수거 돕기

M What are you doing, Jenny?

W I'm playing a computer game.

M You play games too often.

W No, I don't. I _____ _____ _____, so I just started playing now.

M Your mother _____ _____ _____ _____ since she got home from work. Why don't you help her?

W All right. What is she doing now?

M She is busy _____ _____ _____.

W Okay, I'll help her.

09

대화를 듣고, 남자가 대화 직후에 할
일로 가장 적절한 것을 고르시오.

① 기타 수업 가기
② 새 유니폼 구입하기
③ 경기 일정 변경하기
④ 축구 유니폼 세탁하기
⑤ 축구 경기장 가기

M Oh no! The school changed my soccer team's schedule.

W Did they? When's your next game?

M It _____ _____ _____ be next week, but they changed it to tomorrow!

W That's fine. You don't have guitar lessons tomorrow, do you?

M No. But my uniform is dirty. It's _____ _____ _____ from the last game.

W Oh, you can't wear it like that.

M No. I need to _____ _____ _____ _____.

W All right. Go do that now.

10

대화를 듣고, 여자가 대화 직후에 할
일로 가장 적절한 것을 고르시오.

① 저녁 준비하기
② 약속 시각 변경하기
③ 치과 예약하기
④ 칫솔 구입하기
⑤ 식당 예약 취소하기

M I need to _____ _____ _____.

W What's wrong? Do you have a toothache?

M Yes, I do. _____ _____ _____. I don't think I can go to dinner with you tonight.

W Don't worry about that.

M But didn't you _____ _____ _____ at a nice restaurant?

W I did, but _____ _____ _____ _____ _____. You need to see your dentist as soon as possible.

M You're right. Thanks for understanding.

A

다음 영어 어휘나 표현의 뜻을 우리말로 쓰세요.

01 scared

02 math

03 quit

04 lecture

05 dirty

06 dentist

07 toothache

08 garden

09 go for a swim

10 cancel

11 do housework

12 go hiking

13 separate

14 flashlight

15 right away

16 trash

B

우리말에 맞는 영어 어휘나 표현을 [보기]에서 찾아 쓰세요.

| 보기 | mud | make a list | chance | day off | get ~ fixed |
| | while | take a lesson | extreme | break | have ~ delivered |

01 진흙

02 ~하는 동안에

03 고장 내다

04 ~을 수리받다

05 목록을 만들다

06 수업을 듣다

07 기회

08 (근무 또는 일을) 쉬는 날

09 극한의

10 ~을 배달시키다

대화 장소·숫자 정보

유형 설명

대화를 듣고, 대화가 이루어지는 장소나 시각, 금액 등의 숫자 정보를 파악하는 유형이다. 대화의 상황을 통해 대화가 이루어지는 장소를 파악하는 문제와, 특정한 시각이나 지불해야 할 금액을 고르는 문제가 출제된다.

지시문 유형

· 대화를 듣고, 두 사람이 대화하는 장소로 가장 적절한 곳을 고르시오.
· 대화를 듣고, 인터넷 수리 기사가 방문할 시각을 고르시오.
· 대화를 듣고, 여자가 지불해야 할 금액으로 가장 적절한 것을 고르시오.

기출 표현 맛보기

대화 장소

· How about going to the Chinese restaurant next to the theater after the movie?
· I bought this picture book yesterday. But there's a problem with it.

숫자 정보

· We can send someone at one, three, or five in the afternoon.
· There are shows at one, four, and seven o'clock.
· Your total is 10 dollars. For here or to go?

주요 어휘·표현 미리보기

다음을 듣고, [보기]에서 알맞은 어휘나 표현을 찾아 쓰세요.   정답 및 해설 p. 12

	보기	
ⓐ sorry for	ⓑ purpose	ⓒ after school	ⓓ fit in
ⓔ take a look at	ⓕ a lot of	ⓖ heavy traffic	ⓗ seem to

01 Let me _____ it. 그거 한번 보자.

02 We went camping _____. 우리는 방과 후에 캠핑을 갔어.

03 You _____ know the answer. 너는 답을 아는 것 같아.

04 This toy doesn't _____ the box. 이 장난감은 그 상자에 맞지 않아.

05 I'm _____ the late reply. 답이 늦어서 미안해.

06 There's always _____ on this street. 이 도로는 항상 교통량이 많아.

07 There are _____ books on the table. 탁자 위에 많은 책이 있어.

08 What's the _____ of your visit to India? 인도를 방문하신 목적이 무엇인가요?

- 대화 장소를 묻는 문제의 경우, 장소 파악에 중요한 단서가 되는 주제나 화제를 잘 파악하며 들어야 해요.
- 숫자 정보를 묻는 문제의 경우, 대화 도중에 수치가 변경되거나 계산이 필요한 경우가 많으므로 숫자 정보들을 빠짐없이 메모하세요.

01

대화를 듣고, 두 사람이 대화하는 장소로 가장 적절한 곳을 고르시오.

① 은행   ② 병원   ③ 학교
④ 체육관   ⑤ 관광 안내소

W Welcome! What can I do for you?

M Hi! I'd like to look around the city today. 정답 단서

W Okay, do you need a city tour map?

M Yes, please. Are there any famous places to visit?

W There are Gyeongbokgung Palace and the National Museum nearby.

M I see. Can I also find Korean restaurants on the map?

W Sure. The map has all kinds of useful information.

M Great. Thanks a lot.

대화 장소는 보통 직접적으로 언급되지 않아. 장소명이 아닌 대화의 내용에 집중하자!

02

대화를 듣고, 여자가 지불해야 할 금액으로 가장 적절한 것을 고르시오.

① $20   ② $22   ③ $23   ④ $24   ⑤ $25

W Hi, I'd like to buy this book.

M Hi. It's $20.

W Okay. Oh! These bookmarks are so pretty. How much are they?

M The one with the rainbow is $2. The one with the clover is $3. They're all handmade. 오답 함정

W My daughter would like the one with the clover. I'll get it with the book.

M Okay. It'll be $20 for the book and $3 for the bookmark.

W Here's my credit card.

서점에서 책과 책갈피를 고르는 내용이야.

ANSWER

01 도시를 둘러보고 싶다는 남자에게 여자가 관광 안내 지도를 건네주며 명소를 안내하고 있으므로 두 사람이 대화하는 장소로 ⑤가 알맞다.

02 여자는 책($20)과 클로버가 그려진 책갈피($3)를 구입하겠다고 했으므로 여자가 지불해야 할 금액은 ③이다.

LISTENING PRACTICE

일반 속도

빠른 속도

01

대화를 듣고, 두 사람이 대화하는 장소로 가장 적절한 곳을 고르시오.

① 학교   ② 도서관   ③ 우체국
④ 공항   ⑤ 컴퓨터실

02

대화를 듣고, 두 사람이 대화하는 장소로 가장 적절한 곳을 고르시오.

① 약국   ② 병원   ③ 교실
④ 양호실   ⑤ 카페

03

대화를 듣고, 두 사람이 대화하는 장소로 가장 적절한 곳을 고르시오.

① 비행기   ② 공항   ③ 호텔
④ 전시회장   ⑤ 여행사

04

대화를 듣고, 남자가 지불해야 할 금액으로 가장 적절한 것을 고르시오.

① $25   ② $40   ③ $50
④ $80   ⑤ $130

고난도

05

대화를 듣고, 여자가 잠실역에 도착할 시각을 고르시오.

① 4:00 p.m.   ② 4:05 p.m.   ③ 4:40 p.m.
④ 4:45 p.m.   ⑤ 5:00 p.m.

06 대화를 듣고, 두 사람이 대화하는 장소로 가장 적절한 곳을 고르시오.

① 여행사   ② 호텔   ③ 관광 안내소
④ 백화점   ⑤ 부동산 중개소

07 대화를 듣고, 두 사람이 대화하는 장소로 가장 적절한 곳을 고르시오.

① 식료품점   ② 은행   ③ 서비스 센터
④ 전자제품 판매점   ⑤ 집

08 대화를 듣고, 여자가 지불해야 할 금액으로 가장 적절한 것을 고르시오.

① $5   ② $7   ③ $9
④ $10   ⑤ $12

09 대화를 듣고, 축구 경기가 끝난 시각을 고르시오.

① 5:30 p.m.   ② 7:00 p.m.   ③ 7:30 p.m.
④ 8:00 p.m.   ⑤ 9:00 p.m.

10 대화를 듣고, 남자가 받은 거스름돈으로 가장 적절한 것을 고르시오.

① $30   ② $35   ③ $50
④ $65   ⑤ $70

DICTATION

정답 단서 오답 함정

일반 속도

빠른 속도

01

대화를 듣고, 두 사람이 대화하는 장소로 가장 적절한 곳을 고르시오.

① 학교　　② 도서관
③ 우체국　④ 공항
⑤ 컴퓨터실

M How may I help you?

W I have some books that I need to send to a school in the U.S.

M All right. Will they _____ _____ _____ _____?

W Let me check. *[pause]* Yes, it's big enough.

M Good. If _____ _____ _____ _____, I recommend our express service.

W Well, how long will it take to get there _____ _____ _____?

M Seven days.

W How much will it cost?

M _____ _____ _____ this. *[pause]* It will cost $15.

W Okay, I'll use regular mail.

02

대화를 듣고, 두 사람이 대화하는 장소로 가장 적절한 곳을 고르시오.

① 약국　　② 병원
③ 교실　　④ 양호실
⑤ 카페

W Excuse me.

M Yes? What's the matter?

W I _____ _____ _____ _____. It started bothering me during class.

M Let me see. Please _____ _____ _____. Uh-oh... Your throat is swollen. It looks painful.

W What should I do?

M I'll give you a pill. Take it now. But you should _____ _____ _____ after school today.

W Okay, thank you.

M And drink a lot of water. It will help.

03

대화를 듣고, 두 사람이 대화하는 장소로 가장 적절한 곳을 고르시오.

① 비행기　② 공항
③ 호텔　　④ 전시회장
⑤ 여행사

M Can I see your passport, please?

W Yes, here you are.

M What is _____ _____ _____ _____ _____ to our country?

W I'm a photographer. I'll travel around France, taking pictures of the beautiful scenery.

M How long _____ _____ _____ _____?

W I plan to be here for three months.

M Okay. _____ _____ _____.

W Thank you.

04

대화를 듣고, 남자가 지불해야 할 금액으로 가장 적절한 것을 고르시오.

① $25   ② $40
③ $50   ④ $80
⑤ $130

W May I help you?

M I like these blue jeans. How much are they?

W They're $80.

M _____ _____ _____.

W They're a new product, so they cost a bit more. But all the pants in that section over there are 50% off.

M Really? I'll _____ _____ _____ _____ them. *[pause]* Oh! These are nice. The tag says they are $50.

W That's the _____ _____. You can take 50% off of that.

M Great! I'll take them.

고난도

05

대화를 듣고, 여자가 잠실역에 도착할 시각을 고르시오.

① 4:00 p.m.   ② 4:05 p.m.
③ 4:40 p.m.   ④ 4:45 p.m.
⑤ 5:00 p.m.

W Excuse me, sir.

M Yes? How can I help you?

W _____ _____ _____ _____ _____ to get to Jamsil Station from here?

M Let me see. There are 20 stops between this station and Jamsil Station. So it will take 40 minutes.

W That's _____ _____ _____ _____! I need to be there by five.

M Well, it's four o'clock, and there's a train that _____ _____ _____ _____.

W Oh, great. I'll take that one. Thank you!

06

대화를 듣고, 두 사람이 대화하는 장소로 가장 적절한 곳을 고르시오.

① 여행사   ② 호텔
③ 관광 안내소   ④ 백화점
⑤ 부동산 중개소

W Excuse me. I have some questions.

M Okay. What can I help you with?

W I was looking at apartments _____ _____ _____ yesterday. Is the one in Everville still available?

M Sorry, it's already been sold.

W Oh! I _____ _____ _____ _____.

M But we _____ _____ _____ _____ for sale. Why don't I show you some of them?

W Sure. But I want one that's _____ _____ _____ _____.

M Okay.

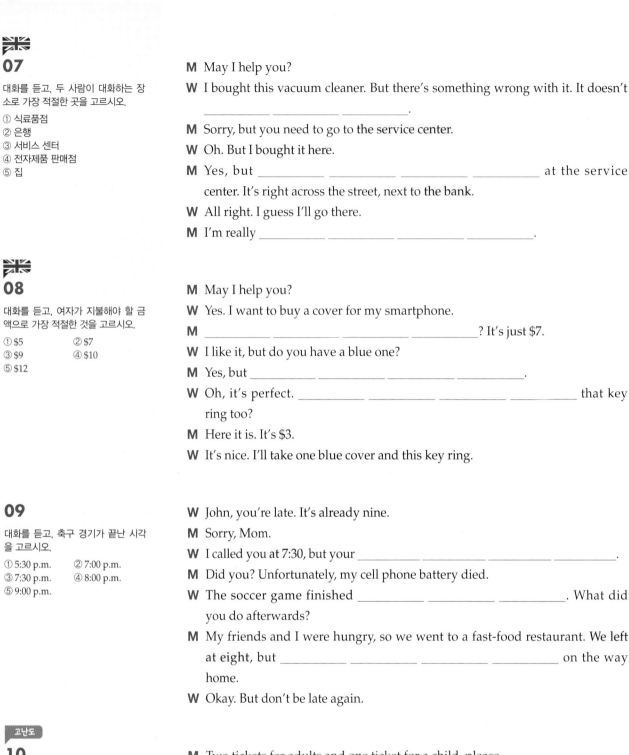

07

대화를 듣고, 두 사람이 대화하는 장소로 가장 적절한 곳을 고르시오.

① 식료품점
② 은행
③ 서비스 센터
④ 전자제품 판매점
⑤ 집

M May I help you?

W I bought this vacuum cleaner. But there's something wrong with it. It doesn't _____ _____ _____.

M Sorry, but you need to go to the service center.

W Oh. But I bought it here.

M Yes, but _____ _____ _____ _____ at the service center. It's right across the street, next to the bank.

W All right. I guess I'll go there.

M I'm really _____ _____ _____ _____.

08

대화를 듣고, 여자가 지불해야 할 금액으로 가장 적절한 것을 고르시오.

① $5   ② $7
③ $9   ④ $10
⑤ $12

M May I help you?

W Yes. I want to buy a cover for my smartphone.

M _____ _____ _____ _____? It's just $7.

W I like it, but do you have a blue one?

M Yes, but _____ _____ _____ _____.

W Oh, it's perfect. _____ _____ _____ _____ that key ring too?

M Here it is. It's $3.

W It's nice. I'll take one blue cover and this key ring.

09

대화를 듣고, 축구 경기가 끝난 시각을 고르시오.

① 5:30 p.m.   ② 7:00 p.m.
③ 7:30 p.m.   ④ 8:00 p.m.
⑤ 9:00 p.m.

W John, you're late. It's already nine.

M Sorry, Mom.

W I called you at 7:30, but your _____ _____ _____ _____.

M Did you? Unfortunately, my cell phone battery died.

W The soccer game finished _____ _____ _____. What did you do afterwards?

M My friends and I were hungry, so we went to a fast-food restaurant. We left at eight, but _____ _____ _____ _____ on the way home.

W Okay. But don't be late again.

10

고난도

대화를 듣고, 남자가 받은 거스름돈으로 가장 적절한 것을 고르시오.

① $30   ② $35
③ $50   ④ $65
⑤ $70

M Two tickets for adults and one ticket for a child, please.

W Okay. If you are a member, you can get 30% off.

M Unfortunately, I'm not a member. How much are the tickets?

W They'll be _____ _____ _____.

M Hmm... Is there any way you can _____ _____ _____ _____?

W If you enter the park after 5:00 p.m., you can _____ _____ _____ _____. It's 4:30 now.

M Oh, that's good. Then I'll wait. Here's a hundred dollars.

W Here are your tickets and change. Please stand over there until it's time.

A 다음 영어 어휘나 표현의 뜻을 우리말로 쓰세요.

01 pill

02 scenery

03 bother

04 regular price

05 recommend

06 tag

07 inconvenience

08 product

09 be located

10 afterwards

11 key ring

12 swollen

13 photographer

14 painful

15 vacuum cleaner

16 passport

B 우리말에 맞는 영어 어휘나 표현을 [보기]에서 찾아 쓰세요.

| 보기 | blue jeans   stop   cost   turn off   in total
          for sale   repair   work   available   on the way home

01 작동되다

02 정거장

03 (전기 등을) 끄다

04 팔려고 내놓은

05 청바지

06 값이 ~이다

07 수리

08 구할[이용할] 수 있는

09 모두 합해서

10 집에 가는[오는] 길에

특정 정보

담화나 대화를 듣고, 문제에서 요구하는 특정 정보를 찾는 유형이다. 주로 날씨를 묻는 문제가 출제되며, 여행 갈 도시, 발표할 나라, 주문할 음식, 학교 축제에서 참여할 활동 등 세부 내용에 관한 문제도 출제된다.

지시문 유형
- 다음을 듣고, 목요일의 날씨로 가장 적절한 것을 고르시오.
- 대화를 듣고, 남자가 발표할 나라로 가장 적절한 것을 고르시오.
- 대화를 듣고, 여자가 영상 제작에서 맡은 일로 가장 적절한 것을 고르시오.

기출 표현 맛보기

날씨
- It is raining now, but it is going to be sunny this afternoon.
- From Monday to Tuesday, it will be cold because of strong winds, so you may want to wear warm clothes.

기타
- Well, actually I've changed my mind. I decided to introduce Germany. (발표할 나라)
- I wrote the script of the video. (영상 제작에서 맡은 일)

주요 어휘·표현 미리보기

다음을 듣고, [보기]에서 알맞은 어휘나 표현을 찾아 쓰세요.

정답 및 해설 p. 15

| 보기 |
| ⓐ rides her bike | ⓑ at first | ⓒ clears up | ⓓ temperatures |
| ⓔ go sightseeing | ⓕ humid | ⓖ is supposed to | ⓗ let me know |

01 I hope it _____ soon. 곧 날씨가 개면 좋겠어.

02 I don't like to _____. 나는 관광하는 것을 좋아하지 않아.

03 He didn't like me _____. 그는 처음에는 나를 좋아하지 않았어.

04 She _____ every morning. 그녀는 매일 아침 자전거를 타.

05 The weather _____ be nice all week. 일주일 내내 날씨가 화창하겠습니다.

06 If you have a question, please _____. 질문이 있으시면 저에게 알려주세요.

07 It was really hot and _____ this summer. 이번 여름은 정말 덥고 습했어.

08 _____ will be lower than they are today. 기온이 오늘보다 낮겠습니다.

01

다음을 듣고, 부산의 오늘 날씨로 가장 적절한 것을 고르시오.

①   ②   ③    ④    ⑤

M   Good morning! This is today's weather. In Seoul, it will rain all day long. In Daejeon, it is cloudy this morning but it will snow a lot in the afternoon. In Busan, you will see a sunny sky all day. It will be a good day for a picnic. Thank you very much.

오답 함정
정답 단서

여러 도시 중에서
'부산'을 지칭하는 말이
나올 때 귀 기울여봐!

02

대화를 듣고, 두 사람이 여행 갈 도시로 가장 적절한 것을 고르시오.

① 경주   ② 전주   ③ 남원   ④ 서울   ⑤ 부산

W   Honey. Where are we going for the weekend?
M   How about going to Busan? The beach is beautiful.
W   Well, we already went there last summer.
M   Then, what about Jeonju or Namwon? They have some beautiful historical sites.
W   Hmm... Namwon sounds good. I've never been there. I've always been interested in history.
M   Okay. I'll book the train tickets.

남자가 제안한 도시 중
여자는 어느 곳이
좋다고 했지?

ANSWER
01 부산은 하루 종일 화창한 하늘을 볼 것이라고 했으므로 부산의 오늘 날씨로 ②가 알맞다.
02 여자는 남자가 제안한 도시 중 남원이 좋다고 했으므로 두 사람이 여행 갈 도시로 ③이 알맞다.

LISTENING PRACTICE

점수 _____ / 10문항

 일반 속도 빠른 속도

01 다음을 듣고, 주말의 날씨로 가장 적절한 것을 고르시오.

①   ②   ③   ④   ⑤

고난도
02 다음을 듣고, 샌디에이고의 오늘 날씨로 가장 적절한 것을 고르시오.

①   ②   ③   ④   ⑤

03 대화를 듣고, 여자가 매일 아침에 하는 운동으로 가장 적절한 것을 고르시오.

① 맨손 체조　　　　② 조깅　　　　③ 자전거 타기
④ 근력 운동　　　　⑤ 줄넘기

04 대화를 듣고, 여자가 Amy에게 줄 선물로 가장 적절한 것을 고르시오.

① 꽃　　　　② 토스터　　　　③ 수건
④ 머그잔　　　　⑤ 세제

05 대화를 듣고, 남자가 대화 직후에 먹을 음식으로 가장 적절한 것을 고르시오.

① 사과　　　　② 바나나　　　　③ 닭고기 샐러드
④ 파스타　　　　⑤ 쿠키

06 다음을 듣고, 오타와의 내일 날씨로 가장 적절한 것을 고르시오.

①  ②   ③   ④   ⑤

07 다음을 듣고, 금요일의 날씨로 가장 적절한 것을 고르시오.

①   ②   ③   ④   ⑤

08 대화를 듣고, 남자가 제주도에서 주로 이용한 교통수단으로 가장 적절한 것을 고르시오.

① 택시　　　　　　　　② 도보　　　　　　　　③ 관광버스
④ 자동차　　　　　　　⑤ 자전거

09 대화를 듣고, 남자가 편의점에서 구매할 음식으로 가장 적절한 것을 고르시오.

① 김밥　　　　　　　　② 샌드위치　　　　　　③ 라면
④ 사탕　　　　　　　　⑤ 쿠키

고난도
10 대화를 듣고, 여자가 제일 먼저 공부할 과목으로 가장 적절한 것을 고르시오.

① 수학　　　　　　　　② 역사　　　　　　　　③ 영어
④ 국어　　　　　　　　⑤ 과학

DICTATION

정답 단서 오답 함정

 일반 속도 빠른 속도

01

다음을 듣고, 주말의 날씨로 가장 적절한 것을 고르시오.

① ② ③ ④ ⑤

고난도

02

다음을 듣고, 샌디에이고의 오늘 날씨로 가장 적절한 것을 고르시오.

① ② ③ ④ ⑤

03

대화를 듣고, 여자가 매일 아침에 하는 운동으로 가장 적절한 것을 고르시오.

① 맨손 체조 ② 조깅
③ 자전거 타기 ④ 근력 운동
⑤ 줄넘기

04

대화를 듣고, 여자가 Amy에게 줄 선물로 가장 적절한 것을 고르시오.

① 꽃 ② 토스터
③ 수건 ④ 머그잔
⑤ 세제

M Welcome to the Weather Center. This is your Thursday weather report. There will be _____ _____, but there is little chance that it will rain. It will start raining tomorrow, however, and the rain will last throughout the weekend. _____ _____ _____ _____ next week. So if you're planning a picnic, _____ _____ _____ till next week.

W I'm Christina Lee, and here's today's weather forecast. If you live in San Diego, be careful. There will be thunderstorms _____ _____ _____ this afternoon. It will be foggy in Los Angeles, but it _____ _____ _____ _____. And in San Francisco there will be sunny skies _____ _____ _____. Have a great day, everyone!

M What's up, Cathy? You look great these days. Did you join a gym?
W No, but I have _____ _____ _____ _____.
M Wow! How can you exercise every morning?
W It was _____ _____ _____. But I soon got used to it.
M What kind of exercise do you do? Do you go jogging?
W No. I just _____ _____ _____ for 30 minutes before school.
M Sounds fun!

W Dan, did you _____ _____ _____ for Amy's housewarming party tomorrow?
M Yes. I bought a pretty mug for her.
W That's a good gift, but I don't know what to get her.
M How about buying some flowers? She likes flowers.
W I'd like to give her _____ _____. What does she need?
M She said that she _____ _____ _____ _____. Why don't you buy her some?
W Okay! That sounds perfect.

05

대화를 듣고, 남자가 대화 직후에 먹을 음식으로 가장 적절한 것을 고르시오.

① 사과　　　　② 바나나
③ 닭고기 샐러드　④ 파스타
⑤ 쿠키

M _____ _____ _____ tonight, Mom?

W We're having pasta with chicken. But we're not eating until seven o'clock.

M Really? I'm hungry already. I can't wait two hours.

W Why don't you have a snack? I _____ _____ _____ this morning.

M Fruit? Don't we have any cookies?

W We do, but I think you _____ _____ _____ _____. How about an apple?

M All right. But can I have a banana instead?

W Sure. There are some on the kitchen table.

M Thanks, Mom.

06

다음을 듣고, 오타와의 내일 날씨로 가장 적절한 것을 고르시오.

① 　②
③ 　④
⑤

M These are the world weather forecasts for tomorrow. In Seoul and Beijing, it will be _____ _____ _____ _____ _____. In Tokyo, it will be cold and windy, but it _____ _____ _____. Wellington will have a warm, sunny day. In Ottawa, the temperature will drop, and _____ _____ _____ _____. It will be foggy in London, but _____ _____ _____ _____ all day in Paris.

07

다음을 듣고, 금요일의 날씨로 가장 적절한 것을 고르시오.

① 　②
③ 　④
⑤

W Good evening. This is the weekly weather report. _____ _____ _____ _____ later tonight, and tomorrow it will be sunny all day. We're _____ _____ _____ on Wednesday and Thursday. On Friday, it will not rain, but there will be _____ _____ _____ _____. The sky is supposed to _____ _____ _____ _____ _____, however. It will be a good time to enjoy outdoor activities.

08

대화를 듣고, 남자가 제주도에서 주로 이용한 교통수단으로 가장 적절한 것을 고르시오.

① 택시   ② 도보
③ 관광버스   ④ 자동차
⑤ 자전거

W How was your vacation on Jeju Island?

M It was great! I _____ _____ _____ _____ _____ there.

W Wow! That must have been fun! When I went to Jeju, I traveled around in a tour bus.

M Yes, that's the easiest way to _____ _____.

W I also saw many tourists taking taxis there, but it's very expensive.

M That's true.

W Were there any problems during your trip?

M It was _____ _____ _____, so biking around was difficult.

09

대화를 듣고, 남자가 편의점에서 구매할 음식으로 가장 적절한 것을 고르시오.

① 김밥   ② 샌드위치
③ 라면   ④ 사탕
⑤ 쿠키

M I need to _____ _____ _____, but I'm in a hurry. Let's stop by a convenience store.

W Okay. What will you get?

M Maybe some instant ramen. And I'll buy some cookies or candy _____ _____.

W That doesn't sound like a very good lunch.

M I guess not. _____ _____ _____ _____?

W When I'm _____ _____ _____, I usually get a sandwich or some gimbap.

M Oh, gimbap is a good idea! I'll get that.

고난도
10

대화를 듣고, 여자가 제일 먼저 공부할 과목으로 가장 적절한 것을 고르시오.

① 수학   ② 역사
③ 영어   ④ 국어
⑤ 과학

W My final exams start next week. I have so many subjects to study.

M What will you start with? I _____ _____ _____ science.

W I'm not taking a science class this year. English and history are _____ _____ _____.

M What about math? That's an important class.

W Yes, but I'll _____ _____ _____ _____. I feel pretty confident about it.

M Then I'd start with whichever class you're _____ _____ _____ _____.

W Good idea. I'll start with history and then study English next.

M Sounds good. Let me know if you need help.

A

다음 영어 어휘나 표현의 뜻을 우리말로 쓰세요.

01 tourist

02 dry

03 dessert

04 drop

05 thunderstorm

06 shine

07 lightning

08 practical

09 foggy

10 expensive

11 weekly

12 outdoor

13 confident

14 convenience store

15 subject

16 enough

B

우리말에 맞는 영어 어휘나 표현을 [보기]에서 찾아 쓰세요.

| 보기 | in a hurry   whichever   heavy snow   throughout   get used to |
| | suggest   last   stop by   shower   housewarming party |

01 내내

02 계속되다

03 폭설

04 집들이

05 소나기

06 급히, 바쁜

07 ~에 잠시 들르다

08 제안하다

09 어느 ~이든

10 ~에 익숙해지다

언급하지 않은 내용

유형 설명 대화나 담화를 듣고, 언급하지 않은 것을 찾는 유형이다. 주로 특정 행사나 프로그램 등에 대해 언급하지 않은 내용을 고르는 문제가 출제된다.

지시문 유형
- 대화를 듣고, 두 사람이 Study Together 프로그램에 대해 언급하지 <u>않은</u> 것을 고르시오.
- 대화를 듣고, 두 사람이 재즈 축제에 대해 언급하지 <u>않은</u> 것을 고르시오.
- 다음을 듣고, 남자가 Job Experience Day에 대해 언급하지 <u>않은</u> 것을 고르시오.
- 다음을 듣고, 여자가 사자에 대해 언급하지 <u>않은</u> 것을 고르시오.

기출 표현 맛보기
- To sign up, fill out the form and give it to your class leader by this Wednesday. (신청 마감일)
- Students from Hankuk University will come to our middle school. They will help us with Korean and math for free. It's only for second graders. (신청 가능 과목, 대상 학년)

주요 어휘·표현 미리보기

다음을 듣고, [보기]에서 알맞은 어휘나 표현을 찾아 쓰세요.   정답 및 해설 p. 18

| 보기 |
| ⓐ was founded | ⓑ invite you to | ⓒ is held | ⓓ was built |
| ⓔ come check out | ⓕ provided | ⓖ named after | ⓗ fasten |

01 The school ＿＿＿＿＿＿ 50 years ago. 그 학교는 50년 전에 설립되었어.

02 The music festival ＿＿＿＿＿＿ every year. 그 음악 축제는 매년 열립니다.

03 Don't forget to ＿＿＿＿＿＿ your seat belt. 안전벨트 매는 걸 잊지 마.

04 I'll ＿＿＿＿＿＿ my house. 너를 우리 집에 초대할게.

05 ＿＿＿＿＿＿ our new place. 우리의 새로운 공간을 보러 오세요.

06 The history museum ＿＿＿＿＿＿ in 1889. 그 역사 박물관은 1889년에 지어졌어.

07 He was ＿＿＿＿＿＿ his uncle. 그는 삼촌의 이름을 따서 이름 지었어.

08 The airline ＿＿＿＿＿＿ us with a hotel room. 그 항공사는 우리에게 호텔 객실을 제공했어.

・ 먼저 지시문과 선택지를 읽고, 주의해서 들어야 할 내용이 무엇인지 파악하세요.
・ 보통 선택지 순서대로 내용이 언급되므로, 들려주는 내용과 선택지를 비교하며 오답을 지워 나가세요.
・ 대화문의 경우, What, When, Where, How 등 의문사로 시작하는 질문과 그에 대한 대답을 유의해서 들어야 해요.

01

대화를 듣고, 남자가 Space Camp에 대해 언급하지 <u>않은</u> 것을 고르시오.

① 주최 기관　　　　② 개최 기간　　　　③ 참가 대상
④ 활동 내용　　　　⑤ 참가 비용

M　Do you know that Midam University will run a Space Camp?
W　No, I don't. When is it?
M　It's from July 2 to the 6.
W　Can we join the camp?
M　Sure, it's for middle school students.
W　Sounds good. What can we do there?
M　We can look at stars through telescopes.
W　Cool. What else can we do?
M　We can wear spacesuits and try space foods.

우주 캠프 프로그램에 관한
대화야. 여자의 질문과 그에 대한
남자의 대답에 귀 기울여 보자.

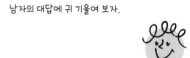

02

다음을 듣고, 여자가 학교 축제에 대해 언급하지 <u>않은</u> 것을 고르시오.

① 장소　　　　② 공연 내용　　　　③ 점심시간
④ 축제 시작 시간　　　　⑤ 복장

W　Hello, Maru Middle School students. I have an announcement about our school festival. As you know, it will be held in the gym tomorrow. There will be performances such as dancing, singing, and a magic show. The festival will start at 10:00 a.m. Please come to school by 9:30 a.m. Don't forget to wear your school uniform. See you tomorrow.

학교 축제에 대한 담화로,
선택지 내용이 거의 매 문장에
차례로 등장하고 있어.

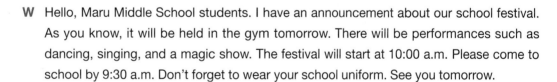

ANSWER

01 선택지 순서대로 주최 기관, 개최 기간, 참가 대상, 활동 내용은 언급했지만 참가 비용은 언급하지 않았으므로 정답은 ⑤이다.

02 선택지 순서대로 장소, 공연 내용, 축제 시작 시간, 복장은 언급했지만 점심시간은 언급하지 않았으므로 정답은 ③이다.

LISTENING PRACTICE

일반 속도

빠른 속도

01 대화를 듣고, 여자가 San Diego Sharks팀에 대해 언급하지 <u>않은</u> 것을 고르시오.

① 종목   ② 창단 시기   ③ 경기 장소
④ 로고   ⑤ 팀 규모

02 대화를 듣고, 남자가 파티에 대해 언급하지 <u>않은</u> 것을 고르시오.

① 개최 요일   ② 장소   ③ 참여 인원
④ 제공 음식   ⑤ 시작 시각

고난도
03 대화를 듣고, 여자가 항공기에 대해 언급하지 <u>않은</u> 것을 고르시오.

① 기종   ② 일일 운항 횟수   ③ 수용 가능 인원
④ 제작 연도   ⑤ 비행 속도

04 대화를 듣고, 남자가 하는 일로 언급하지 <u>않은</u> 것을 고르시오.

① 수업하기   ② 학생의 개인 문제 돕기   ③ 숙제 검사하기
④ 학회 참석하기   ⑤ 시험 문제 출제하기

고난도
05 다음을 듣고, 여자가 Eileen's Hats에 대해 언급하지 <u>않은</u> 것을 고르시오.

① 대상 고객   ② 위치   ③ 개업 연도
④ 영업시간   ⑤ 휴무일

06 대화를 듣고, 두 사람이 카페에 대해 언급하지 <u>않은</u> 것을 고르시오.

① 이름   ② 위치   ③ 주요 메뉴
④ 폐점 시간   ⑤ 규모

07 대화를 듣고, 두 사람이 그림에 대해 언급하지 <u>않은</u> 것을 고르시오.

① 그림 소재   ② 화가   ③ 제작 연도
④ 제작 기법   ⑤ 원본 소장처

08 대화를 듣고, 남자가 퀴즈 대회에 대해 언급하지 <u>않은</u> 것을 고르시오.

① 개최 요일   ② 대회 장소   ③ 1등 상품
④ 참가자 수   ⑤ 참가 신청 방법

09 다음을 듣고, 남자가 바나나에 대해 언급하지 <u>않은</u> 것을 고르시오.

① 재배 지역   ② 모양   ③ 색깔
④ 어원   ⑤ 열량

10 다음을 듣고, 여자가 헬스장에 대해 언급하지 않은 것을 고르시오.

① 이름   ② 위치   ③ 개장 시기
④ 무료 강좌   ⑤ 이용료

DICTATION

 일반 속도
 빠른 속도

01

대화를 듣고, 여자가 San Diego Sharks팀에 대해 언급하지 <u>않은</u> 것을 고르시오.

① 종목   ② 창단 시기
③ 경기 장소   ④ 로고
⑤ 팀 규모

M Hi, Danielle. _____ _____ _____ _____ _____?

W It says, "San Diego Sharks." They're my favorite baseball team.

M I've never heard of them. Where do they play their games?

W _____ _____ _____ _____ just two years ago. They play at Oceanview Stadium. I go there several times a week.

M You must really like them!

W Yes, I do. I've met all 30 players _____ _____ _____!

02

대화를 듣고, 남자가 파티에 대해 언급하지 않은 것을 고르시오.

① 개최 요일   ② 장소
③ 참여 인원   ④ 제공 음식
⑤ 시작 시각

M I'd like to _____ _____ _____ _____ _____ on Saturday, Nancy.

W What kind of party is it?

M It's a barbecue party. _____ _____ _____ _____ in my backyard.

W Barbecue? Sounds delicious.

M Yes. _____ _____ hamburgers and hot dogs. It starts at 5:00 p.m.

W Great! I will definitely come!

M I'm happy to hear that! I'll see you on Saturday.

고난도
03

대화를 듣고, 여자가 항공기에 대해 언급하지 않은 것을 고르시오.

① 기종
② 일일 운항 횟수
③ 수용 가능 인원
④ 제작 연도
⑤ 비행 속도

W _____ _____ Flight 234 to Honolulu.

M Thank you. Can I ask some questions about this airplane?

W Sure. What do you want to know?

M Well, what kind is it and how many people _____ _____ _____?

W It's an Airbus A340, and it can carry 370 people.

M Wow! It's really big.

W Yes, it is. It was built in 2007 and can _____ _____ _____ _____ 900 km/h.

M That's fast! Thank you for the information.

W You're welcome. Now please sit down and _____ _____ _____ _____.

04

대화를 듣고, 남자가 하는 일로 언급하지 <u>않은</u> 것을 고르시오.

① 수업하기
② 학생의 개인 문제 돕기
③ 숙제 검사하기
④ 학회 참석하기
⑤ 시험 문제 출제하기

W Do you like being a teacher, Sam?
M Yes. I _____ _____ _____ in the classroom.
W But doesn't that get boring?
M I do other things as well. I also help students with _____ _____ _____.
W Oh, I see.
M And I _____ _____ _____ _____ and make tests after my classes are over!
W Wow! You must be very busy.
M I am! But I still love my job.

고난도

05

다음을 듣고, 여자가 Eileen's Hats에 대해 언급하지 <u>않은</u> 것을 고르시오.

① 대상 고객   ② 위치
③ 개업 연도   ④ 영업시간
⑤ 휴무일

W Eileen's Hats is the best place to buy hats in Chicago. The owner of the store _____ _____ _____ his grandmother, who wore a different hat every day. _____ _____ _____ _____ Michigan Avenue and has been selling all kinds of hats since 1987. _____ _____ _____ _____ from 10:00 a.m. to 10:00 p.m., but is closed every Wednesday. If you're _____ _____ _____ _____, come on a Sunday—every hat is 10% off.

06

대화를 듣고, 두 사람이 카페에 대해 언급하지 <u>않은</u> 것을 고르시오.

① 이름   ② 위치
③ 주요 메뉴   ④ 폐점 시간
⑤ 규모

W There's a great new café across the street from the post office.
M _____ _____ _____ food or just coffee?
W They serve coffee, cake, and sandwiches.
M Sounds good. Let's go together after our swimming class.
W Unfortunately, _____ _____ _____ _____. It closes at 7:00 p.m.
M Well, then we can go with our classmates after school.
W Yes, but it's really small. There are _____ _____ _____. Why don't you and I go alone?
M Okay!

07

대화를 듣고, 두 사람이 그림에 대해 언급하지 <u>않은</u> 것을 고르시오.
① 그림 소재　② 화가
③ 제작 연도　④ 제작 기법
⑤ 원본 소장처

W I like this painting of sunflowers. Do you know who painted it?
M Yes. _____ _____ _____ _____ Vincent van Gogh.
W Was it? I really like the colors. Almost everything is yellow.
M Yes. He painted it in 1888. He painted many sunflower paintings that year.
W Did he _____ _____ _____?
M Yes, he did. I would like to have that painting in my house.
W You can buy a postcard of the painting _____ _____ _____ _____ _____.

08

대화를 듣고, 남자가 퀴즈 대회에 대해 언급하지 <u>않은</u> 것을 고르시오.
① 개최 요일　② 대회 장소
③ 1등 상품　④ 참가자 수
⑤ 참가 신청 방법

M I'm going to _____ _____ _____ a quiz contest about robots next Monday!
W Really? Where is it?
M It's at the school library. _____ _____ is a new smartphone!
W Well, I hope you win.
M Me too. But 26 other students have also entered it.
W Don't worry. If you study hard _____ _____ _____, you'll do well.

09

다음을 듣고, 남자가 바나나에 대해 언급하지 <u>않은</u> 것을 고르시오.
① 재배 지역　② 모양
③ 색깔　④ 어원
⑤ 열량

M The banana is a popular fruit _____ _____ _____ _____. It is long and curved like a boomerang. When _____ _____ _____, it changes from green to yellow _____ _____ _____. But it is yellowish white on the inside. The average banana contains between 90 and 120 calories.

10

다음을 듣고, 여자가 헬스장에 대해 언급하지 <u>않은</u> 것을 고르시오.
① 이름　② 위치
③ 개장 시기　④ 무료 강좌
⑤ 이용료

W Hello, everyone! _____ _____ _____ the Parkside Gym, a new health club that opened last week. We have the newest training machines. Also, we _____ _____ _____ free classes, including yoga and Pilates. You can _____ _____ _____ a special one-month membership for just $24. If you are interested in fitness, sign up online _____ _____ _____ _____.

정답 및 해설 p. 20

A 다음 영어 어휘나 표현의 뜻을 우리말로 쓰세요.

01 personal

02 across

03 definitely

04 outside

05 backyard

06 contain

07 tropical country

08 average

09 first prize

10 delicious

11 look for

12 ripe

13 stadium

14 owner

15 seat belt

16 take part in

B 우리말에 맞는 영어 어휘나 표현을 [보기]에서 찾아 쓰세요.

| 보기 | fitness | give lessons | curved | serve | enter |
| | bargain | membership | alone | aboard | say |

01 참가하다

02 (음식 등을) 제공하다

03 건강, 신체 단련

04 싼 물건, 특가품

05 다른 사람 없이

06 탑승한

07 곡선의, 약간 휜

08 수업하다

09 ~라고 쓰여 있다

10 회원권, 회원(자격)

유형 설명 담화를 듣고, 중심 내용을 파악하는 유형이다. 주로 설명하거나 안내하는 내용이 무엇인지 묻는 문제가 출제된다.

지시문 유형 다음을 듣고, 여자가 하는 말의 내용으로 가장 적절한 것을 고르시오.

기출 표현 맛보기
· The drone-making class can give you some helpful information! (수업 홍보)
· For your safety, please pay attention and follow these rules while you're using the roller coaster. (안전 수칙)

주요 어휘·표현 미리보기

다음을 듣고, [보기]에서 알맞은 어휘나 표현을 찾아 쓰세요.   정답 및 해설 p. 21

| 보기 |
| ⓐ plenty of | ⓑ be delayed | ⓒ in common | ⓓ understanding |
| ⓔ feed | ⓕ rest | ⓖ focus on | ⓗ permission |

01 Our train will _____ by an hour. 우리 열차는 한 시간 지연될 것입니다.

02 She came back after a few days of _____. 그녀는 며칠간의 휴식 후에 돌아왔어.

03 My aunt and I have many things _____. 우리 이모와 나는 공통점이 많아.

04 Do I need to get _____ from my parents? 저희 부모님께 허락을 받아야 하나요?

05 Please _____ me. 저에게 집중해 주십시오.

06 Thank you for your _____ and help. 이해와 협조 감사합니다.

07 There are _____ candy shops in this city. 이 도시에는 많은 사탕 가게가 있어.

08 When should I _____ the dog? 개에게 언제 먹이를 줘야 하나요?

- 먼저 선택지를 읽고, 어떤 주제나 화제의 내용이 나올지 예상해 보세요.
- 담화의 일부 내용이 아닌 내용 전체를 포괄할 수 있는 선택지를 골라야 해요.

01

다음을 듣고, 여자가 하는 말의 내용으로 가장 적절한 것을 고르시오.

① 감사하는 삶의 자세
② 다양한 문화의 이해
③ 가족 여행의 즐거움
④ 신속한 지진 대피 요령
⑤ 규칙적인 생활의 중요성

오답 함정

W Let me tell you a story about a girl living in Nepal. She lost her family in an earthquake. At that time, many people offered to help her. After that, she felt like the luckiest person in the world. I used to complain a lot before I read her story. But the story made me thankful. Now, I try my best to be thankful for everything in my life. 정답 단서

여자가 네팔에 사는 소녀 이야기를 들려주며 자신이 느낀 점을 말하고 있어.

02

다음을 듣고, 남자가 하는 말의 내용으로 가장 적절한 것을 고르시오.

① 선거 공약
② 전학생 소개
③ 학생증 발급
④ 급식실 공사
⑤ 체육대회 일정

M Hello, Mirae Middle School students. My name is Taeyang Jung. If I become your student leader, I will make our sports day more fun with a variety of activities. Also, I will make new clubs. And, I will make our school cleaner and safer. So, please choose me to be your next student leader. Thank you.

남자가 학생들에게 몇 가지 실천을 약속하면서 자신을 학생회장으로 뽑아 달라고 말하고 있어.

ANSWER

01 여자는 네팔에 사는 소녀 이야기를 언급하며 모든 일에 감사하는 자세를 갖도록 최선을 다해야겠다고 말하고 있으므로 여자가 하는 말의 내용으로 ①이 알맞다.

02 남자는 자신이 학생회장이 된다면 학생들을 위해 어떤 일들을 실행할지 약속하며 투표해 줄 것을 호소하고 있으므로 남자가 하는 말의 내용으로 ①이 알맞다.

LISTENING PRACTICE

점수 _____ / 10문항

일반 속도

빠른 속도

01 다음을 듣고, 남자가 하는 말의 내용으로 가장 적절한 것을 고르시오.

① 보고서 주제 선정 방법
② 스트레스 자가 진단법
③ 시험을 잘 보는 비결
④ 식단 관리 방법
⑤ 일정 관리 요령

02 다음을 듣고, 여자가 하는 말의 내용으로 가장 적절한 것을 고르시오.

① 활주로 공사 일정 안내
② 비행기 결항 안내
③ 비상착륙 시 대처 방법
④ 비행기 출발 지연 안내
⑤ 기내 수하물 반입 규정

03 다음을 듣고, 남자가 하는 말의 내용으로 가장 적절한 것을 고르시오.

① 단체 활동의 즐거움
② 경청하는 자세의 중요성
③ 존경받는 리더 되기
④ 낯가림 개선 방법
⑤ 무대 공포증 극복 방법

04 다음을 듣고, 여자가 하는 말의 내용으로 가장 적절한 것을 고르시오.

① 수영장 안전 수칙
② 수영 강습 수강 안내
③ 수영장 개장 안내
④ 수상 안전 요원 모집
⑤ 주민센터 자원봉사자 모집

고난도
05 다음을 듣고, 남자가 하는 말의 내용으로 가장 적절한 것을 고르시오.

① 신문 제작 공정
② 이면지 활용법
③ 인터넷 신문의 장점
④ 올바른 나무 심기 방법
⑤ 신문 재활용의 이점

06 다음을 듣고, 여자가 하는 말의 내용으로 가장 적절한 것을 고르시오.

① 가게 이전   ② 가게 폐점
③ 업종 변경   ④ 공식 온라인 쇼핑몰 개점
⑤ 도서 할인

07 다음을 듣고, 남자가 하는 말의 내용으로 가장 적절한 것을 고르시오.

① 수족관 새 단장 안내   ② 공연 티켓 할인 정보
③ 상어 쇼 관람 안내   ④ 수중 사진전 소개
⑤ 동물 먹이 주기 체험 안내

08 다음을 듣고, 여자가 하는 말의 내용으로 가장 적절한 것을 고르시오.

① 효과적인 체중 감량 방법   ② 스트레스 해소에 좋은 음식
③ 전자기기 중독 예방법   ④ 규칙적인 운동의 중요성
⑤ 소아 비만의 원인

고난도
09 다음을 듣고, 남자가 하는 말의 내용으로 가장 적절한 것을 고르시오.

① 학업 스트레스의 대표적 증상   ② 미래 설계의 중요성
③ 효율적인 시간 관리 방법   ④ 전공 선택의 기준
⑤ 과목 편식 현상의 심각성

10 다음을 듣고, 여자가 하는 말의 내용으로 가장 적절한 것을 고르시오.

① 재활용의 중요성   ② 환경 오염의 심각성
③ 일회용품 사용의 문제점   ④ 분리수거 시 유의 사항
⑤ 음식물 쓰레기 배출 방법

DICTATION

정답 단서 오답 함정

일반 속도

빠른 속도

01

다음을 듣고, 남자가 하는 말의 내용
으로 가장 적절한 것을 고르시오.

① 보고서 주제 선정 방법
② 스트레스 자가 진단법
③ 시험을 잘 보는 비결
④ 식단 관리 방법
⑤ 일정 관리 요령

M Some students worry about tests but don't know _____ _____ _____ on them. Here are some useful tips. First of all, _____ _____ _____ of the most important topics to study. Second, study hard before the test, but _____ _____ _____ _____ the night before. Third, eat a good breakfast on the day of the test. And finally, answer the easy questions first. Then _____ _____ _____ with the harder ones.

02

다음을 듣고, 여자가 하는 말의 내용
으로 가장 적절한 것을 고르시오.

① 활주로 공사 일정 안내
② 비행기 결항 안내
③ 비상착륙 시 대처 방법
④ 비행기 출발 지연 안내
⑤ 기내 수하물 반입 규정

W May I have your attention, please? Because of problems with the runway, our departure _____ _____ _____ by about thirty minutes. We are very sorry for the delay. The plane will take off as soon as _____ _____ _____. Again, we would like to apologize for the delay. Thank you for _____ _____ _____ _____.

03

다음을 듣고, 남자가 하는 말의 내용
으로 가장 적절한 것을 고르시오.

① 단체 활동의 즐거움
② 경청하는 자세의 중요성
③ 존경받는 리더 되기
④ 낯가림 개선 방법
⑤ 무대 공포증 극복 방법

M Most people who are popular have something in common. They would rather _____ _____ _____ than speak about themselves. People _____ _____ _____ _____. And when you listen to others well, they feel that they are understood by you. This will also make them feel that you respect them. For these reasons, _____ _____ often have better relationships.

04

다음을 듣고, 여자가 하는 말의 내용
으로 가장 적절한 것을 고르시오.

① 수영장 안전 수칙
② 수영 강습 수강 안내
③ 수영장 개장 안내
④ 수상 안전 요원 모집
⑤ 주민센터 자원봉사자 모집

W Hello, students! I would like to let you know about _____ _____ _____ _____ _____. The community center needs ten lifeguards this summer. The position is part-time, and employees will earn _____ _____ _____ _____. If you're interested, please visit our website _____ _____ _____. Thank you for your time!

고난도

05

다음을 듣고, 남자가 하는 말의 내용
으로 가장 적절한 것을 고르시오.

① 신문 제작 공정
② 이면지 활용법
③ 인터넷 신문의 장점
④ 올바른 나무 심기 방법
⑤ 신문 재활용의 이점

M What do you do when you finish _____ _____? Do you just throw it in the trash? Next time, think about this: Up to 200 million trees _____ _____ _____ each year to make newspapers. But by putting old newspapers in a recycling bin, you can _____ _____ _____ _____. In fact, if everyone recycled just one newspaper per week, millions of trees would be saved! It doesn't take much effort, but it can _____ _____ _____ _____.

06

다음을 듣고, 여자가 하는 말의 내용
으로 가장 적절한 것을 고르시오.

① 가게 이전
② 가게 폐점
③ 업종 변경
④ 공식 온라인 쇼핑몰 개점
⑤ 도서 할인

W Here at Robin's Comics, we've been receiving lots of calls from concerned customers. They want to know why our store has closed. But it hasn't closed! We have _____ _____ _____ _____ in the beautiful Springfield Mall. _____ _____ _____ _____ last week. It is much larger, so there are even more great comic books. You can find us _____ _____ _____ the travel agency in the mall. We hope to see you soon!

07

다음을 듣고, 남자가 하는 말의 내용
으로 가장 적절한 것을 고르시오.

① 수족관 새 단장 안내
② 공연 티켓 할인 정보
③ 상어 쇼 관람 안내
④ 수중 사진전 소개
⑤ 동물 먹이 주기 체험 안내

M May I have your attention, please? At 2:00 p.m., there will be a special show. You are invited to _____ _____ _____ _____ the sharks. They will also answer any questions you have _____ _____ _____ _____. But please come to the show early. There aren't many seats, and it's one of _____ _____ _____.

08

다음을 듣고, 여자가 하는 말의 내용
으로 가장 적절한 것을 고르시오.

① 효과적인 체중 감량 방법
② 스트레스 해소에 좋은 음식
③ 전자기기 중독 예방법
④ 규칙적인 운동의 중요성
⑤ 소아 비만의 원인

W These days, even very young children _____ _____ _____.
There are many causes of childhood obesity. First of all, many children don't
_____ _____ _____. They spend too much time playing
games and watching TV. _____ _____ is another problem. Fast
food and soda make kids gain weight quickly. Finally, stress can be a cause of
obesity. Children _____ _____ _____ may overeat to make
themselves feel better.

고난도
09

다음을 듣고, 남자가 하는 말의 내용
으로 가장 적절한 것을 고르시오.

① 학업 스트레스의 대표적 증상
② 미래 설계의 중요성
③ 효율적인 시간 관리 방법
④ 전공 선택의 기준
⑤ 과목 편식 현상의 심각성

M Being a student is a full-time job. There is _____ _____
_____ _____ _____. You have to take tests, read books,
and do homework. But it's never too early to _____ _____
_____ _____ _____. If you are a high school student, or
even a middle school student, you should think about what you enjoy and
_____ _____ _____ _____ _____. This will help
you choose a major and a career later in life.

10

다음을 듣고, 여자가 하는 말의 내용
으로 가장 적절한 것을 고르시오.

① 재활용의 중요성
② 환경 오염의 심각성
③ 일회용품 사용의 문제점
④ 분리수거 시 유의 사항
⑤ 음식물 쓰레기 배출 방법

W Everyone knows that recycling is important for protecting the environment.
However, _____ _____ _____ _____ _____
can sometimes cause problems. To do it right, you need to _____,
_____, _____ _____ _____ that came in contact with
food. When you _____ _____ _____ like pizza boxes, tear
off the greasy parts. And _____ _____ _____ _____
non-recyclable parts like lids, labels, or wrappers.

A 다음 영어 어휘나 표현의 뜻을 우리말로 쓰세요.

01 patience

02 throw

03 departure

04 take off

05 respect

06 million

07 effort

08 employee

09 earn

10 topic

11 opportunity

12 recycle

13 environment

14 relationship

15 protect

16 come in contact with

B 우리말에 맞는 영어 어휘나 표현을 [보기]에서 찾아 쓰세요.

보기	concerned	remove	choose	obesity	make a difference
	childhood	major	tear off	overeat	take one's time

01 전공

02 비만

03 걱정하는, 염려하는

04 차이를 만들다

05 제거하다

06 어린 시절

07 시간을 들이다

08 선택하다

09 과식하다

10 ~을 떼어 내다

유형 설명	대화나 담화를 듣고, 내용이 일치하지 않는 것을 찾는 유형이다. 들려주는 내용과 선택지의 내용이 일치하지 않는 것을 고르는 문제가 출제된다.
지시문 유형	· 대화를 듣고, Better Photo 행사에 대한 내용과 일치하지 <u>않는</u> 것을 고르시오. · 대화를 듣고, 과학 캠프에 대한 내용과 일치하지 <u>않는</u> 것을 고르시오. · 다음을 듣고, 여자의 동아리에 대한 내용과 일치하지 <u>않는</u> 것을 고르시오.
기출 표현 맛보기	· We're going to stay here for 2 days. (4일 동안 여기에 머물 것이다.) · I came here last month with my family. (1년 전에 한국에 왔다.) · But he came back from Japan last Tuesday. (지난 금요일에 돌아왔다.)

주요 어휘·표현 미리보기

다음을 듣고, [보기]에서 알맞은 어휘나 표현을 찾아 쓰세요.   정답 및 해설 p. 23

	보기		
ⓐ on weekdays	ⓑ off	ⓒ are required	ⓓ apply for
ⓔ fluent in	ⓕ daily	ⓖ not allowed	ⓗ keep in touch

01 She's _____ three different languages. 그녀는 세 가지 언어를 유창하게 해.

02 I usually go to bed early _____. 나는 보통 평일에 일찍 잠자리에 들어.

03 Do you still _____ with her? 그녀와 아직도 연락하고 지내니?

04 The museum is open _____. 박물관은 매일 문을 엽니다.

05 He's _____ today. 그는 오늘 쉬어.

06 I'd like to _____ the job. 나는 그 일에 지원하고 싶어.

07 Computer skills _____ for the job. 그 일은 컴퓨터 실력을 필요로 해.

08 You are _____ to swim here. 여기에서는 수영하실 수 없습니다.

기출로 유형 익히기

- 먼저 지시문과 선택지를 읽고, 주의해서 들어야 할 내용이 무엇인지 파악하세요.
- 보통 선택지 순서대로 내용이 언급되므로, 들려주는 내용과 선택지를 비교해가며 오답을 지워 나가세요.
- 대화문에서는 What, When, Where, How 등 의문사로 시작하는 질문과 그에 대한 대답을 유의해서 들어야 해요.

01

대화를 듣고, 여자가 다녀온 여행에 대한 내용과 일치하지 <u>않는</u> 것을 고르시오.

① Singapore에 다녀왔다.　② 여행 기간 내내 비가 왔다.　③ 4일 동안 머물렀다.
④ 여행지에서 친구와 만났다.　⑤ 유명한 식당에 다녀왔다.

M　Hey, Kate. How was your summer vacation?
W　Hi, Minjun. It was wonderful. My family went to Singapore. The weather was beautiful all the time.
M　Singapore? Wow, how long did you stay there?
W　For four days.
M　I see. What did you do there?
W　We met my friend, Ming and went to a famous restaurant together.
M　Oh, a famous restaurant? How was it?
W　The food was really delicious. We had seafoods and traditional noodles.

정답 단서
남자의 물음에 대한
여자의 답변과 선택지를
대조해 보자.

02

다음을 듣고, Highlands Zoo에 대한 내용과 일치하지 <u>않는</u> 것을 고르시오.

① 전 세계에서 온 많은 종류의 동물들이 있다.
② 중국에서 온 판다 두 마리가 있다.
③ 오늘 판다를 볼 수 있다.
④ 동물들에게 약간의 먹이를 줄 수 있다.
⑤ 동물 우리에 물건을 던지면 안 된다.

M　Thank you for visiting the Highlands Zoo. We have many kinds of animals from all over the world. Let me tell you some special news before you look around the zoo. Two pandas arrived from China a month ago and you can see them today. Before we start, please remember you must not give any food to the animals. Also, you must not throw anything into the cage. Are you ready? Let's go!

동물원 방문객을
대상으로 한
안내사항이야.

ANSWER　01 여자가 여행 기간 내내 날씨가 좋았다고 했으므로 내용과 일치하지 않는 선택지는 ②이다.
02 동물들에게 어떤 먹이도 주어서는 안 된다고 했으므로 내용과 일치하지 않는 선택지는 ④이다.

LISTENING PRACTICE

점수 _____ / 10문항

일반 속도   빠른 속도

01 대화를 듣고, 여자가 방학 동안 한 일에 대한 내용과 일치하지 <u>않는</u> 것을 고르시오.

① 4주 동안 호주에서 지냈다.
② 평일에는 영어 수업을 들었다.
③ 주말에는 여행을 했다.
④ 호주의 자연에 관한 책을 읽었다.
⑤ 학교 친구들을 여럿 사귀었다.

02 대화를 듣고, 두 사람의 통화 내용과 일치하지 <u>않는</u> 것을 고르시오.

① Sandra Kim은 부재중이다.
② 남자는 회의 일정을 알려주기 위해 전화했다.
③ 회의는 금요일에 열릴 것이다.
④ 회의는 오후 4시에 끝날 예정이다.
⑤ 회의 장소는 Bexco Center이다.

03 대화를 듣고, 두 사람에 대한 내용과 일치하지 <u>않는</u> 것을 고르시오.

① 두 사람의 10번째 결혼기념일은 이번 주이다.
② 여자는 남자를 위해 선물을 준비했다.
③ 이번 주 금요일에 함께 음식점에 갈 것이다.
④ 남자가 예약한 음식점은 여자의 생일에 갔던 곳이다.
⑤ 두 사람이 가기로 한 음식점은 전망이 좋다.

04 다음을 듣고, 오디션에 대한 내용과 일치하지 <u>않는</u> 것을 고르시오.

① 8세에서 15세 사이의 여자아이만 모집한다.
② 노래와 춤 실력을 갖추어야 한다.
③ 경력이 없어도 지원할 수 있다.
④ 5월 11일에 열릴 예정이다.
⑤ 반드시 온라인으로 등록해야 한다.

05 다음을 듣고, Sala Spanish Restaurant에 대한 내용과 일치하지 <u>않는</u> 것을 고르시오.

① 도심에 자리하고 있다.
② 스페인 음식과 멕시코 음식을 판매한다.
③ 휴무 없이 365일 영업한다.
④ 폐점 시각은 저녁 11시이다.
⑤ 점심시간에는 할인된 가격에 음식을 맛볼 수 있다.

06 대화를 듣고, 여자의 이사에 대한 내용과 일치하지 <u>않는</u> 것을 고르시오.

① 여자는 오늘 온종일 이삿짐을 쌌다.

② 이사 날짜는 내일이다.

③ 현재 사는 집은 강 근처에 있다.

④ 이사할 집은 현재 사는 집에서 멀지 않다.

⑤ 이사할 집에는 여자의 방이 있다.

07 대화를 듣고, 두 사람의 대화 내용과 일치하지 <u>않는</u> 것을 고르시오.

① 남자는 토요일에 연극을 볼 것이다.

② 남자는 연극을 좋아하지 않는다.

③ 남자의 형이 연극의 조연을 맡았다.

④ 공연은 7시 30분에 시작한다.

⑤ Beth와 Victor도 공연을 보러 갈 예정이다.

고난도
08 대화를 듣고, 구인 광고에 대한 내용과 일치하지 <u>않는</u> 것을 고르시오.

① 시간제 근로자를 모집하고 있다.

② 합격자는 국제학생처에서 근무하게 될 것이다.

③ 학생이 아닌 사람도 지원할 수 있다.

④ 영어를 유창하게 구사해야 한다.

⑤ 이번 주 금요일 이전까지 지원을 완료해야 한다.

고난도
09 다음을 듣고, 남자가 본 영화에 대한 내용과 일치하지 <u>않는</u> 것을 고르시오.

① 코미디 장르이다.　　　　　　　② 미국인 감독이 연출한 작품이다.

③ 다수의 유명 배우가 출연했다.　　④ 상영 시간은 2시간 30분이다.

⑤ 남자는 영화를 만족스럽게 보지 못했다.

10 다음을 듣고, 기숙사 규칙에 대한 내용과 일치하지 <u>않는</u> 것을 고르시오.

① 방을 비울 때는 항상 문단속을 해야 한다.

② 밤 10시에 건물 문이 잠긴다.

③ 반려동물을 데리고 올 수 없다.

④ 방에서 취사를 할 수 없다.

⑤ 방문객 출입은 허용되지 않는다.

DICTATION

정답 및 해설 pp. 23-26

정답 단서 오답 함정

 일반 속도   빠른 속도

01

대화를 듣고, 여자가 방학 동안 한 일에 대한 내용과 일치하지 <u>않는</u> 것을 고르시오.

① 4주 동안 호주에서 지냈다.
② 평일에는 영어 수업을 들었다.
③ 주말에는 여행을 했다.
④ 호주의 자연에 관한 책을 읽었다.
⑤ 학교 친구들을 여럿 사귀었다.

M Hey, Minhye! How was your vacation?

W It was fantastic. I stayed in Australia _____ _____ _____.

M What did you do there?

W I _____ _____ _____ on weekdays. And I traveled on weekends.

M That sounds fun. Where did you go?

W I went to a lot of popular places in Sydney and Melbourne.

M Wow! What else did you do?

W I read books about Australian history. And I _____ _____ _____ _____ at my school.

02

대화를 듣고, 두 사람의 통화 내용과 일치하지 <u>않는</u> 것을 고르시오.

① Sandra Kim은 부재중이다.
② 남자는 회의 일정을 알려주기 위해 전화했다.
③ 회의는 금요일에 열릴 것이다.
④ 회의는 오후 4시에 끝날 예정이다.
⑤ 회의 장소는 Bexco Center이다.

[Telephone rings.]

W Sandra Kim's office. How can I help you?

M This is Perry Johnson. Can I talk to Ms. Kim?

W Sorry, _____ _____. She won't be back until Thursday. Can I _____ _____ _____?

M Yes, I called to let her know _____ _____ _____.

W What kind of meeting is it?

M It's a business meeting. It will be on Friday, September 25, and it'll begin at 4:00 p.m.

W _____ _____ _____ _____ _____?

M At Bexco Center.

03

대화를 듣고, 두 사람에 대한 내용과 일치하지 <u>않는</u> 것을 고르시오.

① 두 사람의 10번째 결혼기념일은 이번 주이다.
② 여자는 남자를 위해 선물을 준비했다.
③ 이번 주 금요일에 함께 음식점에 갈 것이다.
④ 남자가 예약한 음식점은 여자의 생일에 갔던 곳이다.
⑤ 두 사람이 가기로 한 음식점은 전망이 좋다.

M Susan, you didn't forget our 10th _____ _____ this Friday, did you?

W Of course not. I have a small gift for you.

M Really? Well, I _____ _____ _____ at a steak restaurant on Friday.

W Oh! The restaurant we went to on your birthday?

M Yes. Is that okay?

W Yes! I love that place. _____ _____ _____ _____, and the food is good, too.

M Great!

72

04

다음을 듣고, 오디션에 대한 내용과 일치하지 <u>않는</u> 것을 고르시오.

① 8세에서 15세 사이의 여자아이만 모집한다.
② 노래와 춤 실력을 갖추어야 한다.
③ 경력이 없어도 지원할 수 있다.
④ 5월 11일에 열릴 예정이다.
⑤ 반드시 온라인으로 등록해야 한다.

W The Sunshine Children's Theater will be _____ _____ for our weekly performances of *The Lion King*. We are looking for boys and girls _____ _____ _____ eight to fifteen who can sing and dance. _____ _____ _____ is required. The auditions will be held on May 11, and you must sign up on our website to participate.

05

다음을 듣고, Sala Spanish Restaurant에 대한 내용과 일치하지 <u>않는</u> 것을 고르시오.

① 도심에 자리하고 있다.
② 스페인 음식과 멕시코 음식을 판매한다.
③ 휴무 없이 365일 영업한다.
④ 폐점 시각은 저녁 11시이다.
⑤ 점심시간에는 할인된 가격에 음식을 맛볼 수 있다.

M Are you looking for a new, exciting restaurant _____ _____ _____ _____? Then you should visit Sala Spanish Restaurant. You can enjoy delicious Spanish and Mexican food there. The restaurant _____ _____ _____ from 11:00 a.m. to 10:00 p.m. There are also _____ _____ on our lunch specials. Stop by and _____ _____ _____ _____ _____!

06

대화를 듣고, 여자의 이사에 대한 내용과 일치하지 <u>않는</u> 것을 고르시오.

① 여자는 오늘 온종일 이삿짐을 쌌다.
② 이사 날짜는 내일이다.
③ 현재 사는 집은 강 근처에 있다.
④ 이사할 집은 현재 사는 집에서 멀지 않다.
⑤ 이사할 집에는 여자의 방이 있다.

M Wow! You have a lot of boxes!
W Yes. I've been _____ _____ _____. My family is moving tomorrow.
M Really? Will you move far away?
W No. Just to an apartment building _____ _____ _____.
M Oh, that's not far. We can _____ _____ _____ _____. But why do you look so happy?
W I'm excited because I'll _____ _____ _____ _____ for the first time!

07

대화를 듣고, 두 사람의 대화 내용과 일치하지 <u>않는</u> 것을 고르시오.

① 남자는 토요일에 연극을 볼 것이다.
② 남자는 연극을 좋아하지 않는다.
③ 남자의 형이 연극의 조연을 맡았다.
④ 공연은 7시 30분에 시작한다.
⑤ Beth와 Victor도 공연을 보러 갈 예정이다.

[Cell phone rings.]
W Hello?
M Hi, Michelle. It's Charlie. Do you want to _____ _____ _____ this Saturday night?
W A play? I didn't know you liked plays.
M Well, I don't. But my brother Justin is _____ _____ _____ _____. It's called *Dr. Jones*.
W Wow! _____ _____ _____ _____!
M Great! The play starts at 7:30. Beth and Victor are coming too. We can all go together!

08

대화를 듣고, 구인 광고에 대한 내용
과 일치하지 <u>않는</u> 것을 고르시오.

① 시간제 근로자를 모집하고 있다.
② 합격자는 국제학생처에서 근무하
게 될 것이다.
③ 학생이 아닌 사람도 지원할 수 있다.
④ 영어를 유창하게 구사해야 한다.
⑤ 이번 주 금요일 이전까지 지원을
완료해야 한다.

W What are you looking at?

M It's an ad. Our school is looking for _____ _____ _____ this semester.

W What kind of job is it?

M It's an office assistant position at the international student office.

W That sounds great. Can anyone _____ _____ _____?

M You have to be a student who is _____ _____ _____ and open-minded toward diverse cultures.

W _____ _____ _____ _____! How can I apply?

M You have to apply on the school website before this Friday.

W I'll do it right now!

09

다음을 듣고, 남자가 본 영화에 대한 내
용과 일치하지 <u>않는</u> 것을 고르시오.

① 코미디 장르이다.
② 미국인 감독이 연출한 작품이다.
③ 다수의 유명 배우가 출연했다.
④ 상영 시간은 2시간 30분이다.
⑤ 남자는 영화를 만족스럽게 보지 못
했다.

M Welcome to my one-minute _____ _____. Yesterday I went to see a new movie called *Mountain Man*. It's a comedy that _____ _____ _____ a Canadian director. There are many famous movie stars in it. Unfortunately, it _____ _____ _____ _____. The biggest problem was its length—it was two and a half hours long. Also, there was _____ _____ _____ and bad language. I give it just one star.

10

다음을 듣고, 기숙사 규칙에 대한 내
용과 일치하지 <u>않는</u> 것을 고르시오.

① 방을 비울 때는 항상 문단속을 해
야 한다.
② 밤 10시에 건물 문이 잠긴다.
③ 반려동물을 데리고 올 수 없다.
④ 방에서 취사를 할 수 없다.
⑤ 방문객 출입은 허용되지 않는다.

W There are some _____ _____ _____. First, always lock your room door when you leave. Second, the door to the building closes at 10:00 p.m., so don't be late. Third, _____ _____ _____ _____. Fourth, you cannot cook in your room. Lastly, you can have visitors, but you must _____ _____ _____ in advance.

A

다음 영어 어휘나 표현의 뜻을 우리말로 쓰세요.

01 discount

02 on weekends

03 international

04 assistant

05 previous

06 downtown

07 in advance

08 title role

09 semester

10 enjoyable

11 lock

12 experience

13 diverse

14 rule

15 performance

16 violence

B

우리말에 맞는 영어 어휘나 표현을 [보기]에서 찾아 쓰세요.

보기	dormitory	description	fit	open-minded	far away
	participate	meeting	director	for the first time	give ~ a try

01 회의

02 열린 마음의

03 적합하다

04 설명

05 기숙사

06 멀리

07 감독

08 ~을 한번 해 보다

09 참가하다

10 처음으로

UNIT 9 목적·이유

유형 설명

대화를 듣고, 특정 행동을 하는 목적이나 이유를 파악하는 유형이다. 주로 전화를 건 목적과 특정 장소에 간 목적을 묻는 문제가 출제된다. 또한, 화자의 특정 행동에 대한 이유를 묻는 문제가 출제되기도 한다.

지시문 유형

· 대화를 듣고, 여자가 전화를 건 목적으로 가장 적절한 것을 고르시오.

· 대화를 듣고, 남자가 체육관에 가는 목적으로 가장 적절한 것을 고르시오.

· 대화를 듣고, 여자가 남자와 함께 갈 수 <u>없는</u> 이유로 가장 적절한 것을 고르시오.

· 대화를 듣고, 남자가 꽃을 산 이유로 가장 적절한 것을 고르시오.

기출표현맛보기

목적

· **W** Oh, are you playing another basketball game with your friends?

　M No, I'm going there to practice dancing.

이유

· **W** Wow, they're beautiful! Is it your mom's birthday?

　M No. Actually, my mom is opening a clothing shop today. I bought these flowers to congratulate her.

주요 어휘·표현 미리보기

다음을 듣고, [보기]에서 알맞은 어휘나 표현을 찾아 쓰세요.　　　　정답 및 해설 p. 26

| 보기 |
| ⓐ charged | ⓑ can't help | ⓒ at least | ⓓ height |
| ⓔ complain about | ⓕ attend | ⓖ apologize | ⓗ business trip |

01 This is my first _____. 이번이 나의 첫 출장이야.

02 Don't _____ the food. 음식에 대해 불평하지 말아라.

03 Once I start laughing, I _____ it. 나는 한번 웃기 시작하면 어쩔 수 없어.

04 I _____ for my mistake. 내 실수에 대해 사과할게.

05 Let me check your _____ and weight. 키와 몸무게를 재 볼게요.

06 She only _____ me half price. 그녀는 나에게 반값만 청구했어.

07 My kids _____ the same class. 우리 아이들은 같은 수업에 참석해.

08 Call me _____ one hour before your visit. 적어도 방문 한 시간 전에 전화해.

기출로 유형 익히기

- 전화를 건 목적을 파악하는 문제의 경우, 자신이 누구인지 밝히거나 상대의 안부를 묻고 난 후에 바로 전화를 건 목적이 나오는 경우가 많으므로 그 부분을 집중해서 들어야 해요.
- 특정 장소에 간 목적이나 이유를 고르는 문제의 경우, 먼저 지시문을 읽고 누구의 목적, 또는 이유를 묻고 있는지 확인하세요. 대화 상대가 다른 내용을 언급하며 오답을 유도하기도 하므로 주의해야 해요.

01

대화를 듣고, 여자가 도서관에 온 목적으로 가장 적절한 것을 고르시오.

① 잡지를 만들기 위해서   ② 책을 반납하기 위해서   ③ 과학 수업을 듣기 위해서
④ 책장 청소를 돕기 위해서   ⑤ 사회 프로젝트를 하기 위해서

M   Hi, Alice.
W   Hi, Karl. What are you doing here in the library?
M   I'm doing my volunteer work. I am cleaning up bookshelves. What about you?   오답 함정
W   Well, I'm here to work on my social studies project. 정답 단서
M   What is your project about?
W   It is about saving children who need clean water in Africa.
M   Oh, that's an interesting topic for a social studies project.

남자와 여자가
도서관에 온 목적이 모두
언급되었네.

02

대화를 듣고, 남자가 마스크를 써야 하는 이유로 가장 적절한 것을 고르시오.

① 황사가 있어서   ② 햇빛이 강해서   ③ 감기에 걸려서
④ 얼굴을 다쳐서   ⑤ 청소를 해야 해서

W   Hurry up, Minsu. It's time to go to school.
M   Okay, Mom. What time is it?
W   It's almost 7:30.
M   Is it raining outside?
W   No, but it's very cloudy.
M   Look! It's really hard to see outside.
W   I think it is because of the yellow dust.
M   Yeah, I think so, too.
W   Make sure you wear a mask before you go out.

여자가 남자에게 마스크를
권하는 이유가 후반부에
제시되니 끝까지 집중하자.

ANSWER

01 여자는 사회 프로젝트를 하기 위해 도서관에 왔다고 했으므로 여자가 도서관에 온 목적으로 ⑤가 알맞다.

02 여자가 황사가 있는 날 학교에 가는 남자에게 마스크를 쓰라고 했으므로 남자가 마스크를 써야 하는 이유로 ①이 알맞다.

01 대화를 듣고, 남자가 전화를 건 목적으로 가장 적절한 것을 고르시오.

① 요금제를 변경하기 위해서
② 수리 비용을 청구하기 위해서
③ 요금 정정을 요청하기 위해서
④ 국제 전화 서비스를 신청하기 위해서
⑤ 스마트폰으로 고지서를 받기 위해서

02 대화를 듣고, 여자가 전화를 건 목적으로 가장 적절한 것을 고르시오.

① 점심을 함께 먹으러 가기 위해서
② 전시회 티켓을 주기 위해서
③ 약속 시각을 변경하기 위해서
④ 미술 숙제를 확인하기 위해서
⑤ 전시회에 함께 가기 위해서

03 대화를 듣고, 남자가 스웨터를 반품하려는 이유로 가장 적절한 것을 고르시오.

① 같은 옷을 가지고 있어서
② 원하는 소재가 아니어서
③ 몸에 잘 맞지 않아서
④ 상품이 훼손되어 있어서
⑤ 디자인이 마음에 들지 않아서

04 대화를 듣고, 여자가 남자에게 전화를 하지 못한 이유로 가장 적절한 것을 고르시오.

① 휴대전화가 고장 나서
② 휴대전화를 집에 두고 가서
③ 영화를 보던 중이어서
④ 휴대전화가 든 가방을 잃어버려서
⑤ 휴대전화 배터리가 없어서

05 대화를 듣고, 아이가 놀이기구를 탈 수 없는 이유로 가장 적절한 것을 고르시오.

① 나이가 어려서
② 키 제한에 걸려서
③ 높은 곳을 무서워해서
④ 보호자를 동반하지 않아서
⑤ 컨디션이 좋지 않아서

고난도

06 대화를 듣고, 여자가 쇼핑몰에 온 목적으로 가장 적절한 것을 고르시오.

① 영화를 보기 위해서
② 머리를 자르기 위해서
③ 근무를 하기 위해서
④ 친구를 만나기 위해서
⑤ 옷을 구입하기 위해서

고난도

07 대화를 듣고, 남자가 상사에게 메일을 보내는 목적으로 가장 적절한 것을 고르시오.

① 업무를 보고하기 위해서
② 감사의 마음을 전하기 위해서
③ 고객의 불만 사항을 전달하기 위해서
④ 서류 결재를 요청하기 위해서
⑤ 업무 일정을 논의하기 위해서

08 대화를 듣고, 여자가 도쿄에 가는 목적으로 가장 적절한 것을 고르시오.

① 여행을 하기 위해서
② 면접을 보기 위해서
③ 결혼식에 참석하기 위해서
④ 남동생의 집을 방문하기 위해서
⑤ 콘서트를 관람하기 위해서

09 대화를 듣고, 남자가 아침 식사를 거른 이유로 가장 적절한 것을 고르시오.

① 시간이 없어서
② 식재료가 다 떨어져서
③ 급체를 해서
④ 식단 관리를 하는 중이어서
⑤ 건강 검진을 받아야 해서

10 대화를 듣고, 여자가 수학 시험을 보지 <u>않은</u> 이유로 가장 적절한 것을 고르시오.

① 늦잠을 자서
② 시험 장소를 착각해서
③ 시험 일정이 연기되어서
④ 시험 범위가 변경되어서
⑤ 시험 문제가 유출되어서

DICTATION

정답 단서 오답 함정

 일반 속도   빠른 속도

01

대화를 듣고, 남자가 전화를 건 목적으로 가장 적절한 것을 고르시오.

① 요금제를 변경하기 위해서
② 수리 비용을 청구하기 위해서
③ 요금 정정을 요청하기 위해서
④ 국제 전화 서비스를 신청하기 위해서
⑤ 스마트폰으로 고지서를 받기 위해서

[Telephone rings.]

W ST Telecom service center. May I help you?

M Yes. I just got my cell phone bill. I didn't make any overseas calls, but you _____ _____ _____ _____.

W Let me _____ _____ _____. What's your name?

M Paul Anderson.

W *[typing sound]* Yes, we've _____ _____ _____. I apologize for the error. I'll fix it and send you a new bill.

M Excellent. Thanks for your help.

02

대화를 듣고, 여자가 전화를 건 목적으로 가장 적절한 것을 고르시오.

① 점심을 함께 먹으러 가기 위해서
② 전시회 티켓을 주기 위해서
③ 약속 시각을 변경하기 위해서
④ 미술 숙제를 확인하기 위해서
⑤ 전시회에 함께 가기 위해서

[Cell phone rings.]

M Hello?

W Hi, Jeremy. It's Susan. What are you doing?

M I'm _____ _____ _____ have lunch. What's up?

W I have to _____ _____ _____ _____ about the new Picasso exhibition. So I'm going to it this Saturday. Why don't you _____ _____ _____?

M Great. I'd love to.

W Excellent. Let's meet at the subway station at noon.

03

대화를 듣고, 남자가 스웨터를 반품하려는 이유로 가장 적절한 것을 고르시오.

① 같은 옷을 가지고 있어서
② 원하는 소재가 아니어서
③ 몸에 잘 맞지 않아서
④ 상품이 훼손되어 있어서
⑤ 디자인이 마음에 들지 않아서

W What can I do for you?

M I'd like to _____ _____ _____.

W All right. Is there a problem with the sweater? Or is it _____ _____ _____?

M Well, it was a gift, but it fits fine. And there's nothing wrong with it.

W I understand. You just don't like it.

M No, I like it a lot. But I already have _____ _____ _____ _____.

W Oh, that's unfortunate! But you can exchange it for another one.

04

대화를 듣고, 여자가 남자에게 전화를 하지 못한 이유로 가장 적절한 것을 고르시오.

① 휴대전화가 고장 나서
② 휴대전화를 집에 두고 가서
③ 영화를 보던 중이어서
④ 휴대전화가 든 가방을 잃어버려서
⑤ 휴대전화 배터리가 없어서

M There you are! Do you know what time it is?

W I'm sorry, Dad. I know I'm late. But I _____ _____ it.

M You should have _____ _____ _____ _____!

W Sorry, but I couldn't.

M Why not? Did your cell phone's battery die?

W Actually, I lost my bag, and _____ _____ _____ _____ _____.

M I see. Then why are you late?

W My purse was in my bag too. I _____ _____ _____, so I walked home.

05

대화를 듣고, 아이가 놀이기구를 탈 수 없는 이유로 가장 적절한 것을 고르시오.

① 나이가 어려서
② 키 제한에 걸려서
③ 높은 곳을 무서워해서
④ 보호자를 동반하지 않아서
⑤ 컨디션이 좋지 않아서

M Welcome to the Viking King ride.

W One child's ticket, please.

M How old is your daughter?

W She's 9 years old.

M Then I have to _____ _____ _____. She needs to be taller than 130 cm.

W All right.

M [pause] Oh, sorry. She's _____ _____ _____, so she can't go on this ride.

W What if I _____ _____ _____ _____ with her?

M Sorry, ma'am. She can't ride this alone or with you.

06

대화를 듣고, 여자가 쇼핑몰에 온 목적으로 가장 적절한 것을 고르시오.

① 영화를 보기 위해서
② 머리를 자르기 위해서
③ 근무를 하기 위해서
④ 친구를 만나기 위해서
⑤ 옷을 구입하기 위해서

M Sharon? Is that you?

W Oh! Hi, Mark! Long time no see!

M I almost didn't recognize you. You _____ _____ _____ _____ _____.

W I did. So _____ _____ _____ _____ _____ at the mall?

M I'm not shopping. I actually work in the clothes store over there.

W Oh, I didn't know that!

M How about you?

W I'm _____ _____ _____ in front of the movie theater. We're going to have dinner together.

M Oh, okay. Well, I'll see you later. _____ _____ _____ _____!

W I will! Bye, Mark.

07

대화를 듣고, 남자가 상사에게 메일을 보내는 목적으로 가장 적절한 것을 고르시오.

① 업무를 보고하기 위해서
② 감사의 마음을 전하기 위해서
③ 고객의 불만 사항을 전달하기 위해서
④ 서류 결재를 요청하기 위해서
⑤ 업무 일정을 논의하기 위해서

W Are you almost ready, Edward?

M Yes. I just need to _____ _____ _____.

W Who are you writing to?

M My boss.

W Is something wrong? You're not _____ _____ _____ _____, are you?

M No. She sent me a nice gift for my birthday, so I _____ _____ _____ _____.

W Wow! I wish we could switch bosses. I don't like mine.

M I know. You're _____ _____ him.

W Anyway, where should we go for dinner?

M I know a great new restaurant near the subway station.

08

대화를 듣고, 여자가 도쿄에 가는 목적으로 가장 적절한 것을 고르시오.

① 여행을 하기 위해서
② 면접을 보기 위해서
③ 결혼식에 참석하기 위해서
④ 남동생의 집을 방문하기 위해서
⑤ 콘서트를 관람하기 위해서

M I heard you are going to Tokyo.

W Yes, I am. _____ _____ _____.

M How long will you stay there?

W Two days.

M Only two days?

W Yes, I'm just going there to _____ _____ _____ _____.

M Oh! I didn't know that.

W I want to stay longer, but I _____ _____ _____ _____ this Friday.

09

대화를 듣고, 남자가 아침 식사를 거른 이유로 가장 적절한 것을 고르시오.

① 시간이 없어서
② 식재료가 다 떨어져서
③ 급체를 해서
④ 식단 관리를 하는 중이어서
⑤ 건강 검진을 받아야 해서

M Hi, Grace. Do you want to get an early lunch with me right now?

W But it's only 10:45. I'm not hungry for lunch yet.

M Oh, okay. I _____ _____, so I'm really hungry.

W Why did you skip breakfast? Are you on a diet?

M No, I had a medical check-up this morning, so I _____ _____ _____ _____ anything for twelve hours.

W You _____ _____ _____! You should go get a snack.

10

대화를 듣고, 여자가 수학 시험을 보지 않은 이유로 가장 적절한 것을 고르시오.

① 늦잠을 자서
② 시험 장소를 착각해서
③ 시험 일정이 연기되어서
④ 시험 범위가 변경되어서
⑤ 시험 문제가 유출되어서

[Cell phone rings.]

W Hi, Dad! Are you _____ _____ _____ _____?

M Not really. Anyway, I wanted to find out _____ _____ _____ _____ _____ _____.

W Oh! Actually, I didn't take it.

M What? Did you oversleep again?

W No! But _____ _____ _____ _____ _____ for next week.

M I see. Well, I've got to go. My train is leaving soon.

W Okay, Dad! Call me again soon!

A

다음 영어 어휘나 표현의 뜻을 우리말로 쓰세요.

01 starving   **02** recognize

03 get one's hair cut   **04** boss

05 exactly   **06** job interview

07 error   **08** reschedule

09 overseas call   **10** on a diet

11 medical check-up   **12** purse

13 can't wait   **14** exhibition

15 actually   **16** bill

B

우리말에 맞는 영어 어휘나 표현을 [보기]에서 찾아 쓰세요.

	보기		switch	die	return	stay	find out
		almost	review	skip	ride	give ~ a call

01 보고서, 논평   **02** (기계가) 서다, 멎다

03 ~을 알아내다[알게 되다]   **04** 거의

05 거르다, 건너뛰다   **06** 엇바꾸다

07 반품하다   **08** 놀이기구, 타다

09 머물다   **10** ~에게 전화를 걸다

유형 설명   대화를 듣고, 화자 두 사람의 관계를 파악하는 유형이다. 대화가 일어나는 상황을 통해 관계를 알아내는 문제가 출제된다.

지시문 유형   대화를 듣고, 두 사람의 관계로 가장 적절한 것을 고르시오.

기출 표현 맛보기

- W   Does he get along with his classmates?
  M   Of course. He is kind to his friends. Everyone likes him. (학부모 – 교사)

- W   Would you like to exchange it for a smaller size?
  M   Actually, he doesn't like the color, either. So, I'd like to get a refund. (점원 – 고객)

- M   I asked for a room with two single beds.
  W   Certainly. Here is your key and two breakfast coupons. (손님 – 호텔 직원)

주요
어휘·표현
미리보기

다음을 듣고, [보기]에서 알맞은 어휘나 표현을 찾아 쓰세요.   정답 및 해설 p. 29

| 보기 |
| ⓐ try on | ⓑ in the back row | ⓒ check out | ⓓ a bit |
| ⓔ weighs | ⓕ get a refund | ⓖ appointment | ⓗ best seller |

01   This bag is the _____ in our store. 이 가방이 우리 가게에서 베스트셀러에요.

02   We'd better sit _____. 우리 뒷줄에 앉는 게 낫겠어.

03   I have an _____ at 10:00 p.m. 나는 저녁 10시에 약속이 있어.

04   Can I _____ this fur coat? 이 털코트를 입어 봐도 될까요?

05   He _____ only about 23 kg. 그는 몸무게가 약 23kg 밖에 나가지 않아.

06   I'd like to _____ on this hat. 이 모자를 환불받고 싶습니다.

07   I may be _____ late. 나는 조금 늦을지도 모르겠어.

08   I need to _____ some books. 나는 책 몇 권을 대출해야 해.

기출로 유형 익히기

- 먼저 선택지를 읽고, 듣게 될 내용을 예상해 보세요.
- 관계를 파악하기 위해, 대화의 주제나 화제를 파악하는 데 초점을 맞춰야 해요.
- 특정 관계에서 자주 쓰이는 어휘를 미리 익혀 두면 좋아요.

01

대화를 듣고, 두 사람의 관계로 가장 적절한 것을 고르시오.

① 꽃가게 점원 – 손님   ② 축구선수 – 코치
③ 안과의사 – 환자   ④ 은행원 – 고객
⑤ 교사 – 학생

W   Good afternoon. What can I do for you?
M   Good afternoon. I want to order a flower basket for my wife.
W   If you choose the flowers, I can make it for you. 정답 단서
M   Okay. My wife likes roses and tulips.
W   That's a good choice.
M   Can you deliver it to her office?
W   Sure. The total will be 35 dollars.

여자는 남자가 꽃을
고르면 그것으로 꽃 바구니를
만들어 주겠다고 했어.

02

대화를 듣고, 두 사람의 관계로 가장 적절한 것을 고르시오.

① 공원 관리인 – 등산객   ② 잡지사 기자 – 화가
③ 사진작가 – 모델   ④ 작곡가 – 가수
⑤ 의사 – 환자

M   Hello, Kelly Watson. I'm Richard Kim from Q Art Magazine.
W   Nice to meet you, Mr. Kim.
M   Your painting, *Blue Mountain*, has become very popular. Our readers say they feel very relaxed and peaceful when they look at it.
W   Really? I'm so happy to hear that.
M   Where do you get the ideas for your paintings?
W   From nature. I spend a lot of time in mountains and valleys.
M   Oh, I see.   오답 함정

남자가 여자의 그림에 대한
독자들의 평을 전하며 자신의
질문을 덧붙이고 있어.

ANSWER

01 여자는 남자가 주문한 꽃 바구니를 만들어 배달해 주겠다고 했으므로 두 사람의 관계로 ①이 알맞다.
02 여자의 그림에 대해 남자가 인터뷰를 하는 상황이므로 두 사람의 관계로 ②가 알맞다.

LISTENING PRACTICE

점수   / 10문항

일반 속도   빠른 속도

01 대화를 듣고, 두 사람의 관계로 가장 적절한 것을 고르시오.

① 영화관 직원 – 손님   ② 서점 직원 – 손님   ③ 호텔 직원 – 투숙객

④ 백화점 직원 – 손님   ⑤ 도서관 사서 – 이용객

고난도

02 대화를 듣고, 두 사람의 관계로 가장 적절한 것을 고르시오.

① 안경점 직원 – 손님   ② 아내 – 남편   ③ 교사 – 학부모

④ 의사 – 보호자   ⑤ 딸 – 아빠

03 대화를 듣고, 두 사람의 관계로 가장 적절한 것을 고르시오.

① 주유소 직원 – 운전자   ② 경비원 – 주민   ③ 교통경찰 – 운전자

④ 택시 기사 – 승객   ⑤ 자동차 정비사 – 고객

04 대화를 듣고, 두 사람의 관계로 가장 적절한 것을 고르시오.

① 택배기사 – 고객   ② 식당 종업원 – 조리사   ③ 가구점 직원 – 손님

④ 아들 – 엄마   ⑤ 식당 주인 – 손님

05 대화를 듣고, 두 사람의 관계로 가장 적절한 것을 고르시오.

① 백화점 직원 – 손님   ② 여행사 직원 – 손님   ③ 은행원 – 고객

④ 우체국 직원 – 손님   ⑤ 우편배달부 – 수신인

06

대화를 듣고, 두 사람의 관계로 가장 적절한 것을 고르시오.

① 손님 – 여행사 직원　　　② 승객 – 승무원　　　③ 손님 – 기념품 가게 점원
④ 여행객 – 관광 안내소 직원　　　⑤ 투숙객 – 호텔 직원

07

대화를 듣고, 두 사람의 관계로 가장 적절한 것을 고르시오.

① 영화배우 – 매니저　　　② 간호사 – 환자　　　③ 교사 – 학생
④ 미용사 – 손님　　　⑤ 옷 가게 점원 – 손님

🇬🇧
08

대화를 듣고, 두 사람의 관계로 가장 적절한 것을 고르시오.

① 약사 – 손님　　　② 간병인 – 보호자　　　③ 교사 – 학생
④ 아빠 – 딸　　　⑤ 의사 – 환자

09

대화를 듣고, 두 사람의 관계로 가장 적절한 것을 고르시오.

① 환자 – 의사　　　② 손님 – 식당 종업원　　　③ 승객 – 승무원
④ 투숙객 – 호텔 직원　　　⑤ 승객 – 버스 운전사

고난도
10

대화를 듣고, 두 사람의 관계로 가장 적절한 것을 고르시오.

① 디자이너 – 모델　　　② 코치 – 운동선수　　　③ 신발 가게 점원 – 손님
④ 미술 교사 – 학생　　　⑤ 서점 직원 – 손님

DICTATION

정답 단서 오답 함정

일반 속도

빠른 속도

01

대화를 듣고, 두 사람의 관계로 가장 적절한 것을 고르시오.
① 영화관 직원 – 손님
② 서점 직원 – 손님
③ 호텔 직원 – 투숙객
④ 백화점 직원 – 손님
⑤ 도서관 사서 – 이용객

W Can I help you?
M Yes. I'm looking for *The Adventures of Sherlock Holmes*, but I can't find it.
W Let me check the computer system. *[pause]* Oh, it _____ _____ _____ _____.
M When will it be available?
W I think _____ _____ _____ _____ next Wednesday.
M Can I reserve it?
W Sure. You can _____ _____ _____ _____ _____.
M Okay. Thank you.

고난도
02

대화를 듣고, 두 사람의 관계로 가장 적절한 것을 고르시오.
① 안경점 직원 – 손님
② 아내 – 남편
③ 교사 – 학부모
④ 의사 – 보호자
⑤ 딸 – 아빠

W This is our classroom.
M It's very nice. I like the pictures on the wall.
W Your daughter Suzie drew one of them. She is good at many things, but I'm _____ _____ _____ _____. They're still dropping.
M Hmm… Which desk is hers?
W It's over there, _____ _____ _____ _____.
M Aha! Maybe that's the problem. I think Suzie might need glasses.
W You could be right. I will _____ _____ _____ _____ _____ in the front row.
M And I will take her to the eye doctor after school tomorrow.
W That's a good idea.

03

대화를 듣고, 두 사람의 관계로 가장 적절한 것을 고르시오.
① 주유소 직원 – 운전자
② 경비원 – 주민
③ 교통경찰 – 운전자
④ 택시 기사 – 승객
⑤ 자동차 정비사 – 고객

M What seems to be the problem?
W My car _____ _____ _____ _____ while I was driving to work.
M I see. Have you had this problem before?
W No, this was the first time.
M Okay. I'll have to _____ _____ _____ _____.
W How long will it take?
M It will probably take a few hours.
W Oh, I guess I'll _____ _____ _____ _____.

04

대화를 듣고, 두 사람의 관계로 가장 적절한 것을 고르시오.

① 택배기사 – 고객
② 식당 종업원 – 조리사
③ 가구점 직원 – 손님
④ 아들 – 엄마
⑤ 식당 주인 – 손님

M There's a problem with table five's food.

W What did they order?

M The chicken soup. They said _____ _____ _____.

W Maybe I added too much salt. _____ _____ _____ and apologize, please. I will make it again.

M All right. And are the sandwiches for table two ready yet?

W Yes. Here you are. You can _____ _____ _____.

05

대화를 듣고, 두 사람의 관계로 가장 적절한 것을 고르시오.

① 백화점 직원 – 손님
② 여행사 직원 – 손님
③ 은행원 – 고객
④ 우체국 직원 – 손님
⑤ 우편배달부 – 수신인

W Good afternoon. How may I help you?

M Hi. I'd like to _____ _____ _____ to Canada.

W Okay. Please _____ _____ _____ _____ _____. What's in it?

M There are some clothes and toys in it.

W I see. It weighs 2 kg. How would you like to send it?

M _____ _____ _____, please. How long will it take?

W About two days. And it will cost $30.

M All right. Here you are.

06

대화를 듣고, 두 사람의 관계로 가장 적절한 것을 고르시오.

① 손님 – 여행사 직원
② 승객 – 승무원
③ 손님 – 기념품 가게 점원
④ 여행객 – 관광 안내소 직원
⑤ 투숙객 – 호텔 직원

M Hi. I don't know if you remember me.

W Ah, yes. You _____ _____ _____ to Japan. Did you get our message about the earthquake in Japan?

M Yes, I did. Has the tour _____ _____?

W Unfortunately, yes. We just made the decision.

M Can I _____ _____ _____?

W Of course. Or we could reschedule the tour.

M I'll take the refund.

07

대화를 듣고, 두 사람의 관계로 가장 적절한 것을 고르시오.

① 영화배우 – 매니저
② 간호사 – 환자
③ 교사 – 학생
④ 미용사 – 손님
⑤ 옷 가게 점원 – 손님

M Do you _____ _____ _____?

W Yes. My name is Kim Minji.

M Okay. Come in and have a seat. What can I do for you?

W I'd like to _____ _____ _____ _____. Do you think brown hair would look good on me?

M Yes, I think brown hair would suit you well.

W Great! I also want to _____ _____ _____ _____.

M How long?

W Shoulder length would be good.

08

대화를 듣고, 두 사람의 관계로 가장
적절한 것을 고르시오.

① 약사 – 손님
② 간병인 – 보호자
③ 교사 – 학생
④ 아빠 – 딸
⑤ 의사 – 환자

M Hello, Sejin. Are you _____ _____ _____?
W Yes. I haven't gotten better since the last time I saw you.
M So what's the problem?
W I still _____ _____ _____.
M Did you take the pills I _____ _____ _____?
W I did, but they haven't helped.
M Let me _____ _____ _____. *[pause]* I'll give you a shot today. Get lots of rest and come back if the fever doesn't go down.

09

대화를 듣고, 두 사람의 관계로 가장
적절한 것을 고르시오.

① 환자 – 의사
② 손님 – 식당 종업원
③ 승객 – 승무원
④ 투숙객 – 호텔 직원
⑤ 승객 – 버스 운전사

M Excuse me. Can I _____ _____ _____ _____, please?
W Of course. Are you not feeling well?
M I'm all right. I just feel a bit cold.
W Should I _____ _____ _____ _____ too?
M Oh, yes, please. By the way, _____ _____ _____ _____ at Incheon Airport?
W We will be there in thirty minutes.
M I see. Thank you.
W You're welcome. Please wait a moment. I'll be right back.

고난도

10

대화를 듣고, 두 사람의 관계로 가장
적절한 것을 고르시오.

① 디자이너 – 모델
② 코치 – 운동선수
③ 신발 가게 점원 – 손님
④ 미술 교사 – 학생
⑤ 서점 직원 – 손님

M Are you looking for something?
W Yes. I'd like to buy _____ _____ _____ _____.
M Okay. How about these ones? They are our best sellers.
W Hmm… I like the design, but I don't like the color. Do you have them _____ _____ _____?
M Yes, they also come in white and gray. They're over here.
W I think the white pair looks better. Can I _____ _____ _____?
M Sure. What size do you wear?
W I wear a size 7.
M Let me _____ _____ _____ _____ _____.

A 다음 영어 어휘나 표현의 뜻을 우리말로 쓰세요.

01 salty _____ **02** package _____

03 scale _____ **04** engine _____

05 reserve _____ **06** clothes _____

07 look good on _____ **08** earthquake _____

09 running shoes _____ **10** length _____

11 strange _____ **12** make a noise _____

13 add _____ **14** express mail _____

15 have a fever _____ **16** package tour _____

B 우리말에 맞는 영어 어휘나 표현을 [보기]에서 찾아 쓰세요.

보기	grade	extra	prescribe	temperature	make a decision
	suit	order	front	feel well	give ~ a shot

01 처방하다 _____ **02** 체온, 온도 _____

03 건강 상태가 좋다 _____ **04** 앞의 _____

05 추가의, 여분의 _____ **06** ~에게 어울리다 _____

07 성적 _____ **08** ~에게 주사를 놓다 _____

09 결정하다 _____ **10** 주문하다 _____

부탁·제안한 일

대화를 듣고, 화자가 상대에게 부탁한 일이나 제안한 일을 고르는 유형이다. 주로 대화가 일어나는 상황을 통해 한 사람이 다른 사람에게 부탁 또는 제안한 일을 파악하는 문제가 출제된다.

지시문 유형

- 대화를 듣고, 여자가 남자에게 부탁한 일로 가장 적절한 것을 고르시오.
- 대화를 듣고, 남자가 여자에게 제안한 일로 가장 적절한 것을 고르시오.

기출표현맛보기

부탁한 일

- Can you go and buy some sugar now? I'll give you money. (설탕 사오기)
- Could you book a ticket for me? (티켓 예매하기)

제안한 일

- Why don't you look at some blogs and read reviews? (블로그 평 보기)

주요
어휘·표현
미리보기

다음을 듣고, [보기]에서 알맞은 어휘나 표현을 찾아 쓰세요.   정답 및 해설 p. 32

| 보기 |

ⓐ dressed ⓑ show you around ⓒ on vacation ⓓ print out
ⓔ weather report ⓕ handle ⓖ an aisle seat ⓗ keeping a blog

01 Please _____ the photos by tomorrow. 그 사진들을 내일까지 출력해주세요.

02 I've been _____ for five years. 나는 5년째 블로그를 하고 있어.

03 You're well _____ today. 너 오늘 옷 잘 차려입었네.

04 I'll choose _____. 저는 통로 쪽 좌석을 선택할게요.

05 She's _____ now. 그녀는 지금 휴가 중이야.

06 I can _____ it within two days. 나는 그것을 이틀 안에 처리할 수 있어.

07 Let me _____ my house. 너에게 우리 집을 구경시켜 줄게.

08 Did you hear the _____ this morning? 오늘 아침에 일기 예보 들었니?

- 먼저 지시문을 읽고, 두 화자 중 누가 부탁/제안한 일을 파악해야 할지 확인하세요.
- 부탁한 일은 'Can I / Can you / Could you / Will you / Would you / Please ~', 제안한 일은 'How about / Why don't you / If you'로 시작하는 표현에 집중해야 해요.
- 이미 한 일이나 상대방이 한 일 등이 함정일 수 있으니 주의하세요.

01

대화를 듣고, 여자가 남자에게 부탁한 일로 가장 적절한 것을 고르시오.

① 병원에 함께 가기　　② 태권도 가르치기　　③ 만화책 가져오기
④ 옷 챙겨오기　　⑤ 책 반납하기

[Cell phone rings.]

W Hello, Ryan.

M Hi, Minju. Are you okay? How's your leg?

W It's getting better, but I'm a little bored in the hospital.

M Glad to hear you're feeling better. I'm going to visit you tomorrow after my Taekwondo lesson. Do you need anything?　　오답 함정

W Umm... I want to read something fun. Could you bring me some of your comic books?　　정답 단서

M Of course. I'll bring you some tomorrow.

W Thanks. See you then.

> 병원에 입원 중인 여자가 남자에게 지루함을 달랠 만한 물건을 부탁하는 내용이야.

02

대화를 듣고, 남자가 여자에게 제안한 일로 가장 적절한 것을 고르시오.

① 규칙적인 생활하기　　② 스케줄 앱 사용하기　　③ 자기계발 도서 읽기
④ 병원 진료 예약하기　　⑤ 스마트폰으로 강의 듣기

M Jiyoung, what's wrong? You look worried.

W I didn't give my homework to the teacher yesterday.

M What happened? Did you forget to do it?

W Yeah. I often forget things these days.

M That's too bad.

W What should I do?

M How about using a schedule app on your smart phone? It might help you remember what to do.

W That's a good idea. I'll download one on my phone.

> 근래에 해야 할 일을 자주 잊는다는 여자에게 남자가 스마트폰을 활용할 것을 제안하는 내용이야.

 ANSWER

01 여자가 남자에게 만화책을 가져와 줄 수 있냐고 했으므로 여자가 남자에게 부탁한 일은 ③이다.

02 남자가 여자에게 스마트폰의 스케줄 앱을 사용하면 해야 할 일을 기억하는 데 도움이 될 거라고 했으므로 남자가 여자에게 제안한 일은 ②이다.

LISTENING PRACTICE

점수 _____ / 10문항

일반 속도

빠른 속도

01 대화를 듣고, 남자가 여자에게 부탁한 일로 가장 적절한 것을 고르시오.

① 선물 포장하기
② 수족관 함께 가기
③ 기념품 사 오기
④ 선물 함께 고르기
⑤ 케이크 사 오기

02 대화를 듣고, 여자가 남자에게 부탁한 일로 가장 적절한 것을 고르시오.

① 버스 시간 확인하기
② 학교에 데려다주기
③ 세탁소에 교복 맡기기
④ 거실 청소하기
⑤ 공책 찾기

03 대화를 듣고, 남자가 여자에게 부탁한 일로 가장 적절한 것을 고르시오.

① 여행 책자 빌려주기
② 여동생에게 시내 구경시켜 주기
③ 숙소 추천하기
④ 공항에 여동생 마중 나가기
⑤ 공항 차편 알아보기

04 대화를 듣고, 여자가 남자에게 부탁한 일로 가장 적절한 것을 고르시오.

① 블로그 게시물 읽어보기
② 영화평 검토하기
③ 블로그 개설하기
④ 블로그 주소 알려주기
⑤ 영화 상영관 알아보기

05 대화를 듣고, 남자가 여자에게 제안한 일로 가장 적절한 것을 고르시오.

① 소풍 계획 짜기
② 도시락 준비하기
③ 할머니 댁 방문하기
④ 일기 예보 확인하기
⑤ 야외에서 산책하기

06 대화를 듣고, 여자가 남자에게 부탁한 일로 가장 적절한 것을 고르시오.

① 농구 연습 시간 변경하기　　② 약 가져다주기
③ 병원에 데려다주기　　④ 휴대전화 가져다주기
⑤ 병원 진료 예약하기

07 대화를 듣고, 남자가 여자에게 부탁한 일로 가장 적절한 것을 고르시오.

① 개 산책시키기　　② 욕실 청소하기
③ 욕실 세면대 수리하기　　④ 개 목욕시키기
⑤ 배관공에게 전화하기

고난도
08 대화를 듣고, 여자가 남자에게 부탁한 일로 가장 적절한 것을 고르시오.

① 안전벨트 매기　　② 좌석 바꿔주기
③ 좌석 아래로 짐 옮기기　　④ 비행기 창문 덮개 열기
⑤ 담요 가져다주기

고난도
09 대화를 듣고, 남자가 여자에게 제안한 일로 가장 적절한 것을 고르시오.

① 콜택시 부르기　　② 지하철로 환승하기
③ 회의실 예약하기　　④ 회의 시간 변경하기
⑤ 회의 자료 출력하기

10 대화를 듣고, 여자가 남자에게 제안한 일로 가장 적절한 것을 고르시오.

① 목소리 낮추기　　② 함께 수학 공부하기
③ 연극 연습 장소 옮기기　　④ 연극 오디션 참가하기
⑤ 연극 연습 일정 바꾸기

DICTATION

정답 단서 오답 함정

일반 속도

빠른 속도

01

대화를 듣고, 남자가 여자에게 부탁한
일로 가장 적절한 것을 고르시오.
① 선물 포장하기
② 수족관 함께 가기
③ 기념품 사 오기
④ 선물 함께 고르기
⑤ 케이크 사 오기

[Cell phone rings.]

M Hello?

W Hello, Paul. It's Linda. Would you like to go to the aquarium together on Sunday?

M Sorry, but I can't. This Sunday is my mother's birthday.

W Really? Did you _____ _____ _____ _____?

M No, I'm going to the mall tomorrow, but I don't know _____ _____ _____ _____. Would you come with me?

W Tomorrow is Friday, right? Okay. I know _____ _____ _____ _____.

M Great. I'll pick you up tomorrow.

02

대화를 듣고, 여자가 남자에게 부탁한
일로 가장 적절한 것을 고르시오.
① 버스 시간 확인하기
② 학교에 데려다주기
③ 세탁소에 교복 맡기기
④ 거실 청소하기
⑤ 공책 찾기

M Aren't you dressed yet? You're going to miss your bus.

W Sorry, Dad! I'm looking for my science notebook.

M It _____ _____ _____ _____ somewhere. Maybe it's in the living room.

W Could you please _____ _____ _____ while I put on my school uniform? It has a green cover.

M Sure, honey. And if you miss your bus, I'll _____ _____ _____ to school.

W Thanks, Dad! I'll hurry!

03

대화를 듣고, 남자가 여자에게 부탁한
일로 가장 적절한 것을 고르시오.
① 여행 책자 빌려주기
② 여동생에게 시내 구경시켜 주기
③ 숙소 추천하기
④ 공항에 여동생 마중 나가기
⑤ 공항 차편 알아보기

[Cell phone rings.]

W Hello?

M Hey, Mina. It's Mark. You still live in Chicago, don't you?

W Yes, I do. Are you coming to visit?

M No, but my sister is. Could you _____ _____ _____ _____ _____?

W Sure! Does she _____ _____ _____ _____ the airport?

M No, that's okay. I'll give her your number, and she'll call you from her hotel.

W All right. Is she coming here to study?

M No, she's _____ _____ _____.

04

대화를 듣고, 여자가 남자에게 부탁한
일로 가장 적절한 것을 고르시오.

① 블로그 게시물 읽어보기
② 영화평 검토하기
③ 블로그 개설하기
④ 블로그 주소 알려주기
⑤ 영화 상영관 알아보기

W Do you _____ _____ _____, Ethan?

M No. I used to, but it was too much work. How about you?

W I do, but I don't think my blog is very interesting.

M What do you write about?

W Movies and music. Would you _____ _____ _____?

M Sure, I'd love to. Give me the address.

W Thanks! I'll send it to you by cell phone message. I want to _____ _____ _____.

05

대화를 듣고, 남자가 여자에게 제안한
일로 가장 적절한 것을 고르시오.

① 소풍 계획 짜기
② 도시락 준비하기
③ 할머니 댁 방문하기
④ 일기 예보 확인하기
⑤ 야외에서 산책하기

M I think we should _____ _____ _____ tomorrow.

W Why? I already prepared all of the food.

M Look at the clouds. I think it's going to rain tonight.

W I don't think so. Can you _____ _____ _____ _____ right now?

M Sure, let me check. Hmm… In most areas, there _____ _____ _____ _____ tomorrow.

W Oh no! I was looking forward to spending the day outside.

M Then how about _____ _____ _____ _____? We can enjoy your food while looking at the view from the terrace.

W That's a good idea. I'm sure Grandma will be glad to see us.

06

대화를 듣고, 여자가 남자에게 부탁한
일로 가장 적절한 것을 고르시오.

① 농구 연습 시간 변경하기
② 약 가져다주기
③ 병원에 데려다주기
④ 휴대전화 가져다주기
⑤ 병원 진료 예약하기

W Oh, _____ _____ _____ _____.

M You must have twisted it during the basketball game. Here, sit down on the sofa.

W Thanks. I might need to see a doctor.

M Would you like me to make an appointment?

W I'll do it. But can you _____ _____ _____? It's in my room.

M Okay. Just stay there. You shouldn't be _____ _____.

07

대화를 듣고, 남자가 여자에게 부탁한
일로 가장 적절한 것을 고르시오.

① 개 산책시키기
② 욕실 청소하기
③ 욕실 세면대 수리하기
④ 개 목욕시키기
⑤ 배관공에게 전화하기

W What are you doing? The bathroom is a mess!

M The sink broke. I'm _____ _____ _____ _____.

W Oh no. Do you need any help?

M No, that's okay. I can handle it.

W All right. But weren't you going to take the dog _____ _____ _____?

M Yes, but I _____ _____ _____. Can you do it for me?

W Sure. Be careful. If you can't fix it, just call a plumber.

M I will.

08

대화를 듣고, 여자가 남자에게 부탁한
일로 가장 적절한 것을 고르시오.

① 안전벨트 매기
② 좌석 바꿔주기
③ 좌석 아래로 짐 옮기기
④ 비행기 창문 덮개 열기
⑤ 담요 가져다주기

M The plane is going to _____ _____ _____.

W Yes! We're starting to move.

M In two hours, we'll be in Tokyo!

W I'm a bit nervous. I should _____ _____ _____ _____.

M Yes. And put your bag under the seat.

W Okay, I will.

M The view will be great once we're in the air.

W Would you _____ _____ _____ _____? I want to look out the window.

M I thought you wanted an aisle seat so you could get to the bathroom easily.

W I did. But I _____ _____ _____!

09

대화를 듣고, 남자가 여자에게 제안한
일로 가장 적절한 것을 고르시오.

① 콜택시 부르기
② 지하철로 환승하기
③ 회의실 예약하기
④ 회의 시간 변경하기
⑤ 회의 자료 출력하기

[Cell phone rings.]

W Hello?

M Hi, Rachel. Are you _____ _____ _____ _____ _____ _____?

W Yes, but the traffic is really bad. I've been in a taxi for thirty minutes already.

M Why did you decide to take a taxi?

W I was _____ _____ _____. I thought it would be faster.

M Hmm. Why don't you get out now and _____ _____ _____? It is faster this time of day.

W Good idea. Oh, could you _____ _____ _____ _____ for the meeting?

M Sure. How many copies do you need?

W At least ten.

M Okay. But please hurry. The meeting starts in twenty minutes.

10

대화를 듣고, 여자가 남자에게 제안한
일로 가장 적절한 것을 고르시오.

① 목소리 낮추기
② 함께 수학 공부하기
③ 연극 연습 장소 옮기기
④ 연극 오디션 참가하기
⑤ 연극 연습 일정 바꾸기

W What are you guys doing here?

M We're _____ _____ _____ _____ _____.

W Oh! I didn't know you were in the play.

M We're not yet. But there are auditions tomorrow.

W I see. I'm actually studying math in the classroom next door. _____ _____ _____ _____ that I can't concentrate.

M Sorry. This was the only empty classroom.

W Why don't you _____ _____ _____ _____ _____? It is usually empty after school.

M Okay, we'll move. We won't need to _____ _____ _____ there.

W Thanks. Good luck with your auditions, guys!

A

다음 영어 어휘나 표현의 뜻을 우리말로 쓰세요.

01 noisy

02 put on

03 address

04 plumber

05 aquarium

06 nervous

07 usually

08 prepare

09 ankle

10 opinion

11 school uniform

12 practice

13 take a taxi

14 see a doctor

15 keep one's voice down

16 change one's mind

B

우리말에 맞는 영어 어휘나 표현을 [보기]에서 찾아 쓰세요.

| 보기 | miss | mess | spend | concentrate | Would you mind ~? |
| | copy | somewhere | careful | for a walk | look forward to v-ing |

01 엉망인 상태

02 (책 등의 한) 부

03 집중하다

04 (시간을) 보내다

05 놓치다

06 산책 삼아

07 어딘가에

08 ~하는 것을 고대하다

09 조심하는

10 ~해도 될까요?

마지막 말에 대한 응답

대화를 듣고, 화자의 마지막 말에 대한 알맞은 응답을 고르는 유형이다. 내용의 전체적인 흐름을 파악하여 대화의 마지막 말에 이어질 응답으로 적절한 것을 묻는 문제가 출제된다.

대화를 듣고, 여자의 마지막 말에 이어질 남자의 말로 가장 적절한 것을 고르시오.

- **W** Eating too fast is not good for your health.
  M Right, I'll remember that.

- **M** School festival? When is it?
  W It's next Friday.

다음을 듣고, [보기]에서 알맞은 어휘나 표현을 찾아 쓰세요.　　　　　　　　정답 및 해설 p. 36

| 보기 |
| ⓐ in need | ⓑ playing the guitar | ⓒ work part-time | ⓓ get on |
| ⓔ pick out | ⓕ have in mind | ⓖ left a message | ⓗ wonder if |

01 Someone _____ on my phone. 누군가 내 전화기에 메시지를 남겼어.

02 I _____ you can help me. 네가 나를 도와줄 수 있는지 궁금해.

03 Where did you _____ this bus? 이 버스를 어디에서 탔니?

04 We have to _____ a scarf for her. 우리는 그녀에게 줄 스카프를 골라야 해.

05 You're very good at _____! 너 기타 정말 잘 친다!

06 What kind of gift do you _____? 어떤 종류의 선물을 생각하고 있어?

07 They sent money to children _____. 그들은 어려움에 처한 아이들에게 돈을 보냈어.

08 I _____, three days a week. 나는 일주일에 세 번 아르바이트를 해.

• 먼저 영어로 제시된 선택지를 읽고, 의미를 파악해 두세요.
• 대화의 전반적인 내용을 파악하는 동시에 화자의 마지막 말을 주의 깊게 들으세요. 특히 마지막 말이 질문이라면 의문사를 놓치지 마세요.

01

대화를 듣고, 남자의 마지막 말에 이어질 여자의 말로 가장 적절한 것을 고르시오.

Woman: _____

① Turn right, please.　　　　② He doesn't have to.
③ Where are you from?　　　④ How can I get there?
⑤ Jogging could be good.

M　Can you believe it? We have no school next week!
W　Yeah, it's already summer vacation.
M　Time goes by so fast!
W　Right. Do you have any special plans for the vacation?
M　Well, I plan to exercise at least three times a week.
W　Awesome! What kind of exercise are you going to do?
M　I didn't decide yet. Can you recommend something?
W　_____

남자가 여름 방학
동안 어떤 운동을 할지
아직 못 정했다고 하네.

02

대화를 듣고, 여자의 마지막 말에 이어질 남자의 말로 가장 적절한 것을 고르시오.

Man: _____

① Enjoy your meal.　　　　② See you next time.
③ Have a wonderful time.　④ Text him that you are sorry.
⑤ Of course, I'll be there on time.

W　Chris, I have something to tell you.
M　What is it, Mina?
W　I had some trouble with Danny.
M　What happened?
W　I forgot to do my part of the group project, so we couldn't finish it in time.
M　Really?
W　Yeah, so I think he's angry at me.
M　He must be upset. Did you try to call him?
W　I did, but he didn't answer my call. What should I do?
M　_____

여자가 그룹 프로젝트
중에 잘못을 해서 친구가
화가 났다고 하네.

ANSWER

01　남자가 여름 방학 때 일주일에 최소 세 번 운동할 계획인데 어떤 운동을 할지 못 정했다며 추천해 달라고 했으므로 그에 대한 여자의 응답으로 ⑤가 알맞다.

02　여자가 자신의 불찰로 인해 화가 난 친구가 전화를 받지 않는다며 어떻게 하면 좋을지 물었으므로 그에 대한 남자의 응답으로 ④가 알맞다.

LISTENING PRACTICE

점수 _____ / 12문항

일반 속도   빠른 속도

[01-02] 대화를 듣고, 여자의 마지막 말에 이어질 남자의 말로 가장 적절한 것을 고르시오.

01

Man: _____

① It'll take about an hour.

② Sorry for keeping you waiting.

③ I'll see her tomorrow evening.

④ Okay, I'll see you after my swimming lesson.

⑤ That would be better. I'll be there at 5:00.

02

Man: _____

① Just some books.

② I bought it last month.

③ She has long, curly black hair.

④ It's dark brown, and it has two pockets.

⑤ I can't find my backpack anywhere.

[03-04] 대화를 듣고, 남자의 마지막 말에 이어질 여자의 말로 가장 적절한 것을 고르시오.

03

Woman: _____

① Not really. But I work part-time.

② I want to take a guitar class, too.

③ I usually walk for half an hour.

④ Yes, I like working in the cafeteria.

⑤ I do my homework in the library.

고난도
04

Woman: _____

① They can help me with my project.

② Okay. I'll move it before they arrive.

③ Sorry, but I'm too busy with my project.

④ Dinner will be ready at 6:30.

⑤ All right. I'll meet you then.

[05-06] 대화를 듣고, 여자의 마지막 말에 이어질 남자의 말로 가장 적절한 것을 고르시오.

05

Man: _____

① It's 4:30 now.

② Thank you for your present.

③ Sorry, I don't have any money.

④ Great. She's often late for school.

⑤ Actually, I already have one.

고난도

06

Man: _____

① Were you too scared to ride it?

② I'll let you know when I get back.

③ I've ridden it several times.

④ Why don't you believe me?

⑤ Yes, I was terrified!

[07-08] 대화를 듣고, 남자의 마지막 말에 이어질 여자의 말로 가장 적절한 것을 고르시오.

07

Woman: _____

① Yes, this is she speaking.

② That's okay. I'll call his cell phone later.

③ The line is busy right now.

④ I think you have the wrong number.

⑤ There's no way to contact him.

08

Woman: _____

① Okay, I'll buy both of them.

② Do you have that in other colors?

③ Then I'll take the green one.

④ Sure. I think blue would look good on you.

⑤ Sorry, but we don't have any black jackets.

[09-10] 대화를 듣고, 여자의 마지막 말에 이어질 남자의 말로 가장 적절한 것을 고르시오.

09　　　　Man: _____

① Mine is broken too.

② I don't need it anymore.

③ Really? That's very kind of you.

④ Oh, can you fix it right now?

⑤ I forgot to charge the laptop.

10　　　　Man: _____

① Yes. I want to volunteer to help them.

② There is nothing I can do about it now.

③ Why don't we go camping this weekend?

④ Thank you for giving me the items that I really needed.

⑤ Sounds good. I'll look around for some items to donate.

[11-12] 대화를 듣고, 남자의 마지막 말에 이어질 여자의 말로 가장 적절한 것을 고르시오.

11　　　　Woman: _____

① Take this pill twice a day.

② Don't worry. You'll be all right.

③ It's not far from here. Take a bus.

④ He said you should eat a balanced diet.

⑤ The surgery was a complete success.

12　　　　Woman: _____

① Yes, she is a good teacher.

② I met her last semester.

③ Every Tuesday and Thursday at 1:00 p.m.

④ I've already taken that class.

⑤ The classroom is on the fourth floor.

DICTATION

정답 단서 오답 함정

일반 속도

빠른 속도

01

대화를 듣고, 여자의 마지막 말에 이어질 남자의 말로 가장 적절한 것을 고르시오.

Man: _____

① It'll take about an hour.
② Sorry for keeping you waiting.
③ I'll see her tomorrow evening.
④ Okay, I'll see you after my swimming lesson.
⑤ That would be better. I'll be there at 5:00.

M What are you doing this Saturday?

W I have a swimming lesson at 11:00 a.m. But it ends at 12:00 p.m.

M Then how about _____ _____ _____ _____ _____ in the afternoon?

W Okay. Do you have a specific movie in mind?

M Yes. I _____ _____ _____ _____ *The Last Wish.*

W That sounds like fun. What time shall we meet?

M The movie starts at 6:30. _____ _____ _____ _____ in front of MV Cinema.

W Why don't we _____ _____ _____ _____ than that and have dinner too?

M _____

02

대화를 듣고, 여자의 마지막 말에 이어질 남자의 말로 가장 적절한 것을 고르시오.

Man: _____

① Just some books.
② I bought it last month.
③ She has long, curly black hair.
④ It's dark brown, and it has two pockets.
⑤ I can't find my backpack anywhere.

[Telephone rings.]

W Hello. How may I help you?

M Hi. I _____ _____ _____ on the subway this morning.

W I see. Which line did you take?

M I took Line 4. I got on at Seoul Station and got off at Sadang.

W Can you tell me _____ _____ _____ _____ _____?

M I guess it was around 9:30.

W All right. What does _____ _____ _____ _____?

M _____

03

대화를 듣고, 남자의 마지막 말에 이어질 여자의 말로 가장 적절한 것을 고르시오.

Woman: _____

① Not really. But I work part-time.
② I want to take a guitar class, too.
③ I usually walk for half an hour.
④ Yes, I like working in the cafeteria.
⑤ I do my homework in the library.

M Oh, hi, Jamie. _____ _____ _____ _____!

W Hi, Dan! It's been ages. How have you been?

M Good. I've been learning how to _____ _____ _____.

W Wow! Is it fun?

M Yes, it is. How about you?

W I'm doing okay. But I have been really busy these days.

M Do you have _____ _____ _____ _____ _____?

W _____

04

대화를 듣고, 남자의 마지막 말에 이어질 여자의 말로 가장 적절한 것을 고르시오.

Woman: _____

① They can help me with my project.
② Okay. I'll move it before they arrive.
③ Sorry, but I'm too busy with my project.
④ Dinner will be ready at 6:30.
⑤ All right. I'll meet you then.

M Hailey, what's that on the kitchen table?

W It's my science project. It's a model of a volcano.

M It's great, but my friends are _____ _____ _____.

W So? You can just go in your room.

M There are five of us, and we're going to _____ _____ _____ _____. We need the table.

W Okay. I'll _____ _____ _____ _____ _____. But not right now.

M Why not?

W The paint is still wet. It's almost dry, though.

M Well, my friends _____ _____ _____ at 6:00.

W _____

05

대화를 듣고, 여자의 마지막 말에 이어질 남자의 말로 가장 적절한 것을 고르시오.

Man: _____

① It's 4:30 now.
② Thank you for your present.
③ Sorry, I don't have any money.
④ Great. She's often late for school.
⑤ Actually, I already have one.

W Hey, Alex. What are you doing here?

M I'm _____ _____ _____ _____ for my younger sister. Her birthday is next week.

W Do you have something in mind?

M No. I'm not sure _____ _____ _____.

W Look at this doll! It's so pretty. How about buying it for her?

M No, she _____ _____ _____ _____ already.

W Then how about this alarm clock? It's really cute.

M _____

06

대화를 듣고, 여자의 마지막 말에 이어질 남자의 말로 가장 적절한 것을 고르시오.

Man: _____

① Were you too scared to ride it?
② I'll let you know when I get back.
③ I've ridden it several times.
④ Why don't you believe me?
⑤ Yes, I was terrified!

M Guess where I'm going this weekend.

W I have no idea. Where?

M Wonderland Amusement Park! My parents are taking me!

W You're kidding! _____ _____ _____ _____ before?

M No, I haven't. How about you?

W I haven't either. But my friends say it has a great roller coaster.

M Yes! I heard it's very high and _____ _____ _____.

W Everyone says that it's really scary. I _____ _____ _____ _____.

M _____

07

대화를 듣고, 남자의 마지막 말에 이어질 여자의 말로 가장 적절한 것을 고르시오.

Woman: _____

① Yes, this is she speaking.
② That's okay. I'll call his cell phone later.
③ The line is busy right now.
④ I think you have the wrong number.
⑤ There's no way to contact him.

[Telephone rings.]

M Hello? This is Spotlight Offices.

W Hello. May I speak to Brad, please?

M I'm sorry, he's _____ _____ _____ _____. Can I ask who is calling?

W This is his sister, Lisa. I called his cell phone several times, but _____ _____ _____.

M Oh, he _____ _____ _____ on his desk.

W Do you know when the meeting will be over?

M Maybe in thirty minutes. Would you like to _____ _____ _____?

W _____

08

대화를 듣고, 남자의 마지막 말에 이어질 여자의 말로 가장 적절한 것을 고르시오.

Woman: _____

① Okay, I'll buy both of them.
② Do you have that in other colors?
③ Then I'll take the green one.
④ Sure. I think blue would look good on you.
⑤ Sorry, but we don't have any black jackets.

W Hi. Can I help you find something?

M Sure, thanks. I'm looking for a jacket.

W How about this green jacket? It's a new arrival.

M Do you have that _____ _____ _____ _____?

W Yes. Here's a large one. Would you like to _____ _____ _____?

M Yes, please. *[pause]* Hmm... The size is okay, but I don't think _____ _____ _____ _____.

W It also comes in blue and black. What do you think?

M Oh, they both look nice. Could you _____ _____ _____ _____ _____?

W _____

09

대화를 듣고, 여자의 마지막 말에 이어질 남자의 말로 가장 적절한 것을 고르시오.

Man: _____

① Mine is broken too.
② I don't need it anymore.
③ Really? That's very kind of you.
④ Oh, can you fix it right now?
⑤ I forgot to charge the laptop.

W What's wrong, Allen?

M I was writing an English essay on my laptop, and it _____ _____ _____.

W Hmm. Do you think it's because of a virus?

M I don't know. I can't _____ _____ _____.

W I think you should take it to the service center.

M Right, but I need a laptop to _____ _____ _____. It's due next Monday.

W I can _____ _____ _____ _____ until yours is fixed.

M _____

10

대화를 듣고, 여자의 마지막 말에 이어질 남자의 말로 가장 적절한 것을 고르시오.

Man: _____

① Yes. I want to volunteer to help them.
② There is nothing I can do about it now.
③ Why don't we go camping this weekend?
④ Thank you for giving me the items that I really needed.
⑤ Sounds good. I'll look around for some items to donate.

M Did you hear about the flood that happened in West Virginia?

W Yes, it's awful. Thousands of people _____ _____ _____.

M Is there any way we can help?

W I heard that **volunteers** are collecting items _____ _____ _____ _____ _____.

M What kinds of items _____ _____ _____ _____?

W Tents, sleeping bags, blankets, clothes, and things like that.

M That makes sense. They need those.

W We can send some goods together. I have a couple of sleeping bags and blankets.

M _____

11

대화를 듣고, 남자의 마지막 말에 이어질 여자의 말로 가장 적절한 것을 고르시오.

Woman: _____

① Take this pill twice a day.
② Don't worry. You'll be all right.
③ It's not far from here. Take a bus.
④ He said you should eat a balanced diet.
⑤ The surgery was a complete success.

W _____ _____ _____, Larry. What's wrong?

M I got the results from the medical check-up I had last week.

W Oh. I hope everything is okay.

M Well, I _____ _____ _____ _____. I need to see a doctor.

W Really? Does your stomach hurt?

M I've _____ _____ _____ _____, I guess.

W When will you see the doctor?

M Next week. I'm worried. _____ _____ it's a disease?

W _____

12

대화를 듣고, 남자의 마지막 말에 이어질 여자의 말로 가장 적절한 것을 고르시오.

Woman: _____

① Yes, she is a good teacher.
② I met her last semester.
③ Every Tuesday and Thursday at 1:00 p.m.
④ I've already taken that class.
⑤ The classroom is on the fourth floor.

W Which class are you going to take?

M I _____ _____ _____. What about you?

W My friend told me that Mrs. Green's English class is really good.

M Hmm... I don't know Mrs. Green. _____ _____ _____ _____ _____?

W She is very tall, and she has black hair.

M Oh! I've seen her before. She seems nice.

W Yes, she is. I'll probably _____ _____ _____.

M When is it?

W _____

정답 및 해설 p. 41

UNIT 12 어휘·표현 다지기

A

다음 영어 어휘나 표현의 뜻을 우리말로 쓰세요.

01 several ____________
02 lend ____________
03 volcano ____________
04 awful ____________
05 probably ____________
06 specific ____________
07 wet ____________
08 disease ____________
09 surgery ____________
10 volunteer ____________
11 success ____________
12 stomachache ____________
13 scary ____________
14 complete ____________
15 flood ____________
16 new arrival ____________

B

우리말에 맞는 영어 어휘나 표현을 [보기]에서 찾아 쓰세요.

보기	seem	essay	contact	balanced	have no idea
	model	charge	get off	collect	look down

01 내리다, 하차하다 ____________
02 전혀 모르다 ____________
03 연락하다 ____________
04 ~인 것 같다 ____________
05 충전하다 ____________
06 균형 잡힌 ____________
07 (짧은 논문식) 과제물 ____________
08 우울해 보이다 ____________
09 모으다 ____________
10 모형 ____________

www.nebooks.co.kr

Section

2

실전 모의고사

1-6 회

시험 직전 모의고사

1-2 회

점수 _____ / 20문항

 일반 속도
 빠른 속도

01 다음을 듣고, 목요일의 날씨로 가장 적절한 것을 고르시오.

① ② ③
④ ⑤

02 대화를 듣고, 여자가 맡긴 여행용 가방으로 가장 적절한 것을 고르시오.

① ② ③
④ ⑤

03 대화를 듣고, 여자의 심정으로 가장 적절한 것을 고르시오.

① excited   ② upset   ③ happy
④ nervous   ⑤ surprised

04 대화를 듣고, 남자가 어제 한 일로 가장 적절한 것을 고르시오.

① 겨울옷 세탁 맡기기   ② 유리창 청소하기
③ 이불 빨래하기   ④ 새 커튼 달기
⑤ 바닥 청소하기

05 대화를 듣고, 두 사람이 대화하는 장소로 가장 적절한 곳을 고르시오.

① 음식점   ② 기차   ③ 버스 터미널
④ 극장   ⑤ 비행기

06 대화를 듣고, 여자의 마지막 말의 의도로 가장 적절한 것을 고르시오.

① 충고   ② 칭찬   ③ 격려
④ 동의   ⑤ 사과

07 대화를 듣고, 남자가 미술사 과제를 위해 선택한 화가를 고르시오.

① 폴 세잔   ② 폴 고갱   ③ 에두아르 마네
④ 클로드 모네   ⑤ 빈센트 반 고흐

08 대화를 듣고, 남자가 대화 직후에 할 일로 가장 적절한 것을 고르시오.

① 설거지하기   ② 거실 청소하기
③ 텔레비전 보기   ④ 역에 마중 나가기
⑤ 기차 시간 알아보기

09 대화를 듣고, 남자가 마술 쇼에 대해 언급하지 않은 것을 고르시오.

① 장소   ② 공연 시간   ③ 공연 날짜
④ 티켓 가격   ⑤ 예매 방법

10 다음을 듣고, 남자가 하는 말의 내용으로 가장 적절한 것을 고르시오.

① 일정 관리 요령   ② 목표 달성 방법
③ 목표 설정 전략   ④ 일의 우선순위 정하는 법
⑤ 마감일 준수의 중요성

11 다음을 듣고, Summer Rock Festival에 대한 내용과 일치하지 않는 것을 고르시오.

① 올해는 올림픽공원에서 열릴 예정이다.
② 축제 기간은 총 3일이다.
③ 일일권은 15,000원이다.
④ 티켓은 현장 구매만 가능하다.
⑤ 스무 팀 이상의 밴드가 공연할 예정이다.

🇬🇧
12 대화를 듣고, 남자가 전화를 건 목적으로 가장 적절한 것을 고르시오.

① 수리 관련 문의를 하기 위해서
② 환불을 요청하기 위해서
③ 물건을 교환하기 위해서
④ 배송 지연에 항의하기 위해서
⑤ 제품 정보에 대해 문의하기 위해서

고난도
13 대화를 듣고, 여자가 지불해야 할 금액으로 가장 적절한 것을 고르시오.

① $27　② $30　③ $32
④ $35　⑤ $55

14 대화를 듣고, 두 사람의 관계로 가장 적절한 것을 고르시오.

① 감독 – 운동선수　② 식당 점원 – 손님
③ 입국심사관 – 여행객　④ 미술관 직원 – 관람객
⑤ 공연장 직원 – 관람객

15 대화를 듣고, 남자가 여자에게 제안한 일로 가장 적절한 것을 고르시오.

① 병원 가기　② 진통제 복용하기
③ 스트레칭하기　④ 전문 마사지 받기
⑤ 충분한 수면 취하기

🇬🇧
16 대화를 듣고, 남자가 영국에 가는 이유로 가장 적절한 것을 고르시오.

① 영어 공부를 하기 위해서
② 관광을 하기 위해서
③ 축구 경기를 보기 위해서
④ 친구를 만나기 위해서
⑤ 축구를 배우기 위해서

17 다음 그림의 상황에 가장 적절한 대화를 고르시오.

①　②　③　④　⑤

고난도
18 다음을 듣고, 남자가 얼룩말에 대해 언급하지 <u>않은</u> 것을 고르시오.

① 서식지　② 먹이　③ 생김새
④ 수명　⑤ 줄무늬의 기능

[19-20] 대화를 듣고, 여자의 마지막 말에 이어질 남자의 말로 가장 적절한 것을 고르시오.

19 Man: _____

① Yes. Can I see your library card?
② Sure. I'll bring it to school tomorrow.
③ That's too bad. I'll try again.
④ Sorry. You should read the book first.
⑤ No. I didn't think it was very good.

🇬🇧
20 Man: _____

① These are sold out.
② I'll pick it up tomorrow afternoon.
③ Then I'll come first thing in the morning.
④ Why don't you come and see me?
⑤ In that case, I'll take two.

DICTATION

정답 단서 오답 함정

일반 속도

빠른 속도

01 ◀ 특정 정보

다음을 듣고, 목요일의 날씨로 가장
적절한 것을 고르시오.

W Good morning. I'm Kylie Johnson. Here's the weekday weather for Miami. It will be hot and **sunny** on both Monday and Tuesday. Make sure _____ _____ _____ _____! It will remain hot on Wednesday, but the skies will be **cloudy**. On Thursday, it will be _____ _____ _____. Finally, it will be **rainy** all day on Friday. So _____ _____ _____!

02 ◀ 그림 묘사

대화를 듣고, 여자가 맡긴 여행용 가
방으로 가장 적절한 것을 고르시오.

M Hi. Can I help you?

W Yes. I left my bag in your storage room this morning. I'd like to pick it up.

M All right. _____ _____ _____ it?

W Yes. It is rectangular. And it has four wheels and _____ _____ _____ _____.

M Okay. There's **one with a thick stripe on it**. Is that one yours?

W No, it doesn't have a stripe. But it has _____ _____ _____ _____ _____.

M Ah, I see it. Can I see your ID, please?

03 ◀ 심정

대화를 듣고, 여자의 심정으로 가장
적절한 것을 고르시오.

① excited ② upset
③ happy ④ nervous
⑤ surprised

M Hello, Maria. You look very nice today.

W Thank you. But look at _____ _____ _____ _____ _____.

M Oh! There's mud all over it. What happened?

W _____ _____ _____ _____ _____ and splashed it. I think it is ruined.

M That's too bad. Maybe it can be dry-cleaned.

W Maybe. I just wish people would _____ _____ _____.

04 ◀ 한 일

대화를 듣고, 남자가 어제 한 일로 가장 적절한 것을 고르시오.

① 겨울옷 세탁 맡기기
② 유리창 청소하기
③ 이불 빨래하기
④ 새 커튼 달기
⑤ 바닥 청소하기

W It's so warm and sunny today! Spring is almost here!

M I know. There are so many things to do.

W Yes. I _____ _____ _____ _____ yesterday. How about you?

M I _____ _____ _____ _____ to the dry cleaner's.

W I think I'll clean my apartment windows today.

M That's a good idea! I'm going to _____ _____ _____.

05 ◀ 대화 장소

대화를 듣고, 두 사람이 대화하는 장소로 가장 적절한 곳을 고르시오.

① 음식점   ② 기차
③ 버스 터미널   ④ 극장
⑤ 비행기

M Excuse me. Can I _____ _____ _____ _____, please?

W Certainly. I'll bring it right over. And please _____ _____ _____ _____. We'll be landing soon.

M Okay. What will the local time be _____ _____ _____?

W It will be about nine o'clock in the morning.

M Thank you very much.

W You're welcome, sir.

06 ◀ 의도

대화를 듣고, 여자의 마지막 말의 의도로 가장 적절한 것을 고르시오.

① 충고   ② 칭찬
③ 격려   ④ 동의
⑤ 사과

M Are you going to the concert in the park tonight?

W Yes. I'm really _____ _____ _____ _____. It's going to be great!

M That's what I heard. I think I might go too.

W Oh! Did you buy a ticket already?

M No, not yet. They're _____ _____ _____, are they?

W Actually, they are. They've been sold out since last week.

M Oh no. I really wanted to go.

W You should _____ _____ _____ _____ _____ next time.

대화를 듣고, 남자가 미술사 과제를
위해 선택한 화가를 고르시오.
① 폴 세잔   ② 폴 고갱
③ 에두아르 마네   ④ 클로드 모네
⑤ 빈센트 반 고흐

M Hi, Erica. What are you reading?

W It's a book about famous architects and artists.

M Oh, are you preparing for your art history project? Which artist did you choose?

W Claude Monet. I really like _____ _____ _____ _____ _____. You chose Paul Gauguin, right?

M I thought about it, but I chose Vincent van Gogh instead. I want to _____ _____ _____ _____ _____.

W That's a great choice! He's _____ _____ _____ _____ _____.

대화를 듣고, 남자가 대화 직후에 할
일로 가장 적절한 것을 고르시오.
① 설거지하기
② 거실 청소하기
③ 텔레비전 보기
④ 역에 마중 나가기
⑤ 기차 시간 알아보기

W What are you doing, John?

M I'm watching TV, Mom.

W Your grandparents will arrive in a few hours. Can you _____ _____ _____?

M Okay. Do you want me to _____ _____ _____ _____ to meet them?

W No, that's okay. I will _____ _____ _____ around three o'clock. But let's clean the house together first.

M All right. I'll _____ _____ _____ _____.

W Thanks. I'll do the dishes.

대화를 듣고, 남자가 마술 쇼에 대해
언급하지 않은 것을 고르시오.
① 장소   ② 공연 시간
③ 공연 날짜   ④ 티켓 가격
⑤ 예매 방법

W Hey, Tim! What did you do yesterday?

M I went to a magic show. It was amazing!

W Oh, I've never seen a live magic show before. Where was it held?

M _____ _____ _____ _____ the Merlin Theatre. I had a seat in the front row, so I could watch the magician's tricks up close.

W Wow. That must have been exciting.

M Yes. It _____ _____ _____ but I felt it was too short. I highly recommend seeing it.

W Are there more performances?

M The show runs until August 15. You can _____ _____ _____ _____.

116

10 ◀ 주제 · 화제

다음을 듣고, 남자가 하는 말의 내용으로 가장 적절한 것을 고르시오.

① 일정 관리 요령
② 목표 달성 방법
③ 목표 설정 전략
④ 일의 우선순위 정하는 법
⑤ 마감일 준수의 중요성

M Do you have things that you _____ _____ _____? Then there are four steps you should take. First, _____ _____ _____. Next, make detailed plans. Third, set deadlines for _____ _____ _____. Finally, give yourself a nice gift whenever you complete each step.

11 ◀ 내용 불일치

다음을 듣고, Summer Rock Festival에 대한 내용과 일치하지 않는 것을 고르시오.

① 올해는 올림픽공원에서 열릴 예정이다.
② 축제 기간은 총 3일이다.
③ 일일권은 15,000원이다.
④ 티켓은 현장 구매만 가능하다.
⑤ 스무 팀 이상의 밴드가 공연할 예정이다.

W The annual Summer Rock Festival will be held at Olympic Park this year. It will _____ _____ _____ _____, from August 3 to August 5. A one-day ticket costs just 15,000 won, and all tickets _____ _____ _____ _____. More than twenty bands from _____ _____ _____ _____ will be playing. Don't miss this fantastic event!

12 ◀ 목적

대화를 듣고, 남자가 전화를 건 목적으로 가장 적절한 것을 고르시오.

① 수리 관련 문의를 하기 위해서
② 환불을 요청하기 위해서
③ 물건을 교환하기 위해서
④ 배송 지연에 항의하기 위해서
⑤ 제품 정보에 대해 문의하기 위해서

[Telephone rings.]
W This is Game World. How can I help you?
M There's something wrong with a game I ordered from you.
W _____ _____ _____ _____ the problem with it?
M It was delivered today, but the disc is scratched.
W Oh, I'm sorry. We will _____ _____ _____ _____.
M Actually, _____ _____ _____ _____.
W I see. Let me talk to my manager. Please wait one moment.
M Okay.

13 ◀ 숫자 정보

대화를 듣고, 여자가 지불해야 할 금액으로 가장 적절한 것을 고르시오.

① $27
② $30
③ $32
④ $35
⑤ $55

M Welcome to High Market. We're _____ _____ _____ today with discounts of up to 50% off.

W That's great. This picture frame is pretty. How much is it?

M _____ _____ _____, it's $27.

W Hmm... That's _____ _____ _____ _____. What about this tablecloth?

M It's normally $50, but it's 50% off today.

W Great. How about this bar of soap?

M It was originally $5, but it's also half off.

W Okay. I'll take _____ _____ _____ _____ and one tablecloth.

14 ◀ 화자 간 관계

대화를 듣고, 두 사람의 관계로 가장 적절한 것을 고르시오.

① 감독 – 운동선수
② 식당 점원 – 손님
③ 입국심사관 – 여행객
④ 미술관 직원 – 관람객
⑤ 공연장 직원 – 관람객

W Can I see your ticket, please?

M Here you are.

W Thank you. But you can't bring food and drinks _____ _____ _____.

M But I bought this food at the store right next to this stadium.

W Sorry, you can't take _____ _____ _____ inside.

M Oh, I didn't know that. What should I do?

W You can eat it before you _____ _____ _____ _____.

M Okay, I'll come back when I finish eating then.

15 ◀ 제안한 일

대화를 듣고, 남자가 여자에게 제안한 일로 가장 적절한 것을 고르시오.

① 병원 가기
② 진통제 복용하기
③ 스트레칭하기
④ 전문 마사지 받기
⑤ 충분한 수면 취하기

M Are you okay, Lisa? You don't look good.

W My back is _____ _____ _____.

M Have you seen a doctor?

W No. It isn't serious. I have been _____ _____ _____ reading at my desk recently.

M I see. Sitting for too long _____ _____ _____ _____.

W Right. But I just need to take some pain medicine. Then I'll feel better.

M Hmm. How about _____ _____ _____ instead? It will help relax your back muscles.

W Oh, that's actually a good idea.

16 ◀ 이유

대화를 듣고, 남자가 영국에 가는 이유로 가장 적절한 것을 고르시오.

① 영어 공부를 하기 위해서
② 관광을 하기 위해서
③ 축구 경기를 보기 위해서
④ 친구를 만나기 위해서
⑤ 축구를 배우기 위해서

W Where are you going on vacation, Nicholas?

M I'm going to England.

W Really? Do you have **friends** there?

M No, I don't. I just want to _____ _____ _____ at a famous stadium.

W Oh. So you won't _____ _____?

M Probably not. I won't _____ _____ _____.

W Well, I hope you have fun.

17 ◀ 그림 상황에 적절한 대화

다음 그림의 상황에 가장 적절한 대화를 고르시오.

①   ②   ③   ④   ⑤

① **M** Excuse me. I think you _____ _____.

   W Oh. Thank you very much.

② **M** Sorry, but _____ _____ _____ _____.

   W All right. I guess I'll sit somewhere else.

③ **M** Can you tell me where the nearest bus stop is?

   W Go two blocks and make a left at the bank.

④ **M** I'm going to _____ _____ _____ _____.

   W Why? Did you forget something on the bus?

⑤ **M** _____ _____ _____, taking the subway or taking the bus?

   W The bus is usually faster.

고난도

18 ◀ 언급하지 않은 내용

다음을 듣고, 남자가 얼룩말에 대해 언급하지 않은 것을 고르시오.

① 서식지   ② 먹이
③ 생김새   ④ 수명
⑤ 줄무늬의 기능

M Zebras are animals found in many parts of Africa. They eat mostly grass. Although they look like horses, they _____ _____ _____ black and white stripes. Zebras live together _____ _____ _____ _____ up to 1,000 animals. When lions attack these groups, the _____ _____ _____. This helps the zebras escape.

대화를 듣고, 여자의 마지막 말에 이어질 남자의 말로 가장 적절한 것을 고르시오.

Man: _____

① Yes. Can I see your library card?
② Sure. I'll bring it to school tomorrow.
③ That's too bad. I'll try again.
④ Sorry. You should read the book first.
⑤ No. I didn't think it was very good.

M Have you seen the movie *The Adventure of Sam*?
W Yes, I saw it last weekend. I love the main actor.
M So do I. His _____ _____ _____.
W I really liked the storyline, too.
M Did you know it's _____ _____ _____ _____? The novel is also interesting.
W Do you have the novel? _____ _____ _____ _____?
M _____

대화를 듣고, 여자의 마지막 말에 이어질 남자의 말로 가장 적절한 것을 고르시오.

Man: _____

① These are sold out.
② I'll pick it up tomorrow afternoon.
③ Then I'll come first thing in the morning.
④ Why don't you come and see me?
⑤ In that case, I'll take two.

W How may I help you, sir?
M I saw your ad. I want to buy one of the smartphones on sale.
W I'm sorry, but they've _____ _____ _____ already.
M Really? Will you be getting more?
W Yes, we'll get more tonight. But they'll _____ _____ _____ in the morning again.
M Wow! They must be popular. Can you _____ _____ _____ _____? I'll come by tomorrow.
W Sorry, we can't do that.
M _____

A

다음 영어 어휘나 표현의 뜻을 우리말로 쓰세요.

01 sore

02 rectangular

03 highly

04 whenever

05 deadline

06 grass

07 floor

08 achieve

09 task

10 detailed

11 purchase

12 muscle

13 finally

14 scratch

15 originally

16 local

B

우리말에 맞는 영어 어휘나 표현을 [보기]에서 찾아 쓰세요.

| 보기 | ruin | splash | attack | architect | sunscreen |
| | land | annual | escape | remain | pain medicine |

01 계속 ~이다

02 진통제

03 엉망으로 만들다

04 건축가

05 착륙하다

06 공격하다

07 자외선 차단제

08 매년의

09 달아나다, 탈출하다

10 (물·흙탕물 등을) 튀기다

01 다음을 듣고, 모스크바의 오후 날씨로 가장 적절한 것을 고르시오.

02 대화를 듣고, 남자가 구입할 운동화로 가장 적절한 것을 고르시오.

03 대화를 듣고, 남자의 심정으로 가장 적절한 것을 고르시오.

① nervous   ② happy   ③ lonely
④ worried   ⑤ shy

🇬🇧
04 대화를 듣고, 남자가 지난 주말에 한 일로 가장 적절한 것을 고르시오.

① 바닷가 가기   ② 놀이공원 가기
③ 사진 정리하기   ④ 야구 경기 관람하기
⑤ 수영장 가기

05 대화를 듣고, 두 사람이 대화하는 장소로 가장 적절한 곳을 고르시오.

① 영화관   ② 학교   ③ 공연장
④ 기차   ⑤ 가구점

06 대화를 듣고, 남자의 마지막 말의 의도로 가장 적절한 것을 고르시오.

① 허가   ② 사과   ③ 요청
④ 충고   ⑤ 거절

07 대화를 듣고, 여자가 가져갈 필요가 없는 물건으로 가장 적절한 것을 고르시오.

① 선크림   ② 모자   ③ 선글라스
④ 샌드위치   ⑤ 수영복

🇬🇧
08 대화를 듣고, 남자가 대화 직후에 할 일로 가장 적절한 것을 고르시오.

① 뉴스 확인하기   ② 학교에 아이 데려다주기
③ 기차 시간 확인하기   ④ 열차 사고 신고하기
⑤ 상사에게 전화하기

고난도
09 대화를 듣고, 두 사람이 가이드 안내 관광에 대해 언급하지 않은 것을 고르시오.

① 만남 시각   ② 인원   ③ 비용
④ 만남 장소   ⑤ 복장

고난도
10 다음을 듣고, 여자가 하는 말의 내용으로 가장 적절한 것을 고르시오.

① 감정 조절 방법
② 건강 관리의 중요성
③ 감정을 표현해야 하는 이유
④ 타인의 감정을 존중하는 자세
⑤ 거짓말을 하지 말아야 하는 이유

11 대화를 듣고, 남자의 여행 계획에 대한 내용과 일치하지 <u>않는</u> 것을 고르시오.

① 유럽에만 갈 예정이다.
② 두 나라를 방문할 것이다.
③ 총 여행 기간은 2주이다.
④ 스위스에서는 호텔에 머물 것이다.
⑤ 스위스에서는 패러글라이딩을 하러 갈 것이다.

12 대화를 듣고, 여자가 도서관에 가는 목적으로 가장 적절한 것을 고르시오.

① 책을 빌리기 위해서
② 책을 예약하기 위해서
③ 시험공부를 하기 위해서
④ 아르바이트를 하기 위해서
⑤ 조별 과제를 하기 위해서

13 대화를 듣고, 남자가 지불해야 할 금액으로 가장 적절한 것을 고르시오.

① $40   ② $45   ③ $50
④ $55   ⑤ $60

14 대화를 듣고, 두 사람의 관계로 가장 적절한 것을 고르시오.

① 호텔 직원 – 손님   ② 음식점 종업원 – 손님
③ 변호사 – 의뢰인   ④ 도서관 사서 – 학생
⑤ 여행사 직원 – 손님

15 대화를 듣고, 여자가 남자에게 부탁한 일로 가장 적절한 것을 고르시오.

① 우산 사 오기   ② 정류장에 데리러 나오기
③ 우산 빌려주기   ④ 버스 요금 대신 지불하기
⑤ 일기 예보 확인하기

16 대화를 듣고, 여자가 옷을 반품한 이유로 가장 적절한 것을 고르시오.

① 제품에 하자가 있어서   ② 색이 잘 어울리지 않아서
③ 가격이 비싸서   ④ 옷이 커서
⑤ 생각한 소재가 아니어서

17 다음 그림의 상황에 가장 적절한 대화를 고르시오.

①   ②   ③   ④   ⑤

18 다음을 듣고, 남자가 Fun City에 대해 언급하지 <u>않</u>은 것을 고르시오.

① 개장일   ② 소재지   ③ 입장 가능 연령
④ 휴무일   ⑤ 입장료

[19-20] 대화를 듣고, 남자의 마지막 말에 이어질 여자의 말로 가장 적절한 것을 고르시오.

19 Woman: _____

① Non-smoking, please.
② A table for two, please.
③ That would be fine.
④ I'm not ready to order yet.
⑤ I apologize for the inconvenience.

20 Woman: _____

① Good job! I'll join you.
② Yes, I'm going to school.
③ Sounds great. See you there.
④ Yes. Would you like to join me?
⑤ Sorry, I'm busy on Sundays.

DICTATION

일반 속도

빠른 속도

01 ◀ 특정 정보

다음을 듣고, 모스크바의 오후 날씨로 가장 적절한 것을 고르시오.

①
②
③
④
⑤

M Good morning. I'm John Harris, and this is the world weather forecast for today. It will be cold and cloudy in New York, but it won't **rain**. Vancouver will _____ _____ _____, _____ _____. In Moscow, they're _____ _____ _____ starting in the afternoon. But if you live in Beijing, you'll be able to _____ _____ _____ _____.

02 ◀ 그림 묘사

대화를 듣고, 남자가 구입할 운동화로 가장 적절한 것을 고르시오.

①
②
③
④
⑤

M Hello. I'd like to buy a new pair of sneakers for my daughter. She's thirteen.

W Okay. These are the latest models. They are all very popular with girls _____ _____ _____. How about these ones with small, pink hearts?

M I think she would like them. But they are _____ _____ _____ _____ _____ she has now.

W Then how about buying a pair _____ _____ _____ on them?

M That's a good idea! I'll get _____ _____ _____ _____.

W Great choice! Your daughter will love them.

03 ◀ 심정

대화를 듣고, 남자의 심정으로 가장 적절한 것을 고르시오.

① nervous   ② happy
③ lonely   ④ worried
⑤ shy

M Hi, Mom! I'm home!

W How was _____ _____ _____ _____, Chris?

M It was good! I _____ _____ _____ _____ today.

W I told you that your new classmates would like you.

M You were right. I thought it would be really hard to make friends at a new school. But everyone was _____ _____ _____ _____. I had a lot of fun today.

W I'm glad to hear that.

04 ◀ 한 일

대화를 듣고, 남자가 지난 주말에 한 일로 가장 적절한 것을 고르시오.

① 바닷가 가기
② 놀이공원 가기
③ 사진 정리하기
④ 야구 경기 관람하기
⑤ 수영장 가기

M Hey, Peggy. What are you doing?
W Oh, hi, Richard. I'm looking at some pictures on my phone.
M Pictures? Can I see them?
W Sure. I went to an amusement park last weekend, so I _____ _____ _____ _____ _____.
M Wow! It looks like you had a really good time.
W Yes, I did. By the way, _____ _____ _____. Did you go to the beach?
M No, I _____ _____ _____ _____ _____ last weekend.

05 ◀ 대화 장소

대화를 듣고, 두 사람이 대화하는 장소로 가장 적절한 곳을 고르시오.

① 영화관　② 학교
③ 공연장　④ 기차
⑤ 가구점

M I think _____ _____ _____ _____.
W Yes, you're right. Thank you for coming with me.
M You're welcome. And thanks for _____ _____ _____ _____. So what is this play about?
W It's about two classmates who become best friends.
M It sounds interesting. Oh, they're _____ _____ _____ _____!
W It must be about to start.

06 ◀ 의도

대화를 듣고, 남자의 마지막 말의 의도로 가장 적절한 것을 고르시오.

① 허가　② 사과
③ 요청　④ 충고
⑤ 거절

M What are you doing in my room, Gina?
W Oh! I'm sorry! I didn't think _____ _____ _____.
M I was downstairs helping Mom with the laundry.
W I didn't know that. I was looking for your bus card.
M My bus card? Why? _____ _____ _____ _____?
W Yes. I looked everywhere, but I can't find it.
M Mine is on my desk. You're _____ _____ _____ _____.

대화를 듣고, 여자가 가져갈 필요가
없는 물건으로 가장 적절한 것을 고르
시오.

① 선크림   ② 모자
③ 선글라스   ④ 샌드위치
⑤ 수영복

M Hey, Ann! My family is _____ _____ _____ _____
this weekend. Would you like to join us?

W Sounds great! Is there anything that I _____ _____ _____?

M Hmm... We will go swimming, so bring your bathing suit. You should also
bring sunglasses and a hat.

W Okay. _____ _____?

M Bringing waterproof sunscreen would be a good idea.

W All right. What about sandwiches and juice?

M No, we will bring enough for everyone.

대화를 듣고, 남자가 대화 직후에 할
일로 가장 적절한 것을 고르시오.

① 뉴스 확인하기
② 학교에 아이 데려다주기
③ 기차 시간 확인하기
④ 열차 사고 신고하기
⑤ 상사에게 전화하기

[Cell phone rings.]

M Hello?

W Hi, honey. Where are you?

M I'm walking to the train station. Is everything okay?

W Yes, I just _____ _____ _____ _____ at school. But
I heard that there's a problem with the trains.

M Oh, really?

W Yes, the news said _____ _____ _____ _____. So
there are long delays.

M That's terrible. I need to call my boss and _____ _____ _____
_____ _____.

W All right. I'll talk to you later.

대화를 듣고, 두 사람이 가이드 안내
관광에 대해 언급하지 않은 것을 고르
시오.

① 만남 시각   ② 인원
③ 비용   ④ 만남 장소
⑤ 복장

[Telephone rings.]

W Hello, this is BK Tours. How may I help you?

M I'd like a guided tour of the Grand Palace next Monday morning. Would that
be possible?

W Yes, it would be. _____ _____ _____ will go?

M A group of five people.

W Okay. It costs forty dollars per person, _____ _____ _____
_____.

M Sounds good. Do you offer hotel pickup?

W We sure do. What hotel are you staying at?

M Riverside Hotel.

W We will _____ _____ _____ at your hotel. And please
remember, _____ _____ _____ long pants and shirts with
long sleeves during the tour.

M Oh, I see. Okay.

고난도

10 ◀ 주제 · 화제

다음을 듣고, 여자가 하는 말의 내용으로 가장 적절한 것을 고르시오.

① 감정 조절 방법
② 건강 관리의 중요성
③ 감정을 표현해야 하는 이유
④ 타인의 감정을 존중하는 자세
⑤ 거짓말을 하지 말아야 하는 이유

W People often worry about _____ _____ _____. Even if they are very sad, they try to hide it. But if you _____ _____ _____ _____, it could harm your health. People who show their emotions are less likely to _____ _____ _____. Also, our emotions help other people understand us better. For these reasons, it's always best to _____ _____ _____ _____ _____.

11 ◀ 내용 불일치

대화를 듣고, 남자의 여행 계획에 대한 내용과 일치하지 않는 것을 고르시오.

① 유럽에만 갈 예정이다.
② 두 나라를 방문할 것이다.
③ 총 여행 기간은 2주이다.
④ 스위스에서는 호텔에 머물 것이다.
⑤ 스위스에서는 패러글라이딩을 하러 갈 것이다.

W Are you _____ _____ _____ next week?
M Yes. I'm going to Germany and Switzerland.
W That's great. For how long?
M I'll spend one week in each country.
W Where are you going to stay?
M I _____ _____ _____ in Switzerland, but I'll stay with a friend in Germany.
W I see. I visited Switzerland last year. I went paragliding in the mountains!
M Really? I'm _____ _____ _____ _____, but I'll just go hiking there.

12 ◀ 목적

대화를 듣고, 여자가 도서관에 가는 목적으로 가장 적절한 것을 고르시오.

① 책을 빌리기 위해서
② 책을 예약하기 위해서
③ 시험공부를 하기 위해서
④ 아르바이트를 하기 위해서
⑤ 조별 과제를 하기 위해서

W Hi, Jack. Where are you going?
M I'm going to the library.
W Oh, I'm going to the library, too.
M Are you going there to _____ _____ _____ _____ _____?
W No. I _____ _____ _____ last week. The library called this morning and said _____ _____ _____ _____. Why are you going to the library?
M You didn't know? I _____ _____ _____.
W Really? That's interesting.

대화를 듣고, 남자가 지불해야 할 금액으로 가장 적절한 것을 고르시오.

① $40   ② $45
③ $50   ④ $55
⑤ $60

W Did you _____ _____ _____?

M Yes. It was excellent. I'd like to pay now.

W Sure. You had the seafood pasta, a potato pizza, and two hot coffees, right?

M That's right.

W Okay. _____ _____ _____ $55.

M Well, the pasta is $15, the pizza is $25, and the coffee is $5 per cup. So I think it should be $50.

W You need to _____ _____ _____ _____ at our restaurant.

M Oh, I see. Here's my credit card.

대화를 듣고, 두 사람의 관계로 가장 적절한 것을 고르시오.

① 호텔 직원 – 손님
② 음식점 종업원 – 손님
③ 변호사 – 의뢰인
④ 도서관 사서 – 학생
⑤ 여행사 직원 – 손님

[Telephone rings.]

M Hello. How may I help you?

W I'd like to confirm my reservation. My name is Park Sumi.

M Let me check… It's a single room _____ _____ _____, from May 10 to the 12. Is that correct?

W Yes, it is. _____ _____ _____, doesn't it?

M Yes, a buffet breakfast will be served at 7:00 a.m.

W Okay. _____ _____ _____ _____ _____ _____ on the tenth?

M Any time after 1:00 p.m.

대화를 듣고, 여자가 남자에게 부탁한 일로 가장 적절한 것을 고르시오.

① 우산 사 오기
② 정류장에 데리러 나오기
③ 우산 빌려주기
④ 버스 요금 대신 지불하기
⑤ 일기 예보 확인하기

[Telephone rings.]

M Hello?

W Hi, Dad. Have you _____ _____ _____ _____?

M Yes. It's raining really hard! The weather forecast said it would be sunny all day.

W I know. So I didn't _____ _____ _____ me.

M That's terrible. Where are you now?

W I'm on the bus. Could you _____ _____ _____ _____ _____?

M Sure, honey. I'll be there in fifteen minutes.

W Thank you, Dad!

16 ◀ 이유

대화를 듣고, 여자가 옷을 반품한 이유로 가장 적절한 것을 고르시오.

① 제품에 하자가 있어서
② 색이 잘 어울리지 않아서
③ 가격이 비싸서
④ 옷이 커서
⑤ 생각한 소재가 아니어서

M Are you going to wear your new red dress tonight?
W No. I _____ _____ to the department store.
M Why? I thought you liked it.
W I _____ _____ _____. It was a very pretty dress.
M Was it too **expensive**?
W No. But it was _____ _____ _____ _____ _____.
M Oh, that's too bad.

17 ◀ 그림 상황에 적절한 대화

다음 그림의 상황에 가장 적절한 대화를 고르시오.

① ② ③ ④ ⑤

① **W** Can you help us find our seats?
　 M Sure. Can I _____ _____ _____?
② **W** Excuse me, but I think _____ _____ _____ _____ _____.
　 M Oh, I'm sorry. I read the number wrong.
③ **W** How about _____ _____ _____ _____ tomorrow?
　 M I'm afraid I can't. I'll be very busy.
④ **W** Hello. How can I help you today?
　 M Hi. I'd like to _____ _____ _____.
⑤ **W** Which seat should we purchase?
　 M Hmm... Let's get seats in Row H.

18 ◀ 언급하지 않은 내용

다음을 듣고, 남자가 Fun City에 대해 언급하지 <u>않은</u> 것을 고르시오.

① 개장일
② 소재지
③ 입장 가능 연령
④ 휴무일
⑤ 입장료

M A new amusement park opened on June 10. It's called Fun City, and _____ _____ _____ Ottawa. It has the tallest roller coaster in Canada. There are also three pools. _____ _____ _____ _____ from 10:00 a.m. to 10:00 p.m., six days a week. It is _____ _____ _____. Tickets cost $20 each. Come to Fun City today!

19 ◀ 마지막 말에 대한 응답

대화를 듣고, 남자의 마지막 말에 이
어질 여자의 말로 가장 적절한 것을
고르시오.

Woman: _____

① Non-smoking, please.
② A table for two, please.
③ That would be fine.
④ I'm not ready to order yet.
⑤ I apologize for the inconvenience.

[Telephone rings.]

M Hello, Green House Restaurant. May I help you?

W Yes, I'd like to _____ _____ _____.

M Okay. For what time and how many people?

W A table for two at seven o'clock this evening.

M Oh, I'm sorry. There are _____ _____ _____ at that time.

W What time _____ _____ then?

M There's a table available at eight o'clock.

W _____

20 ◀ 마지막 말에 대한 응답

대화를 듣고, 남자의 마지막 말에 이
어질 여자의 말로 가장 적절한 것을
고르시오.

Woman: _____

① Good job! I'll join you.
② Yes, I'm going to school.
③ Sounds great. See you there.
④ Yes. Would you like to join me?
⑤ Sorry, I'm busy on Sundays.

M What do you like to do on Sundays?

W I _____ _____ _____ _____ and eat a big breakfast.

M That _____ _____ _____. What else do you do?

W I usually volunteer at a children's hospital _____ _____ _____.

M That's great! Are you going there this Sunday, too?

W _____

A

다음 영어 어휘나 표현의 뜻을 우리말로 쓰세요.

01 emotion _____

02 sleeve _____

03 laundry _____

04 illness _____

05 latest _____

06 shoelace _____

07 suffer from _____

08 confirm _____

09 downstairs _____

10 include _____

11 tax _____

12 midterm exam _____

13 hide _____

14 delay _____

15 correct _____

16 offer _____

B

우리말에 맞는 영어 어휘나 표현을 [보기]에서 찾아 쓰세요.

보기	similar to	hold	hard	bathing suit	entrance fee
	drop ~ off	express	possible	waterproof	be about to-v

01 입장료 _____

02 수영복 _____

03 방수의 _____

04 ~을 내려주다 _____

05 ~와 비슷한 _____

06 심하게, 많이 _____

07 표현하다 _____

08 가능한 _____

09 계속 붙들다 _____

10 막 ~하려는 참이다 _____

01 다음을 듣고, 전주의 내일 날씨로 가장 적절한 것을 고르시오.

02 대화를 듣고, 두 사람이 보고 있는 사진으로 가장 적절한 것을 고르시오.

03 대화를 듣고, 남자의 심정으로 가장 적절한 것을 고르시오.
① curious ② bored ③ thankful
④ relaxed ⑤ excited

04 대화를 듣고, 여자가 점심시간에 한 일로 가장 적절한 것을 고르시오.
① 운동하기 ② 병원 진료받기
③ 파스타 요리하기 ④ 은행 업무 보기
⑤ 냉장고 청소하기

05 대화를 듣고, 두 사람이 대화하는 장소로 가장 적절한 곳을 고르시오.
① 호텔 ② 공항 ③ 기차역
④ 주차장 ⑤ 지하철역

06 대화를 듣고, 여자의 마지막 말의 의도로 가장 적절한 것을 고르시오.
① 감사 ② 거절 ③ 요청
④ 충고 ⑤ 동의

07 대화를 듣고, 여자가 빌릴 물건으로 가장 적절한 것을 고르시오.
① 담요 ② 침낭 ③ 손전등
④ 텐트 ⑤ 구급상자

08 대화를 듣고, 여자가 대화 직후에 할 일로 가장 적절한 것을 고르시오.
① 지하철 타러 가기 ② 경찰에 신고하기
③ 분실물 보관소 가기 ④ 카드 분실 신고하기
⑤ 부모님께 연락하기

고난도
09 대화를 듣고, 여자가 동아리에 대해 언급하지 않은 것을 고르시오.
① 활동 내용 ② 모임 장소 ③ 가입 대상
④ 인원 ⑤ 모임 주기

10 다음을 듣고, 남자가 하는 말의 내용으로 가장 적절한 것을 고르시오.
① 다양한 직업 체험
② 취업의 어려움
③ 온라인 적성 검사 응시 방법
④ 구직 시 충분한 정보 수집의 필요성
⑤ 직업 안내소에서 하는 일

고난도

11 대화를 듣고, 여자에 대한 내용과 일치하지 <u>않는</u> 것을 고르시오.

① 작년에 캐나다에 다녀왔다.
② 친척이 거주 중인 도시에서 지냈다.
③ 6개월간 현지 학교에 다니며 영어를 배웠다.
④ 외국인 친구들을 많이 사귀었다.
⑤ 프랑스인 친구와 함께 프랑스어를 공부했다.

12 대화를 듣고, 여자가 전화를 건 목적으로 가장 적절한 것을 고르시오.

① 예약을 변경하기 위해서
② 예약을 취소하기 위해서
③ 의사의 처방전을 받기 위해서
④ 진료 시간을 물어보기 위해서
⑤ 진료 예약을 하기 위해서

13 대화를 듣고, 남자가 지불해야 할 금액으로 가장 적절한 것을 고르시오.

① $32   ② $64   ③ $70
④ $75   ⑤ $80

14 대화를 듣고, 두 사람의 관계로 가장 적절한 것을 고르시오.

① 경찰 – 운전자   ② 택시 기사 – 승객
③ 경비원 – 방문객   ④ 호텔 직원 – 손님
⑤ 부동산 중개인 – 세입자

15 대화를 듣고, 남자가 여자에게 부탁한 일로 가장 적절한 것을 고르시오.

① 회의 일정 알려주기   ② 음식점 예약하기
③ 보고서 복사하기   ④ 회의실 예약하기
⑤ 간식 준비하기

16 대화를 듣고, 여자가 약속 시간에 늦은 이유로 가장 적절한 것을 고르시오.

① 접촉 사고가 있어서   ② 휴대전화를 찾아야 해서
③ 길이 막혀서   ④ 내비게이션을 수리받아야 해서
⑤ 길을 잃어버려서

17 다음 그림의 상황에 가장 적절한 대화를 고르시오.

①   ②   ③   ④   ⑤

18 다음을 듣고, 남자가 운동회 날에 대해 언급하지 <u>않은</u> 것을 고르시오.

① 날짜   ② 시작 시각   ③ 복장
④ 경기 종목   ⑤ 시상

[19-20] 대화를 듣고, 남자의 마지막 말에 이어질 여자의 말로 가장 적절한 것을 고르시오.

19 Woman: _____

① Never do that again.
② Don't worry. It'll be fine.
③ Please say hello to her for me.
④ How about going to a musical with me?
⑤ What restaurant are you going to?

20 Woman: _____

① That's too bad. I wanted to see him.
② It was nice to see her yesterday.
③ He had a great time at the party.
④ Sehoon likes Minji's cooking, too.
⑤ Her new apartment is 20 minutes from here.

DICTATION

일반 속도

빠른 속도

01 ◀ 특정 정보

다음을 듣고, 전주의 내일 날씨로 가장 적절한 것을 고르시오.

W Good morning! It's time for our weather forecast for tomorrow. It will be **sunny** and warm in Daegu. The sun will be very strong, so everyone should _____ _____ _____ before leaving the house. In Jeonju, it will be _____ _____ _____. It will be windy in Busan, and there will be a _____ _____ in the evening.

02 ◀ 그림 묘사

대화를 듣고, 두 사람이 보고 있는 사진으로 가장 적절한 것을 고르시오.

M How was your weekend? Did you go to the zoo?

W No, I didn't. Look at this photo.

M Oh! You went to the beach! Who is that girl _____ _____ _____ _____?

W That's my sister. She's _____ _____ _____ _____ because she's so happy.

M And that's you sitting on a towel in front of the palm tree.

W Yes. I'm _____ _____ _____ _____.

M You look great!

03 ◀ 심정

대화를 듣고, 남자의 심정으로 가장 적절한 것을 고르시오.

① curious ② bored
③ thankful ④ relaxed
⑤ excited

W Are you packing to go back to England?

M Yes. _____ _____ _____.

W Be careful not to forget anything important.

M I will. By the way, I _____ _____ _____ _____.

W Oh! Can I open it now?

M Yes. I wanted to give you something for _____ _____ _____.

W These gloves are great. Thank you!

M You're welcome. You really _____ _____ _____ like part of your family.

04 ◀ 한 일

대화를 듣고, 여자가 점심시간에 한 일로 가장 적절한 것을 고르시오.

① 운동하기
② 병원 진료받기
③ 파스타 요리하기
④ 은행 업무 보기
⑤ 냉장고 청소하기

W I'm so hungry!

M Why? Lunch was only an hour ago.

W I skipped lunch today.

M Oh. Did you _____ _____ _____ during lunch?

W No, I went to the bank to _____ _____ _____ _____ _____.

M The lines are always much longer during lunchtime.

W I know, but I couldn't do it any other time.

M I see. I _____ _____ _____ _____ in the office refrigerator. Would you like some?

W Yes! Thank you so much.

05 ◀ 대화 장소

대화를 듣고, 두 사람이 대화하는 장소로 가장 적절한 곳을 고르시오.

① 호텔　　② 공항
③ 기차역　　④ 주차장
⑤ 지하철역

W Excuse me, are you Park Minsung?

M Yes, I am. Are you Sue Johnson?

W Yes, I'm your tour guide. Welcome to Chicago. I thought I missed you.

M Sorry. It took a while to _____ _____ _____.

W That's all right. _____ _____ _____ _____?

M It was very long. I'm glad to finally be here.

W I'm glad you're here, too. I have a car outside. I'll _____ _____ _____ _____ _____.

M Thanks.

06 ◀ 의도

대화를 듣고, 여자의 마지막 말의 의도로 가장 적절한 것을 고르시오.

① 감사　　② 거절
③ 요청　　④ 충고
⑤ 동의

[Cell phone rings.]

W Hi, Mike! How are you?

M Hi, Janet. I'm doing well. How did you do on the English test?

W I _____ _____ _____ _____! I'm so happy.

M That's great! We should celebrate. Do you have any plans tonight?

W I'm not doing anything. What do you _____ _____ _____?

M Would you like to have dinner with me? I heard that the new Italian restaurant on Oxford Street is good.

W That sounds great, but I _____ _____ _____ _____ _____. Maybe next time.

대화를 듣고, 여자가 빌릴 물건으로
가장 적절한 것을 고르시오.

① 담요   ② 침낭
③ 손전등   ④ 텐트
⑤ 구급상자

M Are you getting ready for the camping trip, Chloe?

W Yes, Dad. I'm almost done.

M The weather report said that it would be _____ _____ _____ all weekend.

W Then I should bring a warm blanket.

M And _____ _____ _____ _____ _____. What else did you pack?

W I packed clothes, water, snacks, and a lantern.

M What about a tent?

W I don't need to _____ _____ _____. I can rent one at the campsite.

M Good. Oh, make sure you take your first aid kit too.

W Okay, I will.

대화를 듣고, 여자가 대화 직후에 할
일로 가장 적절한 것을 고르시오.

① 지하철 타러 가기
② 경찰에 신고하기
③ 분실물 보관소 가기
④ 카드 분실 신고하기
⑤ 부모님께 연락하기

M Where are you going, Ashley?

W I _____ _____ _____ on the subway. I'm going to look for it.

M Oh. Did you try the subway _____ _____ _____?

W I did, but it wasn't there.

M I'm sorry to hear that. What was in it?

W All my money and a credit card.

M That's terrible. Why don't you call and _____ _____ _____ _____ first? Somebody might use it.

W That's a good idea. I should call now.

대화를 듣고, 여자가 동아리에 대해
언급하지 않은 것을 고르시오.

① 활동 내용   ② 모임 장소
③ 가입 대상   ④ 인원
⑤ 모임 주기

W I've recently started a poetry club with a couple of classmates. Is there any chance you might be interested?

M Well, what does the club do?

W We _____ _____ _____ _____ together and discuss their themes. We sometimes write poems too.

M Can anyone just join the club?

W It is _____ _____ _____ _____ with a love of poetry. So far, we have six members, including me.

M How often does the club meet?

W _____ _____ _____. We meet on the last Saturday of every month. Will you join?

M I'll think about it.

10 ◀ 주제 · 화제

다음을 듣고, 남자가 하는 말의 내용으로 가장 적절한 것을 고르시오.

① 다양한 직업 체험
② 취업의 어려움
③ 온라인 적성 검사 응시 방법
④ 구직 시 충분한 정보 수집의 필요성
⑤ 직업 안내소에서 하는 일

M It's difficult to _____ _____ _____ _____. There are many kinds of jobs. There are even some you don't know about. That's why you should gather _____ _____ _____ _____ _____ before choosing a career. You can find a lot of _____ _____ _____. Also, visiting local job centers is a good idea. The people there will help you. You can learn about the jobs that _____ _____ _____.

고난도

11 ◀ 내용 불일치

대화를 듣고, 여자에 대한 내용과 일치하지 <u>않는</u> 것을 고르시오.

① 작년에 캐나다에 다녀왔다.
② 친척이 거주 중인 도시에서 지냈다.
③ 6개월간 현지 학교에 다니며 영어를 배웠다.
④ 외국인 친구들을 많이 사귀었다.
⑤ 프랑스인 친구와 함께 프랑스어를 공부했다.

M Your English is so good, Sejin! Did you _____ _____?
W Thank you! I studied in Vancouver, Canada last year. My uncle lives there.
M Wow! How long were you there?
W Six months. I went to school there, and I made a lot of _____ _____ _____ _____.
M That's great!
W My closest friend was from France. After meeting her, I want to study French, too.
M It sounds like you _____ _____ _____ _____.
W I really did!

---

12 ◀ 목적

대화를 듣고, 여자가 전화를 건 목적으로 가장 적절한 것을 고르시오.

① 예약을 변경하기 위해서
② 예약을 취소하기 위해서
③ 의사의 처방전을 받기 위해서
④ 진료 시간을 물어보기 위해서
⑤ 진료 예약을 하기 위해서

[Telephone rings.]
M Good morning. This is Smile Dental Clinic.
W Hi. I'd like to _____ _____ _____ with Dr. Green.
M Sure. May I have your name?
W I'm Amy Davis. _____ _____ _____ by Dr. Green before.
M Okay. When would you like to see him?
W _____ _____ _____ _____, please. My tooth hurts so much that I can't chew anything.
M I see. _____ _____ _____ on Thursday at 10:00 a.m.?
W Is it possible to come sooner?
M Then how about Wednesday at 3:00 p.m.?
W Okay, that's fine.

M Hello, I want to see a play, but I'm _____ _____ _____ _____ _____.

W When would you like to see the play?

M At 1:00 p.m. on Saturday.

W The ticket price is $40.

M Can I _____ _____ _____ to get a 20% discount?

W No, that's only for weekdays. But if you _____ _____ _____ _____, you can get a $5 discount on each ticket.

M I have one. I would like two tickets, please.

W Great. Here are your tickets. Enjoy the performance!

14 ◀ 화자 간 관계

대화를 듣고, 두 사람의 관계로 가장 적절한 것을 고르시오.

① 경찰 – 운전자
② 택시 기사 – 승객
③ 경비원 – 방문객
④ 호텔 직원 – 손님
⑤ 부동산 중개인 – 세입자

M Wait a minute. Do you live in this apartment building?

W No, I'm a visitor.

M _____ _____ _____ _____?

W My friend just moved here, and I was invited to her housewarming party.

M I should check _____ _____ _____ _____. Which apartment does your friend live in? I need to check my list.

W She's in 106. And my name is Valerie Smith.

M *[pause]* Okay, you're _____ _____ _____. Go ahead.

15 ◀ 부탁한 일

대화를 듣고, 남자가 여자에게 부탁한 일로 가장 적절한 것을 고르시오.

① 회의 일정 알려주기
② 음식점 예약하기
③ 보고서 복사하기
④ 회의실 예약하기
⑤ 간식 준비하기

W Good morning, Don.

M Hi, Peggy. Our meeting is _____ _____ _____ _____.

W Oh, good. Do we need to order some coffee and donuts for the meeting?

M Hmm… No. We'll _____ _____ _____ right after lunch.

W All right. *[pause]* Where are you going?

M I need to copy this report. While I'm gone, could you _____ _____ _____ _____ from 2:00 p.m. to 3:00 p.m.?

W Sure.

16 ◀ 이유

대화를 듣고, 여자가 약속 시간에 늦은
이유로 가장 적절한 것을 고르시오.

① 접촉 사고가 있어서
② 휴대전화를 찾아야 해서
③ 길이 막혀서
④ 내비게이션을 수리받아야 해서
⑤ 길을 잃어버려서

W Sorry I'm late. Have you been waiting very long?

M For about 40 minutes. I ＿＿＿＿＿ ＿＿＿＿＿ ＿＿＿＿＿ ＿＿＿＿＿.

W Sorry. I left my cell phone at home.

M I thought you ＿＿＿＿＿＿＿＿＿＿＿＿＿＿＿＿＿＿＿. Why are you so late?

W I tried to take a different route, but ＿＿＿＿＿ ＿＿＿＿＿ ＿＿＿＿＿.

M Don't you have a navigation system?

W Not anymore. ＿＿＿＿＿ ＿＿＿＿＿.

M Oh, sorry to hear that. Anyway, I'm hungry. Let's get some pizza.

17 ◀ 그림 상황에 적절한 대화

다음 그림의 상황에 가장 적절한 대화
를 고르시오.

① ② ③ ④ ⑤

① **W** What's wrong? You don't look good.
  M I ＿＿＿＿＿＿＿＿＿＿＿＿＿＿＿＿＿.
② **W** Do you want me to ＿＿＿＿＿ ＿＿＿＿＿ ＿＿＿＿＿ for you?
  M No thanks. I feel better now.
③ **W** My stomach feels upset. I think I ate something bad.
  M I see. ＿＿＿＿＿ ＿＿＿＿＿ ＿＿＿＿＿ three times a day.
④ **W** Is there a pharmacy near here?
  M Yes. Go straight two blocks and turn left.
⑤ **W** I think I'm getting the flu.
  M Why don't you ＿＿＿＿＿ ＿＿＿＿＿ ＿＿＿＿＿? I'll go with you.

18 ◀ 언급하지 않은 내용

다음을 듣고, 남자가 운동회 날에 대
해 언급하지 않은 것을 고르시오.

① 날짜   ② 시작 시각
③ 복장   ④ 경기 종목
⑤ 시상

M Good morning, students! The sports day ＿＿＿＿＿ ＿＿＿＿＿ ＿＿＿＿＿ ＿＿＿＿＿ May 4. It will start at nine o'clock in the morning, and you will need to come to school by 8:40. ＿＿＿＿＿ ＿＿＿＿＿ ＿＿＿＿＿ ＿＿＿＿＿ your PE uniform and trainers. A variety of games and activities will be waiting for you. There will also be ＿＿＿＿＿ ＿＿＿＿＿ ＿＿＿＿＿ ＿＿＿＿＿. I'm sure that everyone will have a great time!

19 ◀ 마지막 말에 대한 응답

대화를 듣고, 남자의 마지막 말에 이어질 여자의 말로 가장 적절한 것을 고르시오.

Woman: _____

① Never do that again.
② Don't worry. It'll be fine.
③ Please say hello to her for me.
④ How about going to a musical with me?
⑤ What restaurant are you going to?

W _____ _____ _____, Matt. Is everything okay?
M Well, I have a date with Somin tonight.
W What are you going to do _____ _____ _____?
M I'm going to take her out to dinner. Then we're going to a musical.
W That sounds like a great plan. I don't understand _____ _____ _____.
M Well, what if she doesn't like me? What if I _____ _____ _____?
W _____

20 ◀ 마지막 말에 대한 응답

대화를 듣고, 남자의 마지막 말에 이어질 여자의 말로 가장 적절한 것을 고르시오.

Woman: _____

① That's too bad. I wanted to see him.
② It was nice to see her yesterday.
③ He had a great time at the party.
④ Sehoon likes Minji's cooking, too.
⑤ Her new apartment is 20 minutes from here.

W I _____ _____ _____ the party tonight.
M I'm looking forward to it, too. There will be a lot of good food.
W Yes. Minji is an excellent cook! Do you think Sehoon will _____ _____ _____ _____?
M No. I asked him to come, but he said he _____ _____ _____.
W Why? Does he _____ _____ _____?
M Yes, he needs to help his sister move tonight.
W _____

A

다음 영어 어휘나 표현의 뜻을 우리말로 쓰세요.

01 skip lunch

02 severe

03 anxious

04 credit card

05 celebrate

06 silly

07 discuss

08 pharmacy

09 lost and found

10 luggage

11 abroad

12 useful

13 chew

14 theme

15 poem

16 lantern

B

우리말에 맞는 영어 어휘나 표현을 [보기]에서 찾아 쓰세요.

| 보기 | leftover | make it | route | first aid kit | checking account |
| | recently | confused | treat | get lost | a variety of |

01 최근에

02 여러 가지의

03 경로

04 구급상자

05 헷갈리는

06 나머지의, 남은

07 예금 계좌

08 길을 잃다

09 치료하다

10 (모임 등에) 가다[참석하다]

01 다음을 듣고, 로마의 내일 날씨로 가장 적절한 것을 고르시오.

02 대화를 듣고, 여자가 구입할 필통으로 가장 적절한 것을 고르시오.

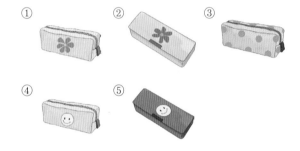

03 대화를 듣고, 남자의 심정으로 가장 적절한 것을 고르시오.

① proud 　② pleased 　③ regretful
④ surprised 　⑤ bored

04 대화를 듣고, 남자가 어제 한 일로 가장 적절한 것을 고르시오.

① 영화 보기 　② 이사하기 　③ 친구 만나기
④ 결혼식 가기 　⑤ 기숙사 알아보기

05 대화를 듣고, 두 사람이 대화하는 장소로 가장 적절한 곳을 고르시오.

① 산 　② 전망대 　③ 장난감 가게
④ 놀이공원 　⑤ 비행기

06 대화를 듣고, 여자의 마지막 말의 의도로 가장 적절한 것을 고르시오.

① 사과 　② 충고 　③ 동의
④ 거절 　⑤ 허가

07 대화를 듣고, 남자가 아직 한국에서 방문하지 않은 곳으로 가장 적절한 것을 고르시오.

① 경주 　② 제주 　③ 부산
④ 서울 　⑤ 전주

08 대화를 듣고, 여자가 대화 직후에 할 일로 가장 적절한 것을 고르시오.

① 헬스장에 전화하기 　② 운동하러 가기
③ 헬스장 위치 알려주기 　④ 할인 쿠폰 양도하기
⑤ 온라인으로 헬스 등록하기

고난도
09 대화를 듣고, 두 사람이 주차장에 대해 언급하지 않은 것을 고르시오.

① 위치 　② 규모 　③ 이용 가능 시간
④ 요금 　⑤ 할인 정보

10 다음을 듣고, 여자가 하는 말의 내용으로 가장 적절한 것을 고르시오.

① 로그인 오류 시 대처 방법
② 비밀번호 분실 시 재설정 방법
③ 보이스 피싱 대처법
④ 주기적인 비밀번호 변경의 필요성
⑤ 보안 프로그램 설치 안내

11 대화를 듣고, 남자의 말에 대한 내용과 일치하지 않는 것을 고르시오.

① 오늘 아침 4시 30분에 일어났다.
② 다음 달에 중요한 야구 시합이 있다.
③ 매일 세 시간씩 야구 연습을 한다.
④ 학교 시작하기 전에 야구 연습을 한다.
⑤ 우천 시에는 야구 연습이 취소된다.

12 대화를 듣고, 남자가 전화를 건 목적으로 가장 적절한 것을 고르시오.

① 어버이날 행사에 대해 문의하기 위해서
② 배송 예정일을 확인하기 위해서
③ 꽃바구니를 주문하기 위해서
④ 주문 내용을 변경하기 위해서
⑤ 화환 비용에 대해 문의하기 위해서

13 대화를 듣고, 여자가 지불해야 할 금액으로 가장 적절한 것을 고르시오.

① $15 　　② $20 　　③ $25
④ $30 　　⑤ $35

14 대화를 듣고, 두 사람의 관계로 가장 적절한 것을 고르시오.

① 의사 – 간호사　　② 교수 – 학생
③ 스키 강사 – 수강생　　④ 의사 – 환자
⑤ 경비원 – 주민

15 대화를 듣고, 여자가 남자에게 부탁한 일로 가장 적절한 것을 고르시오.

① 선물 골라주기　　② 기념품 사다 주기
③ 전시회 같이 가기　　④ 생일 파티 참석하기
⑤ 사진첩 보여주기

16 대화를 듣고, 여자가 교실을 바꾸고 싶어 하는 이유로 가장 적절한 것을 고르시오.

① 교실이 너무 좁아서　　② 냉방이 잘 안 되어서
③ 피아노가 고장 나서　　④ 피아노 두 대가 필요해서
⑤ 방음이 잘 안 되어서

17 다음 그림의 상황에 가장 적절한 대화를 고르시오.

① 　　② 　　③ 　　④ 　　⑤

18 다음을 듣고, 여자가 구인 광고에 대해 언급하지 않은 것을 고르시오.

① 직무　　② 지원 자격　　③ 근무 시간
④ 지원 마감일　　⑤ 연락처

[19-20] 대화를 듣고, 남자의 마지막 말에 이어질 여자의 말로 가장 적절한 것을 고르시오.

19 Woman: _____

① No, I don't need one.
② Yes, if you have a receipt.
③ There's nothing wrong with them.
④ They will be fixed in a few days.
⑤ Thanks, but that's not necessary.

고난도
20 Woman: _____

① I don't feel well today.
② I look forward to attending my new school.
③ I'm afraid that I would hurt his feelings.
④ I don't have problems with my classmates.
⑤ I haven't seen him for a long time.

DICTATION

정답 단서 오답 함정

일반 속도 빠른 속도

01 ◀ 특정 정보

다음을 듣고, 로마의 내일 날씨로 가장 적절한 것을 고르시오.

①
②
③
④
⑤

W Good evening. Here is tomorrow's weather forecast for Western Europe. There will be some _____ _____ _____ _____ tomorrow. It will rain in London for most of the day. Paris has been _____ _____ _____, and it will remain cloudy tomorrow. Rome is going to _____ _____ _____, _____ _____. Finally, there is a chance of snow in Berlin tomorrow.

02 ◀ 그림 묘사

대화를 듣고, 여자가 구입할 필통으로 가장 적절한 것을 고르시오.

①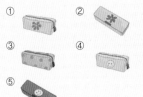
②
③
④
⑤

W I'm going to buy one of these pencil cases.
M Which one? I like _____ _____ _____.
W I'm going to get a cloth one _____ _____ _____ _____ _____.
M I see. I like the one with the happy face on it.
W So do I. But I will get _____ _____ _____ _____ on it.
M Oh, that's nice too.

03 ◀ 심정

대화를 듣고, 남자의 심정으로 가장 적절한 것을 고르시오.
① proud   ② pleased
③ regretful   ④ surprised
⑤ bored

W Is _____ _____ _____, Tom?
M Sort of, but it's nothing important.
W Come on. Tell me. What's wrong?
M Well, I had an argument with Jimin today. I _____ _____ _____ _____, and she got upset. I shouldn't have done that.
W It's okay. If _____ _____ _____ _____ tomorrow, she'll forgive you.
M Okay. I'll do that tomorrow morning. Thank you, Mom.

04 ◀ 한 일

대화를 듣고, 남자가 어제 한 일로 가장 적절한 것을 고르시오.

① 영화 보기　　② 이사하기
③ 친구 만나기　④ 결혼식 가기
⑤ 기숙사 알아보기

[Cell phone rings.]

W Hello?

M Hi, it's Eric.

W Oh, hi! Are you _____ _____ _____ _____ into your dormitory room?

M Actually, I did that yesterday. I _____ _____ _____ cleaning my room today.

W It would have been good if I could have helped you out. I had to _____ _____ _____ _____.

M That's okay. I understand. How about having dinner together tonight?

W That would be great.

05 ◀ 대화 장소

대화를 듣고, 두 사람이 대화하는 장소로 가장 적절한 곳을 고르시오.

① 산　　　　　② 전망대
③ 장난감 가게　④ 놀이공원
⑤ 비행기

M Look at those clouds! They are so beautiful!

W I know. The view is amazing! I still can't believe _____ _____ _____ _____ _____.

M Wow, look at how small the houses are down there!

W Yes, they look like dollhouses.

M Aren't we _____ _____ _____ _____ _____?

W What time is it?

M It's 1:45 p.m.

W Oh. You're right. The pilot will _____ _____ _____ soon.

06 ◀ 의도

대화를 듣고, 여자의 마지막 말의 의도로 가장 적절한 것을 고르시오.

① 사과　　② 충고
③ 동의　　④ 거절
⑤ 허가

M We need to hurry. Let's _____ _____ _____ now.

W Wait! There isn't a crosswalk here.

M I know, but the crosswalk is _____ _____ _____. We don't have time.

W Isn't it dangerous? We could be hit by a car.

M Don't worry. There isn't a lot of traffic today.

W That doesn't matter. You should _____ _____ _____ _____.

◀ 특정 정보

대화를 듣고, 남자가 아직 한국에서
방문하지 않은 곳으로 가장 적절한 것
을 고르시오.

① 경주 　　② 제주
③ 부산 　　④ 서울
⑤ 전주

W How do you like Korea so far?

M It's beautiful.

W What places _____ _____ _____ _____?

M Many places. I was just in Seoul and Gyeongju.

W Great! I recommend you also visit Jeju and Busan. Those cities _____ _____ _____.

M Oh, I went to Jeju when I first came to Korea, and I was in Busan last weekend.

W So where _____ _____ _____ _____?

M I'm going to Jeonju tomorrow.

08 ◀ 할 일

대화를 듣고, 여자가 대화 직후에 할
일로 가장 적절한 것을 고르시오.

① 헬스장에 전화하기
② 운동하러 가기
③ 헬스장 위치 알려주기
④ 할인 쿠폰 양도하기
⑤ 온라인으로 헬스 등록하기

W Did you know there's a new gym across the street?

M Yeah, I know. I have already been working out there.

W Wow! You're fast! I'm going to the gym to register now.

M Actually, you can _____ _____ _____ if you sign up online.

W Oh, really?

M They're _____ _____ _____ _____ right now. You can get 20% off on their website.

W That sounds good. I'll _____ _____ _____.

고난도

09 ◀ 언급하지 않은 내용

대화를 듣고, 두 사람이 주차장에 대
해 언급하지 않은 것을 고르시오.

① 위치 　　　　② 규모
③ 이용 가능 시간　④ 요금
⑤ 할인 정보

W This area is always crowded. Where should I park?

M There is a parking lot _____ _____ _____ _____ that building.

W Oh yeah? Is it a big parking lot?

M Not really, but I guess around twenty cars could park there.

W _____ _____ _____ _____ _____?

M Let me check. [pause] It's 1,000 won for the first thirty minutes and 500 won for every additional ten minutes.

W Don't you think _____ _____ _____ _____?

M Oh, electric car drivers like you can _____ _____ _____ _____ _____.

W Nice. Let's go there, then.

10 ◀ 주제 · 화제

다음을 듣고, 여자가 하는 말의 내용으로 가장 적절한 것을 고르시오.

① 로그인 오류 시 대처 방법
② 비밀번호 분실 시 재설정 방법
③ 보이스 피싱 대처법
④ 주기적인 비밀번호 변경의 필요성
⑤ 보안 프로그램 설치 안내

W A few days ago, _____ _____ _____. Someone logged into my messenger account and asked my friends for money. When I _____ _____ _____ _____, I couldn't. I realized somebody had stolen my password. In order to _____ _____ _____ _____ to you, you should change your passwords frequently. It's a good idea to _____ _____ _____ at least once every three months.

11 ◀ 내용 불일치

대화를 듣고, 남자의 말에 대한 내용과 일치하지 <u>않는</u> 것을 고르시오.

① 오늘 아침 4시 30분에 일어났다.
② 다음 달에 중요한 야구 시합이 있다.
③ 매일 세 시간씩 야구 연습을 한다.
④ 학교 시작하기 전에 야구 연습을 한다.
⑤ 우천 시에는 야구 연습이 취소된다.

W You look tired, Harry.
M I got up at 4:30 this morning.
W Four thirty? Why did you _____ _____ _____ _____?
M We have an important baseball game next month, so our team was practicing. We all gather at 5:30 every morning and _____ _____ _____ _____.
W Every morning?
M Yes, before school starts. We even practice in the rain.
W That must be hard, but I'm sure _____ _____ _____ _____.

12 ◀ 목적

대화를 듣고, 남자가 전화를 건 목적으로 가장 적절한 것을 고르시오.

① 어버이날 행사에 대해 문의하기 위해서
② 배송 예정일을 확인하기 위해서
③ 꽃바구니를 주문하기 위해서
④ 주문 내용을 변경하기 위해서
⑤ 화환 비용에 대해 문의하기 위해서

[Telephone rings.]
W Shari's Shop. How may I help you?
M Can I _____ _____ _____ for May 8?
W Sure. _____ _____ _____ _____ some flowers for Parents' Day?
M That's right. I heard you deliver baskets of flowers.
W We do. It's $40 for a large basket, and $30 for a small one.
M Great! I'd like to have a large basket _____ _____ _____ _____ _____.

13 ◀ 숫자 정보

대화를 듣고, 여자가 지불해야 할 금
액으로 가장 적절한 것을 고르시오.

① $15   ② $20
③ $25   ④ $30
⑤ $35

W Hi, how much are those gloves?

M Do you mean these leather ones? They're $35.

W _____ _____ _____. What about the wool gloves?

M They are _____ _____ _____. They are $30.

W That's still too expensive.

M Well, we _____ _____ _____. They are really warm, and they're only $15.

W Wow! That's $20 cheaper than the leather ones. I'll take them.

14 ◀ 화자 간 관계

대화를 듣고, 두 사람의 관계로 가장
적절한 것을 고르시오.

① 의사 – 간호사
② 교수 – 학생
③ 스키 강사 – 수강생
④ 의사 – 환자
⑤ 경비원 – 주민

M Hello. It's been a while since I've seen you.

W Yes, I've been busy. But now I _____ _____ _____ _____.

M I see. How long have you had it?

W For about one week. It started after I went skiing.

M Please _____ _____ _____ _____. *[pause]* Oh, yes. It seems your throat is red and swollen. Remember to _____ _____ _____ _____ _____.

W Okay.

15 ◀ 부탁한 일

대화를 듣고, 여자가 남자에게 부탁한
일로 가장 적절한 것을 고르시오.

① 선물 골라주기
② 기념품 사다 주기
③ 전시회 같이 가기
④ 생일 파티 참석하기
⑤ 사진첩 보여주기

M I'm going to _____ _____ _____ tomorrow. Would you like to come with me?

W I wish I could, but my grandmother's birthday is this weekend.

M So why can't you come tomorrow?

W I need to buy her something. I _____ _____ _____ _____ tomorrow.

M That's too bad. I think you'd enjoy the photos.

W I think so, too. Could you _____ _____ _____ _____ from the museum's gift shop?

M Sure. I promise I will.

16 ◀ 이유

대화를 듣고, 여자가 교실을 바꾸고 싶어 하는 이유로 가장 적절한 것을 고르시오.

① 교실이 너무 좁아서
② 냉방이 잘 안 되어서
③ 피아노가 고장 나서
④ 피아노 두 대가 필요해서
⑤ 방음이 잘 안 되어서

M Hi, Minju. Are your students _____ _____ _____ _____ _____ tomorrow?

W Actually, there is a small problem with my classroom.

M What's wrong with it? Is the air conditioner _____ _____ _____ again?

W No, that's fine. But I only have one piano.

M Really? I have two pianos in my classroom.

W You do? Can we _____ _____ then? Two of my students are playing a duet.

M Sure. I don't mind.

W Thanks!

17 ◀ 그림 상황에 적절한 대화

다음 그림의 상황에 가장 적절한 대화를 고르시오.

① ② ③ ④ ⑤

① **M** Good afternoon. How can I help you?
   W I'm trying to find Gate 17.
② **M** Do you need me to _____ _____ _____ at the airport?
   W No, I'll just take a taxi home.
③ **M** Welcome back! Did you _____ _____ _____ _____?
   W Yes! I have so many stories to tell you.
④ **M** Excuse me. What time will we be landing?
   W We should be arriving in about one hour.
⑤ **M** Have you _____ _____ _____ _____?
   W Not yet. I'll do that tomorrow morning.

18 ◀ 언급하지 않은 내용

다음을 듣고, 여자가 구인 광고에 대해 언급하지 않은 것을 고르시오.

① 직무   ② 지원 자격
③ 근무 시간   ④ 지원 마감일
⑤ 연락처

W Our company is looking for a computer engineer. We need someone who can _____ _____ _____ _____. We're looking for someone with more than two years of work experience _____ _____ _____. The hours are 9:00 a.m. to 6:00 p.m., Monday to Friday. If you _____ _____ _____ _____ _____, please call us at 555-1352.

19 ◀ 마지막 말에 대한 응답

대화를 듣고, 남자의 마지막 말에 이어질 여자의 말로 가장 적절한 것을 고르시오.

Woman: _____

① No, I don't need one.
② Yes, if you have a receipt.
③ There's nothing wrong with them.
④ They will be fixed in a few days.
⑤ Thanks, but that's not necessary.

W Hi. How can I help you?

M I bought these wireless speakers here yesterday, but there's _____ _____ _____ _____.

W What seems to be the problem?

M They only work for a few minutes, and then _____ _____ _____.

W Did you check the battery?

M Yes, the battery is fine. I even _____ _____ _____.

W I see. In that case, you can exchange them.

M Actually, can I just _____ _____ _____?

W _____

고난도

20 ◀ 마지막 말에 대한 응답

대화를 듣고, 남자의 마지막 말에 이어질 여자의 말로 가장 적절한 것을 고르시오.

Woman: _____

① I don't feel well today.
② I look forward to attending my new school.
③ I'm afraid that I would hurt his feelings.
④ I don't have problems with my classmates.
⑤ I haven't seen him for a long time.

M _____ _____ _____ _____ at your new school?

W Well, not really.

M Are you _____ _____ _____ _____?

W No, I've already made some friends.

M Do you like your teachers?

W Yes, they're all nice to me. The problem is one of my classmates, Taehyeon. He's nice, but he's very talkative during class. I can't _____ _____ _____ _____.

M Why don't you tell him?

W _____

A

다음 영어 어휘나 표현의 뜻을 우리말로 쓰세요.

01 crosswalk

02 argument

03 forgive

04 frequently

05 additional

06 out of order

07 competition

08 realize

09 prevent

10 parking lot

11 talkative

12 work experience

13 promise

14 steal

15 register

16 crowded

B

우리말에 맞는 영어 어휘나 표현을 [보기]에서 찾아 쓰세요.

| 보기 | arrive | sign up | work out | place an order | get ready to-v |
| | matter | wireless | regretful | mind | dormitory |

01 후회하는

02 ~할 준비를 하다

03 도착하다

04 무선의

05 중요하다

06 기숙사

07 운동하다

08 등록하다

09 상관하다

10 주문하다

점수   / 20문항

일반 속도

빠른 속도

01 다음을 듣고, 크리스마스 날의 날씨로 가장 적절한 것을 고르시오.

① ② ③
④ ⑤

02 대화를 듣고, 두 사람이 구입할 커튼으로 가장 적절한 것을 고르시오.

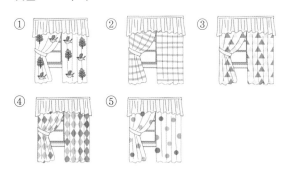

① ② ③
④ ⑤

03 대화를 듣고, 남자의 심정으로 가장 적절한 것을 고르시오.

① nervous   ② surprised   ③ bored
④ excited   ⑤ upset

🇬🇧
04 대화를 듣고, 여자가 지난 주말에 한 일로 가장 적절한 것을 고르시오.

① 아르바이트하기   ② 머리 자르기
③ 콘택트렌즈 사기   ④ 놀이공원 가기
⑤ 안과 검진받기

05 대화를 듣고, 두 사람이 대화하는 장소로 가장 적절한 곳을 고르시오.

① 건물 옥상   ② 해수욕장   ③ 스키장
④ 놀이공원   ⑤ 스케이트장

06 대화를 듣고, 남자의 마지막 말의 의도로 가장 적절한 것을 고르시오.

① 요청   ② 사과   ③ 동의
④ 허가   ⑤ 충고

07 대화를 듣고, 여자가 교환하려는 물건으로 가장 적절한 것을 고르시오.

① 치마   ② 블라우스   ③ 바지
④ 원피스   ⑤ 티셔츠

🇬🇧
08 대화를 듣고, 남자가 대화 직후에 할 일로 가장 적절한 것을 고르시오.

① 문과 창문 잠그기
② 모든 전기 플러그 뽑기
③ 신문 배달 중지 요청하기
④ 이웃에게 우편물 수거 부탁하기
⑤ 우체국에 전화하기

09 대화를 듣고, 두 사람이 벼룩시장에 대해 언급하지 않은 것을 고르시오.

① 일시   ② 장소
③ 입장료   ④ 입장 수익금 사용처
⑤ 판매 품목

🇬🇧
10 다음을 듣고, 남자가 하는 말의 내용으로 가장 적절한 것을 고르시오.

① 학업 스트레스와 행복지수의 상관관계
② 청소년기 또래의 영향력
③ 학생의 균형 잡힌 생활의 필요성
④ 운동 시간이 학업성적에 미치는 영향
⑤ 자투리 시간 관리 방법

고난도

11 다음을 듣고, Ray's Gym에 대한 내용과 일치하지 <u>않는</u> 것을 고르시오.

① 근처에 초등학교가 있다.
② 평일 영업은 오전 6시에 시작한다.
③ 일요일은 평일보다 문을 일찍 닫는다.
④ 형제자매를 대상으로 한 할인 행사를 진행하고 있다.
⑤ 할인을 받기 위해서는 최소 3개월 이상 등록해야 한다.

12 대화를 듣고, 여자가 전화를 건 목적으로 가장 적절한 것을 고르시오.

① 약속을 어긴 것을 사과하기 위해서
② 감사의 마음을 전하기 위해서
③ 응급실 상황을 알려주기 위해서
④ 약속 시각을 변경하기 위해서
⑤ 병문안을 가자고 제안하기 위해서

고난도

13 대화를 듣고, 현재 시각을 고르시오.

① 2:10 p.m.　② 2:30 p.m.　③ 2:40 p.m.
④ 2:50 p.m.　⑤ 3:00 p.m.

14 대화를 듣고, 두 사람의 관계로 가장 적절한 것을 고르시오.

① 의사 – 환자　　② 코치 – 선수
③ 아빠 – 딸　　　④ 감독 – 배우
⑤ 프로 게이머 – 팬

15 대화를 듣고, 여자가 남자에게 부탁한 일로 가장 적절한 것을 고르시오.

① 장 보기　　　　② 샌드위치 만들기
③ 샌드위치 가져다주기　④ 테니스 가르쳐주기
⑤ 슈퍼마켓까지 태워주기

16 대화를 듣고, 남자가 여자와 함께 등산을 갈 수 <u>없는</u> 이유로 가장 적절한 것을 고르시오.

① 동생 병문안을 가야 해서
② 누나가 아기를 낳을 예정이라서
③ 갓 태어난 조카를 보러 가야 해서
④ 출근을 해야 해서
⑤ 삼촌 댁에 가야 해서

17 다음 그림의 상황에 가장 적절한 대화를 고르시오.

①　　②　　③　　④　　⑤

18 다음을 듣고, 여자가 핼러윈 파티에 대해 언급하지 <u>않</u>은 것을 고르시오.

① 일시　　　② 장소　　　③ 입장료
④ 프로그램 내용　⑤ 경품 종류

[19-20] 대화를 듣고, 남자의 마지막 말에 이어질 여자의 말로 가장 적절한 것을 고르시오.

19 Woman: _____

① Will you go with me?
② Thanks for the information.
③ Because I'm not feeling well.
④ I've seen all of the famous places.
⑤ I'm going to stay for five more days.

고난도

20 Woman: _____

① The coffeemakers are on sale.
② Her party is on Saturday at 4:00 p.m.
③ That's a good idea. I'll call her now.
④ I can't go to the party. I have other plans.
⑤ What if she doesn't like my present?

DICTATION

정답 단서 오답 함정

일반 속도

빠른 속도

01 ◀ 특정 정보

다음을 듣고, 크리스마스 날의 날씨로
가장 적절한 것을 고르시오.

① ②
③ ④
⑤

M Good morning! This is Steve Shepard from the Weather Channel. It's going to _____ _____ _____, but it will stop by six o'clock tonight. If you're planning to travel today, I advise you to wait until tomorrow morning. The _____ _____ _____ _____ tonight. On Christmas Eve, it will be cold and sunny. It will be windy on Christmas Day, but it won't _____ _____ _____ until the day after Christmas.

02 ◀ 그림 묘사

대화를 듣고, 두 사람이 구입할 커튼
으로 가장 적절한 것을 고르시오.

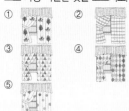

① ②
③ ④
⑤

W Honey, I want to get some curtains for our new house. The ones we have now are so old.

M Okay. Do you have a _____ _____ _____ _____?

W How about the ones with the triangle pattern? They're really cute.

M I don't like those. I think the ones with birds and trees on them will be _____ _____ _____.

W But those would _____ _____ _____.

M What about the curtains with diamonds on them?

W Those look great!

03 ◀ 심정

대화를 듣고, 남자의 심정으로 가장
적절한 것을 고르시오.

① nervous ② surprised
③ bored ④ excited
⑤ upset

W Hi, Greg. I can tell from your smile that you have good news.

M I do! I _____ _____ _____ _____!

W Wow! That's great.

M Yes. The coach said I have to _____ _____ _____. And training will be hard.

W That sounds tough.

M I know, but I still really want to play! It's been my dream to be _____ _____ _____ _____.

04 ◀ 한 일

대화를 듣고, 여자가 지난 주말에 한 일로 가장 적절한 것을 고르시오.

① 아르바이트하기
② 머리 자르기
③ 콘택트렌즈 사기
④ 놀이공원 가기
⑤ 안과 검진받기

W How was your weekend, Max?

M It was good. I _____ _____ _____ _____ last Saturday. I'm working at an amusement park.

W That sounds great! By the way, do you _____ _____ _____ about me?

M Hmm… Did you ~~_____ _____ _____ _____~~?

W No, I'm wearing glasses. I bought them this afternoon.

M They're stylish! Do you usually wear contacts?

W No, I _____ _____ _____ _____ last weekend and the doctor said I needed glasses.

05 ◀ 대화 장소

대화를 듣고, 두 사람이 대화하는 장소로 가장 적절한 곳을 고르시오.

① 건물 옥상　② 해수욕장
③ 스키장　④ 놀이공원
⑤ 스케이트장

W I've been waiting all year for this.

M But _____ _____ _____ _____. Are you sure it's safe?

W Of course it is. Let's go!

M I don't want to. I'm really scared.

W Come on. It's not hard. Just _____ _____ _____ _____ _____.

M But this slope seems very steep.

W It's not as steep as it looks. And once you move forward, you will be able to _____ _____ _____ _____ without effort.

06 ◀ 의도

대화를 듣고, 남자의 마지막 말의 의도로 가장 적절한 것을 고르시오.

① 요청　② 사과
③ 동의　④ 허가
⑤ 충고

M Did you hear that we're doing group projects?

W Oh, that sounds great. Who do you want as your teammates?

M Honestly, I'm not sure. I usually _____ _____ _____.

W Really? May I ask why?

M I hate it when someone in the group doesn't work as hard as everyone else.

W I understand. But it's important to learn _____ _____ _____ _____ with people and communicate with them.

M I guess you're right. Maybe this project can help me _____ _____ _____ _____ _____.

대화를 듣고, 여자가 교환하려는 물건으로 가장 적절한 것을 고르시오.

① 치마　　② 블라우스
③ 바지　　④ 원피스
⑤ 티셔츠

[Telephone rings.]

M Hello. This is Queen's Closet. How may I help you?

W Hello. My name is Katy Parker. I sent you an email about my order of a blouse and skirt.

M I will look for it. Has your order not arrived yet?

W Oh, I got it today. But you _____ _____ _____ _____.

M I'm sorry to hear that. Can I have your order number, please?

W Sure. It's 230315. The skirt is the right size, but the blouse is _____ _____ _____ _____.

M Let me check your email. *[pause]* Oh, we did _____ _____ _____. You ordered a size 55, but that's a 66.

W Right. Can I _____ _____ _____?

M Sure. Please just send it back. We'll send you the right one today.

대화를 듣고, 남자가 대화 직후에 할 일로 가장 적절한 것을 고르시오.

① 문과 창문 잠그기
② 모든 전기 플러그 뽑기
③ 신문 배달 중지 요청하기
④ 이웃에게 우편물 수거 부탁하기
⑤ 우체국에 전화하기

W Hey, Ted! Are you ready for your vacation?

M I think so. I'm just worried about _____ _____ _____ while I'm gone.

W It should be okay. Just _____ _____ _____ _____ all the doors and windows.

M I already did.

W Okay. Have you asked a neighbor to _____ _____ _____ _____ _____?

M Actually, the post office will hold my mail while I'm gone.

W Good. You should also _____ _____ before you leave.

M Oh! I didn't think of that. I should do that right now.

대화를 듣고, 두 사람이 벼룩시장에 대해 언급하지 <u>않은</u> 것을 고르시오.

① 일시
② 장소
③ 입장료
④ 입장 수익금 사용처
⑤ 판매 품목

W Have you made any plans for this weekend, Jack?

M I'll _____ _____ _____ _____ _____ this Saturday. It's open from 10:00 a.m. to 1:00 p.m.

W That sounds fun! Is it _____ _____?

M No, the admission fee is $2. But the money will be donated to an animal hospital.

W Oh, that sounds great.

M It is! And a variety of used jewelry, toys, and clothes _____ _____ _____ _____.

W I'll have to stop by!

10 ◀ 주제·화제

다음을 듣고, 남자가 하는 말의 내용으로 가장 적절한 것을 고르시오.
① 학업 스트레스와 행복지수의 상관관계
② 청소년기 또래의 영향력
③ 학생의 균형 잡힌 생활의 필요성
④ 운동 시간이 학업성적에 미치는 영향
⑤ 자투리 시간 관리 방법

M Everyone knows that students must study hard. But they must do other things, too. Their lives _____ _____ _____. In fact, it's important to socialize with friends at school. Also, students need to exercise every day. They also _____ _____ _____ to stay healthy. Students are happier and more successful in school when they are both _____ _____ _____ _____.

고난도

11 ◀ 내용 불일치

다음을 듣고, Ray's Gym에 대한 내용과 일치하지 <u>않는</u> 것을 고르시오.
① 근처에 초등학교가 있다.
② 평일 영업은 오전 6시에 시작한다.
③ 일요일은 평일보다 문을 일찍 닫는다.
④ 형제자매를 대상으로 한 할인 행사를 진행하고 있다.
⑤ 할인을 받기 위해서는 최소 3개월 이상 등록해야 한다.

W Ray's Gym _____ _____ _____ Harriet Street next to Woodfield Elementary School. It's open from 6:00 a.m. to 11:00 p.m. on weekdays. On Saturdays, the gym closes at 6:00 p.m., and it _____ _____ _____ _____. The gym currently _____ _____ _____ _____ for siblings. If two siblings join the gym together and _____ _____ _____ more than three months, they can each register for an additional month for free.

12 ◀ 목적

대화를 듣고, 여자가 전화를 건 목적으로 가장 적절한 것을 고르시오.
① 약속을 어긴 것을 사과하기 위해서
② 감사의 마음을 전하기 위해서
③ 응급실 상황을 알려주기 위해서
④ 약속 시각을 변경하기 위해서
⑤ 병문안을 가자고 제안하기 위해서

[Cell phone rings.]
M Hello?
W Hi, Ben.
M Jenny, is everything okay? I waited for you at the theater for an hour yesterday.
W I had to _____ _____ _____ _____.
M Really? What happened?
W When I was leaving my house to meet you, I suddenly _____ _____ _____ _____ _____.
M That's terrible. Are you all right now?
W I'm okay, but I'm still in the hospital. Sorry that I couldn't _____ _____ yesterday.

13 ◀ 숫자 정보

대화를 듣고, 현재 시각을 고르시오.

① 2:10 p.m.　　② 2:30 p.m.
③ 2:40 p.m.　　④ 2:50 p.m.
⑤ 3:00 p.m.

W What time does the movie start?

M At three.

W Really? We're so early.

M Yeah. I wanted to leave at 2:10 because there is usually _____ _____ _____ _____.

W But it only took us twenty minutes today.

M I know! Since we're _____ _____ _____, I'm going to get some popcorn.

W Okay. Let's meet back here ten minutes _____ _____ _____ _____.

M Sounds good.

14 ◀ 화자 간 관계

대화를 듣고, 두 사람의 관계로 가장 적절한 것을 고르시오.

① 의사 – 환자
② 코치 – 선수
③ 아빠 – 딸
④ 감독 – 배우
⑤ 프로 게이머 – 팬

M How are you feeling today, Cindy?

W I'm _____ _____ _____. I want to play in today's game.

M Are you really ready to play soccer? I think you need more rest.

W I'm fine. The doctor said I can start exercising _____ _____ _____ _____ _____.

M Playing in a game is too dangerous. I'm going to ask Jessica to _____ _____ _____ today.

W All right. But can I at least practice with the team?

M Hmm… I'll let you, but don't _____ _____ _____ _____.

W Okay.

15 ◀ 부탁한 일

대화를 듣고, 여자가 남자에게 부탁한 일로 가장 적절한 것을 고르시오.

① 장 보기
② 샌드위치 만들기
③ 샌드위치 가져다주기
④ 테니스 가르쳐주기
⑤ 슈퍼마켓까지 태워주기

W Matt, are you busy?

M Not now, but I'm going to play tennis later.

W Then can you _____ _____ _____ _____?

M What is it?

W I'm going to make sandwiches later today, so I need some eggs and other groceries.

M Do you want me to _____ _____ _____ _____?

W No, you don't need to. But could you _____ _____ _____ _____ to the supermarket?

M All right. I'll _____ _____ _____ on my way to the tennis court.

W Great!

16 ◀ 이유

대화를 듣고, 남자가 여자와 함께 등산을 갈 수 없는 이유로 가장 적절한 것을 고르시오.

① 동생 병문안을 가야 해서
② 누나가 아기를 낳을 예정이라서
③ 갓 태어난 조카를 보러 가야 해서
④ 출근을 해야 해서
⑤ 삼촌 댁에 가야 해서

[Cell phone rings.]

W Hello?

M Hi, Whitney.

W What's up, Carl? We're still meeting at 10:00 a.m. to go hiking, right?

M Actually, I have to _____ _____ _____. Something came up.

W That's disappointing. Do you have to go to work?

M No, my sister _____ _____ _____ a baby boy last night. My family is going to see him today.

W Oh, wow! Congratulations on becoming an uncle!

M Thanks. I'm _____ _____ _____ _____ my new nephew.

17 ◀ 그림 상황에 적절한 대화

다음 그림의 상황에 가장 적절한 대화를 고르시오.

① ② ③ ④ ⑤

① **M** I'm interested in renting a swan boat, but I'm not sure _____ _____ _____ _____.

W It costs 20,000 won for 40 minutes.

② **M** I want to swim in the lake. Do you think we can?

W The sign says that people can't swim in the lake. It's too dirty.

③ **M** Can I _____ _____ _____?

W Sure. If you don't have a fishing pole, you can rent one over there.

④ **M** What are we going to do for our picnic?

W We're going to _____ _____ _____ _____ _____ _____.

⑤ **M** What kind of bird is that?

W It's a swan. They like to swim in the lake during the summer.

18 ◀ 언급하지 않은 내용

다음을 듣고, 여자가 핼러윈 파티에 대해 언급하지 않은 것을 고르시오.

① 일시   ② 장소
③ 입장료   ④ 프로그램 내용
⑤ 경품 종류

W Good morning, students! _____ _____ _____ _____ _____ that our school Halloween party is going to be on Friday, October 31 from 4:00 to 8:00 p.m. The event will be held in the gym, and _____ _____ _____ for students and teachers. There will be a costume competition and a pie-eating contest. So _____ _____ _____ _____, bring a friend, and have a great time!

19 ◀ 마지막 말에 대한 응답

대화를 듣고, 남자의 마지막 말에 이어질 여자의 말로 가장 적절한 것을 고르시오.

Woman: _____

① Will you go with me?
② Thanks for the information.
③ Because I'm not feeling well.
④ I've seen all of the famous places.
⑤ I'm going to stay for five more days.

W Excuse me. I lost my map. Can I get one here?
M Sure. Here you are. _____ _____ _____ _____ many places so far?
W Not really. I don't know very much about Seoul.
M I'll _____ _____ _____ on the map for you.
W Thanks, but I'm not sure _____ _____ _____ _____.
M Then I recommend taking the tour bus. It'll take you to the most famous places in the city.
W _____

고난도

20 ◀ 마지막 말에 대한 응답

대화를 듣고, 남자의 마지막 말에 이어질 여자의 말로 가장 적절한 것을 고르시오.

Woman: _____

① The coffeemakers are on sale.
② Her party is on Saturday at 4:00 p.m.
③ That's a good idea. I'll call her now.
④ I can't go to the party. I have other plans.
⑤ What if she doesn't like my present?

[Cell phone rings.]
M Hello?
W Hi, Dan. I'm at a home appliance store now.
M Oh, really? What are you doing there?
W I need to _____ _____ _____ _____ for Beth's housewarming party.
M Do you know what she wants?
W Not really. What about a coffeemaker? She _____ _____ _____.
M I think she already has one. You should call her and _____ _____ _____ _____.
W _____

160

A 다음 영어 어휘나 표현의 뜻을 우리말로 쓰세요.

01 currently _____

02 dizzy _____

03 notice _____

04 steep _____

05 emergency room _____

06 particular _____

07 communicate _____

08 disappointing _____

09 mark _____

10 flea market _____

11 admission (fee) _____

12 donate _____

13 develop _____

14 neighbor _____

15 mentally _____

16 advise _____

B 우리말에 맞는 영어 어휘나 표현을 [보기]에서 찾아 쓰세요.

보기	nephew	cabin	fall down	send back	the day after
	unplug	sibling	physically	give birth to	socialize with

01 육체적으로 _____

02 그다음 날 _____

03 오두막집 _____

04 조카 _____

05 쓰러지다 _____

06 ～을 반송하다 _____

07 형제자매 _____

08 (전기) 플러그를 뽑다 _____

09 ～와 사귀다[어울리다] _____

10 (아이)를 낳다 _____

01 다음을 듣고, 수요일 오전의 날씨로 가장 적절한 것을 고르시오.

02 대화를 듣고, 여자가 찾고 있는 교과서 표지로 가장 적절한 것을 고르시오.

03 대화를 듣고, 남자의 심정으로 가장 적절한 것을 고르시오.

① relaxed   ② nervous   ③ excited
④ annoyed   ⑤ proud

04 대화를 듣고, 여자가 오늘 한 일로 가장 적절한 것을 고르시오.

① 요리 수업 듣기   ② 병원 가기   ③ 등산화 사기
④ 수학여행 가기   ⑤ 등산하기

05 대화를 듣고, 두 사람이 대화하는 장소로 가장 적절한 곳을 고르시오.

① 여행사   ② 공항   ③ 기차역
④ 은행   ⑤ 우체국

06 대화를 듣고, 여자의 마지막 말의 의도로 가장 적절한 것을 고르시오.

① 승낙   ② 설득   ③ 거절
④ 충고   ⑤ 감사

07 대화를 듣고, 여자가 여행지에서 하지 않은 일로 가장 적절한 것을 고르시오.

① 시내 전망 구경하기   ② 커피 마시기
③ 하이킹하기   ④ 동물원 가기
⑤ 야구 경기 관람하기

08 대화를 듣고, 남자가 대화 직후에 할 일로 가장 적절한 것을 고르시오.

① 지갑 챙기기   ② 택시 회사에 전화하기
③ 여권 찾아보기   ④ 짐 정리하기
⑤ 비행기 시간 확인하기

09 대화를 듣고, 두 사람이 프린터에 대해 언급하지 않은 것을 고르시오.

① 구입 시기   ② 고장 원인   ③ 가격
④ 제조사   ⑤ 품질 보증 기간

10 다음을 듣고, 남자가 하는 말의 내용으로 가장 적절한 것을 고르시오.

① 폭설 시 대처 요령   ② 열차 출발 지연
③ 막차 시간 연장   ④ 기차표 환불 규정
⑤ 목적지별 플랫폼 위치

고난도

11 대화를 듣고, 여자의 여행에 대한 내용과 일치하지 않는 것을 고르시오.

① 부모님과 함께 여행했다.
② 사흘 연속으로 비가 내렸다.
③ 8일 동안 여행을 했다.
④ 가이드와 동반했다.
⑤ 사원을 관람하는 일정이 있었다.

🇬🇧
12 대화를 듣고, 남자가 백화점에 온 목적으로 가장 적절한 것을 고르시오.

① 아들을 위한 선물을 사기 위해서
② 식료품을 사기 위해서
③ 근무를 하기 위해서
④ 물건을 교환하기 위해서
⑤ 신제품을 구경하기 위해서

고난도
13 대화를 듣고, 여자가 받은 거스름돈으로 가장 적절한 것을 고르시오.

① $1   ② $2   ③ $3
④ $4   ⑤ $5

14 대화를 듣고, 두 사람의 관계로 가장 적절한 것을 고르시오.

① 치과의사 – 환자   ② 동물원 사육사 – 관람객
③ 편의점 직원 – 손님   ④ 교사 – 학생
⑤ 사진작가 – 모델

15 대화를 듣고, 여자가 남자에게 제안한 일로 가장 적절한 것을 고르시오.

① 외식하기   ② 특별한 선물 사기
③ 저녁 메뉴 변경하기   ④ 케이크 주문하기
⑤ 함께 파티 준비하기

🇬🇧
16 대화를 듣고, 남자가 영화를 보러 갈 수 <u>없는</u> 이유로 가장 적절한 것을 고르시오.

① 수학 숙제를 해야 해서
② 수학 시험을 준비해야 해서
③ 가족과 식사하기로 해서
④ 집들이를 준비해야 해서
⑤ 몸이 좋지 않아서

17 다음 그림의 상황에 가장 적절한 대화를 고르시오.

①   ②   ③   ④   ⑤

고난도
18 다음을 듣고, 여자가 피카소에 대해 언급하지 <u>않은</u> 것을 고르시오.

① 출생지   ② 대표작
③ 작품 수   ④ 대표적인 미술 양식
⑤ 사망 나이

[19-20] 대화를 듣고, 남자의 마지막 말에 이어질 여자의 말로 가장 적절한 것을 고르시오.

19 Woman: _____

① Why don't you buy a new helmet?
② Have you been to the ice rink before?
③ Okay, I will wear one next time.
④ Her birthday was last Monday.
⑤ All right. I won't wear my helmet.

🇬🇧
20 Woman: _____

① Yes, what do you have in mind?
② Of course not. She would be happy to do it.
③ No, my mom washed this coat yesterday.
④ It's none of your business.
⑤ Would you mind picking up the coat at the dry cleaner's?

DICTATION

01 ◀ 특정 정보

다음을 듣고, 수요일 오전의 날씨로 가장 적절한 것을 고르시오.

①
②
③
④
⑤

W Hello, everyone! Welcome to our five-day weather forecast. _____ _____ _____ _____ on Monday because of the rain. On Tuesday, we _____ _____ _____ _____ all day. It will be warm and sunny in the morning on Wednesday, but there is a 30 percent chance of _____ _____ in the afternoon. On Thursday and Friday, it will rain all day again.

02 ◀ 그림 묘사

대화를 듣고, 여자가 찾고 있는 교과서 표지로 가장 적절한 것을 고르시오.

①
②
③
④
⑤

M What are you looking for, Rachel?

W I can't find my textbook. It's called *World History*. The title is _____ _____ _____.

M Okay. Is there a picture of the earth under the title?

W No, that's the older edition. My book has a picture of a knight on it.

M I think I remember seeing that around the house. Did you _____ _____ _____ on it?

W Yes, I wrote it _____ _____ _____ of the knight.

M Okay. Let me help you find it.

03 ◀ 심정

대화를 듣고, 남자의 심정으로 가장 적절한 것을 고르시오.

① relaxed
② nervous
③ excited
④ annoyed
⑤ proud

W The results from the singing audition _____ _____ _____ online!

M Oh, I don't want to look! I don't think I passed.

W Really? Why not?

M I _____ _____ _____ at the audition. I forgot some of the lyrics.

W It'll be all right. You have a great voice. I'm sure they loved you.

M Thank you. I guess I should _____ _____ _____.

04 ◀ 한 일

대화를 듣고, 여자가 오늘 한 일로 가장 적절한 것을 고르시오.

① 요리 수업 듣기
② 병원 가기
③ 등산화 사기
④ 수학여행 가기
⑤ 등산하기

M Mom, I'm home. Did you go to your French cooking class today?
W No, _____ _____ _____. The teacher was sick. I went shopping with a friend instead.
M Did you remember to get me _____ _____ _____ _____ _____? I need them _____ _____ _____ _____.
W Yes, I did. I put them in your room.
M Thanks, Mom. You're the best!

05 ◀ 대화 장소

대화를 듣고, 두 사람이 대화하는 장소로 가장 적절한 곳을 고르시오.

① 여행사 ② 공항
③ 기차역 ④ 은행
⑤ 우체국

M Hello. How may I help you?
W Good morning. I would like to _____ _____ _____.
M Okay. Which shipping option would you like? We have air mail, express mail, and standard mail.
W I'm sending a Christmas card to my friend in Sydney, Australia. _____ _____ _____ _____ _____?
M Express mail is the fastest, but it's expensive. I recommend air mail. It will _____ _____ _____ _____ for the card to get to Australia.
W That's fine.

06 ◀ 의도

대화를 듣고, 여자의 마지막 말의 의도로 가장 적절한 것을 고르시오.

① 승낙 ② 설득
③ 거절 ④ 충고
⑤ 감사

M Can you still _____ _____ _____ _____ with me tomorrow, Sally?
W Of course! I'm really looking forward to it. When does it start?
M It starts at two o'clock. But I think we should _____ _____ _____ before the game starts.
W That's a good idea. Let's meet at 12:30.
M _____ _____ _____ _____ _____ Adam to watch the game with us? He really likes soccer.
W Sure! I would like to meet him.

대화를 듣고, 여자가 여행지에서 하지 않은 일로 가장 적절한 것을 고르시오.
① 시내 전망 구경하기
② 커피 마시기
③ 하이킹하기
④ 동물원 가기
⑤ 야구 경기 관람하기

M Hi, Jessica. How was your trip to Seattle?

W It was great!

M I'm glad to hear that. What did you do?

W First, I went to an observation tower. I could _____ _____ _____ _____ from the top!

M That sounds fun! Did you _____ _____ _____ there?

W Yes, I went to a local coffee shop after my friend and I _____ _____.

M Oh, wow. I heard that there are many mountains near Seattle.

W There are! And _____ _____ _____ _____, I went to a baseball game.

대화를 듣고, 남자가 대화 직후에 할 일로 가장 적절한 것을 고르시오.
① 지갑 챙기기
② 택시 회사에 전화하기
③ 여권 찾아보기
④ 짐 정리하기
⑤ 비행기 시간 확인하기

W Are you almost ready, Scott? We should leave soon.

M I'm ready, Mom. I just needed to _____ _____ _____ _____ to my suitcase. When does our flight leave?

W At six. But we should arrive at the airport three hours before the flight.

M I know. Do you know _____ _____ _____ _____? I can't find it in my room.

W Yes, it's in my bag. Did you _____ _____ _____ _____?

M No, I didn't. I'll call them right now.

대화를 듣고, 두 사람이 프린터에 대해 언급하지 않은 것을 고르시오.
① 구입 시기   ② 고장 원인
③ 가격   ④ 제조사
⑤ 품질 보증 기간

M Bella, you look upset. What's wrong?

W My printer _____ _____.

M The one that you bought last October? Did you reset it?

W Yes, but it doesn't work.

M How much did you pay for it?

W Fifty dollars. It's _____ _____ _____ from AZ Electronics.

M Did it come with a warranty?

W Yes. It is _____ _____ _____ _____ _____. So I should be able to get it fixed right away.

10 ◀ 주제 · 화제

다음을 듣고, 남자가 하는 말의 내용으로 가장 적절한 것을 고르시오.

① 폭설 시 대처 요령
② 열차 출발 지연
③ 막차 시간 연장
④ 기차표 환불 규정
⑤ 목적지별 플랫폼 위치

M Ladies and gentlemen, can I _____ _____ _____, please? This announcement is for passengers waiting for the seven o'clock train to Seoul. Because of ~~_____ _____~~ _____ _____ _____, the seven o'clock train to Seoul is delayed. The train will arrive at 7:30. We're very _____ _____ _____ _____. Thank you for your understanding.

고난도

11 ◀ 내용 불일치

대화를 듣고, 여자의 여행에 대한 내용과 일치하지 <u>않는</u> 것을 고르시오.

① 부모님과 함께 여행했다.
② 사흘 연속으로 비가 내렸다.
③ 8일 동안 여행을 했다.
④ 가이드와 동반했다.
⑤ 사원을 관람하는 일정이 있었다.

M Hi, Beth. How was your summer vacation?
W It was awful. I went to Thailand with my parents, but it rained _____ _____ _____ _____ when we were there.
M I'm sorry to hear that. How long were you there?
W Five days.
M What did you do there?
W We _____ _____ _____ _____, and he took us to several famous temples.
M How was that?
W It was okay. The temples were beautiful, but _____ _____ _____ _____.

---

12 ◀ 목적

대화를 듣고, 남자가 백화점에 온 목적으로 가장 적절한 것을 고르시오.

① 아들을 위한 선물을 사기 위해서
② 식료품을 사기 위해서
③ 근무를 하기 위해서
④ 물건을 교환하기 위해서
⑤ 신제품을 구경하기 위해서

M Hi, Nicole. What are you doing at the department store?
W I work here. Today is my first day. What about you? Are you here to ~~_____ _____~~?
M No. I'm here _____ _____ _____ _____ _____.
W What's wrong with it?
M When my son opened the box, a couple of _____ _____ _____.
W Oh, I see. You really need to exchange it for a new one.

13 ◀ 숫자 정보

대화를 듣고, 여자가 받은 거스름돈으로 가장 적절한 것을 고르시오.

① $1   ② $2
③ $3   ④ $4
⑤ $5

M May I take your order?

W Yes. I'll have two donuts and two apple juices.

M Donuts are $2 each, and apple juices are $4 each. But when you _____ _____ _____ _____ today, you get a donut for free.

W Great! Then I _____ _____ _____ _____ _____ one donut, right?

M That's right. For here or to go?

W To go, please.

M Okay. We offer 10% off for to-go orders, so you can _____ _____ _____ _____ .

W Oh, that's good. Here's a $10 bill.

M Thank you. Here's your change.

14 ◀ 화자 간 관계

대화를 듣고, 두 사람의 관계로 가장 적절한 것을 고르시오.

① 치과의사 – 환자
② 동물원 사육사 – 관람객
③ 편의점 직원 – 손님
④ 교사 – 학생
⑤ 사진작가 – 모델

W Hello, Jacob. What's the problem?

M _____ _____ _____ _____ _____ really hurts. I think I might have a cavity.

W Can you open your mouth? *[pause]* You actually _____ _____ _____ .

M Oh, no! I wonder how that happened. I brush regularly.

W How old is your toothbrush?

M Hmm. I'm not sure. Maybe six months old?

W You should _____ _____ _____ every three months.

15 ◀ 제안한 일

대화를 듣고, 여자가 남자에게 제안한 일로 가장 적절한 것을 고르시오.

① 외식하기
② 특별한 선물 사기
③ 저녁 메뉴 변경하기
④ 케이크 주문하기
⑤ 함께 파티 준비하기

W Hey, Vincent. What are you up to?

M I'm _____ _____ _____ for my parents' 30th wedding anniversary. It's this coming Sunday.

W So what's the surprise?

M I'm going to _____ _____ _____ _____ for them.

W Wow, your parents will be very pleased. What are you going to make?

M I'm thinking about making steak, shrimp pasta, and chicken salad.

W Great! And why don't you _____ _____ _____ too? It's a special day.

M That's a good idea. I'm sure they will like that.

16 ◀ 이유

대화를 듣고, 남자가 영화를 보러 갈 수 없는 이유로 가장 적절한 것을 고르시오.

① 수학 숙제를 해야 해서
② 수학 시험을 준비해야 해서
③ 가족과 식사하기로 해서
④ 집들이를 준비해야 해서
⑤ 몸이 좋지 않아서

W Hi, Chris! How did you do _____ _____ _____ _____?

M I only got two answers wrong! I'm so relieved. How about you?

W I did well, too! Do you want to _____ _____ _____ _____ with me to celebrate?

M I wish I could, but I need to get home. I'm going to _____ _____ _____ _____ _____.

W I understand. Maybe next time!

M Definitely! Enjoy your movie.

17 ◀ 그림 상황에 적절한 대화

다음 그림의 상황에 가장 적절한 대화를 고르시오.

① ② ③ ④ ⑤

① **W** What's wrong with your cell phone?
   M It suddenly stopped working, and I don't know why.
② **W** It's _____ _____ _____! I can't concentrate at all.
   M Then why don't we go to the library?
③ **W** I'd like to _____ _____ _____.
   M Sure. Show me your card, please.
④ **W** Why didn't you call me?
   M I _____ _____ _____ _____ _____. I'm really sorry.
⑤ **W** Could you _____ _____ _____, please?
   M Oh, sorry. I'll be quiet.

고난도

18 ◀ 언급하지 않은 내용

다음을 듣고, 여자가 피카소에 대해 언급하지 않은 것을 고르시오.

① 출생지
② 대표작
③ 작품 수
④ 대표적인 미술 양식
⑤ 사망 나이

W Welcome to the art museum, everyone. I'm your tour guide. We're going to see some Picasso paintings today. But first, let me tell you about him. Picasso _____ _____ _____ Spain, but he lived in France for most of his life. He painted about 30,000 _____ _____ _____. Cubism is his most _____ _____ _____. Picasso was 91 years old when he died.

대화를 듣고, 남자의 마지막 말에 이어질 여자의 말로 가장 적절한 것을 고르시오.

Woman: _____

① Why don't you buy a new helmet?
② Have you been to the ice rink before?
③ Okay, I will wear one next time.
④ Her birthday was last Monday.
⑤ All right. I won't wear my helmet.

M Hi, Jenny! _____ _____ _____ _____ at Stacy's birthday party?

W Yes, I did. We went ice skating at **an ice rink** near her house.

M Did you wear a **helmet**? Ice skating _____ _____ _____ _____.

W Don't be silly, Dad. None of the other kids were wearing helmets.

M But you _____ _____ _____ _____. You need to be careful.

W _____

대화를 듣고, 남자의 마지막 말에 이어질 여자의 말로 가장 적절한 것을 고르시오.

Woman: _____

① Yes, what do you have in mind?
② Of course not. She would be happy to do it.
③ No, my mom washed this coat yesterday.
④ It's none of your business.
⑤ Would you mind picking up the coat at the dry cleaner's?

W Hi, Justin. What happened to your coat?

M A truck _____ _____ _____ _____ when I was crossing the street.

W Oh, no. That's too bad. Can you _____ _____ _____ _____?

M No, I don't think I can. I need to take it to **the dry cleaner's**, but _____ _____ _____.

W My mom can clean it for you _____ _____. She has her own dry cleaning **business**.

M Really? She wouldn't **mind**?

W _____

A

다음 영어 어휘나 표현의 뜻을 우리말로 쓰세요.

01 lower	**02** pleased
03 textbook	**04** company
05 suitcase	**06** artistic style
07 cavity	**08** relieved
09 a pair of	**10** warranty
11 replace	**12** track
13 temple	**14** dry cleaner's
15 quite	**16** hire

B

우리말에 맞는 영어 어휘나 표현을 [보기]에서 찾아 쓰세요.

보기	suddenly	part	wonder	passenger	department store
	standard	upset	regularly	dangerous	pay for

01 일반적인, 보통의	**02** 부품
03 궁금하다	**04** 갑자기
05 위험한	**06** 규칙적으로
07 승객	**08** ~에 대한 대금을 지불하다
09 속상한	**10** 백화점

일반 속도

빠른 속도

01 다음을 듣고, 라스베이거스의 오늘 날씨로 가장 적절한 것을 고르시오.

①   ②   ③

④   ⑤

02 대화를 듣고, 두 사람이 보고 있는 사진으로 가장 적절한 것을 고르시오.

①   ②   ③

④   ⑤

03 대화를 듣고, 여자의 심정으로 가장 적절한 것을 고르시오.

① shy   ② excited   ③ nervous
④ bored   ⑤ disappointed

04 대화를 듣고, 여자가 동물 보호소에서 한 일로 가장 적절한 것을 고르시오.

① 고양이 입양하기   ② 고양이 집 청소하기
③ 안내 책자 만들기   ④ 고양이 먹이 주기
⑤ 고양이에게 책 읽어주기

05 대화를 듣고, 두 사람이 대화하는 장소로 가장 적절한 곳을 고르시오.

① 버스 정류소   ② 경찰서   ③ 백화점
④ 학교   ⑤ 세탁소

06 대화를 듣고, 여자의 마지막 말의 의도로 가장 적절한 것을 고르시오.

① 요청   ② 감사   ③ 허가
④ 동의   ⑤ 충고

07 대화를 듣고, 여자가 선택한 과학 프로젝트의 주제로 가장 적절한 것을 고르시오.

① 달의 모양 변화   ② 롤러코스터의 원리
③ 반죽이 부푸는 원리   ④ 태양계의 구성
⑤ 빵을 굽는 순서

08 대화를 듣고, 남자가 대화 직후에 할 일로 가장 적절한 것을 고르시오.

① 생일 파티 가기   ② 테니스 수업 가기
③ 친구 집 가기   ④ 생일 선물 사기
⑤ 설거지하기

09 대화를 듣고, 두 사람이 Author's Friday 행사에 대해 언급하지 않은 것을 고르시오.

① 날짜   ② 장소   ③ 소요 시간
④ 진행 순서   ⑤ 참석 예상 인원

10 다음을 듣고, 남자가 하는 말의 내용으로 가장 적절한 것을 고르시오.

① 과학실 안전 수칙   ② 실험 기구 사용 방법
③ 과학 전시관 관람 안내   ④ 위급 상황 시 대처 방법
⑤ 유해 화학물질 보관 방법

11 다음을 듣고, 조지 워싱턴에 대한 내용과 일치하지 않는 것을 고르시오.

① 미국의 초대 대통령이다.
② 8년간 재임했다.
③ 퇴임 후 버지니아에 홀로 거주했다.
④ 1달러짜리 지폐에 초상이 그려져 있다.
⑤ 67세에 생을 마감했다.

12 대화를 듣고, 남자가 정장 구두를 산 목적으로 가장 적절한 것을 고르시오.

① 학교 댄스파티에서 신기 위해서
② 가족 결혼식 날에 신기 위해서
③ 댄스 수업 때 신기 위해서
④ 결혼 축하 선물로 주기 위해서
⑤ 졸업식 날에 신기 위해서

13 대화를 듣고, 남자가 병원 진료를 받을 시각을 고르시오.

① 10:30 a.m. ② 1:00 p.m. ③ 1:30 p.m.
④ 2:30 p.m. ⑤ 4:00 p.m.

14 대화를 듣고, 두 사람의 관계로 가장 적절한 것을 고르시오.

① 의사 – 환자   ② 카페 종업원 – 손님
③ 승무원 – 승객   ④ 남편 – 아내
⑤ 음식점 종업원 – 손님

15 대화를 듣고, 여자가 남자에게 부탁한 일로 가장 적절한 것을 고르시오.

① 학부모 상담하기   ② 아이 재우기
③ 장난감 사기   ④ 선물 포장하기
⑤ 게임 설치하기

16 대화를 듣고, 남자가 여자의 생일 파티에 갈 수 없는 이유로 가장 적절한 것을 고르시오.

① 아르바이트를 해야 해서
② 휴가 일정과 겹쳐서
③ 가족 행사에 가야 해서
④ 놀이공원에 가야 해서
⑤ 다른 친구를 만나기로 해서

17 다음 그림의 상황에 가장 적절한 대화를 고르시오.

① ② ③ ④ ⑤

18 다음을 듣고, 남자가 돌고래에 대해 언급하지 <u>않은</u> 것을 고르시오.

① 지능 수준   ② 서식지   ③ 개체 수
④ 주요 먹이   ⑤ 수명

[19-20] 대화를 듣고, 여자의 마지막 말에 이어질 남자의 말로 가장 적절한 것을 고르시오.

19 Man: _____

① It's more expensive than I expected.
② Sure. I'll get a dessert menu for you.
③ No, thank you.
④ I'd like you to make it again.
⑤ You don't need to pay for your meal tonight.

20 Man: _____

① It starts at 6:00 p.m.
② It's a brand-new song.
③ We met at 5:00 p.m.
④ It will be held at City Stadium.
⑤ I've liked them for a long time.

일반 속도   빠른 속도

01 다음을 듣고, 수요일의 날씨로 가장 적절한 것을 고르시오.

 ①
②
③
④
⑤

02 대화를 듣고, 여자가 만들고 있는 뜨개질 책 표지로 가장 적절한 것을 고르시오.

①
② Everyone Can Knit
③
Everyone Can Knit   Everyone Can Knit
④ Everyone Can Knit
⑤ Everyone Can Knit

03 대화를 듣고, 남자의 심정으로 가장 적절한 것을 고르시오.

① excited   ② bored   ③ scared
④ lonely   ⑤ tired

04 대화를 듣고, 여자가 오늘 한 일로 가장 적절한 것을 고르시오.

① 생일 카드 쓰기   ② 케이크 만들기
③ 양초 만들기   ④ 그릇 정리하기
⑤ 인터넷 검색하기

05 대화를 듣고, 두 사람이 대화하는 장소로 가장 적절한 곳을 고르시오.

① 약국   ② 병원   ③ 공연장
④ 학교   ⑤ 음식점

06 대화를 듣고, 여자의 마지막 말의 의도로 가장 적절한 것을 고르시오.

① 충고   ② 감사   ③ 위로
④ 요청   ⑤ 거절

07 대화를 듣고, 두 사람이 구입할 물건으로 가장 적절한 것을 고르시오.

① 인형   ② 풍선   ③ 만화책
④ 잠옷   ⑤ 운동화

08 대화를 듣고, 남자가 대화 직후에 할 일로 가장 적절한 것을 고르시오.

① 졸업식 참석하기   ② 야구 연습 가기
③ 꽃 더 사 오기   ④ 리본 사 오기
⑤ 꽃꽂이 수업 가기

09 대화를 듣고, 두 사람이 전시회에 대해 언급하지 <u>않은</u> 것을 고르시오.

① 기간   ② 장소   ③ 작품 수
④ 참여 학생 수   ⑤ 주제

10 다음을 듣고, 남자가 하는 말의 내용으로 가장 적절한 것을 고르시오.

① 불법 주차 경고   ② 자동차 할인 판매 정보
③ 마트 주차장 위치 안내   ④ 고객 서비스 개선 방향
⑤ 장애인 전용 자동차 소개

11 대화를 듣고, 남자가 다녀온 여행에 대한 내용과 일치하지 <u>않는</u> 것을 고르시오.

① 겨울 방학 동안 베트남에 다녀왔다.
② 날씨가 생각보다 추웠다.
③ 6일 동안 머물렀다.
④ 친척 집을 방문하러 하노이에 갔다.
⑤ 베트남 국수 만드는 법을 배웠다.

12 대화를 듣고, 여자가 과학기술 박물관에 가는 목적으로 가장 적절한 것을 고르시오.

① 우주비행사를 만나기 위해서
② 전기 관련 전시를 보기 위해서
③ 신축 건물을 보기 위해서
④ 유명 건축가를 만나기 위해서
⑤ 별을 관측하기 위해서

13 대화를 듣고, 남자가 지불해야 할 금액으로 가장 적절한 것을 고르시오.

① $20　　② $25　　③ $30
④ $35　　⑤ $40

14 대화를 듣고, 두 사람의 관계로 가장 적절한 것을 고르시오.

① 참가자 – 심사위원　　② 엄마 – 아들
③ 학부모 – 교사　　④ 기자 – 과학자
⑤ 공원 관리인 – 등산객

15 대화를 듣고, 여자가 남자에게 부탁한 일로 가장 적절한 것을 고르시오.

① 병원에 데려다주기　　② 차 끓여주기
③ 병원에 전화하기　　④ 약 사다 주기
⑤ 자전거 수리 맡기기

16 대화를 듣고, 여자가 오늘 집에서 점심을 먹을 수 없는 이유로 가장 적절한 것을 고르시오.

① 학교에 가야 해서
② 축구 연습을 해야 해서
③ 친구 집에 가기로 해서
④ 영화를 보러 가야 해서
⑤ 축구 시합이 늦게 끝나서

17 다음 그림의 상황에 가장 적절한 대화를 고르시오.

①　　②　　③　　④　　⑤

18 다음을 듣고, 여자가 교내 장기자랑에 대해 언급하지 <u>않은</u> 것을 고르시오.

① 장기자랑 장소　　② 장기자랑 개최 일시
③ 오디션 날짜　　④ 지원 방법
⑤ 오디션 장소

[19-20] 대화를 듣고, 남자의 마지막 말에 이어질 여자의 말로 가장 적절한 것을 고르시오.

19 Woman: _____

① I wish I could go, but I have other plans.
② No problem! I would be happy to.
③ I don't like Korean food.
④ Do you need some help?
⑤ Thank you for inviting me.

20 Woman: _____

① Jill can't go with us tonight.
② That sounds good. Thanks a lot.
③ Yes. I'll call you after the movie ends.
④ I'm sure you will really like the movie.
⑤ I'm too busy to join you guys tonight.

지은이

NE능률 영어교육연구소

NE능률 영어교육연구소는 혁신적이며 효율적인 영어 교재를 개발하고
영어 학습의 질을 한 단계 높이고자 노력하는 NE능률의 연구조직입니다.

1316 Listening 〈Level 2〉

펴 낸 이	주민홍
펴 낸 곳	서울특별시 마포구 월드컵북로 396(상암동) 누리꿈스퀘어 비즈니스타워 10층
	㈜ NE능률 (우편번호 03925)
펴 낸 날	2024년 1월 5일 개정판 제1쇄 발행
	2024년 5월 15일 제3쇄
전 화	02 2014 7114
팩 스	02 3142 0356
홈 페 이 지	www.neungyule.com
등 록 번 호	제1-68호
I S B N	979-11-253-4291-5
정 가	14,000원

NE 능률

고객센터

교재 내용 문의 : contact.nebooks.co.kr (별도의 가입 절차 없이 작성 가능)
제품 구매, 교환, 불량, 반품 문의 : 02-2014-7114
☎ 전화문의는 본사 업무시간 중에만 가능합니다.

www.nebooks.co.kr

한 발 앞서 시작하는 첫 번째 수능 영어

한 발 앞서 시작하는 중학생을 위한

논리+소재로
수능 영어 감 잡기
기초편

첫 번째
수능 영어

★ 중학생 난이도에 맞게 최신 모의고사 기출 지문 변형
★ 수능 지문의 논리적 전개 학습을 통한 독해력 신장
★ 빈출 소재 학습으로 수능 영어 적응력 향상

NE Waffle
MP3 & 단어장

NE 능률

전국 **온오프 서점** 판매중

중학생을 위한 수능 영어 독해 기본서 첫수

기초편
(중2-3)

유형편
(중3)

실전편
(중3-예비고1)

기초편
· 모의고사&수능 빈출 소재군 학습으로 실전 감잡기
· 수능 지문의 논리적 구조 학습, 직독직해 코너로 독해력 신장

유형편
· 유형별 도식화된 전략 제시로 수능 유형 적응력 향상
· 매 Unit 빈출 어법 포인트를 제공하여 문제 해결력 신장

실전편
· 유형별, 단계별로 제시된 필수 독해 전략으로 수능 독해 마스터
· 6회분 실전 모의고사로 수능 실전 대비 완성

NE능률 교재 MAP

아래 교재 MAP을 참고하여 본인의 현재 혹은 목표 수준에 따라 교재를 선택하세요.
NE능률 교재들과 함께 영어실력을 쑥쑥~ 올려보세요!
MP3 등 교재 부가 학습 서비스 및 자세한 교재 정보는 www.nebooks.co.kr 에서 확인하세요.

듣기
말하기
쓰기

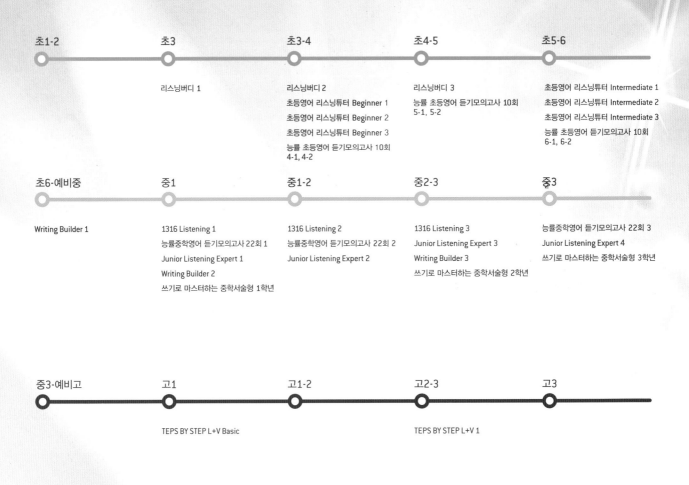

초1-2

초3

리스닝버디 1

초3-4

리스닝버디 2
초등영어 리스닝튜터 Beginner 1
초등영어 리스닝튜터 Beginner 2
초등영어 리스닝튜터 Beginner 3
능률 초등영어 듣기모의고사 10회
4-1, 4-2

초4-5

리스닝버디 3
능률 초등영어 듣기모의고사 10회
5-1, 5-2

초5-6

초등영어 리스닝튜터 Intermediate 1
초등영어 리스닝튜터 Intermediate 2
초등영어 리스닝튜터 Intermediate 3
능률 초등영어 듣기모의고사 10회
6-1, 6-2

초6-예비중

Writing Builder 1

중1

1316 Listening 1
능률중학영어 듣기모의고사 22회 1
Junior Listening Expert 1
Writing Builder 2
쓰기로 마스터하는 중학서술형 1학년

중1-2

1316 Listening 2
능률중학영어 듣기모의고사 22회 2
Junior Listening Expert 2

중2-3

1316 Listening 3
Junior Listening Expert 3
Writing Builder 3
쓰기로 마스터하는 중학서술형 2학년

중3

능률중학영어 듣기모의고사 22회 3
Junior Listening Expert 4
쓰기로 마스터하는 중학서술형 3학년

중3-예비고

고1

TEPS BY STEP L+V Basic

고1-2

고2-3

TEPS BY STEP L+V 1

고3

**수능 이상/
토플 80-89 ·
텝스 327-384점**

TEPS BY STEP L+V 2
RADIX TOEFL Blue Label Listening 1
RADIX TOEFL Blue Label Listening 2

**수능 이상/
토플 90-99 ·
텝스 385-451점**

RADIX TOEFL Black Label Listening 1

**수능 이상/
토플 100 ·
텝스 452점 이상**

TEPS BY STEP L+V 3
RADIX TOEFL Black Label Listening 2

기초부터 실전까지 중학 듣기 완성

1316 LISTENING

정답 및 해설

LEVEL 2

NE 능률

기초부터 실전까지 중학 듣기 완성

1316

1316 LISTENING

정답 및 해설

LEVEL
2

UNIT 1 그림 묘사·그림 상황에 적절한 대화

주요 어휘·표현 미리보기

p. 10

01 ⓕ empty
02 ⓖ permitted to
03 ⓑ prefer
04 ⓓ fell off
05 ⓒ exchange
06 ⓐ instead
07 ⓔ shaped like
08 ⓗ picked

LISTENING PRACTICE

pp. 12-14

01 ② 02 ④ 03 ③ 04 ④ 05 ③ 06 ⑤
07 ② 08 ③ 09 ⑤ 10 ⑤ 11 ④ 12 ②

01 ②

M Which of these postcards should I get?
W I like this one. The beach is beautiful.
M I prefer this one. The moon above the mountain looks great.
W Yes, it does. And there's a small house in front of the mountain.
M Look! There are three sheep in the yard. They're very cute. I'll take that one.

남 이 엽서들 중에서 어떤 것을 사면 될까?
여 나는 이게 좋아. 해변이 아름다워.
남 나는 이게 더 좋은데. 산 위의 달이 멋져 보여.
여 응, 그러네. 그리고 산 앞에 작은 집도 있어.
남 봐! 뜰에 양이 세 마리 있어. 매우 귀엽다. 난 저걸로 할래.

|어휘| postcard [명] 엽서 beach [명] 해변 prefer [동] ~을 더 좋아하다 yard [명] 뜰, 마당

02 ④

W Look at those superheroes on TV. Giant Man is my favorite.
M Giant Man? Which one is he?
W He has long hair.
M Does he have a sword?
W No, he's carrying a big hammer. And there's a star with a "G" inside it on his shirt.
M I see him now. I like his style.

여 TV에 나오는 저 슈퍼 영웅들 좀 봐. 자이언트맨이 내가 제일 좋아하는 영웅이야.
남 자이언트맨? 어떤 게 자이언트맨이야?
여 머리가 길어.
남 검을 가지고 있어?
여 아니, 큰 망치를 가지고 다녀. 그리고 셔츠에 있는 별 안에 'G'가 쓰여 있어.
남 이제 그가 보이네. 그의 스타일이 마음에 들어.

|해설| 여자는 긴 머리에 망치를 들고 있으며, 셔츠의 별 안에 'G'가 쓰여 있는 슈퍼 영웅에 관해 설명하고 있다.

|어휘| superhero [명] 슈퍼 영웅 sword [명] 검 carry [동] 가지고 다니다 hammer [명] 망치

03 ③

① **W** I can't find today's newspaper.
M Did you look on the kitchen table?
② **W** Where is the kitchen?
M It's next to the living room.
③ **W** The refrigerator is empty!
M I guess we need to go to the supermarket.
④ **W** Dinner will be ready in about five minutes.
M Great! I'm really hungry.
⑤ **W** We need to buy a new refrigerator.
M I like that one. Is it on sale?

① **여** 오늘 자 신문을 못 찾겠어요.
남 식탁 위에 봤어요?
② **여** 부엌이 어디죠?
남 거실 옆이에요.
③ **여** 냉장고가 비어 있어요!
남 우리 슈퍼마켓에 가야겠어요.
④ **여** 저녁이 5분 정도 뒤에 다 차려질 거예요.
남 좋아요! 나 정말 배고파요.
⑤ **여** 우리 새 냉장고를 사야 해요.
남 나는 저게 좋네요. 할인 중인가요?

|어휘| newspaper [명] 신문 living room 거실 refrigerator [명] 냉장고 empty [형] 비어 있는 on sale 할인 중인

04 ④

① **M** Can I borrow your bicycle?
W Sure. It's in the garage.
② **M** The doctor is ready to see you.
W Finally! I've been waiting too long.
③ **M** What happened to your elbow?
W I had an accident yesterday.
④ **M** Did you fall off your bicycle?
W Yes, and I hurt my knee.
⑤ **M** Sorry, I can't go bike riding with you.
W Okay, I'll go by myself.

① **남** 네 자전거 좀 빌려도 될까?
여 물론이지. 차고에 있어.
② **남** 의사 선생님이 진료할 준비가 되셨어요.
여 드디어! 너무 오랫동안 기다리고 있었어요.
③ **남** 팔꿈치가 왜 그래?
여 어제 사고가 났었어.
④ **남** 자전거에서 떨어진 거야?
여 응, 그래서 무릎을 다쳤어.
⑤ **남** 미안한데, 나 너랑 자전거 타러 못 가겠어.
여 알았어, 나 혼자 갈게.

|해설| 자전거에서 떨어져서 무릎을 다친 상황과 어울리는 대화는 ④이다.

|어휘| garage [명] 차고 elbow [명] 팔꿈치 have an accident 사고가 나다 fall off 떨어지다 hurt [동] 다치게 하다 knee [명] 무릎 go bike riding 자전거를 타러 가다 by oneself 혼자서

05 ③

M This is my apartment. Do you want to come inside?
W Sure. I really like your front door. It seems old.
M Yes, it is. My favorite part is the window at the top.
W Yes. It's shaped like a half circle. And your apartment number is right below it.
M That's right. And my brother put a sun-shaped sticker below the number.
W It looks really cheerful!

남 여기가 우리 아파트야. 안으로 들어올래?
여 그래. 현관문이 정말 마음에 든다. 오래돼 보이네.
남 응, 맞아. 내가 가장 좋아하는 부분은 맨 위에 있는 창문이야.
여 그래. 반원 모양이네. 그리고 네 아파트 호수가 그 바로 아래에 있구나.
남 맞아. 그리고 내 남동생이 그 숫자 아래에 태양 모양의 스티커를 붙였어.
여 정말 생기 있어 보이네!

|어휘| front door 현관문 seem [동] ~처럼 보이다 at the top 맨 위에 shaped like ~의 모양의 half circle 반원 cheerful [형] 생기 있는

06 ⑤

W Look at this advertisement. It's for an amusement park.
M Is that the name of the amusement park written at the bottom?
W Yes, Fantasy Planet. And that's the park's mascot standing in front of a castle.
M It looks like a big rabbit wearing a dress.
W Yes! Her name is Wendy Rabbit. Look at the two little kids standing next to her.
M They're holding her hands and smiling.
W They look so happy. We should go there someday!
M Sure! It looks like a fun place.

여 이 광고 좀 봐. 놀이공원 광고야.
남 맨 아래에 적힌 게 놀이공원 이름이야?
여 응, Fantasy Planet이야. 그리고 성 앞에 서 있는 건 놀이공원 마스코트고.
남 원피스를 입은 큰 토끼 같아 보이는데.
여 그래! 이름은 Wendy Rabbit이야. 토끼 옆에 서 있는 두 명의 작은 아이들을 봐.
남 토끼의 손을 잡고 웃고 있네.
여 정말 행복해 보인다. 우리 언제 저기 가야겠다!
남 물론이지! 재미있는 곳 같아 보여.

|어휘| advertisement [명] 광고 amusement park 놀이공원 at the bottom 맨 아래에 mascot [명] (행운의) 마스코트 castle [명] 성

07 ②

① **W** What do you think about this painting?
M I think it's unique.
② **W** You can't touch the paintings in the gallery.
M Oh. I'm sorry.
③ **W** Calm down, little boy. Where did you see your mother last?
M I was with her in the lobby.
④ **W** You are not permitted to take pictures in the gallery. The flash will harm the paintings.
M Then can I take a picture without a flash?
⑤ **W** It is so beautiful! Do you know who painted this one?

M I have no idea.

① 여 이 그림에 대해 어떻게 생각해?
남 독특한 것 같아.
② 여 미술관에 있는 그림을 만지면 안 됩니다.
남 아. 죄송해요.
③ 여 진정하렴, 꼬마야. 엄마를 마지막으로 본 게 어디니?
남 엄마와 로비에 있었어요.
④ 여 미술관에서는 사진 촬영이 허용되지 않습니다. 플래시가 그림을 손상시킵니다.
남 그러면 플래시 없이 사진 찍어도 되나요?
⑤ 여 정말 아름답다! 누가 이것을 그렸는지 아니?
남 전혀 모르겠어.

|어휘| unique [형] 독특한 gallery [명] 미술관 calm down 진정하다 permit [동] 허용하다, 허락하다 harm [동] 손상시키다

08 ③

① W I climbed this tree, but I can't get back down.
M I'll come up and help you.
② W Do we have any more apples?
M Sorry, but I think we ate them all already.
③ W I want to pick an apple, but I can't reach it.
M Wait here! I'll go get a ladder.
④ W Eating fruit and vegetables is good for your health.
M I know, but I prefer to eat fast food.
⑤ W Good morning! What can I get for you today?
M I'd like some milk and a piece of apple pie, please.

① 여 나 이 나무에 올라왔는데 다시 내려갈 수가 없어.
남 내가 올라가서 도와줄게.
② 여 우리 사과 더 있어?
남 아쉽게도, 우리가 이미 다 먹은 것 같아.
③ 여 사과를 따고 싶은데 손이 안 닿네.
남 여기서 기다려! 내가 가서 사다리 가져올게.
④ 여 과일과 채소를 먹는 것이 건강에 좋아.
남 알지, 그렇지만 난 패스트푸드를 먹는 게 더 좋아.
⑤ 여 안녕하세요! 오늘은 무엇을 드릴까요?
남 우유와 사과 파이 한 조각 주세요.

|어휘| climb [동] 오르다 pick [동] (과일 등을) 따다 reach [동] (손이) 닿다 ladder [명] 사다리

09 ⑤

M Come in my room for a minute. What do you think of my new desk?
W I like it. There are lots of drawers.
M Yes. There are three on each side. And I put my computer on it.
W I see. But why didn't you put a desk lamp on it too?
M I don't think I really need one.

남 잠깐 내 방으로 들어와 봐. 내 새 책상 어때?
여 마음에 들어. 서랍이 많네.
남 응. 양쪽에 세 칸씩 있어. 그리고 나는 그 위에 컴퓨터도 놓았어.
여 그렇구나. 그런데 왜 탁상용 스탠드는 안 올려놨어?
남 그게 정말 필요할 것 같진 않아서.

|어휘| come in 들어오다 drawer [명] 서랍 desk lamp 탁상용 스탠드

10 ⑤

W Happy birthday, Arthur! This is for you.
M Thanks! Wow, this cake looks great.
W I made it myself. Do you like it? I know you love blueberries.
M I sure do! This little bear in the middle is so cute.
W I wanted to write "Happy Birthday" at first, but it was too hard for me. So I drew that instead.
M Well, the cake looks delicious. Can I taste it now?
W Sure. Go ahead.
M Hmm... *[pause]* This is amazing! I never knew you were such a talented baker.

여 생일 축하해, Arthur! 이거 널 위한 거야.
남 고마워! 와, 이 케이크 정말 멋지다.
여 내가 직접 만들었어. 마음에 들어? 내가 알기로 너 블루베리 정말 좋아하잖아.
남 정말 마음에 들어! 가운데 이 작은 곰이 정말 귀엽다.
여 처음에 "생일 축하해"를 쓰고 싶었는데, 그건 나에게 너무 어려웠어. 그래서 대신 저걸 그렸어.
남 음, 케이크 맛있어 보여. 내가 지금 먹어 봐도 될까?
여 물론이지. 먹어 봐.
남 음… [잠시 후] 놀랍다! 네가 빵을 굽는 데 이렇게 재능이 있는지 전혀 몰랐어.

|어휘| instead [부] 대신에 amazing [형] 놀라운 talented [형] 재능이 있는 baker [명] 제빵사

11 ④

① M Oh no. There is a hole in this shirt.
W Oh, you should go to the customer service center.
② M I got you a shirt. Do you like it?
W Oh, I love it. Thank you!
③ M I need to exchange this shirt for another one.
W Do you want me to come with you?

④ **M** I'd like to return this shirt. There is a hole in it.
W Sure. Could you show me the receipt?
⑤ **M** I don't think this color suits me.
W All right. How about this blue shirt?

① **남** 아 이런. 이 셔츠에 구멍이 있어.
여 아, 너 고객 서비스 센터에 가야겠다.
② **남** 너에게 줄 셔츠를 사 왔어. 마음에 들어?
여 오, 정말 마음에 들어. 고마워!
③ **남** 이 셔츠를 다른 것으로 교환해야 해.
여 내가 같이 가줄까?
④ **남** 이 셔츠를 반품하고 싶습니다. 구멍이 있어요.
여 네. 영수증을 보여 주시겠어요?
⑤ **남** 이 색상은 저에게 어울리지 않는 것 같아요.
여 알겠습니다. 이 파란색 셔츠는 어떠세요?

|어휘| hole [명] 구멍 customer service center 고객 서비스 센터 exchange [동] 교환하다 return [동] 반품하다 receipt [명] 영수증 suit [동] ~에게 어울리다

12 ②

① **W** How can I get to the bus stop?
M Go straight and turn right at the corner.
② **W** The road is packed with cars. What should we do?
M We'd better take the subway, or we'll be late.
③ **W** I'm sorry. There was a lot of traffic.
M That's okay. Please take a seat.
④ **W** Do you want me to drive you to the station?
M No thanks. I'll take a taxi.
⑤ **W** Where should we park our car?
M I don't know. There aren't any parking spots here.

① **여** 버스 정류장에 어떻게 가나요?
남 쭉 가셔서 모퉁이에서 오른쪽으로 도세요.
② **여** 도로가 차들로 꽉 찼어. 어떻게 하지?
남 우리 지하철을 타는 게 좋겠어, 그렇지 않으면 늦을 거야.
③ **여** 죄송해요. 차가 많이 막혔어요.
남 괜찮아요. 자리에 앉으세요.
④ **여** 내가 역까지 태워 줄까?
남 고맙지만 괜찮아. 난 택시를 탈 거야.
⑤ **여** 우리 차를 어디에 주차해야 할까?
남 모르겠어. 여긴 주차 공간이 없어.

|어휘| be packed with ~로 꽉 차다 traffic [명] 교통(량) take a seat 자리에 앉다 drive [동] 태워다 주다 parking spot 주차 공간

어휘·표현 다지기

p. 19

A

01	독특한	02	거실
03	미술관	04	서랍
05	신문	06	영수증
07	사다리	08	오르다
09	팔꿈치	10	자리에 앉다
11	냉장고	12	차고
13	사고가 나다	14	엽서
15	놀이공원	16	광고

B

01	hole	02	harm
03	by oneself	04	reach
05	carry	06	cheerful
07	at the top	08	calm down
09	talented	10	hammer

UNIT 2 심정·의도

주요 어휘·표현 미리보기

p. 20

01	ⓐ the peak season	02	ⓕ bothering
03	ⓓ vote for	04	ⓔ turn down
05	ⓖ the rest	06	ⓑ stayed up late
07	ⓒ pay off	08	ⓗ unforgettable

LISTENING PRACTICE

pp. 22-23

01 ④	02 ②	03 ①	04 ①	05 ④
06 ③	07 ⑤	08 ②	09 ③	10 ①

01 ④

[Telephone rings.]
W Hello, Mama's Pizza. May I help you?
M Yes. I ordered a pizza about an hour ago, but it hasn't been delivered yet.
W Let me check. Can I have your address?
M It's 365 Royal Street.

W Unfortunately, it looks like we made a mistake and forgot about your order.
M You're kidding. My whole family is waiting.
W I'm terribly sorry. We'll deliver it as soon as possible.

[전화벨이 울린다.]
여 여보세요, Mama's Pizza입니다. 도와드릴까요?
남 네. 제가 한 시간 전에 피자를 주문했는데요, 아직도 배달이 안 됐어요.
여 확인해 볼게요. 주소가 어떻게 되시죠?
남 Royal 가 365번지예요.
여 유감스럽게도, 저희가 실수해서 주문을 빠뜨린 것 같습니다.
남 말도 안 돼요. 저희 가족 모두가 기다리고 있다고요.
여 대단히 죄송합니다. 가능한 한 빨리 배달해 드리겠습니다.

|해설| 남자는 한 시간 전에 주문한 피자가 아직 오지 않아 화가 난 상황이다.

|어휘| deliver [동] 배달하다 unfortunately [부] 유감스럽게도 make a mistake 실수하다 whole [형] 전체의 terribly [부] 대단히, 너무 as soon as possible 가능한 한 빨리 **[문제]** relaxed [형] 느긋한 nervous [형] 불안해하는 satisfied [형] 만족하는

02 ②

M How was your vacation? You wanted to go to Italy, didn't you?
W Yes, I really wanted to. But I couldn't go.
M Why not?
W Summer is the peak season in Italy, so flights were too expensive.
M I'm sorry to hear that.
W No, it was okay. I went to China instead. And it was fantastic!
M Really?
W Yes! I tried many kinds of food, and the Great Wall was terrific.

남 휴가는 어땠어? 너 이탈리아 가고 싶어 했었지, 그렇지 않아?
여 응, 정말 가고 싶었지. 그런데 못 갔어.
남 왜 못 갔는데?
여 이탈리아는 여름이 성수기라서, 항공편이 너무 비쌌어.
남 안타깝다.
여 아냐, 괜찮았어. 대신 중국에 갔어. 정말 환상적이더라!
남 정말?
여 응! 다양한 종류의 음식도 먹어보고, 만리장성도 멋졌어.

|어휘| peak season 성수기 the Great Wall 만리장성 terrific [형] 멋진 **[문제]** disappointed [형] 실망한

03 ①

M Why are you smiling, Gina? Do you have good news?
W I just finished talking to my mom.
M What did she say?
W She said that she finally got promoted! She has been waiting for this for a long time.
M That's wonderful! I'm glad her hard work finally paid off.
W Me too. She and I are going out to dinner tonight to celebrate.

남 왜 웃고 있어, Gina? 좋은 소식 있니?
여 엄마랑 방금 이야기를 마쳤어.
남 엄마가 뭐라고 하셨는데?
여 엄마가 드디어 승진하셨대! 오랫동안 승진하길 기다리셨거든.
남 멋지다! 너희 어머니의 노력이 드디어 결실을 거두게 되어서 기쁘다.
여 나도. 오늘 밤에 엄마랑 나는 기념하기 위해 외식하러 갈 거야.

|어휘| get promoted 승진하다 pay off 성과를 올리다, 성공하다 celebrate [동] 기념하다, 축하하다

04 ①

W Hi, Mike. What are you carrying?
M They're posters. They say "Vote for Mike for School President!"
W That's great. Are you putting them up?
M No, I'm taking them down. I can't win this election.
W Why do you say that?
M Because Briana is also running for president. She's more popular than me.
W That doesn't mean you can't win. You still have a chance!

여 안녕, Mike. 뭘 가지고 다니는 거야?
남 포스터야. "학교 회장으로 Mike에게 투표하세요!"라고 적혀 있지.
여 멋지다. 그것들을 붙이는 중이야?
남 아니, 떼고 있어. 난 이 선거에서 당선될 수가 없어.
여 왜 그렇게 말해?
남 왜냐하면 Briana도 회장 선거에 출마했거든. 그 아이가 나보다 더 인기 있어.
여 그렇다고 네가 이기지 못하리란 법은 없지. 너 아직 가능성 있어!

|어휘| vote for ~에 투표하다 president [명] 회장 election [명] 선거 run for ~에 출마하다 popular [형] 인기 있는 chance [명] 가능성

05 ④

M Jenny, why don't you turn down the volume?
W Sorry, I couldn't hear you. What did you say?
M I asked you to turn down the volume.
W Why? I'm using my earphones. You can't hear the music.
M Actually, I can hear it. That means it must be too loud.
W Sorry, I didn't know it was bothering you.
M It's not. I'm just worried about your ears. Loud music can damage them.

남 Jenny, 음량 좀 낮춰줄래?
여 미안, 안 들렸어. 뭐라고 했어?
남 음량 좀 낮춰달라고 했어.
여 왜? 나는 이어폰을 쓰고 있어. 음악이 들리지 않을 텐데.
남 사실, 들려. 그 말은 소리가 너무 크다는 거지.
여 미안, 너를 신경 쓰이게 하는 줄 몰랐어.
남 그게 아니야. 난 단지 네 귀가 걱정스러울 뿐이야. 큰 음악 소리는 귀를 손상시킬 수 있어.

|어휘| turn down (소리 등을) 낮추다 earphone [명] 이어폰 loud [형] 소리가 큰 bother [동] 신경 쓰이게 하다 damage [동] 손상시키다

06 ③

W How was your class today?
M Actually, it didn't go very well.
W Why? What happened?
M I overslept, so I was late.
W Oh no! What did you do last night?
M I stayed up late playing computer games. I couldn't stop!
W That was a big mistake.
M I know. What's worse, I forgot to bring my homework. I shouldn't have stayed up late.
W Well, just make sure you don't do it again.
M I won't. I have definitely learned my lesson.

여 오늘 수업 어땠니?
남 사실 그렇게 잘 흘러가진 않았어.
여 왜? 무슨 일 있었니?
남 늦잠 자서 수업에 늦었거든.
여 아 이런! 어젯밤에 뭐 했는데?
남 컴퓨터 게임을 하면서 늦게까지 깨어 있었어. 멈출 수가 없었어!
여 큰 실수였네.
남 알아. 설상가상으로, 숙제 가져가는 것도 깜빡해버렸어. 밤늦게까지 깨어 있지 말아야 했는데.
여 음, 다시는 그러지 않도록 해.
남 안 그럴 거야. 확실하게 교훈을 얻었어.

|어휘| go well 잘 되어가다 oversleep [동] 늦잠 자다 stay up late 늦게까지 자지 않고 깨어 있다 what's worse 설상가상으로 make sure 반드시 (~하도록) 하다 definitely [부] 확실히 lesson [명] 교훈 **[문제]** regretful [형] 후회하는

07 ⑤

M Hey, Anne. What are you doing?
W I'm just thinking about my future career.
M Really? What would you like to be?
W I'd like to be a French teacher, but my French isn't good enough.
M Just keep studying. It will improve.
W I hope so. I really like French.
M Don't give up. You'll be an expert in no time.
W I don't know. I still have a long way to go.

남 저기, Anne. 뭐 하니?
여 그냥 내 미래의 직업에 대해 생각하고 있어.
남 정말? 뭐가 되고 싶은데?
여 프랑스어 선생님이 되고 싶은데, 내 프랑스어 실력이 그렇게 좋지 않아.
남 그냥 계속 공부해. 나아질 거야.
여 그러면 좋겠다. 나 프랑스어를 정말 좋아하거든.
남 포기하지 마. 곧 전문가가 될 거야.
여 모르겠어. 아직 갈 길이 멀어.

|해설| 여자는 프랑스어 선생님이 되고 싶지만, 프랑스어 실력이 좋지 않아 걱정하고 있다.

|어휘| career [명] 직업 improve [동] 나아지다 give up 포기하다 expert [명] 전문가 in no time 곧 **[문제]** relieved [형] 안도한 joyful [형] 아주 기뻐하는

08 ②

W Hi, Max. Why aren't you at school today?
M It's the anniversary of my school's founding, so all the students and teachers have the day off.
W Oh, that's nice. What are you going to do?
M I have some fun plans. First, I'm going to watch my favorite horror movies. Then I'll go to a baseball game with John this evening.
W Sounds fun! I wish I could join you.

여 안녕, Max. 왜 오늘 학교 안 가고 있니?
남 오늘 개교기념일이라서 학생이랑 선생님 모두 쉬어.
여 아, 그거 좋다. 뭐 할 거야?

남 몇 가지 재미있는 계획이 있어. 먼저, 내가 정말 좋아하는 공포 영화를 볼 거야. 그러고 나서 저녁에 John이랑 야구 경기를 보러 갈 거야.
여 재미있겠다! 나도 함께 할 수 있다면 좋을 텐데.

|해설| 남자는 개교기념일이라 학교에 가지 않아도 된다며 재미있는 계획을 말하고 있다.

|어휘| anniversary [명] 기념일 founding [명] 설립 horror movie 공포 영화 join [동] 함께 하다

09 ③

W Did you go to the school's soccer game yesterday?
M Yes! It was so exciting. Were you there?
W Yes, I was. I didn't expect our school to win. The other team was leading by three goals!
M I know. Everyone was really upset.
W Yes. Our team practices hard every day. I hate to see them lose.
M Fortunately, they didn't!
W That's right! Our team scored several times at the end of the game.
M It was so exciting when they scored the winning goal. It was an unforgettable moment.
W You can say that again!

여 어제 학교 축구 경기 갔었니?
남 응! 아주 흥미진진했어. 너도 있었어?
여 응, 있었어. 나는 우리 학교가 이길 거라고 예상 못했어. 다른 팀이 세 골 앞서고 있었으니까.
남 맞아. 모두 정말 속상해했지.
여 응. 우리 팀은 매일 열심히 연습하잖아. 나는 그들이 지는 걸 보고 싶지 않아.
남 다행스럽게도 지지 않았어!
여 맞아! 우리 팀이 경기 막판에 여러 번 득점했지.
남 결승골을 넣었을 때 정말 신나더라. 잊지 못할 순간이었어.
여 네 말에 전적으로 동의해!

|해설| 'You can say that again.'은 상대방의 말에 동의할 때 쓰는 표현이다.

|어휘| expect [동] 예상하다, 기대하다 lead [동] 앞서다 lose [동] (경기 등에서) 지다 fortunately [부] 다행스럽게도 score [동] 득점하다 winning goal 결승골 unforgettable [형] 잊지 못할 moment [명] 순간

10 ①

M Thanks for helping me with my homework, Hanna.
W No problem. So, do you have any plans for the rest of the day?
M I'm going to meet Sam and Erica at a café.
W Oh! That sounds like a lot of fun.
M How about you? What are you going to do?
W Nothing. I'll probably just go home and watch TV.
M Why don't you come with me instead?

남 숙제 도와줘서 고마워, Hanna.
여 별말을. 그런데 오늘 남은 시간에 무슨 계획 있어?
남 카페에서 Sam과 Erica를 만날 거야.
여 아! 정말 재미있겠는데.
남 너는 어때? 뭐 할 거야?
여 아무것도. 아마 그냥 집에 가서 텔레비전 보겠지.
남 대신 나랑 같이 가지 않을래?

|어휘| rest [명] 나머지 probably [부] 아마

어휘·표현 다지기 p. 27

A

01	함께 하다	02	전체의
03	예상하다, 기대하다	04	대단히, 너무
05	나아지다	06	멋진
07	선거	08	포기하다
09	직업	10	회장
11	손상시키다	12	(경기 등에서) 지다
13	느긋한	14	늦잠 자다
15	전문가	16	만족하는

B

01	get promoted	02	make sure
03	go well	04	in no time
05	make a mistake	06	what's worse
07	score	08	lead
09	as soon as possible	10	run for

UNIT 3 한일·할일

주요 어휘·표현 미리보기 p. 28

01	[g] stick to	02	[e] hurts
03	[a] had a picnic	04	[f] a part-time job
05	[c] hard work	06	[d] answer
07	[h] made a reservation	08	[b] come over to

LISTENING PRACTICE

pp. 30-31

01 ③	02 ③	03 ①	04 ②	05 ④
06 ③	07 ②	08 ⑤	09 ④	10 ⑤

01 ③

M Hey, Ann. Did you have a picnic at Olympic Park last weekend?
W Well, I wanted to, but I couldn't.
M Why not? The weather was perfect!
W David caught a cold, so we decided to go next weekend instead. What did you do last weekend?
M I went paragliding in Danyang.
W Wow! That sounds amazing! Weren't you scared?
M Not at all. I love extreme sports. You should come with me next time.

남 안녕, Ann. 지난 주말에 올림픽 공원으로 소풍 갔었니?
여 음, 가고 싶었는데 못 갔어.
남 왜 못 갔어? 날씨가 환상적이었는데!
여 David가 감기에 걸려서, 대신 다음 주말에 가기로 했어. 너는 지난 주말에 뭐 했니?
남 단양에 패러글라이딩하러 갔었어.
여 와! 멋진데! 안 무서웠어?
남 전혀. 나는 극한 스포츠를 좋아하거든. 다음에 나랑 같이 가자.

|어휘| have a picnic 소풍을 가다 catch a cold 감기에 걸리다 go paragliding 패러글라이딩하러 가다 scared [형] 무서워하는 extreme [형] 극한의

02 ③

M I called you yesterday, but you didn't answer.
W Did you? I didn't have my phone with me. Why did you call?
M I had a question about our math homework.
W Oh, sorry! I was helping my grandmother in her garden.
M That's okay. Mike answered it for me.
W I'm glad to hear that. Mike always knows the answers!

남 어제 너한테 전화했는데, 안 받더라.
여 전화했었어? 나 전화를 안 갖고 있었어. 왜 전화했어?
남 수학 숙제에 관한 질문이 있었거든.
여 아, 미안! 나 할머니 댁 정원에서 할머니를 도와드리던 중이었어.
남 괜찮아. Mike가 답해줬어.
여 잘됐네. Mike는 항상 답을 알고 있지!

|어휘| answer [동] 전화를 받다, 대답하다 [명] 답 math [명] 수학 garden [명] 정원

03 ①

M I'm so hungry!
W Didn't you have lunch?
M No, I didn't have a chance. I broke my phone yesterday while I was roller-skating.
W That's too bad. So did you get it fixed during your lunch break?
M Yes, I did. Did you eat?
W Yes, I went to an Italian restaurant with Brian.
M I see. I think I'll have some spaghetti delivered.

남 정말 배고파!
여 점심 안 먹었니?
남 응, 기회가 없었어. 어제 롤러스케이트를 타다가 휴대전화를 고장 냈거든.
여 정말 안됐다. 그래서 점심시간에 수리받은 거야?
남 응, 맞아. 너는 먹었어?
여 응, Brian이랑 이탈리아 음식점에 갔었어.
남 그렇구나. 나는 스파게티 좀 배달시켜야겠다.

|어휘| chance [명] 기회 break [동] 고장 내다 while [접] ~하는 동안에 get ~ fixed ~을 수리받다 have ~ delivered ~을 배달시키다

04 ②

W Do you have special plans for this weekend?
M Not really. How about you?
W My sister and I are going camping. I can't wait!
M That's great!
W Yes. We'll go hiking and fishing. And we'll have barbecues at night.
M Wow! That sounds fun. But there must be many things that you need to bring.
W Yes. A tent, a flashlight... I think I need to make a list.
M I'll help you make one. Give me a pen!

여 이번 주말에 특별한 계획 있니?
남 그렇지는 않아. 너는?
여 여동생이랑 캠핑하러 갈 예정이야. 기대돼!
남 멋지다!
여 응. 우리는 하이킹이랑 낚시도 하러 갈 거야. 그리고 밤에 바비큐 파티를 할 거야.
남 와! 재미있겠다. 하지만 가져가야 할 게 많겠다.
여 응. 텐트, 손전등… 목록을 만들어야 할 것 같아.

남 내가 만드는 걸 도와줄게. 펜 좀 줘!

|어휘| go hiking 하이킹을 가다 flashlight [명] 손전등 make a list 목록을 만들다

05 ④

W My friends and I are going to a science lecture this afternoon. Why don't you join us?
M I'm afraid I can't. I have to go to my part-time job now.
W That's too bad. Do you work tomorrow, too?
M No, I don't. I have the day off.
W Really? Then why don't we all go to a movie tomorrow?
M That sounds good.
W Let's meet at my apartment and then go to the cinema together.
M Sure.

여 친구들이랑 오늘 오후에 과학 강연에 갈 거야. 우리랑 같이 갈래?
남 아쉽지만 난 못 가. 지금 아르바이트하러 가야 하거든.
여 정말 아쉽다. 내일도 일하니?
남 아니, 안 해. 내일은 쉬는 날이야.
여 정말? 그럼 우리 다 같이 내일 영화 보러 가지 않을래?
남 그거 좋겠다.
여 우리 아파트에서 만난 다음에 같이 영화관으로 가자.
남 좋아.

|어휘| lecture [명] 강연, 강의 part-time job 아르바이트 day off (근무 또는 일을) 쉬는 날

06 ③

W Are you still studying taekwondo, Matt?
M Yes, I am. How about you?
W No, I quit last week. I decided to take dance lessons instead.
M Really? Have you started yet?
W Yes, the first lesson was last night. I enjoyed it a lot.
M Where are the lessons held?
W In a studio above the post office. Do you want to join me?
M No thanks! I'll stick to taekwondo.

여 너 아직도 태권도 배우니, Matt?
남 응, 배워. 너는?
여 안 해, 지난주에 그만뒀어. 대신에 댄스 수업을 듣기로 했어.
남 정말? 벌써 시작했어?
여 응, 첫 수업이 어젯밤이었어. 아주 즐거웠어.
남 수업은 어디서 해?
여 우체국 위에 있는 연습실에서. 나랑 같이 할래?
남 괜찮아! 나는 태권도를 계속할래.

|해설| 여자는 지난주에 태권도를 그만두고 어젯밤부터 댄스 수업을 듣기 시작했다고 했다.

|어휘| quit [동] 그만두다 take a lesson 수업을 듣다 be held 열리다 stick to ~을 계속하다

07 ②

[Cell phone rings.]
M Hello?
W Hello, Henry. This is Amy. Do you want to go for a swim with me?
M No thanks. I'm too tired.
W Why? Did you play soccer before lunch?
M No, I was home all morning.
W If you rested all morning, why are you still tired?
M I didn't rest. I painted my room.
W Oh! That sounds like hard work.
M Yes, it was. But my room looks really good!
W Great! You can show me when I come over to your house.

[휴대전화벨이 울린다.]
남 여보세요?
여 안녕, Henry. 나 Amy야. 나랑 수영하러 갈래?
남 안 될 것 같아. 나 너무 피곤해.
여 왜? 점심 전에 축구 했니?
남 아니, 오전 내내 집에 있었어.
여 오전 내내 쉬었는데 왜 아직도 피곤해?
남 쉬지 않았어. 내 방을 페인트칠했거든.
여 아! 힘든 일 같다.
남 그래, 맞아. 하지만 내 방이 정말 멋져 보여!
여 잘됐네! 내가 너희 집에 들를 때 보여 주면 되겠다.

|해설| 남자는 오전에 축구를 하거나 집에서 쉰 게 아니라 방을 페인트칠했다고 했다.

|어휘| go for a swim 수영하러 가다 rest [동] 쉬다 hard work 힘든 일 come over to ~에 들르다

08 ⑤

M What are you doing, Jenny?
W I'm playing a computer game.
M You play games too often.
W No, I don't. I finished my homework, so I just started

playing now.

M Your mother has been doing housework since she got home from work. Why don't you help her?

W All right. What is she doing now?

M She is busy separating the trash.

W Okay, I'll help her.

남 뭐 하니, Jenny?

여 컴퓨터 게임해요.

남 너 게임을 너무 자주 하는구나.

여 아니에요, 저 안 그래요. 숙제를 끝내서, 이제 막 게임하기 시작했어요.

남 네 엄마는 퇴근하고 집에 온 이후로 집안일을 하고 계셔. 좀 도와드리지 그러니?

여 알았어요. 엄마는 지금 뭐 하세요?

남 쓰레기 분리하느라 바쁘시다.

여 알았어요, 도와드릴게요.

|어휘| do housework 집안일을 하다 separate [동] 분리하다 trash [명] 쓰레기

09 ④

M Oh no! The school changed my soccer team's schedule.

W Did they? When's your next game?

M It was supposed to be next week, but they changed it to tomorrow!

W That's fine. You don't have guitar lessons tomorrow, do you?

M No. But my uniform is dirty. It's covered in mud from the last game.

W Oh, you can't wear it like that.

M No. I need to wash it right away.

W All right. Go do that now.

남 아 이런! 학교에서 저희 축구팀 일정을 바꿨어요.

여 그랬어? 다음 경기가 언제니?

남 원래 다음 주였는데, 내일로 바뀌었어요!

여 괜찮아. 내일 기타 수업도 없잖니, 그렇지?

남 없죠. 하지만 제 유니폼이 더러워요. 지난 경기 때 진흙이 잔뜩 묻었어요.

여 아, 그렇게 입을 수는 없겠네.

남 못 입죠. 지금 당장 빨아야겠어요.

여 알겠어. 지금 가서 하렴.

|어휘| be supposed to-v ~하기로 되어 있다 dirty [형] 더러운 be covered in ~로 덮이다 mud [명] 진흙 right away 지금 당장

10 ⑤

M I need to call my dentist.

W What's wrong? Do you have a toothache?

M Yes, I do. It really hurts. I don't think I can go to dinner with you tonight.

W Don't worry about that.

M But didn't you make a reservation at a nice restaurant?

W I did, but I will cancel it now. You need to see your dentist as soon as possible.

M You're right. Thanks for understanding.

남 치과에 전화해야겠어.

여 무슨 일이야? 치통이 있니?

남 응. 정말 아파. 오늘 밤에 너랑 저녁 식사하러 못 갈 것 같아.

여 그건 걱정하지 마.

남 하지만 근사한 식당을 예약하지 않았어?

여 그랬지만 지금 취소할 거야. 가능한 한 빨리 치과에 가봐야겠다.

남 맞아. 이해해줘서 고마워.

|어휘| dentist [명] 치과 의사, 치과 toothache [명] 치통 hurt [동] 아프다 make a reservation 예약하다 cancel [동] 취소하다

어휘·표현 다지기 p. 35

A

01 무서워하는	02 수학
03 그만두다	04 강연, 강의
05 더러운	06 치과 의사, 치과
07 치통	08 정원
09 수영하러 가다	10 취소하다
11 집안일을 하다	12 하이킹을 가다
13 분리하다	14 손전등
15 지금 당장	16 쓰레기

B

01 mud	02 while
03 break	04 get ~ fixed
05 make a list	06 take a lesson
07 chance	08 day off
09 extreme	10 have ~ delivered

UNIT 4 대화 장소·숫자 정보

주요 어휘·표현 미리보기 p. 36

01 [e] take a look at
02 [c] after school
03 [h] seem to
04 [d] fit in
05 [a] sorry for
06 [g] heavy traffic
07 [f] a lot of
08 [b] purpose

LISTENING PRACTICE

pp. 38-39

01 ③	02 ④	03 ②	04 ①	05 ④
06 ⑤	07 ④	08 ⑤	09 ②	10 ④

01 ③

M How may I help you?
W I have some books that I need to send to a school in the U.S.
M All right. Will they fit in this box?
W Let me check. *[pause]* Yes, it's big enough.
M Good. If you're in a hurry, I recommend our express service.
W Well, how long will it take to get there by regular mail?
M Seven days.
W How much will it cost?
M Let me weigh this. *[pause]* It will cost $15.
W Okay, I'll use regular mail.

남 무엇을 도와드릴까요?
여 미국에 있는 학교에 보내야 할 책이 몇 권 있어요.
남 알겠습니다. 그게 이 상자에 맞을까요?
여 한번 볼게요. [잠시 후] 네, 충분히 크네요.
남 좋습니다. 급하시다면, 특급 우편 서비스를 추천합니다.
여 음, 보통 우편으로 보내는 건 얼마나 걸릴까요?
남 7일 걸립니다.
여 얼마일까요?
남 무게를 재볼게요. [잠시 후] 15달러입니다.
여 네, 보통 우편으로 할게요.

|해설| 우편물 발송에 대한 대화를 하는 것으로 보아 우체국에서 일어나는 상황임을 알 수 있다.

|어휘| fit in ~에 맞다 in a hurry 급히 recommend [동] 추천하다 express service 특급 우편 서비스 regular mail 보통 우편 cost [동] 값이 ~이다 weigh [동] 무게를 달다

02 ④

W Excuse me.
M Yes? What's the matter?
W I have a sore throat. It started bothering me during class.
M Let me see. Please open your mouth. Uh-oh... Your throat is swollen. It looks painful.
W What should I do?
M I'll give you a pill. Take it now. But you should see a doctor after school today.
W Okay, thank you.
M And drink a lot of water. It will help.

여 실례합니다.
남 응? 무슨 일이니?
여 목이 아파요. 수업 중에 괴로움이 시작됐어요.
남 어디 보자. 입을 벌려 보렴. 이런… 목이 부었네. 아프겠구나.
여 어떻게 해야 하죠?
남 알약을 줄게. 지금 그걸 먹으렴. 하지만 오늘 방과 후에 병원에 가 봐야 해.
여 네, 감사합니다.
남 그리고 물을 많이 마시렴. 도움이 될 거야.

|해설| 알약을 주면서 방과 후에 병원에 가 보라는 말로 미루어 보아 양호실에서 일어나는 상황임을 알 수 있다.

|어휘| have a sore throat 목이 아프다 bother [동] 괴롭히다 swollen [형] 부은 painful [형] 아픈 pill [명] 알약 after school 방과 후에 a lot of 많은

03 ②

M Can I see your passport, please?
W Yes, here you are.
M What is the purpose of your visit to our country?
W I'm a photographer. I'll travel around France, taking pictures of the beautiful scenery.
M How long will you stay here?
W I plan to be here for three months.
M Okay. Enjoy your trip.
W Thank you.

남 여권을 보여 주시겠어요?
여 네, 여기 있습니다.
남 우리나라에 방문하신 목적이 무엇인가요?
여 저는 사진작가예요. 아름다운 풍경 사진을 찍으면서 프랑스를 여행할 거예요.

남 여기 얼마나 머무실 예정이죠?
여 석 달 동안 있을 계획입니다.
남 알겠습니다. 즐거운 여행하세요.
여 감사합니다.

|어휘| passport [명] 여권 purpose [명] 목적 photographer [명] 사진작가 scenery [명] 풍경 stay [동] 머물다 plan [동] 계획하다 trip [명] 여행

04 ①

W May I help you?
M I like these blue jeans. How much are they?
W They're $80.
M That's too expensive.
W They're a new product, so they cost a bit more. But all the pants in that section over there are 50% off.
M Really? I'll take a look at them. *[pause]* Oh! These are nice. The tag says they are $50.
W That's the regular price. You can take 50% off of that.
M Great! I'll take them.

여 도와드릴까요?
남 이 청바지가 마음에 드네요. 얼마예요?
여 80달러입니다.
남 너무 비싸네요.
여 신제품이어서 약간 더 비쌉니다. 하지만 저 구역의 모든 바지는 50% 할인하고 있습니다.
남 정말요? 한번 볼게요. [잠시 후] 아! 이거 멋지네요. 가격표에 50달러라고 쓰여 있는데요.
여 그건 정가입니다. 거기서 50% 할인받으실 수 있어요.
남 좋습니다! 이거 살게요.

|어휘| blue jeans 청바지 product [명] 제품 a bit 약간 section [명] 구역 off [부] 할인되어 take a look at ~을 보다 tag [명] 가격표 regular price 정가

05 ④

W Excuse me, sir.
M Yes? How can I help you?
W How long does it take to get to Jamsil Station from here?
M Let me see. There are 20 stops between this station and Jamsil Station. So it will take 40 minutes.
W That's longer than I expected! I need to be there by five.
M Well, it's four o'clock, and there's a train that leaves in five minutes.
W Oh, great. I'll take that one. Thank you!

여 실례합니다.
남 네? 어떻게 도와드릴까요?
여 여기서 잠실역까지 얼마나 걸리나요?
남 어디 봅시다. 이번 역과 잠실역 사이에 20개의 정거장이 있어요. 그러니 40분이 걸릴 겁니다.
여 제가 예상한 것보다 더 오래 걸리네요! 5시까지 그곳에 가야 하거든요.
남 음, 지금 4시 정각인데요, 5분 후에 출발하는 열차가 있네요.
여 아, 좋아요. 그걸 타야겠어요. 감사합니다!

|해설| 여자가 4시 5분에 출발하는 열차를 타면 40분이 걸리므로 4시 45분에 잠실역에 도착할 것이다.

|어휘| station [명] 역 stop [명] 정거장 leave [동] 출발하다, 떠나다

06 ⑤

W Excuse me. I have some questions.
M Okay. What can I help you with?
W I was looking at apartments on your website yesterday. Is the one in Everville still available?
M Sorry, it's already been sold.
W Oh! I should have come sooner.
M But we have some other apartments for sale. Why don't I show you some of them?
W Sure. But I want one that's located near the station.
M Okay.

여 실례합니다. 몇 가지 질문이 있어요.
남 네. 무엇을 도와드릴까요?
여 어제 여기 웹사이트에서 아파트를 보고 있었는데요. Everville에 있는 아파트를 아직 구할 수 있나요?
남 죄송하지만, 그건 이미 팔렸습니다.
여 아! 더 빨리 왔어야 했네요.
남 하지만 매물로 나온 다른 아파트가 좀 있습니다. 그중 일부를 보여 드릴까요?
여 네. 하지만 역 가까이 위치한 곳이었으면 합니다.
남 알겠습니다.

|어휘| available [형] 구할[이용할] 수 있는 for sale 팔려고 내놓은 be located 위치하다

07 ④

M May I help you?
W I bought this vacuum cleaner. But there's something wrong with it. It doesn't seem to work.

M Sorry, but you need to go to the service center.
W Oh. But I bought it here.
M Yes, but all repairs are done at the service center. It's right across the street, next to the bank.
W All right. I guess I'll go there.
M I'm really sorry for the inconvenience.

남 도와드릴까요?
여 제가 이 진공청소기를 샀는데요. 그런데 이게 문제가 있어요. 작동되지 않는 것 같아요.
남 죄송하지만, 서비스 센터에 가셔야 해요.
여 아. 그렇지만 여기서 샀는 걸요.
남 네, 하지만 모든 수리는 서비스 센터에서 하고 있습니다. 센터는 바로 길 건너 은행 옆에 있습니다.
여 알겠습니다. 거기로 가야겠네요.
남 불편을 끼쳐드려 정말 죄송합니다.

|어휘| vacuum cleaner 진공청소기 seem to-v ~처럼 보이다, ~인 것 같다 work [동] 작동되다 repair [명] 수리 sorry for ~을 미안하게 생각하는 inconvenience [명] 불편

08 ⑤

M May I help you?
W Yes. I want to buy a cover for my smartphone.
M How about this one? It's just $7.
W I like it, but do you have a blue one?
M Yes, but it costs $2 more.
W Oh, it's perfect. Would you show me that key ring too?
M Here it is. It's $3.
W It's nice. I'll take one blue cover and this key ring.

남 도와드릴까요?
여 네. 스마트폰 커버를 사고 싶은데요.
남 이건 어떠세요? 7달러밖에 안 해요.
여 마음에 들긴 하는데요, 파란색도 있나요?
남 네, 그런데 그건 2달러 더 비쌉니다.
여 아, 딱 좋아요. 저 열쇠고리도 보여 주시겠어요?
남 여기 있습니다. 3달러입니다.
여 괜찮네요. 파란색 커버 하나랑 이 열쇠고리로 할게요.

|어휘| cover [명] 덮개, 커버 key ring 열쇠고리

09 ②

W John, you're late. It's already nine.
M Sorry, Mom.
W I called you at 7:30, but your phone was turned off.
M Did you? Unfortunately, my cell phone battery died.
W The soccer game finished two hours ago. What did you do afterwards?
M My friends and I were hungry, so we went to a fast-food restaurant. We left at eight, but there was heavy traffic on the way home.
W Okay. But don't be late again.

여 John, 늦었구나. 벌써 9시잖니.
남 죄송해요, 엄마.
여 너에게 7시 30분에 전화했는데, 전화기가 꺼져 있던데.
남 그러셨어요? 공교롭게도, 휴대전화 배터리가 다 됐었거든요.
여 축구 경기는 2시간 전에 끝났잖니. 그 후에 뭐 했니?
남 친구들이랑 저는 배고파서 패스트푸드점에 갔었어요. 8시에 출발했는데, 집에 오는 길에 차가 많았어요.
여 알겠다. 하지만 다신 늦지 말아라.

|어휘| turn off (전기 등을) 끄다 afterwards [부] 그 후에, 나중에 heavy traffic 많은 교통량 on the way home 집에 가는[오는] 길에

10 ④

M Two tickets for adults and one ticket for a child, please.
W Okay. If you are a member, you can get 30% off.
M Unfortunately, I'm not a member. How much are the tickets?
W They'll be $70 in total.
M Hmm... Is there any way you can give me a discount?
W If you enter the park after 5:00 p.m., you can get half off admission. It's 4:30 now.
M Oh, that's good. Then I'll wait. Here's a hundred dollars.
W Here are your tickets and change. Please stand over there until it's time.

남 성인 표 두 장과 어린이 표 한 장 주세요.
여 네. 회원이시면, 30% 할인을 받으실 수 있습니다.
남 유감스럽게도 회원이 아니에요. 표가 얼마죠?
여 모두 합해서 70달러입니다.
남 음… 할인해 주실 수 있는 다른 방법이 있을까요?
여 오후 5시 이후 공원에 들어가시면, 입장료 반액 할인을 받으실 수 있습니다. 지금 4시 30분이네요.
남 아, 그거 좋네요. 그럼 기다릴게요. 여기 100달러예요.
여 여기 표와 거스름돈입니다. 시간이 될 때까지 저쪽에 계십시오.

|해설| 공원 표는 총 70달러인데 오후 5시 이후에 들어가면 반액 할인을 받을 수 있다고 했으므로, 남자가 100달러를 내고 받은 거스름돈은 65달러이다.

|어휘| adult [명] 성인 in total 모두 합해서 discount [명] 할인

admission [명] 입장료　change [명] 거스름돈　it's time 때가[시간이] 되다

어휘·표현 다지기
p. 43

A

01	알약	02	풍경
03	괴롭히다	04	정가
05	추천하다	06	가격표
07	불편	08	제품
09	위치하다	10	그 후에, 나중에
11	열쇠고리	12	부은
13	사진작가	14	아픈
15	진공청소기	16	여권

B

01	work	02	stop
03	turn off	04	for sale
05	blue jeans	06	cost
07	repair	08	available
09	in total	10	on the way home

UNIT 5 특정 정보

주요 어휘·표현 미리보기
p. 44

01	[c] clears up	02	[e] go sightseeing
03	[b] at first	04	[a] rides her bike
05	[g] is supposed to	06	[h] let me know
07	[f] humid	08	[d] Temperatures

LISTENING PRACTICE
pp. 46-47

01 ④	02 ②	03 ③	04 ③	05 ②
06 ③	07 ②	08 ⑤	09 ①	10 ②

01 ④

M Welcome to the Weather Center. This is your Thursday weather report. There will be strong winds, but there is little chance that it will rain. It will start raining tomorrow, however, and the rain will last throughout the weekend. Clear skies are expected next week. So if you're planning a picnic, you'd better wait till next week.

남 기상청입니다. 목요일의 일기 예보를 전해 드리겠습니다. 강한 바람이 불겠지만, 비가 내릴 가능성은 거의 없습니다. 하지만 내일 비가 오기 시작해서 주말 내내 계속되겠습니다. 다음 주에는 맑은 하늘이 예상됩니다. 그러니 나들이를 계획하고 계신다면, 다음 주까지 기다리시는 게 좋겠습니다.

|어휘| last [동] 계속되다　throughout [전] 내내　expect [동] 예상하다

02 ②

W I'm Christina Lee, and here's today's weather forecast. If you live in San Diego, be careful. There will be thunderstorms with dangerous lightning this afternoon. It will be foggy in Los Angeles, but it won't rain until tomorrow. And in San Francisco there will be sunny skies all day long. Have a great day, everyone!

여 저는 Christina Lee이며, 오늘의 일기 예보를 전해 드리겠습니다. 샌디에이고에 계시는 분들은 조심하셔야겠습니다. 오늘 오후에 위험한 번개를 동반한 뇌우가 있을 것입니다. 로스앤젤레스는 안개가 끼겠으나, 비는 내일이 되어서야 내리겠습니다. 그리고 샌프란시스코는 종일 하늘이 맑겠습니다. 모두 좋은 하루 보내시기 바랍니다!

|어휘| weather forecast 일기 예보　thunderstorm [명] 뇌우　lightning [명] 번개　foggy [형] 안개가 낀　not ~ until ... …가 되어서야 ~하다

03 ③

M What's up, Cathy? You look great these days. Did you join a gym?
W No, but I have started exercising every morning.
M Wow! How can you exercise every morning?
W It was difficult at first. But I soon got used to it.
M What kind of exercise do you do? Do you go jogging?
W No. I just ride my bike for 30 minutes before school.
M Sounds fun!

남 어떻게 지내니, Cathy? 요즘 너 좋아 보인다. 헬스장에 등록한 거야?
여 아니, 그렇지만 매일 아침 운동을 하기 시작했어.

남 와! 어떻게 매일 아침 운동을 하니?
여 처음에는 어려웠어. 근데 곧 익숙해지더라.
남 무슨 운동을 해? 조깅하러 가니?
여 아니. 그냥 학교 가기 전에 30분 동안 자전거를 타.
남 재밌겠다!

|어휘| gym [명] 헬스장 exercise [동] 운동하다 [명] 운동 at first 처음에는 get used to ~에 익숙해지다 ride one's bike 자전거를 타다

04 ③

W Dan, did you buy a present for Amy's housewarming party tomorrow?
M Yes. I bought a pretty mug for her.
W That's a good gift, but I don't know what to get her.
M How about buying some flowers? She likes flowers.
W I'd like to give her something practical. What does she need?
M She said that she doesn't have enough towels. Why don't you buy her some?
W Okay! That sounds perfect.

여 Dan, 너 내일 있는 Amy 집들이 선물 샀니?
남 응. 그 애에게 줄 예쁜 머그잔을 샀어.
여 좋은 선물이네, 근데 나는 그 애에게 뭘 사줘야 할지 모르겠어.
남 꽃을 좀 사는 건 어때? 그 애가 꽃 좋아하잖아.
여 뭔가 실용적인 걸 주고 싶어. 그 애는 뭐가 필요할까?
남 수건이 충분하지 않다고 했어. 수건을 좀 사주는 건 어때?
여 그래! 그게 딱 좋겠다.

|해설| 여자는 Amy가 수건이 충분하지 않다는 말을 듣고 수건을 선물하기로 했다.

|어휘| housewarming party 집들이 practical [형] 실용적인 enough [형] 충분한 towel [명] 수건

05 ②

M What's for dinner tonight, Mom?
W We're having pasta with chicken. But we're not eating until seven o'clock.
M Really? I'm hungry already. I can't wait two hours.
W Why don't you have a snack? I bought some fruit this morning.
M Fruit? Don't we have any cookies?
W We do, but I think you should have something healthier. How about an apple?
M All right. But can I have a banana instead?
W Sure. There are some on the kitchen table.
M Thanks, Mom.

남 오늘 저녁은 뭐예요, 엄마?
여 닭고기가 들어간 파스타를 먹을 거야. 그런데 7시나 되어서야 먹을 것 같다.
남 정말요? 전 벌써 배고파요. 2시간 못 기다리겠어요.
여 간식을 먹지 그러니? 오늘 아침에 과일 좀 샀는데.
남 과일이요? 쿠키는 없어요?
여 있지만, 네가 더 몸에 좋은 걸 먹어야 할 것 같은데. 사과는 어떠니?
남 알겠어요. 하지만 대신 바나나 먹어도 돼요?
여 물론이지. 식탁에 몇 개 있어.
남 고마워요, 엄마.

|해설| 남자는 쿠키를 먹고 싶어 했으나 여자가 과일을 권하여 바나나를 먹기로 했다.

|어휘| snack [명] 간식 instead [부] 대신에

06 ③

M These are the world weather forecasts for tomorrow. In Seoul and Beijing, it will be cloudy and rainy all day. In Tokyo, it will be cold and windy, but it will stay dry. Wellington will have a warm, sunny day. In Ottawa, the temperature will drop, and there will be heavy snow. It will be foggy in London, but the sun will shine all day in Paris.

남 내일의 세계 일기 예보입니다. 서울과 베이징은 온종일 흐리고 비가 오겠습니다. 도쿄는 춥고 바람이 불겠지만 비는 오지 않겠습니다. 웰링턴은 따뜻하고 화창한 날이 되겠습니다. 오타와는 기온이 떨어지고 폭설이 오겠습니다. 런던에는 안개가 끼겠지만, 파리에는 온종일 태양이 빛나겠습니다.

|어휘| dry [형] 건조한, 비가 오지 않는 temperature [명] 기온 drop [동] 떨어지다 heavy snow 폭설 shine [동] 빛나다

07 ②

W Good evening. This is the weekly weather report. The rain will stop later tonight, and tomorrow it will be sunny all day. We're expecting some showers on Wednesday and Thursday. On Friday, it will not rain, but there will be a lot of clouds. The sky is supposed to clear up by the weekend, however. It will be a good time to enjoy outdoor activities.

여 안녕하세요. 주간 일기 예보입니다. 비는 오늘 밤 늦게 그치고, 내일은 온종일 맑겠습니다. 수요일과 목요일에는 소나기가 예상됩니다. 금요일에는 비가 오지 않지만, 구름이 많이 끼겠습니다. 하지만 주말에는 하늘이 개겠습니다. 야외 활동을 즐기기에 좋은 시간이 되겠습니다.

|어휘| weekly [형] 주간의 shower [명] 소나기 be supposed to-v ~하기로 되어 있다 clear up (날씨가) 개다 outdoor [형] 야외의 activity [명] 활동

08 ⑤

W How was your vacation on Jeju Island?

M It was great! I went on a bicycle trip there.

W Wow! That must have been fun! When I went to Jeju, I traveled around in a tour bus.

M Yes, that's the easiest way to go sightseeing.

W I also saw many tourists taking taxis there, but it's very expensive.

M That's true.

W Were there any problems during your trip?

M It was hot and humid, so biking around was difficult.

여 제주도에서의 휴가는 어땠니?

남 정말 좋았어! 거기서 자전거 여행을 했어.

여 와! 재밌었겠다! 내가 제주에 갔을 때는 관광버스로 여기저기 여행 다녔는데.

남 그래, 그게 관광하기에 가장 쉬운 방법이지.

여 관광객들이 거기에서 택시 타는 것도 많이 봤는데, 그건 정말 비싸더라.

남 맞아.

여 여행하는 데 어려운 점이 있었니?

남 날씨가 덥고 습해서 자전거를 타고 다니는 게 힘들었어.

|어휘| go on a bicycle trip 자전거 여행을 하다 travel around 여기저기 여행하고 다니다 go sightseeing 관광하다 tourist [명] 관광객 expensive [형] 비싼 humid [형] 습한

09 ①

M I need to get some lunch, but I'm in a hurry. Let's stop by a convenience store.

W Okay. What will you get?

M Maybe some instant ramen. And I'll buy some cookies or candy for dessert.

W That doesn't sound like a very good lunch.

M I guess not. What do you suggest?

W When I'm in a hurry, I usually get a sandwich or some gimbap.

M Oh, gimbap is a good idea! I'll get that.

남 점심을 먹어야 하는데, 시간이 없네. 편의점에 잠시 들르자.

여 그래. 뭐 살 거야?

남 아마 인스턴트 라면. 그리고 후식으로는 쿠키나 사탕을 살 거야.

여 제대로 된 점심이 아닌 것 같은데.

남 아니겠지. 너는 뭘 제안하는데?

여 나는 바쁠 때 대개 샌드위치나 김밥을 먹어.

남 아, 김밥 좋은 생각이네! 그걸 살래.

|해설| 남자는 식사를 제대로 챙겨 먹으라는 여자의 충고를 받아들여 김밥을 사기로 했다.

|어휘| in a hurry 급히, 바쁜 stop by ~에 잠시 들르다 convenience store 편의점 instant [형] 인스턴트의 dessert [명] 후식 suggest [동] 제안하다 usually [부] 보통, 대개

10 ②

W My final exams start next week. I have so many subjects to study.

M What will you start with? I usually start with science.

W I'm not taking a science class this year. English and history are my hardest classes.

M What about math? That's an important class.

W Yes, but I'll save it for last. I feel pretty confident about it.

M Then I'd start with whichever class you're worried about the most.

W Good idea. I'll start with history and then study English next.

M Sounds good. Let me know if you need help.

여 기말고사가 다음 주에 시작해. 공부할 과목이 정말 많아.

남 뭐부터 시작할 거야? 나는 보통 과학으로 시작해.

여 나는 올해 과학 수업을 안 들어. 영어랑 역사가 내가 가장 어려워하는 과목이야.

남 수학은 어떤데? 그거 중요한 과목이잖아.

여 응, 그렇지만 그건 마지막까지 남겨둘 거야. 수학은 꽤 자신 있거든.

남 그럼 나라면 어떤 과목이든 네가 가장 걱정하는 것으로 시작할 거야.

여 좋은 생각이야. 역사로 시작한 다음에 영어를 공부해야겠어.

남 괜찮을 것 같네. 도움이 필요하면 말해.

|어휘| final exam 기말고사 subject [명] 과목 important [형] 중요한 save [동] 남겨두다 pretty [부] 아주, 꽤 confident [형] 자신감 있는 whichever [형] 어느 ~이든 let ~ know ~에게 알리다[말하다]

어휘·표현 다지기

p. 51

A

01 관광객
02 건조한, 비가 오지 않는
03 후식
04 떨어지다
05 뇌우
06 빛나다
07 번개
08 실용적인
09 안개가 낀
10 비싼
11 주간의
12 야외의
13 자신감 있는
14 편의점
15 과목
16 충분한

B

01 throughout
02 last
03 heavy snow
04 housewarming party
05 shower
06 in a hurry
07 stop by
08 suggest
09 whichever
10 get used to

UNIT 6 언급하지 않은 내용

주요 어휘·표현 미리보기

p. 52

01 ⓐ was founded
02 ⓒ is held
03 ⓗ fasten
04 ⓑ invite you to
05 ⓔ Come check out
06 ⓓ was built
07 ⓖ named after
08 ⓕ provided

LISTENING PRACTICE

pp. 54-55

01 ④	02 ③	03 ②	04 ④	05 ①
06 ①	07 ⑤	08 ⑤	09 ④	10 ②

01 ④

M Hi, Danielle. What does your shirt say?
W It says, "San Diego Sharks." They're my favorite baseball team.
M I've never heard of them. Where do they play their games?
W The team was founded just two years ago. They play at Oceanview Stadium. I go there several times a week.
M You must really like them!
W Yes, I do. I've met all 30 players on the team!

남 안녕, Danielle. 네 티셔츠에 뭐라고 쓰여 있는 거야?
여 "San Diego Sharks"라고 쓰여 있어. 내가 가장 좋아하는 야구팀이야.
남 난 한 번도 들어본 적 없어. 어디서 경기해?
여 그 팀은 겨우 2년 전에 창단되었어. Oceanview 경기장에서 경기를 하지. 난 그곳에 일주일에 여러 번 가.
남 너 정말 그 팀을 좋아하는구나!
여 응, 그렇지. 그 팀에 있는 선수 30명을 모두 만나봤어!

|어휘| say [동] ~라고 쓰여 있다 found [동] 창단하다, 설립하다 stadium [명] 경기장

02 ③

M I'd like to invite you to a party on Saturday, Nancy.
W What kind of party is it?
M It's a barbecue party. It will be held in my backyard.
W Barbecue? Sounds delicious.
M Yes. We'll serve hamburgers and hot dogs. It starts at 5:00 p.m.
W Great! I will definitely come!
M I'm happy to hear that! I'll see you on Saturday.

남 토요일에 있을 파티에 너를 초대하고 싶어, Nancy.
여 무슨 파티인데?
남 바비큐 파티야. 우리 집 뒷마당에서 열릴 거야.
여 바비큐? 맛있겠다.
남 응. 우리는 햄버거랑 핫도그를 제공할 거야. 오후 5시에 시작해.
여 좋아! 꼭 갈게!
남 그 말 들으니 기쁘다! 토요일에 보자.

|어휘| invite [동] 초대하다 hold [동] 열다, 개최하다 backyard [명] 뒷마당 delicious [형] 맛있는 serve [동] (음식 등을) 제공하다 definitely [부] 분명히, 확실히

03 ②

W Welcome aboard Flight 234 to Honolulu.
M Thank you. Can I ask some questions about this airplane?
W Sure. What do you want to know?
M Well, what kind is it and how many people does it carry?
W It's an Airbus A340, and it can carry 370 people.
M Wow! It's really big.

W Yes, it is. It was built in 2007 and can travel at speeds over 900 km/h.
M That's fast! Thank you for the information.
W You're welcome. Now please sit down and fasten your seat belt.

여 호놀룰루행 234편에 탑승하신 것을 환영합니다.
남 감사합니다. 이 항공기에 대해 질문을 좀 해도 될까요?
여 물론입니다. 무엇을 알고 싶으세요?
남 음, 기종은 무엇이고, 몇 명이나 수용할 수 있나요?
여 기종은 Airbus A340이고, 370명을 수용할 수 있습니다.
남 와! 정말 크네요.
여 네, 그렇죠. 2007년에 만들어졌고, 시속 900km 이상의 속도로 비행할 수 있습니다.
남 빠르군요! 알려주셔서 감사합니다.
여 별말씀을요. 이제 자리에 앉아 안전벨트를 매주시기 바랍니다.

|어휘| aboard [부] 탑승한 carry [동] 실어 나르다 build [동] 짓다, 만들다 fasten [동] 매다, 채우다 seat belt 안전벨트

04 ④

W Do you like being a teacher, Sam?
M Yes. I enjoy giving lessons in the classroom.
W But doesn't that get boring?
M I do other things as well. I also help students with their personal problems.
W Oh, I see.
M And I have to check homework and make tests after my classes are over!
W Wow! You must be very busy.
M I am! But I still love my job.

여 교사 일은 마음에 드니, Sam?
남 응, 교실에서 수업하는 게 즐거워.
여 그렇지만 그게 싫증 나지는 않고?
남 나는 다른 것들도 하는 걸. 학생들의 개인적인 문제에 도움을 주기도 하고.
여 아, 그렇구나.
남 그리고 수업이 끝난 뒤에는 숙제 검사도 하고 시험 문제도 출제해야 해!
여 와! 매우 바쁘겠네.
남 그렇지! 하지만 그래도 내 직업이 정말 좋아.

|어휘| give lessons 수업하다 personal [형] 개인적인

05 ①

W Eileen's Hats is the best place to buy hats in Chicago. The owner of the store named it after his grandmother, who wore a different hat every day. It is located on Michigan Avenue and has been selling all kinds of hats since 1987. The store is open from 10:00 a.m. to 10:00 p.m., but is closed every Wednesday. If you're looking for a bargain, come on a Sunday—every hat is 10% off.

여 Eileen's Hats는 시카고에서 모자를 사기에 최적의 장소입니다. 가게 주인은 매일 다른 모자를 썼던 자신의 할머니의 이름을 따서 가게 이름을 지었습니다. 가게는 Michigan 가에 위치해 있으며, 1987년 이래로 온갖 모자를 판매해왔습니다. 가게는 오전 10시부터 저녁 10시까지 열지만, 매주 수요일에는 영업을 하지 않습니다. 저렴한 제품을 찾고 계시다면, 일요일에 방문해 주세요. 모든 모자가 10% 할인됩니다.

|어휘| owner [명] 주인, 소유주 name after ~의 이름을 따서 이름 짓다 look for ~을 찾다 bargain [명] 싼 물건, 특가품

06 ①

W There's a great new café across the street from the post office.
M Do they serve food or just coffee?
W They serve coffee, cake, and sandwiches.
M Sounds good. Let's go together after our swimming class.
W Unfortunately, it isn't open late. It closes at 7:00 p.m.
M Well, then we can go with our classmates after school.
W Yes, but it's really small. There are only three tables. Why don't you and I go alone?
M Okay!

여 우체국 건너편에 새로 생긴 근사한 카페가 있더라.
남 음식도 판매하는 거니, 아니면 그냥 커피만 파니?
여 커피, 케이크, 그리고 샌드위치를 판매해.
남 괜찮네. 수영 수업 후에 같이 가자.
여 안타깝게도 늦게까지 열진 않아. 오후 7시에 닫더라고.
남 음, 그러면 방과 후에 우리 반 친구들하고 가면 되겠다.
여 그래, 그런데 거기 정말 작아. 테이블이 세 개뿐이야. 너랑 나만 가는 건 어때?
남 알겠어!

|어휘| across [전] 건너편에 classmate [명] 반 친구 alone [부] 다른 사람 없이

07 ⑤

W I like this painting of sunflowers. Do you know who painted it?
M Yes. It was painted by Vincent van Gogh.

W Was it? I really like the colors. Almost everything is yellow.
M Yes. He painted it in 1888. He painted many sunflower paintings that year.
W Did he use oil paints?
M Yes, he did. I would like to have that painting in my house.
W You can buy a postcard of the painting in the museum gift shop.

여 나는 이 해바라기 그림이 좋아. 누가 그렸는지 알아?
남 응. 그거 빈센트 반 고흐가 그린 거야.
여 그래? 색깔이 정말 마음에 들어. 거의 모든 것이 노란색이야.
남 맞아. 그는 이걸 1888년에 그렸어. 그해에 해바라기 그림을 많이 그렸지.
여 유화 물감을 사용했나?
남 응, 맞아. 우리 집에 저 그림을 두고 싶다.
여 미술관 기념품 가게에서 이 그림의 엽서를 살 수 있어.

|어휘| sunflower [명] 해바라기 oil paint 유화 물감 postcard [명] 엽서

08 ⑤

M I'm going to take part in a quiz contest about robots next Monday!
W Really? Where is it?
M It's at the school library. First prize is a new smartphone!
W Well, I hope you win.
M Me too. But 26 other students have also entered it.
W Don't worry. If you study hard before the contest, you'll do well.

남 나 다음 주 월요일에 로봇 퀴즈 대회에 참가할 거야.
여 정말? 어디서 열리는데?
남 학교 도서관에서. 1등 상품은 새 스마트폰이야!
여 아, 네가 우승하면 좋겠다.
남 나도. 하지만 26명의 다른 학생들도 참가하기로 했는 걸.
여 걱정하지 마. 대회 전에 열심히 공부하면, 잘할 수 있을 거야.

|어휘| take part in ~에 참가하다 first prize 1등 상(품) enter [동] 참가하다

09 ④

M The banana is a popular fruit grown in tropical countries. It is long and curved like a boomerang. When it is ripe, it changes from green to yellow on the outside. But it is yellowish white on the inside. The average banana contains between 90 and 120 calories.

남 바나나는 열대 국가에서 자라는 인기 있는 과일입니다. 그것은 길고 부메랑처럼 휘어 있습니다. 바나나가 익었을 때는, 표면이 초록색에서 노란색으로 변합니다. 하지만 안쪽은 노르스름한 흰색을 띱니다. 바나나는 평균적으로 90~120 칼로리를 함유하고 있습니다.

|어휘| popular [형] 인기 있는 tropical country 열대 국가 curved [형] 곡선의, 약간 휜 ripe [형] 익은 outside [명] 겉(면) yellowish [형] 노르스름한 inside [명] 안쪽 average [형] 평균의 contain [동] 함유하다

10 ②

W Hello, everyone! Come check out the Parkside Gym, a new health club that opened last week. We have the newest training machines. Also, we provide members with free classes, including yoga and Pilates. You can sign up for a special one-month membership for just $24. If you are interested in fitness, sign up online for a quick tour.

여 안녕하세요, 여러분! 지난주에 개장한 새 헬스장인 Parkside 헬스장을 보러 오세요. 저희는 최신 운동 기구를 갖추고 있습니다. 또한, 회원분들에게는 요가와 필라테스를 포함한 무료 강좌를 제공합니다. 단돈 24달러로 특별 1개월 회원권을 신청하실 수 있습니다. 신체 단련에 관심이 있으시다면, 잠시 둘러보러 온라인으로 가입해 주세요.

|어휘| come check out 와서 보다 newest [형] 최신의 training machine 운동 기구 provide [동] 제공하다 including [전] 포함하여 Pilates [명] 필라테스 sign up for ~을 신청[가입]하다 membership [명] 회원권, 회원(자격) fitness [명] 건강, 신체 단련

어휘·표현 다지기 p. 59

A

01	개인적인	02	건너편에
03	분명히, 확실히	04	겉(면)
05	뒷마당	06	함유하다
07	열대 국가	08	평균의
09	1등 상(품)	10	맛있는
11	~을 찾다	12	익은
13	경기장	14	주인, 소유주
15	안전벨트	16	~에 참가하다

B

01	enter	02	serve
03	fitness	04	bargain
05	alone	06	aboard
07	curved	08	give lessons
09	say	10	membership

UNIT 7 주제·화제

주요 어휘·표현 미리보기

p. 60

01	ⓑ be delayed	02	ⓕ rest
03	ⓒ in common	04	ⓗ permission
05	ⓖ focus on	06	ⓓ understanding
07	ⓐ plenty of	08	ⓔ feed

LISTENING PRACTICE

pp. 62-63

01 ③	02 ④	03 ②	04 ④	05 ⑤
06 ①	07 ③	08 ⑤	09 ②	10 ④

01 ③

M Some students worry about tests but don't know how to do well on them. Here are some useful tips. First of all, make a list of the most important topics to study. Second, study hard before the test, but get plenty of rest the night before. Third, eat a good breakfast on the day of the test. And finally, answer the easy questions first. Then take your time with the harder ones.

남 어떤 학생들은 시험을 걱정하지만 어떻게 시험을 잘 볼지 모릅니다. 여기 유용한 몇 가지 조언이 있습니다. 먼저, 공부해야 할 가장 중요한 주제들의 목록을 만드십시오. 둘째, 시험 전에는 열심히 공부하되, 전날 밤에는 푹 쉬십시오. 셋째, 시험 당일에는 아침을 잘 챙겨 드십시오. 그리고 마지막으로, 쉬운 문제부터 먼저 푸십시오. 그러고 나서 더 어려운 문제는 시간을 들여 푸십시오.

|어휘| worry about ~에 대해 걱정하다 topic [명] 주제 plenty of 많은 rest [명] 휴식 breakfast [명] 아침(밥) finally [부] 마지막으로 take one's time 시간을 들이다

02 ④

W May I have your attention, please? Because of problems with the runway, our departure will be delayed by about thirty minutes. We are very sorry for the delay. The plane will take off as soon as we get permission. Again, we would like to apologize for the delay. Thank you for your patience and understanding.

여 주목해 주시겠습니까? 활주로 문제 때문에, 출발이 약 30분 지연될 예정입니다. 지연되어 대단히 죄송합니다. 비행기는 허가를 받는 즉시 이륙하겠습니다. 다시 한번, 지연되어 사과의 말씀을 드립니다. 기다려 주시고 이해해 주셔서 감사합니다.

|어휘| runway [명] 활주로 departure [명] 출발 delay [동] 지연시키다 [명] 지연 take off 이륙하다 permission [명] 허가, 허락 apologize [동] 사과하다 patience [명] 인내 understanding [명] 이해

03 ②

M Most people who are popular have something in common. They would rather listen to others than speak about themselves. People want to be understood. And when you listen to others well, they feel that they are understood by you. This will also make them feel that you respect them. For these reasons, good listeners often have better relationships.

남 인기 있는 대부분의 사람에게는 공통점이 있습니다. 그들은 자기 자신에 대해 말하기보다는 다른 사람의 말을 듣는다는 것입니다. 사람들은 이해받기를 원합니다. 그리고 여러분이 다른 사람의 말을 잘 들어줄 때, 그들은 당신으로부터 이해받고 있다고 느끼게 됩니다. 이것은 또한 그들에게 당신이 그들을 존중한다고 느끼게 할 것입니다. 이런 이유로, 경청하는 사람은 보통 더 좋은 인간관계를 맺습니다.

|해설| 인기 있는 사람들의 공통점은 경청하는 자세라고 말하고 있다.

|어휘| have ~ in common 공통점이 있다 would rather A than B B하기 보다는 차라리 A하겠다 respect [동] 존중하다 reason [명] 이유 relationship [명] 관계

04 ④

W Hello, students! I would like to let you know about an exciting summer job opportunity. The community center needs ten lifeguards this summer. The position is part-time, and employees will earn ten dollars an hour. If you're interested, please visit our website for more information. Thank you for your time!

여 안녕하세요, 학생 여러분! 여러분께 흥미로운 여름 구직 기회에 대해 알려드리려고 합니다. 주민센터에서 올 여름에 수상 안전 요원 10명이 필요합니다. 이 자리는 시간제 근무이며, 요원은 시간당 10달러를 받을 것입니다. 관심 있으시다면, 더 많은 정보를 위해 저희 웹사이트를 방문해 주세요. 시간 내주셔서 감사합니다!

|어휘| opportunity [명] 기회 lifeguard [명] 수상 안전 요원 position [명] (일)자리, 직위 part-time [명] 단시간 근무제, 비상근 employee [명] 고용된 사람 earn [동] (돈을) 벌다 information [명] 정보

05 ⑤

M What do you do when you finish reading a newspaper? Do you just throw it in the trash? Next time, think about this: Up to 200 million trees are cut down each year to make newspapers. But by putting old newspapers in a recycling bin, you can help protect these trees. In fact, if everyone recycled just one newspaper per week, millions of trees would be saved! It doesn't take much effort, but it can make a big difference.

남 신문을 다 읽으면 어떻게 하시나요? 그냥 쓰레기통에 던지나요? 다음번엔 이 점에 대해 생각해 보십시오. 매년 최대 2억 그루의 나무가 신문을 만들기 위해 잘려 나간다는 것을 말입니다. 하지만 헌 신문지를 분리수거함에 넣음으로써 여러분은 이 나무들을 보호하는 데 도움을 줄 수 있습니다. 사실 모든 사람이 매주 신문 한 부씩만 재활용하면, 수백만 그루의 나무를 구할 것입니다! 이것은 많은 노력이 들지는 않지만, 큰 차이를 만들어 낼 수 있습니다.

|어휘| throw [동] 던지다 million [형] 백만의 recycling bin 분리수거함 protect [동] 보호하다 recycle [동] 재활용하다 millions of 수백만의 effort [명] 노력 make a difference 차이를 만들다

06 ①

W Here at Robin's Comics, we've been receiving lots of calls from concerned customers. They want to know why our store has closed. But it hasn't closed! We have moved to a new location in the beautiful Springfield Mall. Our new store opened last week. It is much larger, so there are even more great comic books. You can find us just across from the travel agency in the mall. We hope to see you soon!

여 Robin's Comics에서 걱정하시는 고객님들로부터 전화를 많이 받고 있습니다. 고객님들은 저희 가게가 왜 문을 닫았는지 알고 싶어 하십니다. 하지만 문을 닫은 것이 아닙니다! 저희는 아름다운 Springfield 쇼핑몰의 새로운 장소로 이전하였습니다. 저희 새 매장은 지난주에 문을 열었습니다. 훨씬 커져서, 훨씬 더 많은 만화책을 보유하고 있습니다. 쇼핑몰 안에 있는 여행사 바로 맞은편에서 저희를 찾으실 수 있습니다. 곧 만나 뵙게 되길 바랍니다!

|어휘| receive [동] 받다 concerned [형] 걱정하는, 염려하는 across from ~의 맞은편에 travel agency 여행사

07 ③

M May I have your attention, please? At 2:00 p.m., there will be a special show. You are invited to watch our staff feed the sharks. They will also answer any questions you have about these amazing fish. But please come to the show early. There aren't many seats, and it's one of our most popular shows.

남 주목해 주시겠습니까? 오후 2시에 특별 공연이 있겠습니다. 저희 직원들이 상어에게 먹이를 주는 모습을 보러 와 주시길 바랍니다. 또한, 직원들은 이 놀라운 어류에 대한 모든 질문에 답변을 드릴 것입니다. 하지만 공연에 일찍 와 주시기 바랍니다. 좌석이 많지 않은 데다, 이는 저희의 가장 인기 있는 공연 중 하나이기 때문입니다.

|어휘| feed [동] ~에게 먹이를 주다 amazing [형] 놀라운

08 ⑤

W These days, even very young children have weight problems. There are many causes of childhood obesity. First of all, many children don't get enough exercise. They spend too much time playing games and watching TV. Unhealthy food is another problem. Fast food and soda make kids gain weight quickly. Finally, stress can be a cause of obesity. Children who feel stressed may overeat to make themselves feel better.

여 요즘은 아주 어린 아이들조차 체중 문제를 가지고 있습니다. 소아 비만에는 여러 가지 원인이 있습니다. 무엇보다도, 많은 어린이가 충분한 운동을 하지 않습니다. 아이들은 게임을 하고 TV를 보는 데 너무 많은 시간을 보냅니다. 건강에 해로운 음식은 또 하나의 문제점입니다. 패스트푸드와 탄산음료는 아이들을 빨리 살찌게 만듭니다. 마지막으로, 스트레스가 비만의 원인이 될 수 있습니다. 스트레스를 받는 아이들은 기분을 나아지게 하려고 과식을 할지도 모릅니다.

|어휘| weight [명] 체중 cause [명] 원인 childhood [명] 어린

시절 obesity [명] 비만 unhealthy [형] 건강에 해로운 gain weight 체중이 늘다 overeat [동] 과식하다

09 ②

M Being a student is a full-time job. There is a lot to focus on. You have to take tests, read books, and do homework. But it's never too early to start thinking about the future. If you are a high school student, or even a middle school student, you should think about what you enjoy and what you are good at. This will help you choose a major and a career later in life.

남 학생이라는 것은 아주 힘든 일입니다. 집중해야 할 것이 많으니까요. 시험을 보고, 책을 읽고, 숙제도 해야 합니다. 하지만 미래에 대해 생각하기 시작하는 데 너무 이른 것은 없습니다. 여러분이 고등학생이거나, 심지어 중학생이더라도, 여러분이 무엇을 즐기고 무엇을 잘하는지에 대해 생각해 보아야 합니다. 이것은 여러분이 훗날 전공과 직업을 선택하는 데 도움이 될 것입니다.

|어휘| full-time job 아주 힘든 일, 정규직 focus on ~에 집중하다 choose [동] 선택하다 major [명] 전공 career [명] 직업

10 ④

W Everyone knows that recycling is important for protecting the environment. However, recycling in the wrong way can sometimes cause problems. To do it right, you need to empty, clean, and dry anything that came in contact with food. When you throw away things like pizza boxes, tear off the greasy parts. And be sure to remove non-recyclable parts like lids, labels, or wrappers.

여 환경 보호에 재활용이 중요하다는 것은 모두가 알고 있습니다. 그런데 잘못된 방식으로 재활용하는 것이 때로는 문제를 일으킬 수 있습니다. 이를 제대로 하기 위해, 음식물이 닿았던 것을 비우고 씻어서 말려야 합니다. 피자 상자와 같은 것들을 버릴 때는, 기름이 묻은 부분을 떼어 내십시오. 그리고 뚜껑, 라벨, 포장지와 같이 재활용할 수 없는 부분들을 반드시 제거해 주십시오.

|어휘| environment [명] 환경 cause [동] 일으키다, 야기하다 empty [동] 비우다 dry [동] 말리다 come in contact with ~와 접촉하다 tear off ~을 떼어 내다 greasy [형] 기름이 묻은, 기름기 있는 be sure to-v 반드시 ~하다 remove [동] 제거하다 lid [명] 뚜껑 label [명] 표, 라벨 wrapper [명] 포장지

어휘·표현 다지기

p. 67

A

01 인내	02 던지다
03 출발	04 이룩하다
05 존중하다	06 백만의
07 노력	08 고용된 사람
09 (돈을) 벌다	10 주제
11 기회	12 재활용하다
13 환경	14 관계
15 보호하다	16 ~와 접촉하다

B

01 major	02 obesity
03 concerned	04 make a difference
05 remove	06 childhood
07 take one's time	08 choose
09 overeat	10 tear off

UNIT 8 내용 불일치

주요 어휘·표현 미리보기

p. 68

01 [e] fluent in	02 [a] on weekdays
03 [h] keep in touch	04 [f] daily
05 [b] off	06 [d] apply for
07 [c] are required	08 [g] not allowed

LISTENING PRACTICE

pp. 70-71

01 ④	02 ④	03 ④	04 ①	05 ④
06 ③	07 ③	08 ③	09 ②	10 ⑤

01 ④

M Hey, Minhye! How was your vacation?

W It was fantastic. I stayed in Australia for four weeks.

M What did you do there?

W I took English classes on weekdays. And I traveled on weekends.

M That sounds fun. Where did you go?

W I went to a lot of popular places in Sydney and Melbourne.
M Wow! What else did you do?
W I read books about Australian history. And I made lots of friends at my school.

남 아, 민혜야! 방학은 어떻게 보냈니?
여 환상적이었어. 나 4주 동안 호주에서 지냈어.
남 거기서 뭐 했니?
여 평일에는 영어 수업을 들었어. 그리고 주말에는 여행했어.
남 재미있었겠다. 어디 갔었는데?
여 시드니와 멜버른에 있는 많은 인기 있는 장소에 갔었어.
남 왜! 또 다른 건 뭐 했니?
여 호주 역사에 관한 책을 읽었어. 그리고 학교에서 친구도 많이 사귀었어.

|어휘| fantastic [형] 기막히게 좋은, 환상적인 on weekdays 평일에 on weekends 주말에

02 ④

[Telephone rings.]
W Sandra Kim's office. How can I help you?
M This is Perry Johnson. Can I talk to Ms. Kim?
W Sorry, she's off. She won't be back until Thursday. Can I take a message?
M Yes, I called to let her know about our meeting.
W What kind of meeting is it?
M It's a business meeting. It will be on Friday, September 25, and it'll begin at 4:00 p.m.
W Where will it be held?
M At Bexco Center.

[전화벨이 울린다.]
여 Sandra Kim의 사무실입니다. 무엇을 도와드릴까요?
남 저는 Perry Johnson입니다. 김 사장님과 통화할 수 있을까요?
여 죄송하지만, 오늘 쉬시는 날이에요. 목요일이나 되어야 돌아오실 거예요. 메모 남겨 드릴까요?
남 네, 회의에 대해서 알려드리려고 전화했어요.
여 어떤 회의인가요?
남 업무 회의예요. 9월 25일 금요일에 있을 예정이고, 오후 4시에 시작할 거예요.
여 어디서 열리죠?
남 벡스코 센터에서요.

|해설| 회의는 오후 4시에 끝나는 것이 아니라 시작할 것이라고 했다.

|어휘| off [부] (일 · 근무를) 쉬는 meeting [명] 회의 hold [동] 개최하다

03 ④

M Susan, you didn't forget our 10th wedding anniversary this Friday, did you?
W Of course not. I have a small gift for you.
M Really? Well, I made a reservation at a steak restaurant on Friday.
W Oh! The restaurant we went to on your birthday?
M Yes. Is that okay?
W Yes! I love that place. The view is terrific, and the food is good, too.
M Great!

남 Susan, 이번 주 금요일인 우리 10주년 결혼기념일 잊지 않았죠, 그렇죠?
여 당연히 안 잊었죠. 당신을 위해 작은 선물도 준비했어요.
남 정말이요? 음, 나는 금요일에 스테이크 음식점을 예약했어요.
여 아! 우리가 당신 생일에 갔었던 음식점이요?
남 맞아요. 거기 괜찮아요?
여 네! 그 장소 마음에 들어요. 전망이 훌륭하고, 음식도 맛있잖아요.
남 잘됐네요!

|어휘| forget [동] 잊다 wedding anniversary 결혼기념일 make a reservation 예약하다 view [명] 전망 terrific [형] 훌륭한, 멋진

04 ①

W The Sunshine Children's Theater will be holding auditions for our weekly performances of *The Lion King*. We are looking for boys and girls from the age of eight to fifteen who can sing and dance. No previous experience is required. The auditions will be held on May 11, and you must sign up on our website to participate.

여 Sunshine 아동 극장이 〈라이언 킹〉의 주간 공연을 위한 오디션을 개최합니다. 저희는 노래와 춤이 가능한 8세에서 15세 사이의 남녀 아이를 찾고 있습니다. 이전 경험은 필요하지 않습니다. 오디션은 5월 11일에 열릴 예정이며, 참가하려면 웹사이트에서 등록하셔야 합니다.

|어휘| audition [명] 오디션 performance [명] 공연 previous [형] 이전의 experience [명] 경험 require [동] 필요하다, 필요로 하다 sign up 등록하다 participate [동] 참가하다

05 ④

M Are you looking for a new, exciting restaurant in the downtown area? Then you should visit Sala Spanish

Restaurant. You can enjoy delicious Spanish and Mexican food there. The restaurant is open daily from 11:00 a.m. to 10:00 p.m. There are also daily discounts on our lunch specials. Stop by and give our food a try!

남 도심 지역에서 새롭고 흥미로운 음식점을 찾으십니까? 그렇다면 Sala 스페인 음식점을 방문하세요. 그곳에서 맛있는 스페인 음식과 멕시코 음식을 즐기실 수 있습니다. 식당은 매일 오전 11시부터 저녁 10시까지 엽니다. 매일 할인되는 점심 특선 메뉴도 있습니다. 들러서 저희 음식을 한번 맛보세요!

|어휘| downtown [형] 도심의 area [명] 지역 daily [부] 매일 [형] 매일의 discount [명] 할인 stop by ~에 들르다 give ~ a try ~을 한번 해 보다

06 ③

M Wow! You have a lot of boxes!

W Yes. I've been packing all day. My family is moving tomorrow.

M Really? Will you move far away?

W No. Just to an apartment building near the river.

M Oh, that's not far. We can still keep in touch. But why do you look so happy?

W I'm excited because I'll have my own room for the first time!

남 와! 상자 많다!

여 응. 종일 짐 싸고 있었어. 우리 가족이 내일 이사를 하거든.

남 정말? 멀리 이사 가니?

여 아니. 그냥 강 근처에 있는 아파트로 가.

남 아, 멀지 않네. 우리 계속 연락하며 지낼 수 있겠다. 그런데 왜 그렇게 즐거워 보이는 거야?

여 처음으로 내 방을 갖게 되어서 신나!

|어휘| pack [동] (짐을) 싸다 far away 멀리 far [형] 먼 keep in touch 연락하고 지내다 own [형] 자기 자신의 for the first time 처음으로

07 ③

[Cell phone rings.]

W Hello?

M Hi, Michelle. It's Charlie. Do you want to see a play this Saturday night?

W A play? I didn't know you liked plays.

M Well, I don't. But my brother Justin is playing the title role. It's called *Dr. Jones*.

W Wow! I'd love to go!

M Great! The play starts at 7:30. Beth and Victor are coming too. We can all go together!

[휴대전화벨이 울린다.]

여 여보세요?

남 안녕, Michelle. 나 Charlie야. 이번 토요일 밤에 연극 볼래?

여 연극? 네가 연극 좋아하는 줄은 몰랐네.

남 음, 좋아하진 않아. 그런데 우리 형 Justin이 주인공 역을 맡았거든. 〈Dr. Jones〉라는 연극이야.

여 와! 가고 싶어!

남 잘됐다! 연극은 7시 30분에 시작해. Beth랑 Victor도 올 거야. 우리 다 함께 갈 수 있겠다!

|어휘| play [명] 연극 title role 주인공 역

08 ③

W What are you looking at?

M It's an ad. Our school is looking for a part-time employee this semester.

W What kind of job is it?

M It's an office assistant position at the international student office.

W That sounds great. Can anyone apply for it?

M You have to be a student who is fluent in English and open-minded toward diverse cultures.

W I fit that description! How can I apply?

M You have to apply on the school website before this Friday.

W I'll do it right now!

여 뭐 보고 있니?

남 광고야. 우리 학교에서 이번 학기에 시간제 근로자를 구하고 있네.

여 어떤 일자리인데?

남 국제학생처의 사무 보조원 자리야.

여 괜찮네. 아무나 지원할 수 있는 거야?

남 영어가 유창하고 다양한 문화에 열린 마음을 가지고 있는 학생이어야 해.

여 나 그 설명에 딱 맞아! 어떻게 지원하면 돼?

남 이번 주 금요일 전에 학교 웹사이트에서 지원해야 해.

여 지금 당장 할게!

|해설| 학생이어야 지원할 수 있다고 했다.

|어휘| ad [명] 광고(= advertisement) semester [명] 학기 assistant [명] 보조원, 조수 international [형] 국제적인 apply for ~에 지원하다 fluent [형] 유창한 open-minded [형] 열린 마음의 diverse [형] 다양한 fit [동] 적합하다 description [명] 설명

09 ②

M Welcome to my one-minute movie review. Yesterday I went to see a new movie called *Mountain Man*. It's a comedy that was made by a Canadian director. There are many famous movie stars in it. Unfortunately, it was not very enjoyable. The biggest problem was its length—it was two and a half hours long. Also, there was too much violence and bad language. I give it just one star.

남 저의 1분 영화 평론에 오신 것을 환영합니다. 어제 저는 〈마운틴 맨〉이라는 신작 영화를 보러 갔습니다. 그것은 캐나다인 감독이 연출한 코미디 영화입니다. 영화에는 유명 영화배우들이 많이 나옵니다. 유감스럽게도, 영화는 그렇게 유쾌하지는 않았습니다. 가장 큰 문제는 영화의 길이였는데요, 2시간 30분이나 되었습니다. 또한, 너무 많은 폭력과 욕설이 있었습니다. 저는 그 영화에 별점을 하나만 주겠습니다.

|해설| 캐나다인 감독이 연출한 영화라고 했다.

|어휘| review [명] 평론, 비평 director [명] 감독 enjoyable [형] 유쾌한, 즐거운 length [명] 길이 violence [명] 폭력 bad language 욕설

10 ⑤

W There are some basic dormitory rules. First, always lock your room door when you leave. Second, the door to the building closes at 10:00 p.m., so don't be late. Third, pets are not allowed. Fourth, you cannot cook in your room. Lastly, you can have visitors, but you must ask for permission in advance.

여 몇 가지 기본적인 기숙사 규칙이 있습니다. 첫째, 외출 시에는 항상 방문을 잠그세요. 둘째, 건물 문은 밤 10시에 잠기니, 늦지 마세요. 셋째, 반려동물은 허용되지 않습니다. 넷째, 방에서는 취사를 할 수 없습니다. 마지막으로, 방문객을 들일 수는 있으나, 미리 허락을 구해야 합니다.

|어휘| dormitory [명] 기숙사 rule [명] 규칙 lock [동] 잠그다 allow [동] 허용하다, 허락하다 ask for ~을 청하다 in advance 미리

어휘·표현 다지기

p. 75

A

01 할인	02 주말에
03 국제적인	04 보조원, 조수
05 이전의	06 도심의
07 미리	08 주인공 역
09 학기	10 유쾌한, 즐거운
11 잠그다	12 경험
13 다양한	14 규칙
15 공연	16 폭력

B

01 meeting	02 open-minded
03 fit	04 description
05 dormitory	06 far away
07 director	08 give ~ a try
09 participate	10 for the first time

UNIT 9 목적·이유

주요 어휘·표현 미리보기

p. 76

01 [h] business trip	02 [e] complain about
03 [b] can't help	04 [g] apologize
05 [d] height	06 [a] charged
07 [f] attend	08 [c] at least

LISTENING PRACTICE

pp. 78-79

01 ③	02 ⑤	03 ①	04 ④	05 ②
06 ④	07 ②	08 ③	09 ⑤	10 ③

01 ③

[Telephone rings.]

W ST Telecom service center. May I help you?

M Yes. I just got my cell phone bill. I didn't make any overseas calls, but you charged me for one.

W Let me check your bill. What's your name?

M Paul Anderson.

W *[typing sound]* Yes, we've made a mistake. I apologize for the error. I'll fix it and send you a new bill.

M Excellent. Thanks for your help.

[전화벨이 울린다.]

여 ST 텔레콤 서비스 센터입니다. 도와드릴까요?

남 네. 제가 막 휴대전화 요금 고지서를 받았는데요. 저는 국제 전화를 전혀 이용하지 않았는데, 그것에 대한 요금을 청구하셨더라고요.

여 고객님의 고지서를 확인해 보겠습니다. 성함이 어떻게 되세요?

남 Paul Anderson입니다.

여 [키보드 소리] 네, 저희가 실수를 했네요. 오류에 대해 사과드립니다. 고지서를 정정해서 새 고지서로 보내드리겠습니다.

남 좋아요. 도와주셔서 감사합니다.

|어휘| bill [명] 고지서, 청구서 overseas call 국제 전화 charge [동] 청구하다 apologize [동] 사과하다 error [명] 오류 fix [동] 고치다, 바로잡다

02 ⑤

[Cell phone rings.]

M Hello?

W Hi, Jeremy. It's Susan. What are you doing?

M I'm getting ready to have lunch. What's up?

W I have to write an art review about the new Picasso exhibition. So I'm going to it this Saturday. Why don't you come with me?

M Great. I'd love to.

W Excellent. Let's meet at the subway station at noon.

[휴대전화벨이 울린다.]

남 여보세요?

여 안녕, Jeremy. 나 Susan이야. 뭐 하니?

남 나 점심 먹을 준비 중이야. 무슨 일이야?

여 내가 새로 열린 피카소 전시회에 대한 미술 보고서를 써야 하거든. 그래서 이번 주 토요일에 그곳에 갈 거야. 나랑 같이 가지 않을래?

남 좋아. 가고 싶어.

여 좋았어. 정오에 지하철역에서 만나자.

|어휘| get ready to-v ~하려고 준비를 하다 review [명] 보고서, 논평 exhibition [명] 전시회

03 ①

W What can I do for you?

M I'd like to return this sweater.

W All right. Is there a problem with the sweater? Or is it the wrong size?

M Well, it was a gift, but it fits fine. And there's nothing wrong with it.

W I understand. You just don't like it.

M No, I like it a lot. But I already have exactly the same one.

W Oh, that's unfortunate! But you can exchange it for another one.

여 무엇을 도와 드릴까요?

남 이 스웨터를 반품하고 싶어요.

여 알겠습니다. 스웨터에 문제가 있나요? 아니면 치수가 잘못됐나요?

남 음, 선물이었는데, 몸에 잘 맞아요. 스웨터에 문제가 있는 것도 아니에요.

여 알겠습니다. 그냥 마음에 들지 않으시는 거군요.

남 아니요, 정말 마음에 들어요. 하지만 완전히 똑같은 게 이미 있어서요.

여 아, 유감이네요! 하지만 다른 제품으로 교환하실 수 있어요.

|어휘| return [동] 반품하다 fit [동] (옷 등이) 잘 맞다 fine [부] 잘, 괜찮게 exactly [부] 정확히, 틀림없이 exchange [동] 교환하다

04 ④

M There you are! Do you know what time it is?

W I'm sorry, Dad. I know I'm late. But I couldn't help it.

M You should have at least called me!

W Sorry, but I couldn't.

M Why not? Did your cell phone's battery die?

W Actually, I lost my bag, and my phone was in it.

M I see. Then why are you late?

W My purse was in my bag too. I had no money, so I walked home.

남 너 왔구나! 몇 시인지 아니?

여 죄송해요, 아빠. 늦은 거 알아요. 근데 어쩔 수 없었어요.

남 적어도 나한테 전화는 했어야지!

여 죄송해요, 하지만 그럴 수가 없었어요.

남 왜 못했니? 휴대전화 배터리가 없었니?

여 사실 가방을 잃어버렸는데, 휴대전화가 그 안에 있었어요.

남 알겠다. 그럼 왜 늦은 거니?

여 제 지갑도 가방 안에 있었거든요. 돈이 한 푼도 없어서 집까지 걸어왔어요.

|해설| 여자는 휴대전화가 든 가방을 잃어버려 남자에게 전화를 할 수 없었다.

|어휘| can't help 어쩔 수 없다 at least 적어도 die [동] (기계가) 서다, 멎다 actually [부] 사실 purse [명] 지갑

05 ②

M Welcome to the Viking King ride.

W One child's ticket, please.

M How old is your daughter?

W She's 9 years old.

M Then I have to check her height. She needs to be taller than 130 cm.

W All right.

M *[pause]* Oh, sorry. She's not tall enough, so she can't go on this ride.
W What if I go on the ride with her?
M Sorry, ma'am. She can't ride this alone or with you.

남 바이킹 킹에 오신 것을 환영합니다.
여 아이 표 한 장 주세요.
남 따님이 몇 살인가요?
여 9살이에요.
남 그러면 키를 재봐야겠네요. 130cm 이상이어야 합니다.
여 알겠습니다.
남 [잠시 후] 아, 죄송합니다. 아이 키가 미달이라 이 놀이기구를 탈 수 없겠네요.
여 제가 아이와 함께 타면요?
남 죄송합니다, 손님. 아이 혼자든 고객님과 함께든 탑승할 수 없습니다.

|어휘| ride [명] 놀이기구 [동] 타다 height [명] 키 What if ~? ~라면 어떨까? alone [부] 혼자

06 ④

M Sharon? Is that you?
W Oh! Hi, Mark! Long time no see!
M I almost didn't recognize you. You got your hair cut short.
W I did. So what are you shopping for at the mall?
M I'm not shopping. I actually work in the clothes store over there.
W Oh, I didn't know that!
M How about you?
W I'm meeting a friend in front of the movie theater. We're going to have dinner together.
M Oh, okay. Well, I'll see you later. Give me a call!
W I will! Bye, Mark.

남 Sharon? 너 맞니?
여 아! 안녕, Mark! 오랜만이야!
남 너를 거의 못 알아볼 뻔했어. 머리를 짧게 잘랐구나.
여 그랬지. 너는 쇼핑몰에서 뭘 사고 있어?
남 나 뭐 사러 온 것 아니야. 사실 저기 있는 옷 가게에서 일해.
여 아, 몰랐네!
남 너는?
여 영화관 앞에서 친구를 만날 거야. 같이 저녁 먹으려고.
남 아, 그래. 음, 다음에 보자. 전화 줘!
여 그럴게! 안녕, Mark.

|해설| 여자는 영화관 앞에서 친구를 만나기로 했다.

|어휘| almost [부] 거의 recognize [동] 알아보다 get one's hair cut 머리를 자르다 give ~ a call ~에게 전화를 걸다

07 ②

W Are you almost ready, Edward?
M Yes. I just need to send this email.
W Who are you writing to?
M My boss.
W Is something wrong? You're not having problems at work, are you?
M No. She sent me a nice gift for my birthday, so I want to thank her.
W Wow! I wish we could switch bosses. I don't like mine.
M I know. You're always complaining about him.
W Anyway, where should we go for dinner?
M I know a great new restaurant near the subway station.

여 너 거의 다 준비됐니, Edward?
남 응. 이 이메일만 보내면 돼.
여 누구한테 쓰는 거야?
남 내 상사에게.
여 뭐 잘못됐어? 회사에서 문제 있는 건 아니지, 그렇지?
남 아니야. 내 생일에 좋은 선물을 보내 주셔서 감사를 표하고 싶어서.
여 와! 우리 상사를 서로 바꾸면 좋겠다. 나는 내 상사가 마음에 들지 않거든.
남 알아. 너 항상 그분에 대해 불평하잖아.
여 어쨌든, 저녁 먹으러 어디로 갈까?
남 나 지하철역 근처에 새로 생긴 근사한 식당을 알아.

|어휘| boss [명] 상사 thank [동] 감사를 표하다 switch [동] 엇바꾸다 complain about ~에 대해 불평하다

08 ③

M I heard you are going to Tokyo.
W Yes, I am. I can't wait.
M How long will you stay there?
W Two days.
M Only two days?
W Yes, I'm just going there to attend my brother's wedding.
M Oh! I didn't know that.
W I want to stay longer, but I have a job interview this Friday.

남 너 도쿄에 간다고 들었어.
여 그래, 맞아. 기다려져.
남 거기서 얼마나 머물 거야?
여 이틀.

남 겨우 이틀?
여 응, 난 그냥 남동생 결혼식에 참석하려고 가는 거야.
남 아! 그건 몰랐네.
여 더 오래 머물고 싶지만, 이번 주 금요일에 면접이 있어.

|어휘| can't wait 기다려지다 stay [동] 머물다 attend [동] 참석하다 job interview (취직) 면접

09 ⑤

M Hi, Grace. Do you want to get an early lunch with me right now?
W But it's only 10:45. I'm not hungry for lunch yet.
M Oh, okay. I skipped breakfast, so I'm really hungry.
W Why did you skip breakfast? Are you on a diet?
M No, I had a medical check-up this morning, so I wasn't allowed to eat anything for twelve hours.
W You must be starving! You should go get a snack.

남 안녕, Grace. 지금 나랑 이른 점심 먹을래?
여 하지만 지금 10시 45분밖에 안 됐어. 점심 먹기엔 아직 배가 고프지 않아.
남 아, 그래. 난 아침을 걸러서, 정말 배가 고프거든.
여 왜 아침을 걸렀어? 식이요법 하는 거야?
남 아니, 오늘 아침에 건강 검진이 있어서, 12시간 동안 아무것도 먹을 수 없었어.
여 분명 몹시 허기지겠네! 너 가서 간식 먹어야겠다.

|어휘| skip [동] 거르다, 건너뛰다 on a diet 식이요법을 하는 medical check-up 건강 검진 starving [형] 몹시 허기진

10 ③

[Cell phone rings.]
W Hi, Dad! Are you enjoying your business trip?
M Not really. Anyway, I wanted to find out how your big math test went.
W Oh! Actually, I didn't take it.
M What? Did you oversleep again?
W No! But the teacher rescheduled it for next week.
M I see. Well, I've got to go. My train is leaving soon.
W Okay, Dad! Call me again soon!

[휴대전화벨이 울린다.]
여 안녕하세요, 아빠! 출장은 즐거우세요?
남 그다지. 그건 그렇고 네 중요한 수학 시험이 어땠는지 알고 싶었어.
여 아! 저 사실 시험 안 봤어요.
남 뭐? 너 또 늦잠 잤니?
여 아니요! 선생님께서 다음 주로 일정을 변경하셨거든요.
남 알았다. 음, 그만 끊어야겠다. 기차가 곧 떠나.
여 네, 아빠! 조만간 또 전화주세요!

|어휘| business trip 출장 find out ~을 알아내다[알게 되다] big [형] (중요도가) 큰 oversleep [동] 늦잠 자다 reschedule [동] 일정을 변경하다

어휘·표현 다지기

p. 83

A

01 몹시 허기진	02 알아보다
03 머리를 자르다	04 상사
05 정확히, 틀림없이	06 (취직) 면접
07 오류	08 일정을 변경하다
09 국제 전화	10 식이요법을 하는
11 건강 검진	12 지갑
13 기다려지다	14 전시회
15 사실	16 고지서, 청구서

B

01 review	02 die
03 find out	04 almost
05 skip	06 switch
07 return	08 ride
09 stay	10 give ~ a call

UNIT 10 화자 간 관계

주요 어휘·표현 미리보기

p. 84

01 ⓗ best seller	02 ⓑ in the back row
03 ⓖ appointment	04 ⓐ try on
05 ⓔ weighs	06 ⓕ get a refund
07 ⓓ a bit	08 ⓒ check out

LISTENING PRACTICE

pp. 86-87

01 ⑤	02 ③	03 ⑤	04 ②	05 ④
06 ①	07 ④	08 ⑤	09 ③	10 ③

01 ⑤

W Can I help you?
M Yes. I'm looking for *The Adventures of Sherlock Holmes*, but I can't find it.
W Let me check the computer system. *[pause]* Oh, it has been checked out.
M When will it be available?
W I think it should be available next Wednesday.
M Can I reserve it?
W Sure. You can reserve books on our website.
M Okay. Thank you.

여 도와드릴까요?
남 네. 〈셜록 홈스의 모험〉을 찾고 있는데, 찾을 수가 없어요.
여 컴퓨터상으로 확인해 볼게요. [잠시 후] 아, 그건 대출 중이네요.
남 언제 이용할 수 있나요?
여 다음 주 수요일에는 가능하실 겁니다.
남 그 책 예약할 수 있나요?
여 물론이죠. 저희 홈페이지에서 책을 예약하실 수 있습니다.
남 네. 감사합니다.

|어휘| check out (책을) 대출하다 available [형] 이용할 수 있는 reserve [동] 예약하다

02 ③

W This is our classroom.
M It's very nice. I like the pictures on the wall.
W Your daughter Suzie drew one of them. She is good at many things, but I'm worried about her grades. They're still dropping.
M Hmm… Which desk is hers?
W It's over there, in the back row.
M Aha! Maybe that's the problem. I think Suzie might need glasses.
W You could be right. I will move her to a desk in the front row.
M And I will take her to the eye doctor after school tomorrow.
W That's a good idea.

여 여기가 저희 교실이에요.
남 아주 좋군요. 벽에 걸린 그림들이 마음에 드네요.
여 따님 Suzie가 그중 하나를 그렸어요. 그 애는 다재다능하지만, 성적이 걱정입니다. 계속해서 떨어지고 있어요.
남 음… 어떤 책상이 그 애 것이죠?
여 저기 뒷줄에요.
남 아하! 아마도 그게 문제일 거예요. 제 생각엔 Suzie가 안경이 필요할 것 같거든요.
여 그 말씀이 맞을지도 모르겠네요. Suzie를 앞줄에 있는 책상으로 옮길게요.
남 저는 내일 방과 후에 아이를 안과에 데려가 봐야겠어요.
여 좋은 생각이에요.

|해설| our classroom, your daughter Suzie, grades 등의 말로 미루어 보아, 교사와 학부모 간의 대화임을 알 수 있다.

|어휘| grade [명] 성적 drop [동] 떨어지다 back [형] 뒤의 row [명] (좌석 등의) 줄 front [형] 앞의

03 ⑤

M What seems to be the problem?
W My car made a strange noise while I was driving to work.
M I see. Have you had this problem before?
W No, this was the first time.
M Okay. I'll have to look at the engine.
W How long will it take?
M It will probably take a few hours.
W Oh, I guess I'll take a taxi to work.

남 어떤 문제가 있으시죠?
여 출근길에 운전하고 있는데 제 차에서 이상한 소리가 났어요.
남 그렇군요. 이전에도 이런 문제가 있었나요?
여 아니요, 이번이 처음이었어요.
남 네. 엔진을 봐야겠네요.
여 얼마나 걸릴까요?
남 아마 몇 시간 걸릴 거예요.
여 아, 저는 택시 타고 출근해야겠어요.

|어휘| make a noise 소리를 내다 strange [형] 이상한 engine [명] 엔진 probably [부] 아마

04 ②

M There's a problem with table five's food.
W What did they order?
M The chicken soup. They said it's too salty.
W Maybe I added too much salt. Bring it back and apologize, please. I will make it again.
M All right. And are the sandwiches for table two ready yet?
W Yes. Here you are. You can serve them now.

남 5번 테이블 음식에 문제가 있어요.
여 그분들이 무엇을 주문하셨죠?
남 닭고기 수프요. 너무 짜다고 하시네요.
여 아마 제가 소금을 너무 많이 넣었나 봐요. 다시 가져오고 사과해 주세요. 다시 만들게요.

남 알겠습니다. 그리고 2번 테이블에 나갈 샌드위치는 준비가 다 되었나요?

여 네. 여기 있어요. 지금 가져다드리면 돼요.

|어휘| order [동] 주문하다 salty [형] (맛이) 짠 add [동] 첨가하다 ready [형] 준비가 된 serve [동] (음식 등을) 제공하다

05 ④

W Good afternoon. How may I help you?

M Hi. I'd like to send this package to Canada.

W Okay. Please put it on the scale. What's in it?

M There are some clothes and toys in it.

W I see. It weighs 2 kg. How would you like to send it?

M By express mail, please. How long will it take?

W About two days. And it will cost $30.

M All right. Here you are.

여 안녕하세요. 무엇을 도와드릴까요?

남 안녕하세요. 이 소포를 캐나다로 보내고 싶은데요.

여 네. 그걸 저울 위에 올려 주세요. 그 안에 뭐가 들었나요?

남 안에 옷과 장난감이 있어요.

여 알겠습니다. 무게가 2kg이네요. 어떻게 보내고 싶으세요?

남 빠른 우편으로요. 얼마나 걸릴까요?

여 이틀 정도요. 그리고 비용은 30달러입니다.

남 알겠습니다. 여기 있어요.

|어휘| package [명] 소포 scale [명] 저울 clothes [명] 옷, 의복 weigh [동] 무게가 ~이다 express mail 빠른 우편 cost [동] (값이) ~이다

06 ①

M Hi. I don't know if you remember me.

W Ah, yes. You bought a package tour to Japan. Did you get our message about the earthquake in Japan?

M Yes, I did. Has the tour been canceled?

W Unfortunately, yes. We just made the decision.

M Can I get a refund?

W Of course. Or we could reschedule the tour.

M I'll take the refund.

남 안녕하세요. 저 기억하실지 모르겠네요.

여 아, 네. 일본 패키지여행 상품을 구매하셨죠. 일본 지진에 관한 저희 메시지 받으셨나요?

남 네, 받았어요. 여행이 취소되었나요?

여 안타깝게도 그렇습니다. 저희도 방금 결정했어요.

남 환불받을 수 있을까요?

여 물론이죠. 아니면 여행 일정을 변경해드릴 수도 있고요.

남 환불받을게요.

|어휘| remember [동] 기억하다 package tour 패키지여행 earthquake [명] 지진 cancel [동] 취소하다 make a decision 결정하다 get a refund 환불받다

07 ④

M Do you have an appointment?

W Yes. My name is Kim Minji.

M Okay. Come in and have a seat. What can I do for you?

W I'd like to change my hair color. Do you think brown hair would look good on me?

M Yes, I think brown hair would suit you well.

W Great! I also want to have my hair cut.

M How long?

W Shoulder length would be good.

남 예약하셨나요?

여 네. 제 이름은 김민지입니다.

남 알겠습니다. 들어와서 자리에 앉으세요. 뭘 도와드릴까요?

여 머리 색깔을 바꾸고 싶어요. 갈색 머리가 저에게 잘 어울릴 거라고 생각하세요?

남 네, 갈색 머리는 손님한테 잘 어울릴 거예요.

여 좋아요! 머리도 자르고 싶은데요.

남 얼마나요?

여 어깨 길이가 좋겠어요.

|어휘| appointment [명] 예약, 약속 have a seat 자리에 앉다 look good on ~와 잘 어울리다 suit [동] ~에게 어울리다 length [명] 길이

08 ⑤

M Hello, Sejin. Are you still feeling sick?

W Yes. I haven't gotten better since the last time I saw you.

M So what's the problem?

W I still have a fever.

M Did you take the pills I prescribed for you?

W I did, but they haven't helped.

M Let me take your temperature. *[pause]* I'll give you a shot today. Get lots of rest and come back if the fever doesn't go down.

남 안녕, 세진아. 아직도 아프니?

여 네. 마지막으로 선생님을 뵌 이후로 나아지지를 않네요.

남 그래서 무엇이 문제니?

여 아직도 열이 있어요.

남 내가 처방해 준 약은 먹었니?
여 네, 하지만 도움이 안 됐어요.
남 체온을 재 보자. [잠시 후] 오늘은 주사를 놔 줄게. 푹 쉬고 열이 내리지 않으면 다시 오렴.

|어휘| have a fever 열이 나다 pill [명] 알약 prescribe [동] 처방하다 temperature [명] 체온, 온도 give ~ a shot ~에게 주사를 놓다 rest [명] 휴식

09 ③

M Excuse me. Can I get an extra blanket, please?
W Of course. Are you not feeling well?
M I'm all right. I just feel a bit cold.
W Should I bring you some hot water too?
M Oh, yes, please. By the way, when will we arrive at Incheon Airport?
W We will be there in thirty minutes.
M I see. Thank you.
W You're welcome. Please wait a moment. I'll be right back.

남 실례합니다. 담요를 하나 더 받을 수 있을까요?
여 물론입니다. 몸이 안 좋으신가요?
남 괜찮습니다. 다만 조금 추워서요.
여 따뜻한 물도 좀 가져다드릴까요?
남 아 네, 주세요. 그런데 인천 공항에는 언제 도착하나요?
여 30분 후에 도착할 겁니다.
남 알겠습니다. 감사합니다.
여 천만에요. 잠시만 기다려 주세요. 바로 돌아오겠습니다.

|어휘| extra [형] 추가의, 여분의 feel well 건강 상태가 좋다 a bit 조금, 약간

10 ③

M Are you looking for something?
W Yes. I'd like to buy a pair of running shoes.
M Okay. How about these ones? They are our best sellers.
W Hmm... I like the design, but I don't like the color. Do you have them in other colors?
M Yes, they also come in white and gray. They're over here.
W I think the white pair looks better. Can I try them on?
M Sure. What size do you wear?
W I wear a size 7.
M Let me go get them for you.

남 찾으시는 게 있으세요?
여 네. 운동화 한 켤레를 사고 싶은데요.
남 그러시군요. 이건 어떠세요? 저희의 베스트셀러입니다.
여 음… 디자인은 마음에 드는데, 색이 마음에 안 드네요. 다른 색도 있나요?
남 네, 흰색과 회색도 나옵니다. 여기 있습니다.
여 흰색 운동화가 더 좋아 보이는 것 같아요. 신어 봐도 될까요?
남 그럼요. 어떤 치수를 신으세요?
여 7호를 신어요.
남 가서 가져다드릴게요.

|어휘| running shoes 운동화 best seller 베스트셀러, 잘 나가는 상품 try on ~을 입어[신어] 보다

어휘·표현 다지기

p. 91

A

01	(맛이) 짠	02	소포
03	저울	04	엔진
05	예약하다	06	옷, 의복
07	~와 잘 어울리다	08	지진
09	운동화	10	길이
11	이상한	12	소리를 내다
13	첨가하다	14	빠른 우편
15	열이 나다	16	패키지여행

B

01	prescribe	02	temperature
03	feel well	04	front
05	extra	06	suit
07	grade	08	give ~ a shot
09	make a decision	10	order

UNIT 11 부탁·제안한 일

주요 어휘·표현 미리보기

p. 92

01	[d] print out	02	[h] keeping a blog
03	[a] dressed	04	[g] an aisle seat
05	[c] on vacation	06	[f] handle
07	[b] show you around	08	[e] weather report

LISTENING PRACTICE

pp. 94-95

01 ④	02 ⑤	03 ②	04 ①	05 ③
06 ④	07 ①	08 ②	09 ②	10 ③

01 ④

[Cell phone rings.]

M Hello?

W Hello, Paul. It's Linda. Would you like to go to the aquarium together on Sunday?

M Sorry, but I can't. This Sunday is my mother's birthday.

W Really? Did you buy something for her?

M No, I'm going to the mall tomorrow, but I don't know what to get her. Would you come with me?

W Tomorrow is Friday, right? Okay. I know what mothers usually like.

M Great. I'll pick you up tomorrow.

[휴대전화벨이 울린다.]

남 여보세요?

여 안녕, Paul. 나 Linda야. 일요일에 수족관에 같이 갈래?

남 미안하지만, 못 갈 것 같아. 이번 주 일요일이 어머니 생신이거든.

여 정말? 어머니를 위해서 무언가 샀니?

남 아니, 내일 쇼핑몰에 갈 건데, 어머니께 무엇을 사드려야 할지 모르겠어. 나랑 같이 가 줄래?

여 내일이 금요일이지, 맞지? 알겠어. 난 어머니들께서 보통 무엇을 좋아하시는지 알아.

남 잘됐다. 내일 데리러 갈게.

|어휘| aquarium [명] 수족관 usually [부] 보통, 대개 pick up ~을 태우러 가다

02 ⑤

M Aren't you dressed yet? You're going to miss your bus.

W Sorry, Dad! I'm looking for my science notebook.

M It must be around here somewhere. Maybe it's in the living room.

W Could you please look for it while I put on my school uniform? It has a green cover.

M Sure, honey. And if you miss your bus, I'll give you a ride to school.

W Thanks, Dad! I'll hurry!

남 너 아직 옷 안 입었니? 버스 놓치겠어.

여 죄송해요, 아빠! 제 과학 공책을 찾고 있어요.

남 그거 분명 여기 어딘가에 있을 텐데. 아마 거실에 있을 거야.

여 저 교복 입는 동안 좀 찾아 주시겠어요? 초록색 표지예요.

남 알았다, 얘야. 그리고 버스 놓치면, 내가 학교까지 데려다줄게.

여 고마워요, 아빠! 서두를게요!

|어휘| be dressed 옷을 입다 miss [동] 놓치다 somewhere [부] 어딘가에 put on (옷 등을) 입다 school uniform 교복 give ~ a ride ~을 차로 태워주다

03 ②

[Cell phone rings.]

W Hello?

M Hey, Mina. It's Mark. You still live in Chicago, don't you?

W Yes, I do. Are you coming to visit?

M No, but my sister is. Could you show her around the city?

W Sure! Does she need a ride from the airport?

M No, that's okay. I'll give her your number, and she'll call you from her hotel.

W All right. Is she coming here to study?

M No, she's just on vacation.

[휴대전화벨이 울린다.]

여 여보세요?

남 얘, 미나야. 나 Mark야. 너 아직 시카고에 살지, 그렇지?

여 그래, 맞아. 너 놀러 오려고?

남 아니, 내 여동생이 갈 거야. 그 애한테 시내 구경시켜 줄 수 있니?

여 물론이지! 공항에서 오는 차편이 필요할까?

남 아니, 괜찮아. 내가 그 애한테 네 전화번호를 전해줄 거고, 그 애가 호텔에서 너한테 전화할 거야.

여 알겠어. 그 애는 여기 공부하러 오는 거야?

남 아니, 그냥 휴가 가는 거야.

|어휘| show ~ around ~에게 구경시켜 주다 on vacation 휴가로

04 ①

W Do you keep a blog, Ethan?

M No. I used to, but it was too much work. How about you?

W I do, but I don't think my blog is very interesting.

M What do you write about?

W Movies and music. Would you mind reading it?

M Sure, I'd love to. Give me the address.

W Thanks! I'll send it to you by cell phone message. I want to hear your opinion.

여 너 블로그 하니, Ethan?
남 아니. 했었는데 해야 할 일이 너무 많더라. 너는?
여 나는 하긴 하는데, 내 블로그가 그렇게 흥미로운 것 같진 않아.
남 뭐에 관해 쓰는데?
여 영화랑 음악. 좀 읽어봐 줄래?
남 물론, 그러고 싶어. 주소 좀 알려줘.
여 고마워! 휴대전화 문자로 보낼게. 네 의견을 듣고 싶어.

|해설| 'Would you mind ~?'는 '~해도 될까요?'라는 뜻으로, 상대에게 정중히 부탁하거나 양해를 구할 때 쓰는 표현이다.

|어휘| keep a blog 블로그를 (작성)하다 Would you mind ~? ~해도 될까요? address [명] 주소 opinion [명] 의견

05 ③

M I think we should cancel our picnic tomorrow.
W Why? I already prepared all of the food.
M Look at the clouds. I think it's going to rain tonight.
W I don't think so. Can you check the weather report right now?
M Sure, let me check. Hmm… In most areas, there will be heavy rain tomorrow.
W Oh no! I was looking forward to spending the day outside.
M Then how about visiting Grandma's house instead? We can enjoy your food while looking at the view from the terrace.
W That's a good idea. I'm sure Grandma will be glad to see us.

남 우리 내일 소풍을 취소해야 할 것 같아.
여 왜? 나 이미 음식도 다 준비했는데.
남 구름 좀 봐. 오늘 밤에 비 올 것 같아.
여 나는 안 그럴 것 같은데. 지금 바로 일기 예보를 확인해 줄 수 있어?
남 그래, 확인해 볼게. 음… 대부분의 지역에 내일 많은 비가 내릴 거래.
여 아 이런! 야외에서 하루를 보내기를 고대하고 있었는데.
남 그럼 대신에 할머니 댁을 방문하는 건 어때? 테라스에서의 경관을 보면서 음식을 즐길 수 있잖아.
여 그거 좋은 생각이다. 분명 할머니가 우리를 보시면 기뻐하실 거야.

|어휘| prepare [동] 준비하다 weather report 일기 예보 look forward to v-ing ~하는 것을 고대하다 spend [동] (시간을) 보내다 outside [부] 밖에서

06 ④

W Oh, my ankle really hurts.
M You must have twisted it during the basketball game. Here, sit down on the sofa.
W Thanks. I might need to see a doctor.
M Would you like me to make an appointment?
W I'll do it. But can you get my phone? It's in my room.
M Okay. Just stay there. You shouldn't be walking around.

여 아, 나 발목이 정말 아파.
남 농구 경기 중에 삐었나 봐. 여기 소파에 앉아봐.
여 고마워. 진찰을 받아야 할 것 같아.
남 내가 예약해줄까?
여 내가 할게. 그런데 내 전화기 좀 가져다줄래? 내 방에 있어.
남 그래. 그냥 거기 있어. 너 돌아다니면 안 되겠다.

|어휘| ankle [명] 발목 hurt [동] 아프다, 아프게 하다 twist [동] 삐다, 접질리다 see a doctor 진찰을 받다 make an appointment (진료 · 상담 등을) 예약하다

07 ①

W What are you doing? The bathroom is a mess!
M The sink broke. I'm trying to fix it.
W Oh no. Do you need any help?
M No, that's okay. I can handle it.
W All right. But weren't you going to take the dog for a walk?
M Yes, but I don't have time. Can you do it for me?
W Sure. Be careful. If you can't fix it, just call a plumber.
M I will.

여 뭐 하는 중이에요? 화장실이 엉망이네요!
남 개수대가 망가졌어요. 고쳐보려고 하고 있어요.
여 아 이런. 도와줄까요?
남 아니요, 괜찮아요. 내가 처리할 수 있어요.
여 알았어요. 그런데 산책 삼아 개를 데리고가려던 거 아니었어요?
남 맞아요, 그렇지만 시간이 없어요. 나 대신 해줄래요?
여 알겠어요. 조심해요. 고치기 힘들면, 그냥 배관공을 불러요.
남 그럴게요.

|어휘| mess [명] 엉망인 상태 sink [명] 개수대 handle [동] 처리하다 for a walk 산책 삼아 careful [형] 조심하는 plumber [명] 배관공

08 ②

M The plane is going to take off soon.
W Yes! We're starting to move.
M In two hours, we'll be in Tokyo!
W I'm a bit nervous. I should fasten my seat belt.

M Yes. And put your bag under the seat.
W Okay, I will.
M The view will be great once we're in the air.
W Would you change seats with me? I want to look out the window.
M I thought you wanted an aisle seat so you could get to the bathroom easily.
W I did. But I changed my mind!

남 비행기가 곧 이륙할 거야.
여 그래! 움직이기 시작하네.
남 두 시간 뒤면 우리는 도쿄에 있게 될 거야!
여 나 좀 초조해. 안전벨트를 매야겠다.
남 그래. 그리고 가방을 좌석 아래에 놔.
여 알았어. 그럴게.
남 하늘에 떠 있으면 전망이 근사할 거야.
여 나랑 자리 좀 바꿔 줄래? 창밖을 보고 싶어.
남 화장실에 쉽게 갈 수 있어서 통로 쪽 좌석을 원한 줄 알았는데.
여 그랬지. 하지만 마음이 바뀌었어!

|해설| 여자는 대화 후반부에 남자에게 자리를 바꿔 달라고 부탁했다.

|어휘| take off 이륙하다 nervous [형] 초조해하는 fasten [동] 매다 aisle seat 통로 쪽 좌석 change one's mind ~의 마음을 바꾸다

09 ②

[Cell phone rings.]
W Hello?
M Hi, Rachel. Are you on your way to the meeting?
W Yes, but the traffic is really bad. I've been in a taxi for thirty minutes already.
M Why did you decide to take a taxi?
W I was in a hurry. I thought it would be faster.
M Hmm. Why don't you get out now and take the subway? It is faster this time of day.
W Good idea. Oh, could you print out my report for the meeting?
M Sure. How many copies do you need?
W At least ten.
M Okay. But please hurry. The meeting starts in twenty minutes.

[휴대전화벨이 울린다.]
여 여보세요?
남 안녕하세요, Rachel. 회의에 오는 중인가요?
여 네, 그런데 교통 체증이 정말 심하네요. 벌써 30분째 택시 안에 있어요.
남 왜 택시를 타기로 한 거예요?
여 서둘러 가느라고요. 그게 더 빠를 거라 생각했죠.
남 음. 지금 내려서 지하철을 타지 그래요? 이 시간대에는 그게 더 빨라요.
여 좋은 생각이네요. 아, 제 회의용 보고서 좀 출력해 줄 수 있나요?
남 물론이죠. 몇 부 필요해요?
여 최소한 10부요.
남 알겠어요. 하지만 서둘러 주세요. 20분 뒤에 회의가 시작돼요.

|어휘| take a taxi 택시를 타다 hurry [명] 서두름 [동] 서두르다 print out ~을 출력하다 copy [명] (책 등의 한) 부

10 ③

W What are you guys doing here?
M We're practicing for the school play.
W Oh! I didn't know you were in the play.
M We're not yet. But there are auditions tomorrow.
W I see. I'm actually studying math in the classroom next door. You are so noisy that I can't concentrate.
M Sorry. This was the only empty classroom.
W Why don't you practice in the music room? It is usually empty after school.
M Okay, we'll move. We won't need to keep our voices down there.
W Thanks. Good luck with your auditions, guys!

여 너희 여기서 뭐 하고 있어?
남 우리 교내 연극을 연습하는 중이야.
여 아! 너희가 연극에 출연하는 줄 몰랐네.
남 아직 출연하는 건 아니야. 하지만 내일 오디션이 있어서.
여 그렇구나. 실은 내가 옆 교실에서 수학 공부를 하고 있거든. 너희가 너무 시끄러워서 집중할 수가 없어.
남 미안해. 이게 유일한 빈 교실이었어.
여 음악실에서 연습하지 그래? 거기는 방과 후에 보통 비어 있잖아.
남 알겠어. 우리가 옮길게. 거기선 우리 목소리를 낮출 필요 없겠다.
여 고마워. 너희 오디션 잘 봐!

|어휘| practice [동] 연습하다 noisy [형] 시끄러운 concentrate [동] 집중하다 empty [형] 빈 keep one's voice down 목소리를 낮추다

어휘·표현 다지기

p. 99

A

01 시끄러운
02 (옷 등을) 입다
03 주소
04 배관공
05 수족관
06 초조해하는
07 보통, 대개
08 준비하다

09 발목
10 의견
11 교복
12 연습하다
13 택시를 타다
14 진찰을 받다
15 목소리를 낮추다
16 ~의 마음을 바꾸다

B

01 mess
02 copy
03 concentrate
04 spend
05 miss
06 for a walk
07 somewhere
08 look forward to v-ing
09 careful
10 Would you mind ~?

UNIT 12 마지막 말에 대한 응답

주요 어휘·표현 미리보기

p. 100

01 [g] left a message
02 [h] wonder if
03 [d] get on
04 [e] pick out
05 [b] playing the guitar
06 [f] have in mind
07 [a] in need
08 [c] work part-time

LISTENING PRACTICE

pp. 102-104

01 ⑤	02 ④	03 ①	04 ②	05 ④	06 ②
07 ②	08 ④	09 ③	10 ⑤	11 ②	12 ③

01 ⑤

M What are you doing this Saturday?
W I have a swimming lesson at 11:00 a.m. But it ends at 12:00 p.m.
M Then how about going to see a movie in the afternoon?
W Okay. Do you have a specific movie in mind?
M Yes. I really want to watch *The Last Wish*.
W That sounds like fun. What time shall we meet?
M The movie starts at 6:30. Let's meet at 6:00 in front of MV Cinema.
W Why don't we meet an hour earlier than that and have dinner too?
M That would be better. I'll be there at 5:00.

① It'll take about an hour.
② Sorry for keeping you waiting.
③ I'll see her tomorrow evening.
④ Okay, I'll see you after my swimming lesson.

남 너 이번 주 토요일에 뭐 할 거야?
여 오전 11시에 수영 강습이 있어. 그런데 오후 12시에 끝나.
남 그럼 오후에 영화 보러 가는 거 어때?
여 좋아. 생각해 둔 특정 영화가 있니?
남 응. 난 〈마지막 소원〉을 정말 보고 싶어.
여 그거 재미있겠다. 몇 시에 만날까?
남 영화가 6시 30분에 시작하거든. 6시에 MV Cinema 앞에서 만나자.
여 그보다 한 시간 일찍 만나서 저녁도 먹으면 어때?
남 그게 낫겠다. 5시에 거기로 갈게.

① 한 시간쯤 걸릴 거야.
② 기다리게 해서 미안해.
③ 내일 저녁에 그 애를 만날 거야.
④ 좋아. 수영 수업 끝나고 만나자.

|어휘| have ~ in mind ~을 염두에 두다[생각하다] specific [형] 특정한 in front of ~의 앞에

02 ④

[Telephone rings.]
W Hello. How may I help you?
M Hi. I left my backpack on the subway this morning.
W I see. Which line did you take?
M I took Line 4. I got on at Seoul Station and got off at Sadang.
W Can you tell me what time you got off?
M I guess it was around 9:30.
W All right. What does the backpack look like?
M It's dark brown, and it has two pockets.

① Just some books.
② I bought it last month.
③ She has long, curly black hair.
⑤ I can't find my backpack anywhere.

[전화벨이 울린다.]
여 안녕하세요. 무엇을 도와드릴까요?
남 안녕하세요. 제가 오늘 아침 지하철에 배낭을 두고 내려서요.
여 그러시군요. 몇 호선을 타셨죠?
남 4호선을 탔어요. 서울역에서 타서 사당에서 내렸고요.
여 몇 시에 내리셨는지 말씀해 주실 수 있나요?
남 9시 30분쯤이었던 것 같아요.
여 알겠습니다. 배낭이 어떻게 생겼나요?
남 짙은 갈색이고, 주머니가 두 개 있어요.

① 책 몇 권뿐이에요.

② 지난달에 그걸 샀어요.

③ 그 애는 머리가 길고 검은색 곱슬머리예요.

⑤ 제 배낭을 어디에서도 찾을 수가 없어요.

|어휘| backpack 명 배낭 get on 타다, 승차하다   get off 내리다, 하차하다 [문제] pocket 명 주머니 anywhere 튀 어디에서도

03 ①

M Oh, hi, Jamie. Long time no see!

W Hi, Dan! It's been ages. How have you been?

M Good. I've been learning how to play the guitar.

W Wow! Is it fun?

M Yes, it is. How about you?

W I'm doing okay. But I have been really busy these days.

M Do you have a lot of school work?

W Not really. But I work part-time.

② I want to take a guitar class, too.

③ I usually walk for half an hour.

④ Yes, I like working in the cafeteria.

⑤ I do my homework in the library.

남 오, 안녕, Jamie. 오랜만이야!

여 안녕, Dan! 오랜만이다. 어떻게 지냈니?

남 잘 지냈어. 나는 기타 치는 법을 배우고 있어.

여 와! 그거 재미있니?

남 응, 재미있어. 너는 어떻게 지냈니?

여 잘 지내고 있어. 그런데 요즘에는 정말 바빴어.

남 학교 공부가 많니?

여 그렇진 않아. 하지만 아르바이트를 하거든.

② 나도 기타 강습을 받고 싶어.

③ 나는 보통 30분 동안 걸어.

④ 응, 나는 구내식당에서 일하는 것이 좋아.

⑤ 나는 도서관에서 숙제를 해.

|어휘| It's been ages. 오랜만이야. these days 요즘 [문제] work part-time 아르바이트하다 take a class 수업을 받다

04 ②

M Hailey, what's that on the kitchen table?

W It's my science project. It's a model of a volcano.

M It's great, but my friends are coming over later.

W So? You can just go in your room.

M There are five of us, and we're going to study for a test. We need the table.

W Okay. I'll put it in my room. But not right now.

M Why not?

W The paint is still wet. It's almost dry, though.

M Well, my friends will be here at 6:00.

W Okay. I'll move it before they arrive.

① They can help me with my project.

③ Sorry, but I'm too busy with my project.

④ Dinner will be ready at 6:30.

⑤ All right. I'll meet you then.

남 Hailey, 식탁 위에 있는 게 뭐야?

여 그건 내 과학 과제야. 화산 모형이지.

남 멋지네. 그런데 이따 내 친구들이 올 건데.

여 그래서? 그냥 네 방에 가면 되잖아.

남 우리가 5명인 데다가, 시험공부를 할 거라서. 우리는 그 식탁이 필요해.

여 알았어. 그거 내 방에 둘게. 근데 지금 당장은 안 돼.

남 왜?

여 칠이 아직 덜 말랐어. 거의 마르기는 했지만.

남 음, 내 친구들은 여기에 6시에 올 거야.

여 알았어. 친구들이 오기 전에 옮길게.

① 그들이 내 과제를 도와줄 수 있겠다.

③ 미안하지만, 난 내 과제 때문에 너무 바빠.

④ 저녁은 6시 30분에 다 될 거야.

⑤ 알았어. 그때 만나자.

|어휘| project 명 과제, 프로젝트 model 명 모형 volcano 명 화산 wet 형 젖은 though 튀 하지만

05 ④

W Hey, Alex. What are you doing here?

M I'm looking for a gift for my younger sister. Her birthday is next week.

W Do you have something in mind?

M No. I'm not sure what she likes.

W Look at this doll! It's so pretty. How about buying it for her?

M No, she has too many dolls already.

W Then how about this alarm clock? It's really cute.

M Great. She's often late for school.

① It's 4:30 now.

② Thank you for your present.

③ Sorry, I don't have any money.

⑤ Actually, I already have one.

여 얘, Alex. 여기서 뭐 하고 있니?

남 여동생에게 줄 선물을 찾고 있어. 여동생 생일이 다음 주거든.

여 생각해 둔 것이 있니?
남 아니. 그 애가 뭘 좋아하는지 잘 모르겠어.
여 이 인형 봐! 정말 예쁘다. 동생에게 이 인형을 사주는 게 어때?
남 아냐, 그 애는 이미 인형이 너무 많아.
여 그럼 이 자명종은 어때? 정말 귀여워.
남 좋다. 그 애는 학교에 종종 지각하거든.

① 지금은 4시 30분이야.
② 선물 고마워.
③ 미안, 나는 돈이 하나도 없어.
⑤ 사실, 나 이미 하나 있어.

|해설| 여자가 동생 선물로 자명종을 권하고 있으므로 그 제안에 대한 응답이 와야 한다.

|어휘| alarm clock 자명종 [문제] often [부] 종종

06 ②

M Guess where I'm going this weekend.
W I have no idea. Where?
M Wonderland Amusement Park! My parents are taking me!
W You're kidding! Have you ever been there before?
M No, I haven't. How about you?
W I haven't either. But my friends say it has a great roller coaster.
M Yes! I heard it's very high and goes very fast.
W Everyone says that it's really scary. I wonder if that's true.
M I'll let you know when I get back.

① Were you too scared to ride it?
③ I've ridden it several times.
④ Why don't you believe me?
⑤ Yes, I was terrified!

남 이번 주말에 내가 어디 가는지 맞혀봐.
여 전혀 모르겠어. 어디인데?
남 Wonderland 놀이공원! 부모님께서 데려가 주신대!
여 설마! 전에 거기 가 본 적 있어?
남 아니, 없어. 너는?
여 나도 없어. 하지만 내 친구들이 그러는데 거기 엄청난 롤러코스터가 있대.
남 맞아! 그거 아주 높고 엄청 빨리 간다고 들었어.
여 모든 사람이 그거 진짜 무섭다더라. 그게 사실인지 궁금해.
남 내가 돌아와서 너에게 알려 줄게.

① 그거 너무 무서워서 못 탔니?
③ 나는 그거 여러 번 타봤어.
④ 나를 왜 믿지 못하니?
⑤ 응, 나 무서웠어!

|어휘| have no idea 전혀 모르다 scary [형] 무서운 wonder [동] 궁금해하다 [문제] several [형] 여럿의, 몇몇의 terrified [형] 무서워하는

07 ②

[Telephone rings.]
M Hello? This is Spotlight Offices.
W Hello. May I speak to Brad, please?
M I'm sorry, he's in a meeting now. Can I ask who is calling?
W This is his sister, Lisa. I called his cell phone several times, but he didn't answer.
M Oh, he left his phone on his desk.
W Do you know when the meeting will be over?
M Maybe in thirty minutes. Would you like to leave a message?
W That's okay. I'll call his cell phone later.

① Yes, this is she speaking.
③ The line is busy right now.
④ I think you have the wrong number.
⑤ There's no way to contact him.

[전화벨이 울린다.]
남 여보세요? Spotlight Offices입니다.
여 안녕하세요. Brad와 통화할 수 있을까요?
남 죄송하지만, 지금 회의 중이에요. 누구신지 여쭤봐도 될까요?
여 누나 Lisa인데요. 그 애 휴대전화로 여러 번 전화했는데, 안 받아서요.
남 아, 책상에 전화기를 두고 갔네요.
여 회의가 언제 끝나는지 아시나요?
남 아마 30분 후에요. 메시지 남기시겠어요?
여 괜찮습니다. 나중에 그 애 휴대전화로 다시 걸게요.

① 네, 접니다.
③ 지금 통화 중입니다.
④ 잘못 거신 것 같네요.
⑤ 그에게 연락할 길이 없어요.

|어휘| be over 끝나다 leave a message 메시지를 남기다 [문제] contact [동] 연락하다

08 ④

W Hi. Can I help you find something?
M Sure, thanks. I'm looking for a jacket.
W How about this green jacket? It's a new arrival.

M Do you have that in a size large?
W Yes. Here's a large one. Would you like to try it on?
M Yes, please. *[pause]* Hmm... The size is okay, but I don't think this color suits me.
W It also comes in blue and black. What do you think?
M Oh, they both look nice. Could you pick one out for me?
W Sure. I think blue would look good on you.

① Okay, I'll buy both of them.
② Do you have that in other colors?
③ Then I'll take the green one.
⑤ Sorry, but we don't have any black jackets.

여 안녕하세요. 찾으시는 거 도와드릴까요?
남 네, 고맙습니다. 재킷을 찾고 있는데요.
여 이 녹색 재킷 어떠세요? 신상품이에요.
남 그게 큰 사이즈가 있나요?
여 네. 여기 큰 사이즈 있습니다. 입어 보시겠어요?
남 네. [잠시 후] 음… 사이즈는 괜찮은데, 이 색상이 저에게 어울리지 않는 것 같아요.
여 파란색과 검은색도 있어요. 어떠세요?
남 아, 그 둘 다 좋아 보여요. 저에게 하나를 골라 주시겠어요?
여 네. 파란색이 손님께 잘 어울릴 것 같아요.

① 네, 둘 다 살게요.
② 그거 다른 색도 있나요?
③ 그럼 녹색을 살게요.
⑤ 죄송하지만, 검은색 재킷은 없네요.

|어휘| new arrival 신상품 suit [동] ~에게 어울리다 pick out ~을 고르다

09 ③

W What's wrong, Allen?
M I was writing an English essay on my laptop, and it suddenly stopped working.
W Hmm. Do you think it's because of a virus?
M I don't know. I can't turn it on.
W I think you should take it to the service center.
M Right, but I need a laptop to finish the essay. It's due next Monday.
W I can lend you my laptop until yours is fixed.
M Really? That's very kind of you.

① Mine is broken too.
② I don't need it anymore.
④ Oh, can you fix it right now?
⑤ I forgot to charge the laptop.

여 무슨 일 있어, Allen?
남 노트북 컴퓨터로 영어 에세이를 쓰고 있었는데, 갑자기 작동이 멈췄어.
여 음. 바이러스 때문인 것 같아?
남 모르겠어. 켤 수가 없어.
여 서비스 센터에 가져가야 할 것 같은데.
남 그래, 하지만 에세이를 끝내려면 노트북 컴퓨터가 필요해. 다음 주 월요일까지 해야 하거든.
여 네 것을 고칠 때까지 내 노트북 컴퓨터를 빌려줄 수 있어.
남 진짜? 정말 고마워.

① 내 것도 고장 났어.
② 난 그거 더 이상 필요 없어.
④ 아, 지금 바로 그걸 고칠 수 있니?
⑤ 노트북 컴퓨터 충전하는 걸 잊었어.

|어휘| essay [명] (짧은 논문식) 과제물, 에세이 laptop [명] 노트북 컴퓨터 suddenly [부] 갑자기 turn on ~을 켜다 service center 수리점, 서비스 센터 due [형] 마감 기한이 ~인 lend [동] 빌려주다 fix [동] 고치다 **[문제]** charge [동] 충전하다

10 ⑤

M Did you hear about the flood that happened in West Virginia?
W Yes, it's awful. Thousands of people lost their homes.
M Is there any way we can help?
W I heard that volunteers are collecting items for the people in need.
M What kinds of items can be donated?
W Tents, sleeping bags, blankets, clothes, and things like that.
M That makes sense. They need those.
W We can send some goods together. I have a couple of sleeping bags and blankets.
M Sounds good. I'll look around for some items to donate.

① Yes. I want to volunteer to help them.
② There is nothing I can do about it now.
③ Why don't we go camping this weekend?
④ Thank you for giving me the items that I really needed.

남 웨스트 버지니아 주에서 일어난 홍수 소식 들었니?
여 응, 끔찍해. 수천 명의 사람들이 집을 잃었잖아.
남 우리가 도울 수 있는 무슨 방법이 있을까?
여 자원봉사자들이 어려움에 처한 사람들을 위해 물품을 모으고 있다고 들었어.
남 어떤 종류의 물품들을 기부할 수 있는 거야?
여 텐트, 침낭, 담요, 옷 같은 것들.

남 일리가 있네. 그런 것들이 필요하겠다.
여 우리가 함께 물건들을 보낼 수 있어. 나는 침낭 두어 개와 담요들이 있어.
남 좋아. 기부할 물품들을 좀 찾으러 둘러볼게.

① 응. 나는 그들을 돕기 위해 자원봉사를 하고 싶어.
② 지금 내가 그것에 관해 할 수 있는 게 아무것도 없어.
③ 우리 이번 주말에 캠핑 가는 게 어때?
④ 내가 정말 필요했던 물건들을 줘서 고마워.

|해설| 홍수로 집을 잃은 사람들에게 필요한 물품들을 함께 보낼 것을 제안하고 있으므로, 그 제안에 대한 응답이 와야 한다.

|어휘| flood [명] 홍수 happen [동] 일어나다, 발생하다 awful [형] 끔찍한, 지독한 thousands of 수천의 volunteer [명] 자원봉사자 [동] 자원봉사로 하다 collect [동] 모으다 in need 어려움에 처한 donate [동] 기부하다 sleeping bag 침낭 blanket [명] 담요 a couple of 둘의, 두서너 개의 [문제] look around for ~을 찾기 위해 둘러보다

11 ②

W You look down, Larry. What's wrong?
M I got the results from the medical check-up I had last week.
W Oh. I hope everything is okay.
M Well, I have some stomach problems. I need to see a doctor.
W Really? Does your stomach hurt?
M I've had a few stomachaches, I guess.
W When will you see the doctor?
M Next week. I'm worried. What if it's a disease?
W Don't worry. You'll be all right.

① Take this pill twice a day.
③ It's not far from here. Take a bus.
④ He said you should eat a balanced diet.
⑤ The surgery was a complete success.

여 너 우울해 보여, Larry. 무슨 일 있어?
남 나 지난주에 한 건강 검진 결과를 받았어.
여 아. 다 괜찮았으면 좋겠다.
남 음, 위 문제가 좀 있대. 병원에 가봐야 해.
여 정말? 배가 아파?
남 복통이 몇 번 있긴 했던 것 같아.
여 병원에 언제 갈 거야?
남 다음 주에. 걱정돼. 병에 걸린 거면 어쩌지?
여 걱정하지 마. 괜찮을 거야.

① 하루에 두 번 이 알약을 먹어.
③ 그곳은 여기서 멀지 않아. 버스를 타렴.
④ 그가 말하길 너는 균형 잡힌 식사를 해야 한대.
⑤ 수술은 완벽하게 성공적이었어.

|해설| 남자는 건강 검진 결과가 좋지 않아 병원에 가봐야 한다고 했으므로, 그를 위로하는 응답이 와야 한다.

|어휘| look down 우울해 보이다 stomach [명] 위, 복부 stomachache [명] 위통, 복통 disease [명] 질병, 병 [문제] balanced [형] 균형 잡힌 diet [명] 식사 surgery [명] 수술 complete [형] 완벽한 success [명] 성공

12 ③

W Which class are you going to take?
M I haven't decided yet. What about you?
W My friend told me that Mrs. Green's English class is really good.
M Hmm... I don't know Mrs. Green. What does she look like?
W She is very tall, and she has black hair.
M Oh! I've seen her before. She seems nice.
W Yes, she is. I'll probably take her class.
M When is it?
W Every Tuesday and Thursday at 1:00 p.m.

① Yes, she is a good teacher.
② I met her last semester.
④ I've already taken that class.
⑤ The classroom is on the fourth floor.

여 너 어떤 수업 들을 거니?
남 아직 결정 못 했어. 너는?
여 내 친구가 Green 선생님의 영어 수업이 정말 좋다고 했어.
남 음… 난 Green 선생님을 몰라. 어떻게 생기셨니?
여 키가 매우 크고 검은 머리셔.
남 아! 전에 뵌 적 있어. 좋으신 분 같아.
여 응, 좋으셔. 난 아마 그 선생님 수업을 들을 것 같아.
남 수업이 언젠데?
여 매주 화요일, 목요일 오후 1시야.

① 응, 그분은 좋은 선생님이셔.
② 난 그분을 지난 학기에 만났어.
④ 난 이미 그 수업을 들었어.
⑤ 교실은 4층에 있어.

|어휘| yet [부] 아직 seem [동] ~인 것 같다 probably [부] 아마 [문제] semester [명] 학기 floor [명] 층

A

01	여럿의, 몇몇의	02	빌려주다
03	화산	04	끔찍한, 지독한
05	아마	06	특정한
07	젖은	08	질병, 병
09	수술	10	자원봉사자, 자원봉사로 하다
11	성공	12	위통, 복통
13	무서운	14	완벽한
15	홍수	16	신상품

B

01	get off	02	have no idea
03	contact	04	seem
05	charge	06	balanced
07	essay	08	look down
09	collect	10	model

실전 모의고사 1회

pp. 112-113

01 ①	02 ④	03 ②	04 ①	05 ⑤
06 ①	07 ⑤	08 ②	09 ④	10 ②
11 ④	12 ②	13 ②	14 ⑤	15 ③
16 ③	17 ①	18 ④	19 ②	20 ③

01 ①

W Good morning. I'm Kylie Johnson. Here's the weekday weather for Miami. It will be hot and sunny on both Monday and Tuesday. Make sure you wear your sunscreen! It will remain hot on Wednesday, but the skies will be cloudy. On Thursday, it will be cold and windy. Finally, it will be rainy all day on Friday. So take an umbrella!

여 안녕하세요. Kylie Johnson입니다. 마이애미의 주중 날씨입니다. 월요일과 화요일 모두 덥고 화창하겠습니다. 자외선 차단제를 꼭 바르세요! 수요일에도 계속 덥겠으나, 하늘은 흐리겠습니다. 목요일에는 춥고 바람이 불겠습니다. 마지막으로, 금요일에는 종일 비가 내리겠습니다. 그러니 우산을 챙기시기 바랍니다!

|어휘| weekday 몡 주중, 평일 make sure 반드시 ~하다 sunscreen 몡 자외선 차단제 remain 동 계속 ~이다 finally 면 마지막으로

02 ④

M Hi. Can I help you?

W Yes. I left my bag in your storage room this morning. I'd like to pick it up.

M All right. Can you describe it?

W Yes. It is rectangular. And it has four wheels and a handle on top.

M Okay. There's one with a thick stripe on it. Is that one yours?

W No, it doesn't have a stripe. But it has a pocket on the front.

M Ah, I see it. Can I see your ID, please?

남 안녕하세요. 도와드릴까요?

여 네. 제가 오늘 아침에 보관소에 제 가방을 두었거든요. 찾고 싶어서요.

남 알겠습니다. 어떻게 생겼는지 설명해 주시겠어요?

여 네. 직사각형이에요. 그리고 바퀴가 네 개이고 위에 손잡이가 있어요.

남 네. 굵은 줄무늬 하나가 들어간 가방이 있네요. 그게 손님 건가요?

여 아니요, 줄무늬는 없어요. 하지만 앞쪽에 주머니가 있어요.

남 아, 보이네요. 신분증 좀 볼 수 있을까요?

|어휘| describe 동 묘사하다, 말로 설명하다 rectangular 형 직사각형의 handle 몡 손잡이 thick 형 굵은 stripe 몡 줄무늬 front 몡 앞쪽 ID 몡 신분증

03 ②

M Hello, Maria. You look very nice today.

W Thank you. But look at the bottom of my dress.

M Oh! There's mud all over it. What happened?

W A speeding car drove by and splashed it. I think it is ruined.

M That's too bad. Maybe it can be dry-cleaned.

W Maybe. I just wish people would drive more carefully.

남 안녕, Maria. 너 오늘 매우 멋져 보인다.

여 고마워. 근데 내 원피스 맨 아래 부분 좀 봐.

남 아! 진흙이 다 묻었네. 무슨 일이야?

여 질주하는 차가 지나가면서 튀긴 거야. 원피스가 엉망이 된 것 같아.

남 그거 안됐다. 아마 드라이클리닝을 할 수 있을 거야.

여 아마 그렇겠지. 사람들이 더 조심해서 운전하길 바랄 뿐이야.

|어휘| bottom 몡 맨 아래 부분 mud 몡 진흙 splash 동 (물·흙탕물 등을) 튀기다 ruin 동 엉망으로 만들다 dry-clean 동 드라이클리닝하다

04 ①

W It's so warm and sunny today! Spring is almost here!

M I know. There are so many things to do.

W Yes. I put up new curtains yesterday. How about you?

M I took my winter coats to the dry cleaner's.

W I think I'll clean my apartment windows today.

M That's a good idea! I'm going to wash my floors.

여 오늘 날씨 정말 따뜻하고 화창하다! 봄이 거의 온 것 같아!

남 그러니까. 할 일이 정말 많아.

여 맞아. 나는 어제 커튼을 새로 달았어. 너는?

남 나는 세탁소에 내 겨울 코트들을 맡겼어.

여 난 오늘 아파트 창문을 닦을 생각이야.
남 좋은 생각이다! 나는 바닥 청소해야지.

|어휘| put up ~을 달다 dry cleaner's 드라이클리닝점, 세탁소 floor [명] 바닥

05 ⑤

M Excuse me. Can I have some grape juice, please?
W Certainly. I'll bring it right over. And please fasten your seat belt. We'll be landing soon.
M Okay. What will the local time be when we arrive?
W It will be about nine o'clock in the morning.
M Thank you very much.
W You're welcome, sir.

남 실례합니다. 포도 주스 좀 주시겠어요?
여 물론이죠. 바로 가져다 드리겠습니다. 그리고 안전벨트를 매주시기 바랍니다. 곧 착륙할 예정입니다.
남 네. 도착하면 현지 시각이 몇 시일까요?
여 오전 9시 정도일 겁니다.
남 정말 감사합니다.
여 천만에요, 손님.

|해설| 음료 요청, 안전벨트, 착륙, 현지 시각 등의 단어가 나오므로, 기내에서 대화가 이루어지고 있음을 알 수 있다.

|어휘| fasten [동] 매다 land [동] 착륙하다 local [형] 현지의

06 ①

M Are you going to the concert in the park tonight?
W Yes. I'm really looking forward to it. It's going to be great!
M That's what I heard. I think I might go too.
W Oh! Did you buy a ticket already?
M No, not yet. They're not sold out, are they?
W Actually, they are. They've been sold out since last week.
M Oh no. I really wanted to go.
W You should buy a ticket in advance next time.

남 오늘 밤에 공원에서 하는 콘서트에 갈 거니?
여 응. 콘서트를 정말 고대하고 있어. 멋질 거야!
남 나도 그럴 거라 들었어. 나도 아마 갈 것 같아.
여 아! 표는 이미 샀지?
남 아니, 아직. 매진되지는 않았겠지, 그렇지?
여 사실, 매진이야. 지난주 이후로 매진됐어.
남 아 이런. 나 정말 가고 싶었는데.
여 다음번에는 미리 표를 사도록 해.

|어휘| look forward to ~을 고대하다 sold out (표가) 매진된 actually [부] 사실은 in advance 미리

07 ⑤

M Hi, Erica. What are you reading?
W It's a book about famous architects and artists.
M Oh, are you preparing for your art history project? Which artist did you choose?
W Claude Monet. I really like the way he paints landscapes. You chose Paul Gauguin, right?
M I thought about it, but I chose Vincent van Gogh instead. I want to learn more about his life.
W That's a great choice! He's one of my favorite artists.

남 안녕, Erica. 너 뭐 읽고 있니?
여 유명 건축가와 화가에 관한 책이야.
남 아, 너 미술사 과제 준비 중이니? 어떤 화가를 선택했어?
여 클로드 모네. 나는 그가 풍경을 그리는 방식을 정말 좋아해. 너는 폴 고갱을 골랐잖아, 맞지?
남 그것에 대해 생각해 봤었는데, 대신 빈센트 반 고흐를 선택했어. 그의 삶에 대해 더 알아보고 싶거든.
여 잘 골랐네! 그는 내가 정말 좋아하는 화가 중 한 명이야.

|어휘| architect [명] 건축가 prepare [동] 준비하다 choose [동] 선택하다 paint [동] (그림물감으로) 그리다 landscape [명] 풍경

08 ②

W What are you doing, John?
M I'm watching TV, Mom.
W Your grandparents will arrive in a few hours. Can you help me out?
M Okay. Do you want me to go to the station to meet them?
W No, that's okay. I will pick them up around three o'clock. But let's clean the house together first.
M All right. I'll clean the living room.
W Thanks. I'll do the dishes.

여 뭐 하고 있니, John?
남 텔레비전 보고 있어요, 엄마.
여 할아버지, 할머니께서 몇 시간 뒤에 도착하실 거야. 나 좀 도와줄래?
남 네. 제가 역에 할아버지, 할머니 마중 갈까요?
여 아니, 그건 괜찮아. 내가 3시쯤에 모시러 갈 거야. 그런데 우선 집부터 함께 치우자.
남 알았어요. 제가 거실을 청소할게요.
여 고맙다. 나는 설거지할게.

|해설| 여자가 집 안 청소부터 하자는 말에 남자가 동의하며 거실을 치우겠다고 했다.

|어휘| pick up ~을 데리러 가다 do the dishes 설거지하다

09 ④

W Hey, Tim! What did you do yesterday?
M I went to a magic show. It was amazing!
W Oh, I've never seen a live magic show before. Where was it held?
M It was held at the Merlin Theatre. I had a seat in the front row, so I could watch the magician's tricks up close.
W Wow. That must have been exciting.
M Yes. It lasted two hours but I felt it was too short. I highly recommend seeing it.
W Are there more performances?
M The show runs until August 15. You can book the ticket online.

여 얘, Tim! 어제 뭐 했니?
남 나 마술 쇼에 갔어. 굉장했어!
여 아, 나는 한 번도 실황 마술 쇼를 본 적이 없어. 어디서 열렸니?
남 Merlin Theatre에서 열렸어. 나는 앞줄에 앉아서, 마술사의 마술을 바로 가까이에서 볼 수 있었어.
여 와, 흥미진진했겠다.
남 응. 두 시간 동안 했는데 너무 짧게 느껴졌어. 그걸 보는 걸 정말 추천해.
여 공연이 더 있니?
남 그 쇼는 8월 15일까지 지속돼. 온라인으로 티켓을 예매하면 돼.

|어휘| live [형] 생방송의, 실황의 row [명] (극장 등의 좌석) 줄 trick [명] 마술 up close 바로 가까이에(서) last [동] 지속되다 highly [부] 매우 recommend [동] 추천하다 performance [명] 공연 run [동] 지속되다 book [동] 예약하다

10 ②

M Do you have things that you want to achieve? Then there are four steps you should take. First, set clear goals. Next, make detailed plans. Third, set deadlines for completing each task. Finally, give yourself a nice gift whenever you complete each step.

남 이루고 싶은 것들이 있습니까? 그렇다면 여러분이 밟아야 할 네 가지 단계가 있습니다. 첫째, 분명한 목표를 정하십시오. 다음으로, 세부적인 계획을 세우십시오. 셋째, 각 과업을 끝마치기 위한 기한을 정하십시오. 마지막으로, 각 단계를 마칠 때마다 자신에게 멋진 선물을 주십시오.

|해설| 이루고 싶은 목표를 달성하기 위한 네 단계를 소개하고 있다.

|어휘| achieve [동] 이루다 step [명] 단계 set a goal 목표를 정하다 detailed [형] 세부적인 deadline [명] 기한 complete [동] 끝마치다, 완료하다 task [명] 과업, 일 whenever [접] ~할 때마다

11 ④

W The annual Summer Rock Festival will be held at Olympic Park this year. It will last for three days, from August 3 to August 5. A one-day ticket costs just 15,000 won, and all tickets can be purchased online. More than twenty bands from all over the world will be playing. Don't miss this fantastic event!

여 매년 개최되는 Summer Rock Festival이 올해는 올림픽공원에서 열립니다. 축제는 8월 3일부터 8월 5일까지 3일간 이어집니다. 일일권은 단돈 15,000원이며, 모든 티켓은 온라인에서 구입하실 수 있습니다. 전 세계에서 온 스무 팀 이상의 밴드가 공연을 할 예정입니다. 이 환상적인 행사를 놓치지 마세요!

|어휘| annual [형] 매년의 purchase [동] 구입하다

12 ②

[Telephone rings.]
W This is Game World. How can I help you?
M There's something wrong with a game I ordered from you.
W What seems to be the problem with it?
M It was delivered today, but the disc is scratched.
W Oh, I'm sorry. We will exchange it for you.
M Actually, I'd like a refund.
W I see. Let me talk to my manager. Please wait one moment.
M Okay.

[전화벨이 울린다.]
여 Game World입니다. 무엇을 도와드릴까요?
남 제가 거기서 주문한 게임에 뭔가 문제가 있어서요.
여 무슨 문제인 것 같으세요?
남 오늘 배송받았는데, 판이 긁혀 있네요.
여 아, 죄송합니다. 교환해 드리겠습니다.
남 실은 환불을 원해요.
여 그러시군요. 매니저님께 말씀드리겠습니다. 잠시 기다려 주세요.
남 알겠습니다.

|해설| 남자는 판이 긁혀 있는 게임을 교환하는 것이 아니라 환불받는 것을 원하고 있다.

|어휘| deliver [동] 배달하다 disc [명] 둥글납작한 판, CD, 디스크

scratch [동] 긁다 exchange [동] 교환하다 refund [명] 환불 manager [명] 매니저, 관리인 one moment 잠시

13 ②

M Welcome to High Market. We're having a sale today with discounts of up to 50% off.
W That's great. This picture frame is pretty. How much is it?
M With the discount, it's $27.
W Hmm... That's still a bit expensive. What about this tablecloth?
M It's normally $50, but it's 50% off today.
W Great. How about this bar of soap?
M It was originally $5, but it's also half off.
W Okay. I'll take two bars of soap and one tablecloth.

남 High Market에 오신 것을 환영합니다. 저희는 오늘 최대 50%까지 할인 판매를 하고 있습니다.
여 좋군요. 이 액자 예쁘네요. 얼마예요?
남 할인해서 27달러입니다.
여 음… 그래도 약간 비싸네요. 이 식탁보는 얼마예요?
남 보통 때는 50달러인데, 오늘은 50% 할인됩니다.
여 좋네요. 이 비누는 얼마인가요?
남 원래는 5달러이지만, 그것 역시 반값입니다.
여 알겠습니다. 비누 두 개와 식탁보 하나 주세요.

|해설| 여자는 비누 2개와 식탁보 1개를 구입한다고 했는데 두 제품 모두 50% 할인을 하므로, 여자가 지불할 금액은 $\$2.5 \times 2 + \$25 = \$30$이다.

|어휘| discount [명] 할인 picture frame 액자 still [부] 그런데도 a bit 조금, 약간 tablecloth [명] 식탁보 normally [부] 보통 때는 bar [명] 바, 막대, 개 originally [부] 원래

14 ⑤

W Can I see your ticket, please?
M Here you are.
W Thank you. But you can't bring food and drinks into the stadium.
M But I bought this food at the store right next to this stadium.
W Sorry, you can't take any kind of food inside.
M Oh, I didn't know that. What should I do?
W You can eat it before you enter the concert area.
M Okay, I'll come back when I finish eating then.

여 표 좀 보여주시겠어요?
남 여기 있습니다.
여 감사합니다. 그런데 음식과 음료수는 경기장 안으로 갖고 들어가실 수 없습니다.
남 하지만 이 음식은 경기장 바로 옆에 있는 가게에서 산 건데요.
여 죄송하지만, 어떤 음식도 내부로 반입하실 수 없습니다.
남 아, 몰랐어요. 어떻게 해야 하나요?
여 콘서트 구역에 입장하시기 전에 드시면 됩니다.
남 네, 그럼 먹고 나서 다시 오겠습니다.

|어휘| stadium [명] 경기장 inside [부] 내부에[로] area [명] 구역

15 ③

M Are you okay, Lisa? You don't look good.
W My back is a little sore.
M Have you seen a doctor?
W No. It isn't serious. I have been staying up late reading at my desk recently.
M I see. Sitting for too long can cause back pain.
W Right. But I just need to take some pain medicine. Then I'll feel better.
M Hmm. How about doing some stretching instead? It will help relax your back muscles.
W Oh, that's actually a good idea.

남 괜찮아, Lisa? 너 안 좋아 보여.
여 허리가 조금 아파.
남 병원에 가 봤어?
여 아니, 심각한 건 아니야. 내가 최근에 늦게까지 안 자고 책상에서 책을 읽거든.
남 그렇구나. 너무 오래 앉아 있는 건 허리 통증을 유발할 수 있지.
여 맞아. 그런데 그냥 진통제를 좀 먹어야겠어. 그럼 좋아지겠지.
남 음. 대신 스트레칭을 하는 게 어때? 허리 근육 긴장을 푸는 데 도움이 될 거야.
여 아, 그거 진짜 좋은 생각이다.

|어휘| back [명] 등, 허리 a little 조금 sore [형] 아픈 serious [형] 심각한 stay up late 늦게까지 깨어 있다 cause [동] 유발하다 pain [명] 고통, 아픔 pain medicine 진통제 stretch [동] 스트레칭하다 relax [동] 긴장을 풀다 muscle [명] 근육

16 ③

W Where are you going on vacation, Nicholas?
M I'm going to England.
W Really? Do you have friends there?
M No, I don't. I just want to watch a soccer game at a famous stadium.
W Oh. So you won't go sightseeing?
M Probably not. I won't have enough time.

W Well, I hope you have fun.

여 휴가로 어디 가니, Nicholas?
남 영국에 갈 거야.
여 정말? 거기에 친구가 있어?
남 아니, 없어. 난 그냥 유명 경기장에서 축구 경기를 보고 싶을 뿐이야.
여 아, 그럼 관광은 안 할 거야?
남 아마도. 시간이 충분하지 않을 거야.
여 아, 재미있게 보내길 바랄게.

|어휘| on vacation 휴가로 go sightseeing 관광 가다[하다] have fun 재미있게 보내다

17 ①

① **M** Excuse me. I think you dropped something.
W Oh. Thank you very much.
② **M** Sorry, but this seat is taken.
W All right. I guess I'll sit somewhere else.
③ **M** Can you tell me where the nearest bus stop is?
W Go two blocks and make a left at the bank.
④ **M** I'm going to the lost and found office.
W Why? Did you forget something on the bus?
⑤ **M** Which is faster, taking the subway or taking the bus?
W The bus is usually faster.

① **남** 실례합니다. 뭔가 떨어뜨리신 것 같아요.
여 어머. 정말 감사합니다.
② **남** 죄송하지만, 이 자리는 주인이 있어요.
여 알겠습니다. 다른 어딘가에 앉아야겠네요.
③ **남** 가장 가까운 버스 정류장이 어딘지 알려주시겠어요?
여 두 블록 가셔서 은행에서 좌회전하세요.
④ **남** 나 분실물 보관소에 갈 거야.
여 왜? 버스에 뭐 두고 내렸어?
⑤ **남** 지하철 타는 것과 버스 타는 것 중에 어느 쪽이 더 빨라?
여 보통 버스가 더 빠르지.

|어휘| drop [동] 떨어뜨리다 somewhere [부] 어딘가에 nearest [형] 가장 가까운 lost and found office 분실물 보관소

18 ④

M Zebras are animals found in many parts of Africa. They eat mostly grass. Although they look like horses, they are covered in black and white stripes. Zebras live together in large groups of up to 1,000 animals. When lions attack these groups, the stripes confuse them. This helps the zebras escape.

남 얼룩말은 아프리카의 많은 지역에서 발견되는 동물입니다. 얼룩말은 대개 풀을 먹습니다. 말처럼 생겼지만, 흑백 줄무늬로 덮여 있습니다. 얼룩말은 최대 1,000마리에 이르는 큰 무리를 이루어 함께 삽니다. 사자들이 이 무리를 공격할 때, 줄무늬가 그들을 혼란스럽게 합니다. 이는 얼룩말이 달아나게 돕습니다.

|어휘| mostly [부] 대개 grass [명] 풀, 잔디 up to ~까지 attack [동] 공격하다 confuse [동] 혼란스럽게 하다 escape [동] 달아나다, 탈출하다

19 ②

M Have you seen the movie *The Adventure of Sam*?
W Yes, I saw it last weekend. I love the main actor.
M So do I. His performance was great.
W I really liked the storyline, too.
M Did you know it's based on a novel? The novel is also interesting.
W Do you have the novel? Can I borrow it?
M Sure. I'll bring it to school tomorrow.

① Yes. Can I see your library card?
③ That's too bad. I'll try again.
④ Sorry. You should read the book first.
⑤ No. I didn't think it was very good.

남 영화 〈Sam의 모험〉 봤어?
여 응, 지난 주말에 봤어. 주연 배우가 너무 좋아.
남 나도. 그의 연기가 대단하더라.
여 줄거리도 정말 좋았어.
남 그거 소설을 기반으로 한 거 알고 있었니? 소설도 흥미진진해.
여 그 소설 있어? 빌릴 수 있을까?
남 물론이지. 내일 학교에 가져올게.

① 네. 대출 카드 좀 볼 수 있을까요?
③ 그거 안됐다. 내가 다시 해볼게.
④ 미안. 너는 책 먼저 읽어야겠다.
⑤ 아니. 그게 그렇게 좋은 것 같진 않았어.

|어휘| main actor 주연 배우 performance [명] 연기 storyline [명] 줄거리 be based on ~을 기반으로 하다 novel [명] 소설
[문제] library card (도서관의) 대출 카드

20 ③

W How may I help you, sir?
M I saw your ad. I want to buy one of the smartphones on sale.
W I'm sorry, but they've all been sold already.
M Really? Will you be getting more?

W Yes, we'll get more tonight. But they'll probably sell out in the morning again.
M Wow! They must be popular. Can you keep one for me? I'll come by tomorrow.
W Sorry, we can't do that.
M Then I'll come first thing in the morning.

① These are sold out.
② I'll pick it up tomorrow afternoon.
④ Why don't you come and see me?
⑤ In that case, I'll take two.

여 무엇을 도와드릴까요, 손님?
남 광고를 봤는데요. 할인 판매 중인 스마트폰을 하나 사고 싶어서요.
여 죄송하지만, 그건 이미 전부 품절되었습니다.
남 정말요? 더 입고되나요?
여 네, 오늘 밤에 더 들여올 겁니다. 하지만 아마 아침에는 다시 다 팔릴 것 같아요.
남 와! 인기가 많나 보네요. 제 것 하나 맡아주실 수 있나요? 내일 잠깐 들를게요.
여 죄송하지만, 그렇게는 해드릴 수 없습니다.
남 그럼 아침 일찍 올게요.

① 이건 품절되었습니다.
② 내일 오후에 찾아갈게요.
④ 저를 보러 오시는 게 어때요?
⑤ 그렇다면 두 개 살게요.

|어휘| ad [명] 광고 (= advertisement) come by 잠깐 들르다
[문제] first thing 맨 먼저, 일찍

어휘·표현 다지기

p. 121

A

01	아픈	02	직사각형의
03	매우	04	~할 때마다
05	기한	06	풀, 잔디
07	바닥	08	이루다
09	과업, 일	10	세부적인
11	구입하다	12	근육
13	마지막으로	14	긁다
15	원래	16	현지의

B

01	remain	02	pain medicine
03	ruin	04	architect
05	land	06	attack
07	sunscreen	08	annual
09	escape	10	splash

실전 모의고사 2회

pp. 122-123

01 ②	02 ③	03 ②	04 ④	05 ③
06 ①	07 ④	08 ⑤	09 ①	10 ③
11 ⑤	12 ①	13 ④	14 ①	15 ②
16 ④	17 ②	18 ③	19 ③	20 ④

01 ②

M Good morning. I'm John Harris, and this is the world weather forecast for today. It will be cold and cloudy in New York, but it won't rain. Vancouver will have a cold, windy day. In Moscow, they're expecting heavy snow starting in the afternoon. But if you live in Beijing, you'll be able to enjoy a sunny day.

남 안녕하세요. 저는 John Harris이며, 오늘의 세계 일기 예보를 전해 드리겠습니다. 뉴욕은 춥고 구름이 끼겠으나, 비는 내리지 않겠습니다. 밴쿠버는 춥고 바람 부는 날이 되겠습니다. 모스크바는 오후부터 많은 양의 눈이 예상됩니다. 하지만 베이징에 사시는 분들은 화창한 날을 즐기실 수 있겠습니다.

|어휘| forecast [명] 예보 expect [동] 예상하다

02 ③

M Hello. I'd like to buy a new pair of sneakers for my daughter. She's thirteen.
W Okay. These are the latest models. They are all very popular with girls around that age. How about these ones with small, pink hearts?
M I think she would like them. But they are very similar to the ones she has now.
W Then how about buying a pair without any pattern on them?
M That's a good idea! I'll get this pair with shoelaces.
W Great choice! Your daughter will love them.

남 안녕하세요. 제 딸을 위한 새 운동화 한 켤레를 사고 싶은데요. 딸은 열세 살입니다.
여 네. 이것들이 최신 모델입니다. 모두 그 연령대의 여자아이들에게 매우 인기 있어요. 작은 분홍색 하트가 있는 이 운동화는 어떠세요?
남 딸이 좋아할 것 같네요. 하지만 딸이 지금 갖고 있는 것과 매우 비슷하군요.
여 그러면 아무 무늬 없는 운동화를 구입하시는 건 어떠세요?
남 좋은 생각이에요! 신발끈이 있는 이걸로 할게요.
여 탁월한 선택입니다! 따님이 매우 좋아할 거예요.

|어휘| sneaker [명] 운동화 latest [형] 최신의 similar to ~와 비슷한 pattern [명] 무늬 shoelace [명] 신발끈

03 ②

M Hi, Mom! I'm home!
W How was your first day of school, Chris?
M It was good! I made lots of friends today.
W I told you that your new classmates would like you.
M You were right. I thought it would be really hard to make friends at a new school. But everyone was very nice to me. I had a lot of fun today.
W I'm glad to hear that.

남 다녀왔습니다, 엄마! 저 왔어요!
여 학교 첫날 어땠니, Chris?
남 좋았어요! 오늘 친구를 많이 사귀었어요.
여 새로운 반 친구들이 널 좋아할 거라고 내가 말했잖니.
남 엄마 말씀이 맞았어요. 새 학교에서 친구를 사귀는 게 정말 어려울 거라 생각했어요. 하지만 모두 제게 잘해주더라고요. 오늘 정말 즐거운 시간을 보냈어요.
여 그 말을 들으니 좋구나.

|어휘| make a friend 친구를 사귀다 classmate [명] 반 친구

04 ④

M Hey, Peggy. What are you doing?
W Oh, hi, Richard. I'm looking at some pictures on my phone.
M Pictures? Can I see them?
W Sure. I went to an amusement park last weekend, so I took a lot of pictures.
M Wow! It looks like you had a really good time.
W Yes, I did. By the way, you look tanned. Did you go to the beach?
M No, I went to a baseball game last weekend.

남 얘, Peggy. 뭐 하고 있어?
여 아, 안녕, Richard. 내 전화기에 있는 사진들을 좀 보고 있어.
남 사진? 나도 봐도 돼?
여 물론이지. 지난 주말에 놀이공원에 가서 사진을 많이 찍었어.
남 와! 너 진짜 좋은 시간을 보낸 것 같네.
여 응, 그랬지. 그런데 너 피부가 탄 것 같다. 바닷가에 갔었어?
남 아니, 지난 주말에 야구 경기를 보러 갔었어.

|어휘| take a picture 사진 찍다 by the way 그나저나 tanned [형] (피부가) 햇볕에 탄

05 ③

M I think these are our seats.
W Yes, you're right. Thank you for coming with me.
M You're welcome. And thanks for buying me a ticket. So what is this play about?
W It's about two classmates who become best friends.
M It sounds interesting. Oh, they're turning off the lights!
W It must be about to start.

남 여기가 우리 자리인 것 같아.
여 응, 맞네. 나랑 같이 와줘서 고마워.
남 천만에. 그리고 나에게 표를 사 줘서 고마워. 근데 이 연극은 무슨 내용이야?
여 반 친구 둘이 절친한 사이가 되는 내용이야.
남 재밌겠다. 아, 불이 꺼지고 있어!
여 이제 시작하려나 봐.

|어휘| play [명] 연극 be about to-v 막 ~하려는 참이다

06 ①

M What are you doing in my room, Gina?
W Oh! I'm sorry! I didn't think you were home.
M I was downstairs helping Mom with the laundry.
W I didn't know that. I was looking for your bus card.
M My bus card? Why? Did you lose yours?
W Yes. I looked everywhere, but I can't find it.
M Mine is on my desk. You're welcome to use it.

남 내 방에서 뭐 하는 거야, Gina?
여 아! 미안! 네가 집에 없는 줄 알았어.
남 아래층에서 엄마 빨래하시는 거 도와드리고 있었어.
여 몰랐네. 난 네 버스 카드를 찾고 있었어.
남 내 버스 카드? 왜? 네 것 잃어버렸어?
여 응. 다 찾아봤는데, 못 찾겠어.
남 내 건 내 책상 위에 있어. 자유롭게 써도 괜찮아.

|해설| 남자가 버스 카드가 있는 곳을 알려주며 여자에게 써도 된다고 말하고 있다.

|어휘| downstairs [부] 아래층에서 laundry [명] 세탁물, 세탁 welcome to-v ~을 자유로이 할 수 있는

07 ④

M Hey, Ann! My family is going to the beach this weekend. Would you like to join us?
W Sounds great! Is there anything that I need to bring?
M Hmm... We will go swimming, so bring your bathing

suit. You should also bring sunglasses and a hat.
W Okay. Anything else?
M Bringing waterproof sunscreen would be a good idea.
W All right. What about sandwiches and juice?
M No, we will bring enough for everyone.

남 저기, Ann! 우리 가족은 이번 주말에 해변에 갈 거야. 너도 우리랑 같이 갈래?
여 재밌겠다! 내가 챙겨가야 할 것 있어?
남 음… 수영하러 갈 거니까, 수영복 가져와. 선글라스랑 모자도 가져와야 해.
여 알았어. 다른 건?
남 방수가 되는 자외선 차단제를 가져오는 게 좋을 것 같아.
여 알았어. 샌드위치랑 주스는 어때?
남 아니야, 모두가 먹게 우리가 충분히 가져갈 거야.

|어휘| join [동] 함께하다 bathing suit 수영복 waterproof [형] 방수의

08 ⑤

[Cell phone rings.]
M Hello?
W Hi, honey. Where are you?
M I'm walking to the train station. Is everything okay?
W Yes, I just dropped the kids off at school. But I heard that there's a problem with the trains.
M Oh, really?
W Yes, the news said there was an accident. So there are long delays.
M That's terrible. I need to call my boss and tell him I'll be late.
W All right. I'll talk to you later.

[휴대전화벨이 울린다.]
남 여보세요?
여 안녕, 여보. 어디예요?
남 기차역으로 걸어가고 있어요. 별일 없죠?
여 네, 방금 학교에 애들을 내려줬어요. 근데 열차에 문제가 있다는 얘기를 들었어요.
남 아, 정말요?
여 네, 뉴스에서 사고가 있었다고 하더라고요. 그래서 운행이 많이 지연된대요.
남 큰일이네요. 상사에게 전화해서 늦을 거라고 말해야겠어요.
여 알겠어요. 나중에 얘기해요.

|해설| 남자는 열차 지연 소식을 듣고 상사에게 전화해야겠다고 했다.

|어휘| drop ~ off ~을 내려주다 accident [명] 사고 delay [명] 지연 boss [명] 상사

09 ①

[Telephone rings.]
W Hello, this is BK Tours. How may I help you?
M I'd like a guided tour of the Grand Palace next Monday morning. Would that be possible?
W Yes, it would be. How many people will go?
M A group of five people.
W Okay. It costs forty dollars per person, including the entrance fee.
M Sounds good. Do you offer hotel pickup?
W We sure do. What hotel are you staying at?
M Riverside Hotel.
W We will pick you up at your hotel. And please remember, you must wear long pants and shirts with long sleeves during the tour.
M Oh, I see. Okay.

[전화벨이 울린다.]
여 안녕하세요, BK Tours입니다. 무엇을 도와드릴까요?
남 다음 주 월요일 오전에 Grand Palace 가이드 안내 관광을 하고 싶은데요. 가능할까요?
여 네, 그럴 거예요. 몇 분이 가실 건가요?
남 다섯 명입니다.
여 네. 비용은 입장료를 포함하여 인당 40달러입니다.
남 좋네요. 호텔 픽업 서비스를 제공해 주시나요?
여 물론입니다. 어느 호텔에 머물고 계신가요?
남 Riverside 호텔이요.
여 저희가 호텔로 모시러 가겠습니다. 그리고 관광 시 긴 바지와 긴 소매 셔츠를 입으셔야 한다는 점을 기억해 주세요.
남 아, 그렇군요. 알겠습니다.

|어휘| guided [형] 가이드가 안내[인솔]하는 possible [형] 가능한 per person 1인당 including [전] ~을 포함하여 entrance fee 입장료 offer [동] 제공하다 pickup [명] (사람을) 태우러 감 stay [동] 머물다 sleeve [명] 소매

10 ③

W People often worry about showing their emotions. Even if they are very sad, they try to hide it. But if you hold your feelings inside, it could harm your health. People who show their emotions are less likely to suffer from illness. Also, our emotions help other people understand us better. For these reasons, it's always best to express how you really feel.

여 사람들은 보통 자신의 감정을 드러내는 것에 대해 걱정합니다. 비록 아주 슬플지라도, 그걸 감추려고 하죠. 하지만 감정을 내면에 계속 붙들고 있으면, 건강을 해칠 수 있습니다. 감정을 드러내는 사람은 질병에 시달릴 가능성이 더 적습니다. 또한, 우리의 감정은 다른 사람이 우리를 더 잘 이해할 수 있도록 도와주죠. 이러한 이유로, 당신이 실제로 어떻게 느끼는지 표현하는 것이 언제나 최선입니다.

|해설| 여자는 감정을 표현하는 것의 장점들을 나열하고 있다.

|어휘| show [동] 보이다, 드러내다 emotion [명] 감정 even if 비록 ~일지라도 hide [동] 감추다 hold [동] 계속 붙들다 harm [동] 해치다, 손상시키다 be less likely to-v ~할 가능성이 더 적다 suffer from ~로 고통받다 illness [명] 질병 for these reasons 이러한 이유들로 express [동] 표현하다

11 ⑤

W Are you going on vacation next week?
M Yes. I'm going to Germany and Switzerland.
W That's great. For how long?
M I'll spend one week in each country.
W Where are you going to stay?
M I booked a hotel in Switzerland, but I'll stay with a friend in Germany.
W I see. I visited Switzerland last year. I went paragliding in the mountains!
M Really? I'm going to the mountains, but I'll just go hiking there.

여 너 다음 주에 휴가 갈 거니?
남 응, 독일이랑 스위스에 갈 예정이야.
여 멋지다. 얼마 동안?
남 각 나라에 일주일씩 있을 거야.
여 어디에서 머물 건데?
남 스위스에서는 호텔을 예약했는데, 독일에서는 친구랑 머물려고 해.
여 그렇구나. 나는 작년에 스위스에 갔었어. 산에 패러글라이딩을 하러 가기도 했지!
남 정말? 나도 산에는 갈 건데, 그냥 하이킹만 하러 갈 거야.

|어휘| go paragliding 패러글라이딩하러 가다 go hiking 하이킹하러 가다

12 ①

W Hi, Jack. Where are you going?
M I'm going to the library.
W Oh, I'm going to the library, too.
M Are you going there to study for the midterm exams?
W No. I reserved a book last week. The library called this morning and said it is available now. Why are you going to the library?
M You didn't know? I work there part-time.
W Really? That's interesting.

여 안녕, Jack. 어디 가니?
남 도서관에 가고 있어.
여 아, 나도 도서관 가는 길인데.
남 거기 중간고사 공부하러 가는 거야?
여 아니. 지난주에 책을 예약했거든. 오늘 아침에 도서관에서 전화 왔는데 이제 빌릴 수 있대. 너는 도서관에 왜 가?
남 몰랐구나? 나 거기서 시간제로 일하잖아.
여 정말? 흥미롭네.

|어휘| midterm exam 중간고사 reserve [동] 예약하다 available [형] 이용할 수 있는 work part-time 시간제로 일하다

13 ④

W Did you enjoy the meal?
M Yes. It was excellent. I'd like to pay now.
W Sure. You had the seafood pasta, a potato pizza, and two hot coffees, right?
M That's right.
W Okay. Your total is $55.
M Well, the pasta is $15, the pizza is $25, and the coffee is $5 per cup. So I think it should be $50.
W You need to add 10% for tax at our restaurant.
M Oh, I see. Here's my credit card.

여 식사 맛있게 하셨나요?
남 네. 정말 맛있었어요. 지금 계산할게요.
여 네. 해산물 파스타, 감자 피자, 그리고 따뜻한 커피 두 잔 드신 것 맞으시죠?
남 맞아요.
여 알겠습니다. 총 55달러입니다.
남 음, 파스타가 15달러, 피자가 25달러, 커피가 한 잔에 5달러잖아요. 그러면 50달러가 되어야 하는 것 같은데요.
여 저희 식당에서는 세금으로 10% 더하셔야 합니다.
남 아, 그렇군요. 여기 제 신용카드예요.

|어휘| meal [명] 식사 total [명] 총액, 합계 add [동] 더하다 tax [명] 세금 credit card 신용카드

14 ①

[Telephone rings.]
M Hello. How may I help you?
W I'd like to confirm my reservation. My name is Park Sumi.
M Let me check… It's a single room for two nights, from May 10 to the 12. Is that correct?

W Yes, it is. It includes breakfast, doesn't it?
M Yes, a buffet breakfast will be served at 7:00 a.m.
W Okay. What time can I check in on the tenth?
M Any time after 1:00 p.m.

[전화벨이 울린다.]
남 안녕하세요. 무엇을 도와드릴까요?
여 예약을 확인하고 싶은데요. 제 이름은 박수미예요.
남 확인해보겠습니다… 5월 10일부터 12일까지 2박으로 1인실을 예약하셨네요. 맞나요?
여 네, 맞아요. 조식은 포함이죠?
남 네, 뷔페식 아침 식사가 오전 7시에 제공될 겁니다.
여 알겠습니다. 10일에는 몇 시에 입실할 수 있나요?
남 오후 1시 이후에는 아무 때나 가능합니다.

|어휘| confirm [동] 확인하다 reservation [명] 예약 correct [형] 맞는 include [동] 포함하다 serve [동] 제공하다 check in 입실하다

15 ②

[Telephone rings.]
M Hello?
W Hi, Dad. Have you looked out the window?
M Yes. It's raining really hard! The weather forecast said it would be sunny all day.
W I know. So I didn't bring my umbrella with me.
M That's terrible. Where are you now?
W I'm on the bus. Could you pick me up at the station?
M Sure, honey. I'll be there in fifteen minutes.
W Thank you, Dad!

[전화벨이 울린다.]
남 여보세요?
여 안녕하세요, 아빠. 창밖 보셨어요?
남 그래. 비가 정말 많이 오는구나! 일기 예보에서는 종일 맑을 거라고 했는데.
여 그러니까요. 그래서 저 우산 안 가져왔거든요.
남 큰일이구나. 지금 어디니?
여 버스 안이에요. 정류장으로 저를 데리러 와주실 수 있어요?
남 물론이지, 얘야. 15분 뒤에 거기 도착할 거야.
여 감사해요, 아빠!

|어휘| hard [부] 심하게, 많이

16 ④

M Are you going to wear your new red dress tonight?
W No. I returned it to the department store.
M Why? I thought you liked it.
W I did like it. It was a very pretty dress.
M Was it too expensive?
W No. But it was bigger than I had thought.
M Oh, that's too bad.

남 너 오늘 밤에 새 빨간 원피스 입을 거야?
여 아니. 그거 백화점에 반품했어.
남 왜? 네가 그거 마음에 드는 줄 알았는데.
여 그랬지. 정말 예쁜 원피스였어.
남 너무 비쌌어?
여 아니. 하지만 내가 생각한 것보다 더 크더라고.
남 아, 아쉽네.

|어휘| return [동] 반품하다

17 ②

① W Can you help us find our seats?
M Sure. Can I see your tickets?
② W Excuse me, but I think you're sitting in my seat.
M Oh, I'm sorry. I read the number wrong.
③ W How about going to the movies tomorrow?
M I'm afraid I can't. I'll be very busy.
④ W Hello. How can I help you today?
M Hi. I'd like to change my seat.
⑤ W Which seat should we purchase?
M Hmm... Let's get seats in Row H.

① 여 저희 좌석을 찾는 걸 도와주시겠어요?
남 네. 표를 볼 수 있을까요?
② 여 실례지만, 제 자리에 앉아 계신 것 같아요.
남 아, 죄송합니다. 제가 번호를 잘못 봤네요.
③ 여 내일 영화 보러 가는 거 어때?
남 나는 못 갈 것 같아. 많이 바쁠 거야.
④ 여 안녕하세요. 무엇을 도와드릴까요?
남 안녕하세요. 좌석을 바꾸고 싶어요.
⑤ 여 우리 어떤 좌석을 살까?
남 음… H열에 있는 좌석으로 하자.

|어휘| seat [명] 자리, 좌석 go to the movies 영화를 보러 가다 purchase [동] 구입하다 row [명] 열

18 ③

M A new amusement park opened on June 10. It's called Fun City, and it's located in Ottawa. It has the tallest roller coaster in Canada. There are also three pools. The park is open from 10:00 a.m. to 10:00 p.m., six days a week. It is closed every Monday. Tickets cost $20 each. Come to Fun City today!

남 6월 10일에 새로운 놀이공원이 개장했습니다. 이름은 Fun City이고, 오타와에 위치하고 있습니다. 캐나다에서 가장 높은 롤러코스터가 있는데요. 수영장도 세 군데가 있습니다. 놀이공원은 주 6일 오전 10시부터 밤 10시까지 엽니다. 매주 월요일은 휴무입니다. 표는 장당 20달러입니다. 오늘 Fun City에 오세요!

|어휘| be located in ~에 위치하다

19 ③

[Telephone rings.]

M Hello, Green House Restaurant. May I help you?
W Yes, I'd like to make a reservation.
M Okay. For what time and how many people?
W A table for two at seven o'clock this evening.
M Oh, I'm sorry. There are no tables available at that time.
W What time is available then?
M There's a table available at eight o'clock.
W That would be fine.

① Non-smoking, please.
② A table for two, please.
④ I'm not ready to order yet.
⑤ I apologize for the inconvenience.

[전화벨이 울린다.]

남 안녕하세요, Green House 레스토랑입니다. 무엇을 도와드릴까요?
여 네, 예약을 하고 싶은데요.
남 네. 시간과 인원이 어떻게 되세요?
여 오늘 저녁 7시에 두 명 테이블이요.
남 아, 죄송합니다. 그 시간에는 가능한 테이블이 없습니다.
여 그럼 몇 시가 가능한가요?
남 8시에 가능한 테이블이 있습니다.
여 괜찮겠네요.

① 비흡연석으로 부탁합니다.
② 두 명이 앉을 테이블 부탁합니다.
④ 아직 주문할 준비가 안 됐습니다.
⑤ 불편을 끼쳐드려 죄송합니다.

|어휘| make a reservation 예약하다 [문제] apologize [동] 사과하다 inconvenience [명] 불편

20 ④

M What do you like to do on Sundays?
W I like to sleep late and eat a big breakfast.
M That sounds very relaxing. What else do you do?
W I usually volunteer at a children's hospital in the afternoon.
M That's great! Are you going there this Sunday, too?
W Yes. Would you like to join me?

① Good job! I'll join you.
② Yes, I'm going to school.
③ Sounds great. See you there.
⑤ Sorry, I'm busy on Sundays.

남 일요일에는 뭐 하는 걸 좋아해?
여 늦잠을 자고 푸짐한 아침을 먹는 걸 좋아해.
남 느긋할 것 같다. 또 뭘 해?
여 오후에는 보통 어린이 병원에서 자원봉사를 해.
남 멋지다! 이번 일요일에도 갈 거야?
여 응. 너도 함께 갈래?

① 잘했어! 나도 너랑 함께 할게.
② 응, 나 학교 가.
③ 좋아. 거기서 보자.
⑤ 미안, 나 일요일에는 바빠.

|어휘| relaxing [형] 편한, 마음을 느긋하게 해주는 volunteer [동] 자원봉사하다

어휘·표현 다지기

p. 131

A

01 감정	02 소매
03 세탁물, 세탁	04 질병
05 최신의	06 신발끈
07 ~로 고통받다	08 확인하다
09 아래층에서	10 포함하다
11 세금	12 중간고사
13 감추다	14 지연
15 맞는	16 제공하다

B

01 entrance fee	02 bathing suit
03 waterproof	04 drop ~ off
05 similar to	06 hard
07 express	08 possible
09 hold	10 be about to-v

실전 모의고사 3회

pp. 132-133

01 ②	02 ①	03 ③	04 ④	05 ②
06 ②	07 ④	08 ④	09 ②	10 ④
11 ⑤	12 ⑤	13 ③	14 ③	15 ④
16 ⑤	17 ③	18 ④	19 ②	20 ①

01 ②

W Good morning! It's time for our weather forecast for tomorrow. It will be sunny and warm in Daegu. The sun will be very strong, so everyone should put on sunscreen before leaving the house. In Jeonju, it will be cloudy all day. It will be windy in Busan, and there will be a severe thunderstorm in the evening.

여 좋은 아침입니다! 내일 일기 예보를 전해드릴 시간입니다. 대구는 화창하고 따뜻하겠습니다. 햇볕이 매우 강할 예정이니, 모두 외출하기 전에 자외선 차단제를 바르셔야겠습니다. 전주는 온종일 흐리겠습니다. 부산은 바람이 불고, 저녁에는 심한 뇌우가 내리겠습니다.

|어휘| put on ~을 바르다 severe [형] 극심한 thunderstorm [명] 뇌우

02 ①

M How was your weekend? Did you go to the zoo?
W No, I didn't. Look at this photo.
M Oh! You went to the beach! Who is that girl with the long hair?
W That's my sister. She's jumping in the air because she's so happy.
M And that's you sitting on a towel in front of the palm tree.
W Yes. I'm wearing my new sunglasses.
M You look great!

남 주말 어땠어? 동물원에 갔었어?
여 아니, 안 갔어. 이 사진 좀 봐.
남 아! 해변에 갔었구나! 긴 머리의 저 여자는 누구야?
여 우리 언니야. 언니가 기분이 아주 좋아서 점프하고 있는 거야.
남 그리고 야자수 앞 수건 위에 앉아 있는 건 너구나.
여 맞아. 새로 산 선글라스를 끼고 있지.
남 너 멋지다!

|어휘| palm tree 야자수

03 ③

W Are you packing to go back to England?
M Yes. I'm almost finished.
W Be careful not to forget anything important.
M I will. By the way, I bought this for you.
W Oh! Can I open it now?
M Yes. I wanted to give you something for being so kind.
W These gloves are great. Thank you!
M You're welcome. You really made me feel like part of your family.

여 영국으로 돌아가려고 짐 싸고 있니?
남 네. 거의 끝났어요.
여 중요한 것을 잊지 않도록 주의하렴.
남 그럴게요. 그나저나, 이거 드리려고 샀어요.
여 어머나! 지금 열어봐도 되니?
남 네. 정말 친절하게 대해 주셔서 뭔가 드리고 싶었어요.
여 이 장갑 정말 멋지다. 고맙구나!
남 천만에요. 제가 정말 가족의 일원처럼 느끼게 해 주셨잖아요.

|어휘| pack [동] 짐을 싸다 glove [명] 장갑 [문제] curious [형] 궁금한 bored [형] 지루한 thankful [형] 고맙게 생각하는 relaxed [형] 느긋한

04 ④

W I'm so hungry!
M Why? Lunch was only an hour ago.
W I skipped lunch today.
M Oh. Did you go to the gym during lunch?
W No, I went to the bank to open a new checking account.
M The lines are always much longer during lunchtime.
W I know, but I couldn't do it any other time.
M I see. I have some leftover pasta in the office refrigerator. Would you like some?
W Yes! Thank you so much.

여 정말 배고파!
남 왜? 불과 한 시간 전에 점심시간이었잖아.
여 나 오늘 점심을 걸렀어.
남 아. 점심시간에 헬스장 갔었니?
여 아니, 새 예금 계좌를 개설하려고 은행에 갔었어.
남 점심시간에는 언제나 줄이 훨씬 더 길잖아.
여 맞아, 근데 다른 시간에는 할 수가 없었어.
남 그렇구나. 사무실 냉장고에 남은 파스타가 있어. 좀 줄까?
여 응! 정말 고마워.

|어휘| skip lunch 점심을 거르다 gym [명] 체육관, 헬스장 checking account 예금 계좌 leftover [형] 나머지의, 남은 office [명] 사무실

05 ②

W Excuse me, are you Park Minsung?
M Yes, I am. Are you Sue Johnson?
W Yes, I'm your tour guide. Welcome to Chicago. I thought I missed you.
M Sorry. It took a while to get my luggage.
W That's all right. How was your flight?
M It was very long. I'm glad to finally be here.
W I'm glad you're here, too. I have a car outside. I'll drive you to your hotel.
M Thanks.

여 실례지만, 박민성 씨세요?
남 네, 맞습니다. Sue Johnson 씨세요?
여 네, 제가 손님의 여행 가이드입니다. 시카고에 오신 것을 환영합니다. 손님을 놓친 줄 알았어요.
남 죄송해요. 짐 찾는 데 시간이 한참 걸렸어요.
여 괜찮습니다. 비행은 어떠셨어요?
남 정말 길었어요. 드디어 여기 와서 좋네요.
여 손님이 오셔서 저도 기쁩니다. 밖에 차가 있어요. 호텔로 모셔다드릴게요.
남 감사합니다.

|해설| 여자가 비행기를 타고 온 남자를 마중 나온 것으로 보아 대화가 공항에서 이루어지고 있음을 알 수 있다.

|어휘| luggage [명] 짐, 수화물 flight [명] 비행 outside [부] 밖에

06 ②

[Cell phone rings.]
W Hi, Mike! How are you?
M Hi, Janet. I'm doing well. How did you do on the English test?
W I got a perfect score! I'm so happy.
M That's great! We should celebrate. Do you have any plans tonight?
W I'm not doing anything. What do you have in mind?
M Would you like to have dinner with me? I heard that the new Italian restaurant on Oxford Street is good.
W That sounds great, but I had a really big lunch. Maybe next time.

[휴대전화벨이 울린다.]
여 안녕, Mike! 잘 지내?
남 안녕, Janet! 난 잘 지내고 있어. 영어 시험 어떻게 봤어?
여 만점 받았어! 정말 기뻐.
남 멋지다! 우리 축하해야겠다. 오늘 밤에 무슨 계획 있어?
여 아무것도 안 할 거야. 뭐 생각해둔 거 있어?
남 나랑 저녁 먹을래? Oxford 가에 새로 생긴 이탈리아 음식점이 맛있다고 들었는데.
여 그거 좋긴 한데, 내가 점심을 진짜 푸짐하게 먹었어. 다음에 가자.

|어휘| perfect score 만점 celebrate [동] 기념하다, 축하하다

07 ④

M Are you getting ready for the camping trip, Chloe?
W Yes, Dad. I'm almost done.
M The weather report said that it would be cold and cloudy all weekend.
W Then I should bring a warm blanket.
M And don't forget your sleeping bag. What else did you pack?
W I packed clothes, water, snacks, and a lantern.
M What about a tent?
W I don't need to bring a tent. I can rent one at the campsite.
M Good. Oh, make sure you take your first aid kit too.
W Okay, I will.

남 캠핑 여행 갈 준비하고 있니, Chloe?
여 네, 아빠. 거의 다 됐어요.
남 일기 예보에서 주말 내내 춥고 흐릴 거라고 했단다.
여 그럼 따뜻한 담요를 가져가야겠어요.
남 그리고 침낭도 잊지 말아라. 그 밖에 뭘 챙겼니?
여 옷, 물, 간식, 손전등을 챙겼어요.
남 텐트는?
여 텐트는 가져갈 필요 없어요. 캠핑장에서 하나 빌릴 수 있거든요.
남 잘됐구나. 아, 구급상자도 꼭 가져가렴.
여 네, 그럴게요.

|어휘| blanket [명] 담요 sleeping bag 침낭 lantern [명] 손전등 rent [동] 빌리다, 대여하다 campsite [명] 야영지, 캠핑장 first aid kit 구급상자

08 ④

M Where are you going, Ashley?
W I lost my purse on the subway. I'm going to look for it.
M Oh. Did you try the subway lost and found?
W I did, but it wasn't there.
M I'm sorry to hear that. What was in it?

W All my money and a credit card.
M That's terrible. Why don't you call and report the lost card first? Somebody might use it.
W That's a good idea. I should call now.

남 어디 가는 거야, Ashley?
여 지하철에서 지갑을 잃어버렸어. 찾으러 가는 중이야.
남 아, 지하철 분실물 보관소 가봤어?
여 가봤는데, 거기에 없었어.
남 안타깝네. 안에 뭐 들어있었는데?
여 내 돈 전부랑 신용카드.
남 큰일이네. 전화해서 카드 분실 신고부터 하는 게 어때? 누가 쓸지도 모르잖아.
여 좋은 생각이다. 지금 전화해야겠어.

|어휘| lost and found 분실물 보관소

09 ②

W I've recently started a poetry club with a couple of classmates. Is there any chance you might be interested?
M Well, what does the club do?
W We read our favorite poems together and discuss their themes. We sometimes write poems too.
M Can anyone just join the club?
W It is open to any student with a love of poetry. So far, we have six members, including me.
M How often does the club meet?
W Once a month. We meet on the last Saturday of every month. Will you join?
M I'll think about it.

여 내가 최근에 반 친구들 몇 명과 시 동아리를 만들었거든. 혹시 너 관심 있니?
남 글쎄, 그 동아리는 뭘 하는데?
여 좋아하는 시를 함께 읽고 주제에 대해 토론해. 가끔 시를 쓰기도 하고.
남 아무나 그 동아리에 가입할 수 있니?
여 시를 사랑하는 모든 학생에게 열려 있어. 지금까지는 나를 포함해서 여섯 명의 회원이 있어.
남 그 동아리는 얼마나 자주 만나?
여 한 달에 한 번. 매달 마지막 토요일에 만나. 들어올래?
남 생각해 볼게.

|어휘| recently [부] 최근에 poem [명] (한 편의) 시 discuss [동] 토론하다 theme [명] 주제

10 ④

M It's difficult to choose a future career. There are many kinds of jobs. There are even some you don't know about. That's why you should gather as much information as possible before choosing a career. You can find a lot of useful information online. Also, visiting local job centers is a good idea. The people there will help you. You can learn about the jobs that interest you most.

남 미래의 직업을 선택하는 것은 어렵습니다. 많은 종류의 직업이 있죠. 심지어 여러분이 알지 못하는 것도 있습니다. 그것이 직업을 선택하기 전에 가능한 한 많은 정보를 모아야 하는 이유입니다. 여러분은 온라인에서 유용한 정보를 많이 찾을 수 있습니다. 또한, 지역 직업 안내소를 방문하는 것도 좋은 생각입니다. 그곳 사람들이 여러분을 도와줄 것입니다. 여러분은 여러분의 관심을 가장 많이 끄는 직업들에 대해 알 수 있습니다.

|어휘| future [형] 미래의 career [명] 직업 gather [동] 모으다 as ~ as possible 될 수 있는 대로, 가급적 useful [형] 유용한 local [형] 지역의 interest [동] ~의 관심을 끌다

11 ⑤

M Your English is so good, Sejin! Did you study abroad?
W Thank you! I studied in Vancouver, Canada last year. My uncle lives there.
M Wow! How long were you there?
W Six months. I went to school there, and I made a lot of new friends from other countries.
M That's great!
W My closest friend was from France. After meeting her, I want to study French, too.
M It sounds like you had a wonderful experience.
W I really did!

남 너 영어 정말 잘한다, 세진아! 외국에서 공부했니?
여 고마워! 작년에 캐나다 밴쿠버에서 공부했어. 삼촌이 거기 사시거든.
남 와! 거기서 얼마나 있었어?
여 6개월. 거기서 학교도 다니고, 다른 나라에서 온 친구도 많이 사귀었어.
남 멋지다!
여 가장 친한 친구는 프랑스 출신이었어. 그 친구를 만나고 나니, 나도 프랑스어를 배우고 싶어.
남 멋진 경험을 한 것 같다.
여 정말 그랬어!

|어휘| abroad [부] 해외에서, 해외에 experience [명] 경험

12 ⑤

[Telephone rings.]

M Good morning. This is Smile Dental Clinic.

W Hi. I'd like to make an appointment with Dr. Green.

M Sure. May I have your name?

W I'm Amy Davis. I've been treated by Dr. Green before.

M Okay. When would you like to see him?

W As soon as possible, please. My tooth hurts so much that I can't chew anything.

M I see. Can you come on Thursday at 10:00 a.m.?

W Is it possible to come sooner?

M Then how about Wednesday at 3:00 p.m.?

W Okay, that's fine.

[전화벨이 울린다.]

남 안녕하세요. 스마일 치과입니다.

여 안녕하세요. Green 선생님께 예약을 하고 싶어서요.

남 네. 성함이 어떻게 되시죠?

여 Amy Davis입니다. 전에 Green 선생님께 치료받은 적 있어요.

남 네. 언제 진료받길 원하세요?

여 최대한 빨리요. 이가 너무 아파서 아무것도 씹을 수가 없어요.

남 그러시군요. 목요일 오전 10시에 오실 수 있으세요?

여 더 빨리 가는 게 가능한가요?

남 그럼 수요일 오후 3시에는 어떠세요?

여 네, 좋아요.

|어휘| dental clinic 치과 make an appointment (진료·상담 등을) 예약하다 treat [동] 치료하다 hurt [동] 아프다 chew [동] 씹다

13 ③

M Hello, I want to see a play, but I'm confused about the ticket prices.

W When would you like to see the play?

M At 1:00 p.m. on Saturday.

W The ticket price is $40.

M Can I use this coupon to get a 20% discount?

W No, that's only for weekdays. But if you have a membership card, you can get a $5 discount on each ticket.

M I have one. I would like two tickets, please.

W Great. Here are your tickets. Enjoy the performance!

남 안녕하세요, 연극을 보고 싶은데, 표 가격이 헷갈리네요.

여 언제 연극을 보고 싶으세요?

남 토요일 오후 1시에요.

여 표 가격은 40달러입니다.

남 이 쿠폰을 써서 20% 할인받을 수 있나요?

여 아니요, 그 쿠폰은 평일에만 사용하실 수 있어요. 하지만 회원 카드를 소지하고 계시면, 표 한 장당 5달러를 할인받으실 수 있어요.

남 저 있어요. 표 두 장 주세요.

여 좋습니다. 여기 표 있습니다. 공연 재미있게 보세요!

|해설| 회원 카드로 장당 5달러를 할인받을 수 있으므로 표 두 장을 구입하려는 남자는 총 80달러에서 10달러를 할인받을 수 있다.

|어휘| confused [형] 헷갈리는 discount [명] 할인 weekday [명] 평일 performance [명] 공연

14 ③

M Wait a minute. Do you live in this apartment building?

W No, I'm a visitor.

M What brings you here?

W My friend just moved here, and I was invited to her housewarming party.

M I should check before letting you in. Which apartment does your friend live in? I need to check my list.

W She's in 106. And my name is Valerie Smith.

M *[pause]* Okay, you're on my list. Go ahead.

남 잠시만요. 이 아파트에 사십니까?

여 아니요, 저는 방문객이에요.

남 무슨 일로 오셨나요?

여 제 친구가 여기로 막 이사를 와서, 집들이에 초대받았거든요.

남 들여보내드리기 전에 확인을 해야겠네요. 친구분이 어느 아파트에 사시나요? 명단을 확인해야 합니다.

여 106호입니다. 제 이름은 Valerie Smith고요.

남 [잠시 후] 됐습니다, 명단에 있네요. 들어가십시오.

|어휘| invite [동] 초대하다 housewarming party 집들이 list [명] 목록, 명단

15 ④

W Good morning, Don.

M Hi, Peggy. Our meeting is scheduled for next Tuesday.

W Oh, good. Do we need to order some coffee and donuts for the meeting?

M Hmm... No. We'll have the meeting right after lunch.

W All right. *[pause]* Where are you going?

M I need to copy this report. While I'm gone, could you reserve a conference room from 2:00 p.m. to 3:00 p.m.?

W Sure.

여 좋은 아침이에요, Don.

남 안녕하세요, Peggy. 우리 회의가 다음 주 화요일로 예정되었어요.

여 아, 잘됐네요. 회의를 위해서 커피랑 도넛을 좀 주문해야 할까요?

남 음… 아니요. 점심 직후에 회의를 하니까요.

여 알겠어요. [잠시 후] 어디 가세요?

남 이 보고서를 복사해야 해서요. 제가 가는 동안, 오후 2시부터 3시까지 회의실 예약 좀 해주실래요?

여 그러죠.

|어휘| scheduled ⓐ 예정된 order ⓥ 주문하다 copy ⓥ 복사하다 report ⓝ 보고서 reserve ⓥ 예약하다 conference room 회의실

16 ⑤

W Sorry I'm late. Have you been waiting very long?

M For about 40 minutes. I called you several times.

W Sorry. I left my cell phone at home.

M I thought you had an accident. Why are you so late?

W I tried to take a different route, but I got lost.

M Don't you have a navigation system?

W Not anymore. Mine broke.

M Oh, sorry to hear that. Anyway, I'm hungry. Let's get some pizza.

여 늦어서 미안. 아주 오래 기다렸니?

남 대략 40분 동안. 너한테 전화 여러 번 했는데.

여 미안해. 집에 휴대전화를 놓고 왔어.

남 사고 난 줄 알았잖아. 왜 이렇게 늦은 거야?

여 다른 경로로 오려다가, 길을 잃었어.

남 내비게이션 있지 않아?

여 이젠 없어. 내 것 고장 났거든.

남 아, 안타깝네. 어쨌든 나 배고파. 피자 먹자.

|어휘| accident ⓝ 사고 route ⓝ 경로 get lost 길을 잃다 navigation system 운행 유도 시스템

17 ③

① W What's wrong? You don't look good.

  M I have a stomachache.

② W Do you want me to get some medicine for you?

  M No thanks. I feel better now.

③ W My stomach feels upset. I think I ate something bad.

  M I see. Take these pills three times a day.

④ W Is there a pharmacy near here?

  M Yes. Go straight two blocks and turn left.

⑤ W I think I'm getting the flu.

M Why don't you see a doctor? I'll go with you.

① 여 무슨 일이니? 너 안 좋아 보여.

  남 배가 아파.

② 여 내가 약을 좀 사다 줄까?

  남 아니, 괜찮아. 이제 나았어.

③ 여 속이 안 좋아요. 뭔가 상한 걸 먹은 것 같아요.

  남 그러시군요. 이 알약을 하루 세 번 복용하세요.

④ 여 여기 근처에 약국이 있나요?

  남 네. 두 블록 직진해서 왼쪽으로 도세요.

⑤ 여 나 독감에 걸린 것 같아.

  남 병원에 가는 게 어때? 내가 같이 갈게.

|어휘| stomachache ⓝ 복통 medicine ⓝ 약 stomach ⓝ 위, 배 take ⓥ (약을) 복용하다 pill ⓝ 알약 pharmacy ⓝ 약국 go straight 직진하다 turn left 좌회전하다 flu ⓝ 독감

18 ④

M Good morning, students! The sports day will be held on May 4. It will start at nine o'clock in the morning, and you will need to come to school by 8:40. You should come in your PE uniform and trainers. A variety of games and activities will be waiting for you. There will also be prizes for the winners. I'm sure that everyone will have a great time!

남 좋은 아침입니다, 학생 여러분! 운동회 날이 5월 4일에 개최될 것입니다. 오전 9시에 시작할 예정이므로, 여러분은 8시 40분까지 등교해야 합니다. 체육복과 운동화를 착용하고 와야 합니다. 여러 가지 경기와 활동이 여러분을 기다리고 있을 것입니다. 우승자에게는 상도 있을 것입니다. 분명 모두가 좋은 시간을 보낼 것입니다!

|어휘| sports day 운동회 날 PE uniform 체육복 trainer ⓝ 운동화 a variety of 여러 가지의

19 ②

W You look anxious, Matt. Is everything okay?

M Well, I have a date with Somin tonight.

W What are you going to do on your date?

M I'm going to take her out to dinner. Then we're going to a musical.

W That sounds like a great plan. I don't understand why you're worried.

M Well, what if she doesn't like me? What if I say something silly?

W Don't worry. It'll be fine.

① Never do that again.
③ Please say hello to her for me.
④ How about going to a musical with me?
⑤ What restaurant are you going to?

여 너 불안해 보인다, Matt. 괜찮아?
남 음, 오늘 밤에 소민이랑 데이트가 있거든.
여 데이트 때 뭐 할 거야?
남 소민이를 저녁 식사 자리에 데려갈 거야. 그러고 나서 뮤지컬을 보러 가려고 해.
여 진짜 좋은 계획 같은데. 네가 왜 걱정하는지 이해가 안 돼.
남 음, 그 애가 나를 안 좋아하면 어쩌지? 내가 바보 같은 말을 하면?
여 걱정하지 마. 잘 될 거야.

① 다시는 그렇게 하지 마.
③ 그 애한테 나 대신 안부 인사 전해줘.
④ 나랑 뮤지컬 보러 가는 게 어때?
⑤ 너희 어떤 음식점에 갈 거야?

|어휘| anxious ⓗ 불안해하는 musical ⓝ 뮤지컬 What if ~? ~라면 어쩌지? silly ⓗ 바보 같은, 어리석은 [문제] say hello to ~에게 안부를 전하다

20 ①

W I can't wait for the party tonight.
M I'm looking forward to it, too. There will be a lot of good food.
W Yes. Minji is an excellent cook! Do you think Sehoon will come to the party?
M No. I asked him to come, but he said he can't make it.
W Why? Does he have other plans?
M Yes, he needs to help his sister move tonight.
W That's too bad. I wanted to see him.

② It was nice to see her yesterday.
③ He had a great time at the party.
④ Sehoon likes Minji's cooking, too.
⑤ Her new apartment is 20 minutes from here.

여 오늘 밤 파티가 기다려져.
남 나도 기대하고 있어. 맛있는 음식이 많을 거야.
여 그래. 민지는 요리를 아주 잘하니까! 세훈이가 파티에 올 것 같니?
남 아니. 내가 오라고 했는데, 참석 못 한대.
여 왜? 다른 계획이 있나?
남 응, 오늘 밤에 누나가 이사하는 것을 도와야 한대.
여 정말 아쉽다. 그 애 보고 싶었는데.

② 어제 그 애를 봐서 좋았어.
③ 그 애는 파티에서 좋은 시간을 보냈어.
④ 세훈이도 민지의 요리를 좋아해.
⑤ 그 애의 새로운 아파트는 여기서 20분 거리야.

|어휘| can't wait 기다려지다 make it (모임 등에) 가다[참석하다]

어휘·표현 다지기   p. 141

A

01 점심을 거르다   02 극심한
03 불안해하는   04 신용카드
05 기념하다, 축하하다   06 바보 같은, 어리석은
07 토론하다   08 약국
09 분실물 보관소   10 짐, 수화물
11 해외에서, 해외에   12 유용한
13 씹다   14 주제
15 (한 편의) 시   16 손전등

B

01 recently   02 a variety of
03 route   04 first aid kit
05 confused   06 leftover
07 checking account   08 get lost
09 treat   10 make it

실전 모의고사 4회   pp. 142-143

01 ①	02 ①	03 ③	04 ②	05 ⑤
06 ②	07 ⑤	08 ⑤	09 ③	10 ④
11 ⑤	12 ③	13 ①	14 ④	15 ②
16 ④	17 ③	18 ④	19 ②	20 ③

01 ①

W Good evening. Here is tomorrow's weather forecast for Western Europe. There will be some changes in the weather tomorrow. It will rain in London for most of the day. Paris has been cloudy all week, and it will remain cloudy tomorrow. Rome is going to get some sunny, warm weather. Finally, there is a chance of snow in Berlin tomorrow.

여 안녕하십니까. 서유럽의 내일 일기 예보입니다. 내일은 날씨에 다소 변화가 있겠습니다. 런던은 하루 대부분 비가 내리겠습니다. 파리는 일주일 내내 흐렸는데요, 내일도 계속해서 구름이 끼겠습니다. 로마는 화창하고 따뜻한 날씨가 될 것입니다. 마지막으로, 베를린에는 내일 눈이 올 가능성이 있습니다.

|어휘| remain [동] 계속 ~이다 chance [명] 가능성

02 ①

W I'm going to buy one of these pencil cases.
M Which one? I like the plastic ones.
W I'm going to get a cloth one with a zipper on top.
M I see. I like the one with the happy face on it.
W So do I. But I will get the one with a flower on it.
M Oh, that's nice too.

여 나 이 필통 중에서 하나 살 거야.
남 어떤 거? 나는 플라스틱 필통이 좋은데.
여 나는 상단에 지퍼가 있는 천 필통을 사려고.
남 그렇구나. 나는 웃는 얼굴이 있는 게 마음에 들어.
여 나도. 그렇지만 나는 꽃이 있는 필통을 살 거야.
남 아, 그것도 멋지네.

|어휘| pencil case 필통 cloth [명] 천 on top 맨 위에 face [명] 얼굴

03 ③

W Is something bothering you, Tom?
M Sort of, but it's nothing important.
W Come on. Tell me. What's wrong?
M Well, I had an argument with Jimin today. I made fun of her, and she got upset. I shouldn't have done that.
W It's okay. If you apologize to her tomorrow, she'll forgive you.
M Okay. I'll do that tomorrow morning. Thank you, Mom.

여 신경 쓰이는 일 있니, Tom?
남 그렇긴 한데, 중요한 건 아니에요.
여 그러지 말고. 나에게 말해봐. 뭐가 문제니?
남 음, 지민이랑 오늘 말다툼을 했어요. 제가 놀려서, 지민이 마음이 상했어요. 그러지 말았어야 했는데요.
여 괜찮아. 내일 사과하면, 그 애가 용서해 줄 거야.
남 알겠어요. 내일 아침에 그렇게 할게요. 고마워요, 엄마.

|해설| 남자는 친구를 놀린 자신의 행동을 후회하고 있다.

|어휘| bother [동] 신경 쓰이게 하다, 괴롭히다 argument [명] 언쟁, 말다툼 make fun of ~을 놀리다 upset [형] 마음이 상한, 속상한 apologize [동] 사과하다 forgive [동] 용서하다 **[문제]** proud [형] 자랑스러워하는 pleased [형] 기쁜 regretful [형] 후회하는

04 ②

[Cell phone rings.]
W Hello?
M Hi, it's Eric.
W Oh, hi! Are you getting ready to move into your dormitory room?
M Actually, I did that yesterday. I spent all day cleaning my room today.
W It would have been good if I could have helped you out. I had to go to a wedding.
M That's okay. I understand. How about having dinner together tonight?
W That would be great.

[휴대전화벨이 울린다.]
여 여보세요?
남 안녕, 나 Eric이야.
여 아, 안녕! 기숙사 방으로 들어갈 준비를 하고 있니?
남 실은 어제 들어왔어. 오늘은 내 방 치우느라 하루를 다 보냈네.
여 내가 널 도울 수 있었다면 좋았을 텐데. 나는 결혼식에 가야 했어.
남 괜찮아. 이해해. 오늘 밤에 저녁 식사 같이 하는 거 어때?
여 좋아.

|어휘| get ready to-v ~할 준비를 하다 dormitory [명] 기숙사 spend ~ v-ing …하느라 ~을 보내다 wedding [명] 결혼식

05 ⑤

M Look at those clouds! They are so beautiful!
W I know. The view is amazing! I still can't believe we are in the air.
M Wow, look at how small the houses are down there!
W Yes, they look like dollhouses.
M Aren't we going to land pretty soon?
W What time is it?
M It's 1:45 p.m.
W Oh. You're right. The pilot will make an announcement soon.

남 저 구름 봐! 정말 아름답다!
여 그러니까. 경치가 놀라워! 아직도 우리가 공중에 있다는 게 믿기지 않아.
남 와, 저 밑에 집들이 얼마나 작은지 봐!
여 응, 인형의 집처럼 보인다.
남 우리 이제 곧 착륙하지 않아?
여 몇 시지?
남 오후 1시 45분이야.
여 아, 그렇네. 조종사가 곧 안내 방송하겠다.

|어휘| view [명] 경치 amazing [형] 놀라운 still [부] 아직도, 여전히 in the air 공중에 dollhouse [명] 인형의 집 land [동] 착륙하다 pretty [부] 꽤 make an announcement 발표하다

06 ②

M We need to hurry. Let's cross the road now.
W Wait! There isn't a crosswalk here.
M I know, but the crosswalk is too far away. We don't have time.
W Isn't it dangerous? We could be hit by a car.
M Don't worry. There isn't a lot of traffic today.
W That doesn't matter. You should always use a crosswalk.

남 서둘러야 해. 지금 길 건너자.
여 잠깐만! 여기는 횡단보도가 없잖아.
남 알아, 근데 횡단보도가 너무 멀잖아. 우리 시간 없어.
여 위험하지 않아? 우리 차에 치일 수도 있어.
남 걱정하지 마. 오늘은 교통량이 많지 않으니까.
여 그건 중요하지 않아. 항상 횡단보도를 이용해야 해.

|어휘| hurry [동] 서두르다 cross the road 길을 건너다 crosswalk [명] 횡단보도 dangerous [형] 위험한 hit [동] 치다 traffic [명] 교통량 matter [동] 중요하다

07 ⑤

W How do you like Korea so far?
M It's beautiful.
W What places have you been to?
M Many places. I was just in Seoul and Gyeongju.
W Great! I recommend you also visit Jeju and Busan. Those cities have wonderful beaches.
M Oh, I went to Jeju when I first came to Korea, and I was in Busan last weekend.
W So where will you go next?
M I'm going to Jeonju tomorrow.

여 지금까지 한국은 어떤 것 같아?
남 아름다워.
여 어떤 곳에 가봤어?
남 많은 곳들. 서울과 경주에 있었어.
여 잘했네! 제주랑 부산도 방문하는 것을 추천할게. 그 도시들에는 멋진 해변이 있거든.
남 아, 한국에 처음 왔을 때 제주는 가 봤고, 지난 주말에는 부산에 있었어.
여 그럼 다음에는 어디 갈 거야?
남 내일 전주에 갈 거야.

|어휘| so far 지금까지 place [명] 장소, 곳 recommend [동] 추천하다 city [명] 도시

08 ⑤

W Did you know there's a new gym across the street?
M Yeah, I know. I have already been working out there.
W Wow! You're fast! I'm going to the gym to register now.
M Actually, you can get a discount if you sign up online.
W Oh, really?
M They're having a special offer right now. You can get 20% off on their website.
W That sounds good. I'll sign up now.

여 길 건너편에 새 헬스장 있는 것 알고 있었어?
남 응, 알아. 나는 벌써 거기서 운동하고 있어.
여 와! 빠르다! 나는 지금 등록하러 갈 거야.
남 사실 온라인에서 등록하면 할인받을 수 있어.
여 아, 정말?
남 지금 특별 할인 진행 중이야. 웹사이트에서 20% 할인받을 수 있어.
여 좋다. 지금 등록해야겠어.

|어휘| work out 운동하다 register [동] 등록하다 discount [명] 할인 sign up 등록하다 special offer 특별 할인

09 ③

W This area is always crowded. Where should I park?
M There is a parking lot at the back of that building.
W Oh yeah? Is it a big parking lot?
M Not really, but I guess around twenty cars could park there.
W How much does it cost?
M Let me check. *[pause]* It's 1,000 won for the first thirty minutes and 500 won for every additional ten minutes.
W Don't you think it's a little expensive?
M Oh, electric car drivers like you can get a 50% parking discount.
W Nice. Let's go there, then.

여 이 지역은 항상 혼잡하네. 어디에 주차해야 하지?
남 저 건물 뒤편에 주차장이 있어.
여 아, 그래? 큰 주차장이니?
남 꼭 그렇지는 않은데, 내 생각에 거기 차 20대 정도 주차할 수 있을 것 같아.
여 비용이 얼마야?

남 확인해 볼게. [잠시 후] 최초 30분은 1,000원이고, 추가 10분당 500원이야.
여 조금 비싼 것 같지 않니?
남 아, 너처럼 전기 자동차 운전자는 50% 주차 할인받을 수 있어.
여 좋아. 그럼 거기로 가자.

|어휘| area [명] 지역, 구역 crowded [형] 붐비는, 혼잡한 park [동] 주차하다 parking lot 주차장 additional [형] 추가의 electric car 전기 자동차

10 ④

W A few days ago, something strange happened. Someone logged into my messenger account and asked my friends for money. When I tried to log in, I couldn't. I realized somebody had stolen my password. In order to prevent this from happening to you, you should change your passwords frequently. It's a good idea to change each password at least once every three months.

여 며칠 전에 이상한 일이 일어났습니다. 누군가 제 메신저 계정으로 접속해서 제 친구들에게 돈을 요구했죠. 제가 접속을 하려고 했을 때, 할 수가 없었습니다. 누군가 제 비밀번호를 도용했다는 것을 깨달았어요. 여러분에게 이런 일이 발생하는 것을 막기 위해서는 비밀번호를 자주 변경하셔야 합니다. 적어도 3개월에 한 번씩 각 비밀번호를 변경하는 것이 좋은 방안입니다.

|어휘| happen [동] 일어나다, 발생하다 log into ~에 접속하다 account [명] 계정, 계좌 realize [동] 깨닫다 steal [동] 훔치다, 도용하다 password [명] 비밀번호 prevent [동] 막다 frequently [부] 자주 at least 적어도

11 ⑤

W You look tired, Harry.
M I got up at 4:30 this morning.
W Four thirty? Why did you get up so early?
M We have an important baseball game next month, so our team was practicing. We all gather at 5:30 every morning and practice for three hours.
W Every morning?
M Yes, before school starts. We even practice in the rain.
W That must be hard, but I'm sure it will pay off.

여 너 피곤해 보인다, Harry.
남 오늘 아침에 4시 30분에 일어났거든.
여 4시 30분? 왜 그렇게 일찍 일어났니?
남 우리 팀이 다음 달에 중요한 야구 시합이 있어서, 연습하고 있었어. 매일 아침 5시 30분에 모두 모여서 3시간 동안 연습을 해.
여 매일 아침?
남 응, 학교 시작하기 전에. 심지어 빗속에서도 연습해.
여 그건 분명히 힘들겠지만, 성과가 있을 거라 확신해.

|어휘| gather [동] 모이다 pay off 성과가 있다

12 ③

[Telephone rings.]
W Shari's Shop. How may I help you?
M Can I place an order for May 8?
W Sure. Are you interested in some flowers for Parents' Day?
M That's right. I heard you deliver baskets of flowers.
W We do. It's $40 for a large basket, and $30 for a small one.
M Great! I'd like to have a large basket delivered to my parents' home.

[전화벨이 울린다.]
여 Shari's Shop입니다. 무엇을 도와드릴까요?
남 5월 8일 자로 주문할 수 있을까요?
여 물론이죠. 어버이날을 위한 꽃에 관심 있으신가요?
남 맞습니다. 꽃바구니를 배달해 주신다고 들었습니다.
여 네. 큰 바구니는 40달러이고, 작은 바구니는 30달러입니다.
남 좋네요! 저희 부모님 댁으로 큰 바구니를 배달시키고 싶어요.

|어휘| place an order 주문하다 deliver [동] 배달하다

13 ①

W Hi, how much are those gloves?
M Do you mean these leather ones? They're $35.
W That's too expensive. What about the wool gloves?
M They are a little cheaper. They are $30.
W That's still too expensive.
M Well, we have knitted gloves. They are really warm, and they're only $15.
W Wow! That's $20 cheaper than the leather ones. I'll take them.

여 안녕하세요, 저 장갑은 얼마인가요?
남 이 가죽 장갑 말씀이신가요? 35달러입니다.
여 너무 비싸네요. 그 모직 장갑은요?
남 조금 더 저렴합니다. 30달러예요.
여 그것도 역시 너무 비싸요.
남 음, 니트로 된 장갑이 있는데요. 정말 따뜻하고, 겨우 15달러밖에 안 해요.
여 와! 가죽 장갑보다 20달러 더 싸네요. 그걸로 할게요.

|어휘| leather [형] 가죽의 wool [형] 모직의 cheap [형] 저렴한 knitted [형] 뜨개질한, 니트로 된

14 ④

M Hello. It's been a while since I've seen you.
W Yes, I've been busy. But now I have a sore throat.
M I see. How long have you had it?
W For about one week. It started after I went skiing.
M Please open your mouth wide. *[pause]* Oh, yes. It seems your throat is red and swollen. Remember to drink a lot of hot water.
W Okay.

남 안녕하세요. 오랜만에 뵙네요.
여 네, 계속 바빴어요. 그런데 지금 목이 아파서요.
남 알겠습니다. 목이 아픈 지 얼마나 되셨나요?
여 일주일 정도요. 스키 타러 다녀온 후로 아프기 시작했어요.
남 입을 크게 벌려보세요. [잠시 후] 아, 그렇네요. 목이 빨갛고 부어 올라 보이네요. 따뜻한 물 많이 드시는 것 기억하세요.
여 알겠습니다.

|어휘| have a sore throat 목이 아프다 seem [동] ~인 것처럼 보이다 swollen [형] 부어오른

15 ②

M I'm going to a photography exhibit tomorrow. Would you like to come with me?
W I wish I could, but my grandmother's birthday is this weekend.
M So why can't you come tomorrow?
W I need to buy her something. I have to go shopping tomorrow.
M That's too bad. I think you'd enjoy the photos.
W I think so, too. Could you buy me some postcards from the museum's gift shop?
M Sure. I promise I will.

남 나 내일 사진전에 갈 거야. 나랑 같이 갈래?
여 나도 그러고 싶은데, 우리 할머니 생신이 이번 주말이야.
남 그런데 내일 왜 못 가?
여 할머니께 뭔가 사 드려야 하거든. 내일 쇼핑 가야 해.
남 아쉽다. 네가 사진 좋아할 거라고 생각했는데.
여 나도 그래. 미술관 기념품점에서 나에게 엽서 좀 사다 줄 수 있니?
남 물론이지. 꼭 사다 줄게.

|어휘| photography [명] 사진(술) exhibit [명] 전시회 postcard [명] 엽서 gift shop 기념품점 promise [동] 약속하다

16 ④

M Hi, Minju. Are your students ready for the music competition tomorrow?
W Actually, there is a small problem with my classroom.
M What's wrong with it? Is the air conditioner out of order again?
W No, that's fine. But I only have one piano.
M Really? I have two pianos in my classroom.
W You do? Can we switch classrooms then? Two of my students are playing a duet.
M Sure. I don't mind.
W Thanks!

남 안녕하세요, 민주 선생님. 선생님 반 학생들 내일 음악 경연 대회 준비는 다 되었나요?
여 실은, 저희 교실에 작은 문제가 있어요.
남 뭐가 잘못됐어요? 에어컨이 또 고장 났나요?
여 아니요, 그건 괜찮아요. 그런데 피아노가 한 대밖에 없어요.
남 정말요? 저희 교실에는 피아노가 두 대 있어요.
여 그래요? 그러면 교실을 바꿔 주실 수 있나요? 학생 둘이 이중주를 하거든요.
남 물론이죠. 상관없어요.
여 고마워요!

|해설| 여자는 이중주를 하는 두 학생을 위해 피아노가 두 대 있는 남자의 교실과 자신의 교실을 바꾸고 싶어 한다.

|어휘| competition [명] (경연) 대회 air conditioner 에어컨 out of order 고장 난 switch [동] 바꾸다 play a duet 이중주를 하다 mind [동] 상관하다

17 ③

① **M** Good afternoon. How can I help you?
W I'm trying to find Gate 17.
② **M** Do you need me to pick you up at the airport?
W No, I'll just take a taxi home.
③ **M** Welcome back! Did you have a nice trip?
W Yes! I have so many stories to tell you.
④ **M** Excuse me. What time will we be landing?
W We should be arriving in about one hour.
⑤ **M** Have you booked our flight tickets?
W Not yet. I'll do that tomorrow morning.

① **남** 안녕하세요. 무엇을 도와드릴까요?
여 17번 탑승구를 찾고 있어요.
② **남** 내가 공항으로 너 마중 나갈까?
여 아니요, 그냥 집에 택시 타고 갈게요.
③ **남** 돌아온 걸 환영해! 여행 잘 했니?

여 네! 말씀드리고 싶은 이야기가 정말 많아요.
④ 남 실례합니다. 몇 시에 착륙하나요?
여 대략 한 시간 뒤에 도착할 겁니다.
⑤ 남 우리 항공권 예약했니?
여 아직이요. 내일 아침에 할 거예요.

|어휘| airport [명] 공항 arrive [동] 도착하다 book [동] 예약하다 flight ticket 항공권

18 ④

W Our company is looking for a computer engineer. We need someone who can start work right away. We're looking for someone with more than two years of work experience in the field. The hours are 9:00 a.m. to 6:00 p.m., Monday to Friday. If you are interested in this job, please call us at 555–1352.

여 저희 회사에서 컴퓨터 엔지니어를 구하고 있습니다. 바로 일을 시작할 수 있는 분을 원합니다. 업계에서 2년 이상의 경력이 있는 지원자를 찾고 있습니다. (근무) 시간은 월요일부터 금요일, 오전 9시부터 오후 6시까지입니다. 이 일에 관심이 있으시면, 555–1352로 전화해 주시기 바랍니다.

|어휘| company [명] 회사 work experience 경력 field [명] 분야

19 ②

W Hi. How can I help you?
M I bought these wireless speakers here yesterday, but there's something wrong with them.
W What seems to be the problem?
M They only work for a few minutes, and then they turn off.
W Did you check the battery?
M Yes, the battery is fine. I even tried replacing it.
W I see. In that case, you can exchange them.
M Actually, can I just get a refund?
W Yes, if you have a receipt.

① No, I don't need one.
③ There's nothing wrong with them.
④ They will be fixed in a few days.
⑤ Thanks, but that's not necessary.

여 안녕하세요. 무엇을 도와드릴까요?
남 어제 여기서 이 무선 스피커를 샀는데, 뭔가 문제가 있는 것 같아요.
여 무슨 문제인 것 같으세요?
남 겨우 몇 분 작동하고 나서는 전원이 꺼져요.
여 배터리는 확인하셨나요?
남 네, 배터리는 괜찮아요. 심지어 배터리도 교체했어요.
여 알겠습니다. 그런 경우에는 교환하실 수 있습니다.
남 저, 그냥 환불받을 수 있을까요?
여 네, 영수증을 가지고 계시다면요.

① 아니요, 필요 없어요.
③ 그 물건에는 아무 문제가 없어요.
④ 며칠 뒤에 수리될 겁니다.
⑤ 감사하지만, 그러실 필요 없습니다.

|어휘| wireless [형] 무선의 turn off 꺼지다, 끄다 replace [동] 교체하다, 대체하다 exchange [동] 교환하다 get a refund 환불받다 [문제] receipt [명] 영수증 necessary [형] 필요한

20 ③

M Is everything going well at your new school?
W Well, not really.
M Are you having problems making friends?
W No, I've already made some friends.
M Do you like your teachers?
W Yes, they're all nice to me. The problem is one of my classmates, Taehyeon. He's nice, but he's very talkative during class. I can't concentrate on the class.
M Why don't you tell him?
W I'm afraid that I would hurt his feelings.

① I don't feel well today.
② I look forward to attending my new school.
④ I don't have problems with my classmates.
⑤ I haven't seen him for a long time.

남 새 학교에서는 다 잘 되고 있니?
여 음, 그다지.
남 친구 사귀는 데 문제 있어?
여 아니, 친구는 이미 몇 명 사귀었어.
남 선생님들은 좋아?
여 응, 모두 내게 잘해 주셔. 문제는 우리 반 친구 중 한 명인 태현이야. 얘는 착한데, 수업 시간에 아주 말이 많아. 수업에 집중할 수가 없어.
남 그 애한테 말하지 그래?
여 그 애 기분을 상하게 할까 봐 겁나.

① 오늘 몸이 안 좋아.
② 새로운 학교 다니는 게 기대돼.
④ 반 친구들과는 문제없어.
⑤ 그 애를 오랫동안 보지 못했어.

|어휘| have a problem v-ing ~하는 데 문제가 있다 talkative [형] 수다스러운, 말이 많은 concentrate on ~에 집중하다 [문제] attend [동] ~에 다니다 hurt [동] (감정을) 상하게 하다

어휘·표현 다지기

p. 151

A

01 횡단보도
02 언쟁, 말다툼
03 용서하다
04 자주
05 추가의
06 고장 난
07 (경연) 대회
08 깨닫다
09 막다
10 주차장
11 수다스러운, 말이 많은
12 경력
13 약속하다
14 훔치다, 도용하다
15 등록하다
16 붐비는, 혼잡한

B

01 regretful
02 get ready to-v
03 arrive
04 wireless
05 matter
06 dormitory
07 work out
08 sign up
09 mind
10 place an order

실전 모의고사 5회

pp.152-153

01 ①	02 ④	03 ④	04 ⑤	05 ③
06 ③	07 ②	08 ②	09 ②	10 ③
11 ③	12 ①	13 ②	14 ②	15 ⑤
16 ③	17 ①	18 ⑤	19 ②	20 ③

01 ①

M Good morning! This is Steve Shepard from the Weather Channel. It's going to snow this afternoon, but it will stop by six o'clock tonight. If you're planning to travel today, I advise you to wait until tomorrow morning. The roads will be icy tonight. On Christmas Eve, it will be cold and sunny. It will be windy on Christmas Day, but it won't start snowing again until the day after Christmas.

남 안녕하십니까! 날씨 채널의 Steve Shepard입니다. 오늘 오후에는 눈이 내리겠지만, 오늘 저녁 6시쯤에는 그치겠습니다. 오늘 여행을 계획하고 계신다면, 내일 아침까지 기다려 보시기를 권고드립니다. 오늘 밤에 도로가 얼어붙을 것으로 예상됩니다. 크리스마스이브에는, 춥지만 맑겠습니다. 크리스마스에는 바람이 불겠지만, 눈은 크리스마스 다음 날에서야 다시 오기 시작하겠습니다.

|어휘| advise [동] 권고하다, 충고하다 icy [형] 얼음으로 덮인 the day after 그다음 날

02 ④

W Honey, I want to get some curtains for our new house. The ones we have now are so old.
M Okay. Do you have a particular pattern in mind?
W How about the ones with the triangle pattern? They're really cute.
M I don't like those. I think the ones with birds and trees on them will be good for spring.
W But those would get dirty easily.
M What about the curtains with diamonds on them?
W Those look great!

여 여보, 우리 새집에 달 커튼을 사고 싶어요. 지금 있는 커튼은 무척 오래됐잖아요.
남 그래요. 마음에 둔 특정한 무늬가 있어요?
여 삼각형 무늬가 있는 건 어때요? 정말 귀여워요.
남 나는 그건 마음에 안 들어요. 새와 나무가 있는 게 봄에 좋을 것 같아요.
여 하지만 그 커튼은 쉽게 더러워질 거예요.
남 다이아몬드 무늬가 있는 커튼은 어때요?
여 그거 좋아 보이네요!

|어휘| have ~ in mind ~을 마음에 두다 particular [형] 특정한 pattern [명] 무늬

03 ④

W Hi, Greg. I can tell from your smile that you have good news.
M I do! I made the baseball team!
W Wow! That's great.
M Yes. The coach said I have to practice every day. And training will be hard.
W That sounds tough.
M I know, but I still really want to play! It's been my dream to be on the school team.

여 안녕, Greg. 네 미소를 보니까 좋은 소식이 있는 걸 알겠네.
남 맞아! 나 야구팀에 들어가게 됐어!
여 와! 잘됐다.
남 응. 코치님께서는 내가 매일 연습해야 한다고 말씀하셨어. 그리고 훈련도 힘들 거야.
여 힘들겠다.
남 알아, 그래도 정말 경기하고 싶어! 학교 팀에 들어가는 것은 내 꿈이었어.

|해설| 남자는 자신이 원했던 대로 야구팀에 합류하게 되어 기뻐하고 있다.

|어휘| make a team 팀에 들어가다 training [명] 훈련 hard [형]

어려운, 힘든 tough [형] 힘든

04 ⑤

W How was your weekend, Max?

M It was good. I started my summer job last Saturday. I'm working at an amusement park.

W That sounds great! By the way, do you notice anything different about me?

M Hmm... Did you get a haircut?

W No, I'm wearing glasses. I bought them this afternoon.

M They're stylish! Do you usually wear contacts?

W No, I got my eyes checked last weekend and the doctor said I needed glasses.

여 주말 어떻게 보냈니, Max?

남 잘 보냈어. 나 지난 토요일에 여름 아르바이트를 시작했어. 놀이공원에서 일하고 있어.

여 잘됐다! 그나저나 나 좀 달라진 거 알아챘어?

남 음… 머리 잘랐어?

여 아니, 안경을 쓰고 있잖아. 오늘 오후에 샀어.

남 멋지다! 보통 때는 콘택트렌즈 껴?

여 아니, 지난 주말에 시력 검사를 받았는데 의사 선생님이 내가 안경을 써야 한다고 하시더라고.

|어휘| notice [동] 알아채다 get a haircut 머리를 자르다 stylish [형] 멋진, 유행을 따른 usually [부] 보통, 평상시에 contacts [명] 콘택트렌즈(= contact lens)

05 ③

W I've been waiting all year for this.

M But the course looks dangerous. Are you sure it's safe?

W Of course it is. Let's go!

M I don't want to. I'm really scared.

W Come on. It's not hard. Just take a small step forward.

M But this slope seems very steep.

W It's not as steep as it looks. And once you move forward, you will be able to slide down the slope without effort.

여 나는 일 년 내내 이걸 기다려왔어.

남 그런데 코스가 위험해 보여. 이거 안전한 거 맞아?

여 물론이지. 가자!

남 나는 가고 싶지 않아. 정말 무서워.

여 그러지 말고. 어렵지 않아. 앞으로 발을 조금만 내디뎌봐.

남 하지만 이 슬로프는 아주 가파르게 보여.

여 보이는 것만큼 가파르진 않아. 그리고 일단 앞으로 움직이면, 슬로프를 거뜬히 미끄러져 내려갈 수 있을 거야.

|어휘| scared [형] 무서워하는, 겁먹은 take a step 걸음을 내딛다 forward [부] 앞으로 slope [명] 경사지, 슬로프 steep [형] 가파른 slide down 미끄러져 내려가다 without effort 문제없이, 거뜬히

06 ③

M Did you hear that we're doing group projects?

W Oh, that sounds great. Who do you want as your teammates?

M Honestly, I'm not sure. I usually prefer working alone.

W Really? May I ask why?

M I hate it when someone in the group doesn't work as hard as everyone else.

W I understand. But it's important to learn how to work together with people and communicate with them.

M I guess you're right. Maybe this project can help me develop my teamwork and communication skills.

남 우리 그룹 프로젝트 할 거라는 얘기 들었어?

여 아, 그거 좋다. 누가 팀 동료가 되면 좋겠어?

남 솔직히 잘 모르겠어. 난 보통 혼자 일하는 걸 더 좋아하거든.

여 정말? 왜인지 물어봐도 될까?

남 난 그룹의 누군가가 다른 사람들만큼 열심히 일하지 않으면 싫어.

여 이해해. 하지만 사람들과 함께 일하고 의사소통하는 법을 배우는 것은 중요해.

남 네 말이 맞는 것 같아. 어쩌면 이 프로젝트는 내가 팀워크와 의사소통 기술을 발전시키는 데 도움이 될 수 있을지도 모르겠어.

|어휘| teammate [명] 팀 동료 alone [부] 혼자 important [형] 중요한 communicate [동] 의사소통하다 develop [동] 발전시키다 teamwork [명] 팀워크, 협동 작업 skill [명] 기술

07 ②

[Telephone rings.]

M Hello. This is Queen's Closet. How may I help you?

W Hello. My name is Katy Parker. I sent you an email about my order of a blouse and skirt.

M I will look for it. Has your order not arrived yet?

W Oh, I got it today. But you sent the wrong size.

M I'm sorry to hear that. Can I have your order number, please?

W Sure. It's 230315. The skirt is the right size, but the blouse is too big for me.

M Let me check your email. *[pause]* Oh, we did make a

mistake. You ordered a size 55, but that's a 66.

W Right. Can I exchange the blouse?

M Sure. Please just send it back. We'll send you the right one today.

[전화벨이 울린다.]

남 안녕하세요. Queen's Closet입니다. 무엇을 도와드릴까요?

여 안녕하세요. Katy Parker인데요. 제 블라우스와 치마 주문 관련해서 이메일을 한 통 보냈거든요.

남 찾아볼게요. 주문하신 게 아직 도착하지 않았나요?

여 아, 오늘 받았어요. 그런데 사이즈를 잘못 보내셨어요.

남 죄송합니다. 주문 번호를 알 수 있을까요?

여 네. 230315입니다. 스커트는 맞는 사이즈인데, 블라우스는 저에게 너무 크네요.

남 이메일을 확인해 보겠습니다. [잠시 후] 아, 저희가 실수를 했네요. 55사이즈를 주문하셨는데, 그건 66이네요.

여 맞아요. 블라우스를 교환할 수 있나요?

남 물론입니다. 그건 그냥 반송해 주세요. 맞는 제품을 오늘 보내드리겠습니다.

|어휘| order [명] 주문 [동] 주문하다 arrive [동] 도착하다 yet [부] 아직 make a mistake 실수하다 send back ~을 반송하다

08 ②

W Hey, Ted! Are you ready for your vacation?

M I think so. I'm just worried about leaving my apartment empty while I'm gone.

W It should be okay. Just make sure to lock all the doors and windows.

M I already did.

W Okay. Have you asked a neighbor to take care of your mail?

M Actually, the post office will hold my mail while I'm gone.

W Good. You should also unplug everything before you leave.

M Oh! I didn't think of that. I should do that right now.

여 얘, Ted! 방학 준비는 됐니?

남 그런 것 같아. 떠나 있는 동안에 아파트를 비워두는 게 걱정될 뿐이야.

여 괜찮을 거야. 모든 문이랑 창문을 확실하게 잠가.

남 이미 잠갔어.

여 그래. 이웃한테 우편물 좀 봐달라고 부탁했어?

남 실은 내가 없는 동안 우체국에서 우편물을 보관해줄 거야.

여 잘됐네. 떠나기 전에 전기 플러그도 다 뽑아 놔야 해.

남 아! 그건 생각 못 했네. 지금 당장 해야겠다.

|해설| 남자는 대화 직후에 여자의 충고대로 전기 플러그를 다 뽑을 것이다.

|어휘| empty [형] 빈 neighbor [명] 이웃 hold [동] 보관하다 unplug [동] (전기) 플러그를 뽑다

09 ②

W Have you made any plans for this weekend, Jack?

M I'll work at a flea market this Saturday. It's open from 10:00 a.m. to 1:00 p.m.

W That sounds fun! Is it free admission?

M No, the admission fee is $2. But the money will be donated to an animal hospital.

W Oh, that sounds great.

M It is! And a variety of used jewelry, toys, and clothes will be on sale.

W I'll have to stop by!

여 이번 주말 계획 세웠니, Jack?

남 난 이번 주 토요일에 벼룩시장에서 일할 거야. 오전 10시부터 오후 1시까지 열려.

여 재미있겠다! 무료입장이야?

남 아니, 입장료는 2달러야. 하지만 그 돈은 동물 병원에 기부될 거야.

여 아, 멋지다.

남 맞아! 그리고 여러 가지 중고 보석, 장난감과 옷이 판매될 거야.

여 나도 들러봐야겠다!

|어휘| flea market 벼룩시장 free [형] 무료의 admission (fee) [명] 입장료 donate [동] 기부하다 used [형] 중고의 jewelry [명] 보석 on sale 판매되는, 할인 중인 stop by 들르다

10 ③

M Everyone knows that students must study hard. But they must do other things, too. Their lives should be balanced. In fact, it's important to socialize with friends at school. Also, students need to exercise every day. They also need enough rest to stay healthy. Students are happier and more successful in school when they are both mentally and physically healthy.

남 학생이 공부를 열심히 해야 한다는 것은 누구나 알고 있습니다. 하지만 학생들은 다른 것도 해야 합니다. 그들의 삶은 균형 잡혀야 합니다. 사실, 학교에서 친구들과 어울리는 것은 중요합니다. 또한, 학생들은 매일 운동해야 합니다. 그들은 건강을 유지하기 위해 충분한 휴식도 취할 필요가 있습니다. 정신적으로, 육체적으로 모두 건강할 때, 학생들은 학교에서 더 행복하고 더 성공적일 수 있습니다.

|어휘| balanced [형] 균형 잡힌 in fact 사실은 socialize with

~와 사귀다[어울리다] exercise [동] 운동하다 rest [명] 휴식 stay healthy 건강을 유지하다 successful [형] 성공한, 성공적인 mentally [부] 정신적으로 physically [부] 육체적으로

11 ③

W Ray's Gym is located on Harriet Street next to Woodfield Elementary School. It's open from 6:00 a.m. to 11:00 p.m. on weekdays. On Saturdays, the gym closes at 6:00 p.m., and it doesn't open on Sundays. The gym currently has a special offer for siblings. If two siblings join the gym together and sign up for more than three months, they can each register for an additional month for free.

여 Ray's Gym은 Harriet 가의 Woodfield 초등학교 옆에 위치해 있습니다. 평일에는 오전 6시부터 밤 11시까지 영업합니다. 토요일에는 오후 6시에 닫으며, 일요일에는 영업하지 않습니다. 체육관은 현재 형제자매를 위한 특별 할인 중입니다. 두 명의 형제자매가 함께 3개월 이상 등록하시면, 각각 추가 1개월을 무료로 등록하실 수 있습니다.

|해설| 일요일은 영업하지 않는다고 설명하고 있다.

|어휘| currently [부] 현재 sibling [명] 형제자매 register [동] 등록하다 additional [형] 추가의

12 ①

[Cell phone rings.]

M Hello?

W Hi, Ben.

M Jenny, is everything okay? I waited for you at the theater for an hour yesterday.

W I had to go to the emergency room.

M Really? What happened?

W When I was leaving my house to meet you, I suddenly felt dizzy and fell down.

M That's terrible. Are you all right now?

W I'm okay, but I'm still in the hospital. Sorry that I couldn't make it yesterday.

[휴대전화벨이 울린다.]

남 여보세요?

여 안녕, Ben.

남 Jenny, 다 괜찮은 거야? 어제 영화관에서 널 한 시간 동안 기다렸는데.

여 나 응급실에 가야 했어.

남 정말? 무슨 일이었는데?

여 널 만나려고 집을 나서는데, 갑자기 어지러워서 쓰러졌어.

남 저런. 지금은 괜찮아?

여 괜찮은데, 아직 입원 중이야. 어제 약속 못 지켜서 미안해.

|어휘| emergency room 응급실 dizzy [형] 어지러운 fall down 쓰러지다

13 ②

W What time does the movie start?

M At three.

W Really? We're so early.

M Yeah. I wanted to leave at 2:10 because there is usually a lot of traffic.

W But it only took us twenty minutes today.

M I know! Since we're thirty minutes early, I'm going to get some popcorn.

W Okay. Let's meet back here ten minutes before the movie starts.

M Sounds good.

여 영화 몇 시에 시작해?

남 3시에.

여 정말? 우리 정말 일찍 왔다.

남 응. 평상시에 교통량이 많으니까 2시 10분에 출발하고 싶었거든.

여 근데 오늘은 20분밖에 안 걸렸네.

남 그러니까! 30분 일찍 왔으니까, 난 팝콘 좀 살래.

여 그래. 영화 시작하기 10분 전에 여기서 다시 만나자.

남 좋아.

|해설| 영화는 3시에 시작하는데 두 사람은 영화 시작 30분 전에 도착했다고 했으므로, 현재 시각은 2시 30분이다.

|어휘| traffic [명] 교통량

14 ②

M How are you feeling today, Cindy?

W I'm feeling much better. I want to play in today's game.

M Are you really ready to play soccer? I think you need more rest.

W I'm fine. The doctor said I can start exercising as long as I'm careful.

M Playing in a game is too dangerous. I'm going to ask Jessica to take your place today.

W All right. But can I at least practice with the team?

M Hmm... I'll let you, but don't push yourself too hard.

W Okay.

남 오늘 좀 어떠니, Cindy?

여 저 훨씬 나아졌어요. 오늘 경기에서 뛰고 싶어요.
남 정말 축구 경기를 할 준비됐니? 휴식이 더 필요할 것 같은데.
여 괜찮아요. 의사 선생님께서 제가 조심하기만 하면 운동을 시작해도 된다고 하셨어요.
남 경기에 나가는 건 너무 위험해. 오늘은 Jessica에게 네 자리를 대신하라고 할게.
여 알겠어요. 하지만 최소한 팀과 훈련은 해도 될까요?
남 음… 허락하겠지만, 너무 열심히 애쓰지는 마.
여 알겠어요.

|어휘| take one's place ~의 자리를 대신하다 let [동] 허락하다 push oneself 애쓰다

15 ⑤

W Matt, are you busy?
M Not now, but I'm going to play tennis later.
W Then can you do me a favor?
M What is it?
W I'm going to make sandwiches later today, so I need some eggs and other groceries.
M Do you want me to go grocery shopping?
W No, you don't need to. But could you give me a ride to the supermarket?
M All right. I'll drop you off on my way to the tennis court.
W Great!

여 Matt, 너 바쁘니?
남 지금은 바쁘지 않은데, 이따가 테니스 치러 갈 거야.
여 그러면 내 부탁 좀 들어줄래?
남 뭔데?
여 오늘 이따가 샌드위치 만들 거라, 달걀이랑 다른 식료품이 필요해.
남 내가 장 보러 가길 원하는 거야?
여 아니, 그럴 필요는 없어. 근데 슈퍼마켓까지 나 좀 태워다 줄 수 있어?
남 그래. 테니스장 가는 길에 내려줄게.
여 좋아!

|어휘| do ~ a favor ~의 부탁을 들어주다 grocery [명] 식료품 drop ~ off ~을 내려주다 on one's way to ~로 가는 길에

16 ③

[Cell phone rings.]
W Hello?
M Hi, Whitney.
W What's up, Carl? We're still meeting at 10:00 a.m. to go hiking, right?
M Actually, I have to cancel our plans. Something came up.
W That's disappointing. Do you have to go to work?
M No, my sister gave birth to a baby boy last night. My family is going to see him today.
W Oh, wow! Congratulations on becoming an uncle!
M Thanks. I'm looking forward to meeting my new nephew.

[휴대전화벨이 울린다.]
여 여보세요?
남 안녕, Whitney.
여 무슨 일이야, Carl? 우리 오전 10시에 만나서 하이킹하러 가는 거 맞지?
남 실은, 우리 계획을 취소해야 해. 일이 생겼어.
여 실망스럽다. 출근해야 하는 거야?
남 아니, 우리 누나가 어젯밤에 아들을 낳았거든. 우리 가족은 오늘 아기를 보러 갈 거야.
여 우와! 삼촌 된 걸 축하해!
남 고마워. 새 조카 만나는 걸 고대하는 중이야.

|어휘| cancel [동] 취소하다 disappointing [형] 실망스러운 give birth to (아이)를 낳다 look forward to v-ing ~하기를 고대하다 nephew [명] 조카

17 ①

① **M** I'm interested in renting a swan boat, but I'm not sure how much it costs.
W It costs 20,000 won for 40 minutes.
② **M** I want to swim in the lake. Do you think we can?
W The sign says that people can't swim in the lake. It's too dirty.
③ **M** Can I go fishing here?
W Sure. If you don't have a fishing pole, you can rent one over there.
④ **M** What are we going to do for our picnic?
W We're going to rent a cabin by a lake.
⑤ **M** What kind of bird is that?
W It's a swan. They like to swim in the lake during the summer.

① 남 백조 보트를 빌리고 싶은데, 비용이 얼마인지 모르겠네요.
여 40분에 2만 원입니다.
② 남 호수에서 수영하고 싶다. 우리가 해도 될까?
여 표지판에 호수에서 수영할 수 없다고 쓰여 있어. 물이 너무 더럽대.
③ 남 여기서 낚시해도 되나요?
여 물론이죠. 낚싯대가 없으시면, 저쪽에서 빌리실 수 있어요.

④ 남 우리 소풍 때 뭘 할까?
여 호숫가에 있는 오두막집을 빌릴 예정이야.
⑤ 남 저건 무슨 새야?
여 백조야. 여름에 호수에서 헤엄치는 걸 좋아해.

|어휘| rent [동] 빌리다 sign [명] 표지판 go fishing 낚시하다 fishing pole 낚싯대 cabin [명] 오두막집

18 ⑤

W Good morning, students! I'd like to remind you that our school Halloween party is going to be on Friday, October 31 from 4:00 to 8:00 p.m. The event will be held in the gym, and admission is free for students and teachers. There will be a costume competition and a pie-eating contest. So put on a costume, bring a friend, and have a great time!

여 안녕하세요, 학생 여러분! 우리 학교 핼러윈 파티가 10월 31일 금요일 오후 4시부터 8시까지 열릴 예정임을 다시 한번 알려드립니다. 행사는 체육관에서 개최될 예정이며, 학생과 교사들은 입장료가 무료입니다. 의상 경연 대회와 파이 먹기 대회가 열릴 겁니다. 그러니 의상을 입고 친구를 데려와서 즐거운 시간을 보내세요!

|어휘| remind [동] 상기시키다 event [명] 행사 costume [명] 의상, 분장

19 ②

W Excuse me. I lost my map. Can I get one here?
M Sure. Here you are. Have you been to many places so far?
W Not really. I don't know very much about Seoul.
M I'll mark some places on the map for you.
W Thanks, but I'm not sure how to get around.
M Then I recommend taking the tour bus. It'll take you to the most famous places in the city.
W Thanks for the information.

① Will you go with me?
③ Because I'm not feeling well.
④ I've seen all of the famous places.
⑤ I'm going to stay for five more days.

여 실례합니다. 제가 지도를 잃어버렸는데요. 여기서 하나 얻을 수 있을까요?
남 물론이죠. 여기 있습니다. 그동안 많은 곳을 가보셨나요?
여 그다지요. 제가 서울에 대해 잘 몰라서요.
남 제가 지도에 몇 군데 표시해 드릴게요.
여 감사합니다만, 어떻게 다녀야 할지 모르겠어요.
남 그러면 관광버스 타시는 걸 추천합니다. 관광버스가 시내 명소로 모셔다 드릴 거예요.
여 정보 감사합니다.

① 저랑 함께 가실래요?
③ 제가 몸이 안 좋아서요.
④ 모든 명소들을 봤어요.
⑤ 저는 5일 더 머물 거예요.

|어휘| mark [동] 표시하다 recommend [동] 추천하다 [문제] information [명] 정보

20 ③

[Cell phone rings.]
M Hello?
W Hi, Dan. I'm at a home appliance store now.
M Oh, really? What are you doing there?
W I need to pick out a present for Beth's housewarming party.
M Do you know what she wants?
W Not really. What about a coffeemaker? She really likes coffee.
M I think she already has one. You should call her and ask what she wants.
W That's a good idea. I'll call her now.

① The coffeemakers are on sale.
② Her party is on Saturday at 4:00 p.m.
④ I can't go to the party. I have other plans.
⑤ What if she doesn't like my present?

[휴대전화벨이 울린다.]
남 여보세요?
여 안녕, Dan. 나 지금 가전제품 판매점에 있어.
남 아, 정말? 거기서 뭐 해?
여 Beth의 집들이 선물을 골라야 하거든.
남 그 애가 뭘 갖고 싶어 하는지 알아?
여 글쎄. 커피메이커 어때? 그 애가 커피를 정말 좋아하잖아.
남 내 생각엔 그 애는 이미 가지고 있을 것 같아. 그 애한테 전화해서 뭘 원하는지 물어봐.
여 좋은 생각이야. 지금 전화해야겠어.

① 그 커피메이커는 할인 중이야.
② 그 애의 파티는 토요일 오후 4시에 있어.
④ 나는 파티에 못 가. 다른 계획들이 있어.
⑤ 만약 그 애가 내 선물을 안 좋아하면 어쩌지?

|어휘| home appliance 가정용 전기제품 pick out ~을 고르다

어휘·표현 다지기

p. 161

A

01 현재	02 어지러운
03 알아채다	04 가파른
05 응급실	06 특정한
07 의사소통하다	08 실망스러운
09 표시하다	10 벼룩시장
11 입장료	12 기부하다
13 발전시키다	14 이웃
15 정신적으로	16 권고하다, 충고하다

B

01 physically	02 the day after
03 cabin	04 nephew
05 fall down	06 send back
07 sibling	08 unplug
09 socialize with	10 give birth to

실전 모의고사 6회

pp. 162-163

01 ①	02 ①	03 ②	04 ③	05 ⑤
06 ①	07 ④	08 ②	09 ②	10 ②
11 ③	12 ④	13 ①	14 ①	15 ④
16 ③	17 ⑤	18 ②	19 ③	20 ②

01 ①

W Hello, everyone! Welcome to our five-day weather forecast. It will be humid on Monday because of the rain. On Tuesday, we will have cloudy skies all day. It will be warm and sunny in the morning on Wednesday, but there is a 30 percent chance of rain showers in the afternoon. On Thursday and Friday, it will rain all day again.

여 안녕하세요, 여러분! 5일간의 일기 예보입니다. 월요일에는 비 때문에 습하겠습니다. 화요일에는 종일 구름 낀 하늘을 보게 되실 것입니다. 수요일 아침에는 따뜻하고 화창하겠지만, 오후에는 소나기가 올 가능성이 30%입니다. 목요일과 금요일에는 다시 종일 비가 내리겠습니다.

|어휘| humid [형] 습한 chance [명] 가능성 rain shower 소나기

02 ①

M What are you looking for, Rachel?

W I can't find my textbook. It's called *World History*. The title is on the top.

M Okay. Is there a picture of the earth under the title?

W No, that's the older edition. My book has a picture of a knight on it.

M I think I remember seeing that around the house. Did you write your name on it?

W Yes, I wrote it under the picture of the knight.

M Okay. Let me help you find it.

남 뭐 찾고 있니, Rachel?

여 내 교과서를 못 찾겠어. 〈세계의 역사〉라는 책이야. 맨 위에 제목이 있어.

남 알았어. 제목 아래에 지구 그림이 있니?

여 아니, 그건 구판이야. 내 책은 표지에 기사 그림이 있어.

남 집 어딘가에서 그걸 본 기억이 나는 것 같아. 그 위에 네 이름 써놨니?

여 응, 기사 그림 밑에 써놨어.

남 알겠어. 내가 찾는 거 도와줄게.

|어휘| textbook [명] 교과서 title [명] 제목 earth [명] 지구 edition [명] (출간 횟수를 나타내는) 판 knight [명] (중세의) 기사

03 ②

W The results from the singing audition have been posted online!

M Oh, I don't want to look! I don't think I passed.

W Really? Why not?

M I didn't do well at the audition. I forgot some of the lyrics.

W It'll be all right. You have a great voice. I'm sure they loved you.

M Thank you. I guess I should check the website.

여 노래 오디션 결과가 온라인에 게시됐어!

남 아, 보고 싶지 않아! 나 합격하지 못했을 것 같아.

여 정말? 왜 못해?

남 오디션에서 잘하지 못했거든. 가사 일부를 잊어버렸어.

여 괜찮을 거야. 너는 목소리가 좋잖아. 그들이 너를 마음에 들어 했을 거라고 확신해.

남 고마워. 웹사이트를 확인해 봐야겠어.

|어휘| audition [명] 오디션 post [동] 올리다, 게시하다 pass [동] 합격하다 do well 잘하다 lyrics [명] (노래의) 가사 **[문제]** annoyed [형] 짜증이 난

04 ③

M Mom, I'm home. Did you go to your French cooking class today?

W No, it was canceled. The teacher was sick. I went shopping with a friend instead.

M Did you remember to get me a pair of hiking boots? I need them for my school trip.

W Yes, I did. I put them in your room.

M Thanks, Mom. You're the best!

남 엄마, 저 집에 왔어요. 오늘 프랑스 요리 수업 다녀오셨어요?

여 아니, 그건 취소되었어. 선생님이 아프셨거든. 대신 친구하고 쇼핑했어.

남 저 등산화 한 켤레 사주기로 하신 것 기억하셨죠? 수학여행에 필요해요.

여 그래, 기억했지. 네 방에 두었어.

남 고마워요, 엄마. 엄마가 최고예요!

|어휘| a pair of 한 쌍의 hiking boots 등산화 school trip 수학여행

05 ⑤

M Hello. How may I help you?

W Good morning. I would like to mail this card.

M Okay. Which shipping option would you like? We have air mail, express mail, and standard mail.

W I'm sending a Christmas card to my friend in Sydney, Australia. Which one is the fastest?

M Express mail is the fastest, but it's expensive. I recommend air mail. It will take about two weeks for the card to get to Australia.

W That's fine.

남 안녕하세요. 어떻게 도와드릴까요?

여 안녕하세요. 이 카드를 보내고 싶습니다.

남 네. 어떤 배송 방법으로 하시겠습니까? 저희는 항공 우편, 빠른 우편, 보통 우편이 있습니다.

여 호주 시드니에 있는 친구에게 크리스마스 카드를 보내려고 하거든요. 어떤 게 가장 빠른가요?

남 빠른 우편이 가장 빠르지만 비쌉니다. 항공 우편을 추천할게요. 카드가 호주까지 가는 데 2주 정도 걸릴 거예요.

여 괜찮네요.

|어휘| mail [동] (우편으로) 보내다 [명] 우편 air mail 항공 우편 express mail 빠른 우편 standard [형] 일반적인, 보통의

06 ①

M Can you still go to the soccer game with me tomorrow, Sally?

W Of course! I'm really looking forward to it. When does it start?

M It starts at two o'clock. But I think we should get some lunch before the game starts.

W That's a good idea. Let's meet at 12:30.

M Can I invite my friend Adam to watch the game with us? He really likes soccer.

W Sure! I would like to meet him.

남 내일 나랑 축구 경기 가기로 한 것 아직 가능한 거지, Sally?

여 물론이지! 나 정말 기대돼. 언제 시작하지?

남 2시에 시작해. 하지만 경기가 시작하기 전에 점심을 먹어야 할 것 같아.

여 좋은 생각이야. 12시 30분에 만나자.

남 우리랑 경기 함께 보는 데에 내 친구 Adam을 초대해도 될까? 그 애는 축구를 정말 좋아해.

여 물론이지! 그 애를 만나보고 싶다.

|해설| 남자가 자신의 친구를 초대해도 되냐고 묻자 여자가 그 애를 만나보고 싶다고 대답했다.

|어휘| invite [동] 초대하다

07 ④

M Hi, Jessica. How was your trip to Seattle?

W It was great!

M I'm glad to hear that. What did you do?

W First, I went to an observation tower. I could see the whole city from the top!

M That sounds fun! Did you try the coffee there?

W Yes, I went to a local coffee shop after my friend and I went hiking.

M Oh, wow. I heard that there are many mountains near Seattle.

W There are! And on my last day, I went to a baseball game.

남 안녕, Jessica. 시애틀 여행은 어땠어?

여 대단했어!

남 잘됐다. 뭐 했는데?

여 맨 먼저 전망 탑에 갔어. 꼭대기에서 도시 전체를 볼 수 있었지!

남 재미있었겠다! 거기서 커피도 마셔봤어?

여 응, 친구와 하이킹을 하고 나서 지역 카페에 갔었어.

남 와. 시애틀 근처에는 산이 많다고 들었어.

여 많지! 그리고 마지막 날에는 야구 경기를 보러 갔었어.

|어휘| observation tower 전망 탑 whole [형] 전체의 local [형] 지역의

08 ②

W Are you almost ready, Scott? We should leave soon.
M I'm ready, Mom. I just needed to add a few things to my suitcase. When does our flight leave?
W At six. But we should arrive at the airport three hours before the flight.
M I know. Do you know where my passport is? I can't find it in my room.
W Yes, it's in my bag. Did you call the taxi company?
M No, I didn't. I'll call them right now.

여 너 준비 거의 다 됐니, Scott? 우리 곧 떠나야 해.
남 준비됐어요, 엄마. 여행 가방에 몇 가지만 더 추가하면 됐거든요. 우리 항공편은 언제 떠나요?
여 6시에. 그렇지만 우리는 비행 3시간 전에 공항에 도착해야 해.
남 알아요. 제 여권 어디 있는지 아세요? 제 방에서 찾을 수가 없어요.
여 응, 그거 내 가방에 있어. 택시 회사에 전화는 했니?
남 아니요, 안 했어요. 지금 당장 전화할게요.

|어휘| add [동] 추가하다 suitcase [명] 여행 가방 flight [명] 항공편, 비행 passport [명] 여권 company [명] 회사

09 ②

M Bella, you look upset. What's wrong?
W My printer broke again.
M The one that you bought last October? Did you reset it?
W Yes, but it doesn't work.
M How much did you pay for it?
W Fifty dollars. It's the cheapest model from AZ Electronics.
M Did it come with a warranty?
W Yes. It is under a one year warranty. So I should be able to get it fixed right away.

남 Bella, 너 속상해 보여. 무슨 일이야?
여 내 프린터가 또 고장 났어.
남 지난 10월에 산 프린터? 재설정했니?
여 응, 하지만 작동을 안 해.
남 너 그거 얼마 줬니?
여 50달러. AZ Electronics의 가장 저렴한 모델이야.
남 거기 품질 보증서는 딸려 있었어?
여 응. 1년 품질 보증돼. 그럼 바로 수리 맡겨야겠다.

|어휘| upset [형] 속상한 break [동] 고장 나다 reset [동] 다시 장치하다 work [동] 작동하다 pay for ~에 대한 대금을 지불하다 warranty [명] 품질 보증(서) get fixed 수리 맡기다

10 ②

M Ladies and gentlemen, can I have your attention, please? This announcement is for passengers waiting for the seven o'clock train to Seoul. Because of heavy snow on the tracks, the seven o'clock train to Seoul is delayed. The train will arrive at 7:30. We're very sorry for the delay. Thank you for your understanding.

남 신사숙녀 여러분, 주목해주시겠습니까? 서울행 7시 열차를 기다리시는 승객께 드리는 소식입니다. 선로 위에 쌓인 폭설 때문에, 서울행 7시 열차가 지연되고 있습니다. 열차는 7시 30분에 도착할 예정입니다. 지연되어 대단히 죄송합니다. 양해해 주셔서 감사합니다.

|어휘| announcement [명] 발표, 소식 passenger [명] 승객 track [명] 선로 delay [동] 지연시키다 [명] 지연

11 ③

M Hi, Beth. How was your summer vacation?
W It was awful. I went to Thailand with my parents, but it rained for three days straight when we were there.
M I'm sorry to hear that. How long were you there?
W Five days.
M What did you do there?
W We hired a tour guide, and he took us to several famous temples.
M How was that?
W It was okay. The temples were beautiful, but they were too crowded.

남 안녕, Beth. 여름 휴가 어땠어?
여 끔찍했어. 부모님과 태국에 갔었는데, 우리가 거기 있는 동안 3일 연속으로 비가 왔어.
남 안됐구나. 거기에 얼마나 오래 있었는데?
여 5일.
남 거기서 뭐 했니?
여 여행 가이드를 고용했는데, 그분이 우리를 몇몇 유명한 사원에 데리고 갔어.
남 어땠어?
여 괜찮았어. 사원들은 아름다웠는데, 너무 붐비더라.

|어휘| awful [형] 끔찍한 hire [동] 고용하다 tour guide 여행 가이드 temple [명] 사원

12 ④

M Hi, Nicole. What are you doing at the department store?

W I work here. Today is my first day. What about you? Are you here to buy groceries?

M No. I'm here to exchange this toy car.

W What's wrong with it?

M When my son opened the box, a couple of parts were missing.

W Oh, I see. You really need to exchange it for a new one.

남 안녕, Nicole. 백화점에서 뭐 하고 있니?

여 나 여기서 일해. 오늘이 첫날이야. 너는? 식료품 사려고 왔니?

남 아니. 이 장난감 자동차를 교환하려고 왔어.

여 뭐가 잘못됐어?

남 우리 아들이 상자를 열었는데, 부품 두 서너 개가 없더라고.

여 아, 그렇구나. 정말 새걸로 교환해야겠네.

|어휘| department store 백화점 exchange [동] 교환하다 a couple of 두 서너 개의 part [명] 부품 missing [형] 빠진, 누락된

13 ①

M May I take your order?

W Yes. I'll have two donuts and two apple juices.

M Donuts are $2 each, and apple juices are $4 each. But when you buy any two drinks today, you get a donut for free.

W Great! Then I don't need to pay for one donut, right?

M That's right. For here or to go?

W To go, please.

M Okay. We offer 10% off for to-go orders, so you can get an additional discount.

W Oh, that's good. Here's a $10 bill.

M Thank you. Here's your change.

남 주문하시겠어요?

여 네. 도넛 두 개와 사과 주스 두 잔 주세요.

남 도넛은 하나에 2달러이고, 사과 주스는 한 잔에 4달러입니다. 그런데 오늘 어떤 음료든 두 잔 사시면, 도넛 한 개가 무료예요.

여 좋네요! 그럼 제가 도넛 한 개는 계산할 필요가 없는 거죠, 맞나요?

남 맞습니다. 여기서 드실 건가요, 아니면 가져가실 건가요?

여 가져갈게요.

남 알겠습니다. 포장 주문에는 10% 할인을 제공해 드리니, 추가 할인을 받으실 수 있습니다.

여 아, 잘됐네요. 여기 10달러 지폐예요.

남 감사합니다. 여기 거스름돈입니다.

|해설| 도넛 하나가 무료여서 총 10달러인데 포장 주문은 10% 추가 할인을 받을 수 있다고 했으므로, 여자가 10달러를 내고 받은 거스름돈은 1달러이다.

|어휘| order [명] 주문 each [부] 개마다 offer [동] 제공하다 discount [명] 할인 change [명] 거스름돈

14 ①

W Hello, Jacob. What's the problem?

M One of my back teeth really hurts. I think I might have a cavity.

W Can you open your mouth? *[pause]* You actually have two cavities.

M Oh, no! I wonder how that happened. I brush regularly.

W How old is your toothbrush?

M Hmm. I'm not sure. Maybe six months old?

W You should replace your toothbrush every three months.

여 안녕하세요, Jacob. 무엇이 문제인가요?

남 뒤쪽의 이 중 하나가 정말 아파요. 충치가 있는 것 같아요.

여 입을 벌려 주시겠어요? [잠시 후] 실제로 충치가 두 개 있네요.

남 아, 이런! 어쩌다 그렇게 됐는지 궁금하네요. 저는 규칙적으로 양치하거든요.

여 칫솔을 얼마나 오래 쓰셨나요?

남 음. 확실히는 모르겠어요. 아마 6개월 됐을 걸요?

여 칫솔은 3개월마다 교체해 주셔야 해요.

|어휘| hurt [동] 아프다 cavity [명] 충치 wonder [동] 궁금하다 regularly [부] 규칙적으로 toothbrush [명] 칫솔 replace [동] 교체하다

15 ④

W Hey, Vincent. What are you up to?

M I'm planning a surprise for my parents' 30th wedding anniversary. It's this coming Sunday.

W So what's the surprise?

M I'm going to prepare a romantic dinner for them.

W Wow, your parents will be very pleased. What are you going to make?

M I'm thinking about making steak, shrimp pasta, and chicken salad.

W Great! And why don't you order a cake too? It's a special day.

M That's a good idea. I'm sure they will like that.

여 얘, Vincent. 뭐 하고 있니?
남 우리 부모님의 30번째 결혼기념일을 위해 뜻밖의 선물을 계획하고 있어. 다가오는 이번 주 일요일이야.
여 그래서 뜻밖의 선물이 뭐야?
남 부모님을 위해 낭만적인 저녁 식사를 준비할 거야.
여 와, 너희 부모님이 정말 기뻐하시겠다. 뭘 만들 거니?
남 스테이크, 새우 파스타, 치킨 샐러드를 만들려고 생각 중이야.
여 멋지다! 그리고 케이크도 주문하면 어때? 특별한 날이니까.
남 좋은 생각이야. 분명 두 분이 그걸 좋아하실 거야.

|어휘| surprise [명] 뜻밖의 일[선물] anniversary [명] 기념일 prepare [동] 준비하다 pleased [형] 기쁜

16 ③

W Hi, Chris! How did you do on the math test?
M I only got two answers wrong! I'm so relieved. How about you?
W I did well, too! Do you want to go to a movie with me to celebrate?
M I wish I could, but I need to get home. I'm going to have dinner with my family tomorrow.
W I understand. Maybe next time!
M Definitely! Enjoy your movie.

여 안녕, Chris! 수학 시험 어떻게 봤니?
남 나 딱 두 개 틀렸어! 정말 다행이야. 너는 어때?
여 나도 잘 봤어! 기념으로 나랑 영화 보러 갈래?
남 나도 가고 싶은데, 집에 가야 해. 가족과 함께 저녁을 먹을 거거든.
여 알겠어. 다음에 함께 하자!
남 그렇고말고! 영화 재미있게 봐.

|어휘| math [명] 수학 relieved [형] 안도하는 celebrate [동] 기념하다, 축하하다 definitely [부] 틀림없이, 그렇고말고

17 ⑤

① W What's wrong with your cell phone?
M It suddenly stopped working, and I don't know why.
② W It's too noisy here! I can't concentrate at all.
M Then why don't we go to the library?
③ W I'd like to borrow these books.
M Sure. Show me your card, please.
④ W Why didn't you call me?
M I left my phone at home. I'm really sorry.
⑤ W Could you lower your voice, please?
M Oh, sorry. I'll be quiet.

① 여 휴대전화에 무슨 문제가 있나요?
남 갑자기 작동이 멈췄는데, 이유를 모르겠어요.
② 여 여기 너무 시끄러워! 난 전혀 집중할 수가 없어.
남 그럼 우리 도서관에 가는 게 어때?
③ 여 이 책들을 빌리고 싶은데요.
남 네. 카드를 보여 주세요.
④ 여 왜 나한테 전화 안 했어?
남 집에 내 전화기를 두고 왔어. 정말 미안해.
⑤ 여 목소리를 좀 낮춰 주시겠어요?
남 아, 죄송해요. 조용히 할게요.

|어휘| suddenly [부] 갑자기 noisy [형] 시끄러운 concentrate [동] 집중하다 borrow [동] 빌리다 lower [동] ~을 내리다[낮추다] voice [명] 목소리

18 ②

W Welcome to the art museum, everyone. I'm your tour guide. We're going to see some Picasso paintings today. But first, let me tell you about him. Picasso was born in Spain, but he lived in France for most of his life. He painted about 30,000 works of art. Cubism is his most famous artistic style. Picasso was 91 years old when he died.

여 미술관에 오신 것을 환영합니다, 여러분. 저는 여러분의 여행 가이드입니다. 오늘 우리는 피카소의 그림 몇 점을 볼 예정입니다. 하지만 우선 그에 대해 말씀드리겠습니다. 피카소는 스페인에서 태어났지만, 인생의 대부분을 프랑스에서 보냈습니다. 그는 3만여 점의 미술 작품을 그렸습니다. 입체파는 그의 가장 유명한 미술 양식이죠. 피카소는 사망 당시 91세였습니다.

|어휘| cubism [명] 입체파 artistic style 미술 양식

19 ③

M Hi, Jenny! Did you have fun at Stacy's birthday party?
W Yes, I did. We went ice skating at an ice rink near her house.
M Did you wear a helmet? Ice skating can be quite dangerous.
W Don't be silly, Dad. None of the other kids were wearing helmets.
M But you fall down a lot. You need to be careful.
W Okay, I will wear one next time.

① Why don't you buy a new helmet?
② Have you been to the ice rink before?
④ Her birthday was last Monday.
⑤ All right. I won't wear my helmet.

남 안녕, Jenny! Stacy의 생일 파티에서 재미있게 놀았니?

여 네. 그 애 집 근처 스케이트장에 스케이트 타러 갔었어요.

남 너 헬멧은 썼니? 스케이트 타는 건 꽤 위험할 수 있어.

여 말도 안 돼요, 아빠. 다른 아이들은 아무도 헬멧을 안 썼다고요.

남 하지만 너는 많이 넘어지잖니. 조심해야 해.

여 네, 다음번에는 착용할게요.

① 새 헬멧을 사는 게 어때요?

② 전에 스케이트장에 가보셨어요?

④ 그 애의 생일은 지난 월요일이었어요.

⑤ 알겠어요. 저는 헬멧을 쓰지 않을 거예요.

|어휘| ice rink 스케이트장 quite 🖣 꽤 dangerous 🖲 위험한
silly 🖲 어리석은 fall down 넘어지다

20 ②

W Hi, Justin. What happened to your coat?

M A truck splashed mud on me when I was crossing the street.

W Oh, no. That's too bad. Can you wash it at home?

M No, I don't think I can. I need to take it to the dry cleaner's, but it's too expensive.

W My mom can clean it for you for free. She has her own dry cleaning business.

M Really? She wouldn't mind?

W Of course not. She would be happy to do it.

① Yes, what do you have in mind?

③ No, my mom washed this coat yesterday.

④ It's none of your business.

⑤ Would you mind picking up the coat at the dry cleaner's?

여 안녕, Justin. 너 코트에 무슨 일이야?

남 길을 건너고 있을 때, 트럭 한 대가 나한테 진흙을 튀겼어.

여 아, 이런. 안됐구나. 집에서 세탁할 수 있겠어?

남 아니. 못할 것 같아. 세탁소에 가져가야 할 것 같은데, 그건 너무 비싸.

여 우리 엄마가 무료로 세탁해 주실 수 있을 거야. 엄마가 세탁소를 하시거든.

남 정말? 싫어하지 않으실까?

여 당연히 아니지. 엄마는 기꺼이 해 주실 거야.

① 응, 어떤 것을 생각하고 있니?

③ 아니야, 우리 엄마는 이 코트를 어제 세탁하셨어.

④ 네가 상관할 바 아니야.

⑤ 세탁소에서 코트 좀 찾아와줄 수 있니?

|해설| 엄마가 무료로 옷을 세탁해 줄 거라는 여자의 말에 남자가 주저하고 있으므로, 엄마가 기꺼이 해 주실 거라고 말하는 것이 자연스럽다.

|어휘| splash 🖲 튀기다 mud 🖲 진흙 dry cleaner's 세탁소
mind 🖲 꺼리다

어휘·표현 다지기   p. 171

A

01 ~을 내리다[낮추다]	02 기쁜
03 교과서	04 회사
05 여행 가방	06 미술 양식
07 충치	08 안도하는
09 한 쌍의	10 품질 보증(서)
11 교체하다	12 선로
13 사원	14 세탁소
15 꽤	16 고용하다

B

01 standard	02 part
03 wonder	04 suddenly
05 dangerous	06 regularly
07 passenger	08 pay for
09 upset	10 department store

시험 직전 모의고사 1회
pp. 172-173

01 ④	02 ②	03 ⑤	04 ⑤	05 ②
06 ⑤	07 ③	08 ⑤	09 ③	10 ①
11 ③	12 ②	13 ②	14 ②	15 ④
16 ②	17 ④	18 ③	19 ⑤	20 ①

01 ④

W Hello, this is Rachael from the Weather Channel. Here is today's forecast for the US. It's raining now in New York. In fact, lightning hit some power lines. It's cloudy and rainy in the South, but the skies are clear in Miami. Cities in the Southwest, especially Las Vegas, will have strong winds all day.

여 안녕하세요, 날씨 채널의 Rachael입니다. 오늘 미국의 (일기) 예보입니다. 뉴욕에는 현재 비가 내리고 있는데요. 실제로 번개가 몇몇 송전선을 내리쳤습니다. 남쪽은 구름이 끼고 비가 내리지만, 마이애미의 하늘은 맑습니다. 남서쪽의 도시들, 특히 라스베이거스는 종일 강한 바람이 불겠습니다.

|어휘| forecast 🖲 예보 lightning 🖲 번개 hit 🖲 때리다, 치다

power line 송전선　especially ⓫ 특히

02 ②

W James! Did you enjoy your vacation?

M Yes, it was fun! This is a picture I took with my family in Kyoto.

W That looks like a nice restaurant. What were you eating?

M Miso ramen. It was so delicious!

W I'm sure it was. Who is the girl sitting next to you?

M That's my little sister, Tiffany. She loves Japanese food, so she has a smile on her face.

W It looks like you all had a great time!

여 James! 휴가 잘 보냈니?

남 응, 재미있었어! 이건 교토에서 내가 가족과 찍은 사진이야.

여 저긴 좋은 식당 같아 보여. 뭐 먹고 있었어?

남 미소 라멘. 아주 맛있더라!

여 정말 그랬을 것 같아. 네 옆에 앉아 있는 여자아이는 누구니?

남 내 여동생 Tiffany야. 그 애는 일본 음식을 아주 좋아해서, 얼굴에 미소를 띠고 있어.

여 너희 모두 멋진 시간을 보낸 것 같네!

|어휘| vacation ⓜ 방학, 휴가　delicious ⓗ 맛있는　face ⓜ 얼굴

03 ⑤

W Hurry, Dad! I'm going to be late for my soccer game.

M I'm sorry, Kelly, but your coach just canceled the game. He called a few minutes ago.

W No! Why? It's only raining.

M There is also lightning, so it's too dangerous to play outside.

W But I've been looking forward to this game all week. I can't believe it.

M I know how you feel, but you can play next week.

여 서두르세요, 아빠! 저 축구 경기에 늦겠어요.

남 Kelly, 유감이지만 코치님이 방금 경기를 취소하셨단다. 몇 분 전에 전화하셨어.

여 안 돼요! 왜요? 그냥 비 오는 것뿐이잖아요.

남 번개도 치고 있으니, 야외에서 경기하는 것은 너무 위험하잖니.

여 하지만 저는 일주일 내내 이 경기를 기대했는걸요. 믿을 수가 없어요.

남 네 기분은 알겠지만, 다음 주에 경기할 수 있잖니.

|해설| 여자는 고대하던 축구 경기가 날씨 때문에 취소되자 실망감을 감추지 못하고 있다.

|어휘| cancel ⓥ 취소하다　outside ⓫ 야외에서　look forward to ~을 고대하다

04 ⑤

M Did you have fun at the animal shelter, Brooke?

W Yes, I had a great time. We helped take care of the cats.

M That's great. What did you do? Did you feed them?

W No, other people did that. I read books to them.

M Really? But cats don't understand stories.

W Yes, but they seem to enjoy the sound of my voice.

M Oh, I see.

남 동물 보호소에서 즐겁게 보냈니, Brooke?

여 응, 좋은 시간 보냈어. 우리는 고양이 돌보는 것을 도왔어.

남 멋지다. 뭐 했는데? 고양이에게 먹이를 줬니?

여 아니, 그건 다른 사람들이 했어. 나는 고양이들에게 책을 읽어줬어.

남 정말? 하지만 고양이들은 이야기를 이해할 수 없잖아.

여 그렇지, 하지만 고양이들이 내 목소리 듣는 것을 좋아하는 것처럼 보였어.

남 아, 그렇구나.

|어휘| feed ⓥ 먹이를 주다　understand ⓥ 이해하다

05 ②

W Excuse me, officer. Can you help me?

M Of course. What's the problem?

W My wallet was stolen on the number five bus this morning.

M I'm sorry to hear that. Did you see the person who took it?

W Yes. He wore a cap and a mask. I don't remember anything else.

M What does your wallet look like?

W It's black with a silver buckle in the middle.

M Okay. Please tell me exactly what happened.

여 실례합니다. 경찰관님. 저 좀 도와주실 수 있나요?

남 물론이죠. 무슨 문제죠?

여 제가 오늘 아침에 5번 버스에서 지갑을 도난당했어요.

남 유감입니다. 그걸 가져간 사람을 보셨나요?

여 네. 그 남자는 모자와 마스크를 쓰고 있었어요. 그 외에는 아무것도 기억나지 않아요.

남 지갑은 어떻게 생겼죠?

여 가운데에 은색 버클이 달린 검은색이에요.

남 알겠습니다. 정확히 무슨 일이 일어났는지 저에게 말씀해 주세요.

|어휘| wallet [명] 지갑 steal [동] 훔치다 remember [동] 기억나다 buckle [명] 버클, 잠금장치 exactly [부] 정확히 happen [동] 일어나다, 발생하다

06 ⑤

W Hi, Kyle! What's wrong? You look upset.
M My teacher told me I am failing three of my classes.
W Really? What seems to be the problem?
M I can't concentrate on my schoolwork in class. I always feel sleepy.
W Maybe you need to go to bed earlier.
M But I like staying up to watch TV at night.
W Doing well in school is more important than watching TV.

여 안녕, Kyle! 무슨 일이야? 속상해 보여.
남 우리 선생님께서 내가 세 수업에서 낙제할 거라고 말씀하셨어.
여 정말? 뭐가 문제 같아?
남 수업 때 학업에 집중할 수가 없어. 늘 졸려.
여 아마도 넌 더 일찍 자야 할 것 같아.
남 하지만 난 밤에 안 자고 TV 보는 게 좋아.
여 학교에서 잘하는 게 TV 보는 것보다 더 중요해.

|어휘| fail [동] 낙제하다 concentrate on ~에 집중하다 schoolwork [명] 학업 stay up 안 자다, 깨어 있다

07 ③

M Hi, Becky! What are you doing in the library?
W I'm working on my science project. Have you decided on a topic yet?
M I have. I'm interested in space, so I'm going to draw the different phases of the moon. Your project is about roller coasters, right?
W No, I changed my mind. I want to do a project on baking bread.
M But that's not science.
W Yes, it is! I'm going to explain how dough rises.

남 안녕, Becky! 도서관에서 뭐 하니?
여 과학 과제를 하고 있어. 너는 벌써 주제 정했니?
남 정했어. 나는 우주에 관심이 있어서, 달의 각기 다른 단계들을 그릴 거야. 네 과제는 롤러코스터에 관한 것 맞지?
여 아니, 나 마음을 바꿨어. 제빵에 관한 과제를 하고 싶어.
남 하지만 그건 과학이 아니잖아.
여 아니, 과학이야! 밀가루 반죽이 어떻게 부푸는지 설명할 거야.

|어휘| decide [동] 결정하다 topic [명] 주제 yet [부] 이미, 벌써 draw [동] 그리다 phase [명] 단계 change one's mind 마음을 바꾸다 bake [동] 굽다 dough [명] 밀가루 반죽 rise [동] (빵 · 케이크 등이) 부풀다

08 ⑤

M Mom, I'm going to Tyler's birthday party tomorrow. Will you be able to drop me off at his house?
W Sure. I'll drop you off on the way to my tennis lesson.
M Thanks! But there's a problem.
W What is it?
M I need to buy him a present, but I've spent all my money already.
W Hmm… If you do the dishes, I'll give you ten dollars.
M That's great! I'll wash them right now.

남 엄마, 저 내일 Tyler의 생일 파티에 가요. 그 애 집까지 차로 데려다 주실 수 있으세요?
여 그래. 엄마 테니스 수업 가는 길에 내려줄게.
남 감사해요! 그런데 문제가 하나 있어요.
여 그게 뭔데?
남 그 애에게 선물을 사줘야 하는데, 이미 돈을 다 써버렸어요.
여 음… 네가 설거지를 하면, 10달러를 줄게.
남 좋아요! 지금 당장 설거지할게요.

|어휘| drop ~ off ~을 (차로) 데려다 주다 do the dishes 설거지를 하다

09 ③

[Telephone rings.]
W Hello? Emily Porter speaking.
M Hello, Ms. Porter. This is Cody Evans from Graham Bookstore.
W Oh, how are you?
M Good. I'm calling to remind you of our Author's Friday event on July 15.
W Right. I'm so excited to meet my readers at Graham Bookstore. Does it start at 5:00 p.m.?
M Yes. There will be a Q&A and book signing after your talk.
W Okay. How many people are expected to come?
M We are expecting about eighty people to come.
W Wonderful! See you then.

[전화벨이 울린다.]
여 여보세요? Emily Porter입니다.
남 안녕하세요, Porter 씨. Graham 서점의 Cody Evans입니다.
여 아, 안녕하세요?
남 네. 7월 15일에 있는 Author's Friday 행사에 대해 다시 한번 알려드리려고 전화했습니다.

여 맞아요. Graham 서점에서 제 독자들을 만나게 되어 정말 기쁩니다. 오후 5시에 시작하죠?

남 네. 작가님의 강연 후에 질의응답과 책 사인회가 있을 예정입니다.

여 알겠습니다. 몇 명 정도 올 것으로 예상되나요?

남 80명 정도가 올 것으로 예상하고 있습니다.

여 좋아요! 그때 뵙겠습니다.

|어휘| remind [동] 다시 한번 알려주다 author [명] 작가 book signing 책 사인회 talk [명] 연설, 강연 expect [동] 예상하다

10 ①

M Come in, students! Please listen carefully to the safety rules. First, when you walk into the science room, do not touch any chemicals until I tell you to do so. Second, do not eat or drink anything in the science room. Third, please make sure to clean up your desk before you leave.

남 어서 들어오세요, 학생 여러분! 안전 수칙을 주의 깊게 들어주시기 바랍니다. 먼저, 과학실에 들어올 때는, 제가 만지라고 말할 때까지 어떤 화학물질도 만지지 마세요. 두 번째로, 과학실에서는 어떤 것도 먹거나 마시지 마세요. 세 번째로, 나가기 전에 반드시 본인의 책상을 정리하세요.

|어휘| safety rule 안전 수칙 chemical [명] 화학물질 make sure to-v 반드시 ~하다 clean up ~을 치우다[청소하다]

11 ③

W Good morning, students! I'm Mary from the American History Museum. Today, we're going to learn about George Washington, the first president of the United States. He was in office for eight years. When he retired, he moved to Virginia with his wife, Martha. The one-dollar bill has his face on it. He died when he was 67 years old.

여 좋은 아침입니다, 학생 여러분! 저는 미국 역사박물관에서 나온 Mary입니다. 오늘 우리는 미국 초대 대통령인 조지 워싱턴에 관해 배울 것입니다. 그는 8년 동안 재임했습니다. 그는 퇴임했을 때, 아내 Martha와 함께 버지니아로 이주했죠. 1달러 지폐에는 그의 얼굴이 있습니다. 그는 67세에 사망했습니다.

|해설| 조지 워싱턴은 퇴임할 때, 아내와 함께 버지니아로 갔다고 했다.

|어휘| president [명] 대통령 in office 재직 중인 retire [동] 은퇴하다, 퇴직하다 move [동] 이주하다 bill [명] 지폐

12 ②

W Hi, Luke! What's in the box?

M They're new dress shoes. I just bought them at the mall.

W They're so stylish! Are they for the school dance next Saturday?

M No, my brother is getting married next weekend. I'm going to wear these shoes to his wedding.

W Oh, I see. Where is the ceremony going to be held?

M In Incheon. I'm looking forward to meeting all my relatives.

여 안녕, Luke! 상자에는 뭐가 들었어?

남 새 정장 구두야. 방금 쇼핑몰에서 샀어.

여 정말 멋지다! 다음 주 토요일에 있을 학교 댄스파티를 위한 거니?

남 아니, 우리 형이 다음 주말에 결혼하거든. 형의 결혼식에 이 신발을 신고 갈 거야.

여 아, 그렇구나. 결혼식을 어디서 하시는데?

남 인천에서. 모든 친척을 만나는 게 기대돼.

|어휘| dress shoes 정장 구두 stylish [형] 멋진, 유행을 따른 ceremony [명] 의식, 행사 hold [동] 개최하다 relative [명] 친척

13 ②

[Telephone rings.]

W Dr. Kim's office. How can I help you?

M My left ear really hurts. Can I make an appointment?

W Sure. When would you like to come in?

M Is 10:30 a.m. okay?

W I'm sorry, sir. We're fully booked this morning.

M That's too bad. What about this afternoon?

W That would be fine. The doctor is free at 1:00, 1:30, 2:30, and 4:00.

M Great! The earliest appointment works for me.

W Okay. We'll see you then.

[전화벨이 울린다.]

여 김 의원입니다. 무엇을 도와드릴까요?

남 왼쪽 귀가 정말 아픈데요. 예약할 수 있을까요?

여 물론이죠. 언제 오시고 싶으세요?

남 오전 10시 30분 괜찮은가요?

여 죄송합니다, 손님. 오늘 오전은 예약이 꽉 찼어요.

남 아쉽네요. 오늘 오후는요?

여 괜찮습니다. 의사 선생님께서 1시, 1시 30분, 2시 30분과 4시에 시간이 비네요.

남 좋네요! 저는 가장 빠른 예약이 좋겠어요.

여 알겠습니다. 그럼 그때 뵙겠습니다.

|어휘| hurt [동] 아프다 make an appointment (진료 · 상담 등을) 예약하다 fully [부] 완전히 book [동] 예약하다

14 ②

M Good morning.
W Good morning. I'd like a cappuccino, please.
M I ran out of coffee beans this morning. I'm sorry.
W Oh, no. Do any of your other drinks contain caffeine? I'm so tired today.
M How about black tea? There are many options to choose from.
W I don't like the taste of black tea. It's not sweet enough.
M Adding milk and sugar will make it sweeter.
W Okay, I'll try that!

남 좋은 아침입니다.
여 안녕하세요. 카푸치노 한 잔 주세요.
남 오늘 아침에 커피콩이 바닥났어요. 죄송합니다.
여 아, 이런. 여기 다른 음료들 중 카페인이 포함된 게 있나요? 오늘 제가 정말 피곤해서요.
남 홍차는 어떠세요? 고르실 수 있는 선택권이 많이 있습니다.
여 제가 홍차 맛을 안 좋아해요. 그건 별로 달지가 않아서요.
남 우유와 설탕을 넣으면 더 달아질 겁니다.
여 알겠습니다. 그걸 마셔볼게요!

|어휘| run out of ~이 바닥나다 bean [명] 콩 contain [동] 포함하다 black tea 홍차 option [명] 선택(할 수 있는 것) choose [동] 고르다 taste [명] 맛 add [동] 더하다, 추가하다

15 ④

[Cell phone rings.]
W Honey, I'm on my way home now.
M Wow, you worked really late.
W I know. I had to call a student's parents after school today. Is our son sleeping?
M Yes. By the way, why don't we get him a toy robot for Children's Day tomorrow?
W Actually, I just bought a computer game for him.
M Oh, great. Thanks for doing that!
W Could you wrap it for me tonight?
M Sure. See you at home.

[휴대전화벨이 울린다.]
여 여보, 저 지금 집에 가는 길이에요.
남 와, 정말 늦게까지 일했네요.
여 그래요. 오늘 방과 후에 학생 부모님께 전화해야 했거든요. 우리 아들은 자고 있나요?
남 네. 그나저나, 내일 어린이날에 애한테 장난감 로봇을 사주는 게 어때요?
여 사실, 방금 컴퓨터 게임을 하나 샀어요.
남 아, 잘됐네요. 그렇게 해줘서 고마워요!
여 오늘 밤에 그것 좀 포장해 줄래요?
남 물론이죠. 집에서 봐요.

|어휘| on one's way 도중에 wrap [동] 포장하다, 싸다

16 ②

W Ted! Can you guess why I circled the 15th on this calendar?
M Let me see... *[pause]* Isn't that your birthday?
W That's right! I'm having a party at an amusement park.
M That sounds really fun. I wish I could join you.
W You can't come to the party? Do you have other plans?
M Yes. I'll be on vacation in Cambodia that week.
W I really wanted you to be there, but have a nice trip anyway.

여 Ted! 내가 왜 이 달력 15일에 동그라미를 쳤는지 알겠니?
남 어디 보자… [잠시 후] 그날이 네 생일 아니야?
여 맞아! 나 놀이공원에서 파티할 거야.
남 정말 재미있겠다. 나도 너와 함께하면 좋을 텐데.
여 파티에 못 와? 다른 계획이 있니?
남 응. 나는 그 주에 캄보디아에서 휴가 중일 거야.
여 네가 정말 파티에 오길 바랐는데, 어쨌든 여행 잘 다녀와.

|어휘| guess [동] 추측하다, 알아맞히다 circle [동] 동그라미를 그리다 calendar [명] 달력 amusement park 놀이공원 on vacation 휴가 중인

17 ④

① **M** When does the meeting start?
W It starts at 3:30 p.m.
② **M** Excuse me. May I sit here?
W Sorry. This seat is taken.
③ **M** Can I have a hot dog please?
W Sure. That will be $3.
④ **M** Do you like watching baseball?
W No, I don't. It's boring.
⑤ **M** Can I buy a ticket to the baseball game?
W I'm sorry, sir. They're sold out.

① **남** 회의는 언제 시작하나요?

여	오후 3시 30분에 시작해요.
② 남	실례합니다. 여기 앉아도 되나요?
여	죄송해요. 이 자리는 주인이 있어요.
③ 남	핫도그 하나 주시겠어요?
여	알겠습니다. 3달러입니다.
④ 남	너 야구 경기 보는 것 좋아해?
여	아니, 안 좋아해. 그건 지루해.
⑤ 남	야구 경기 표 살 수 있나요?
여	죄송합니다, 손님. 표가 매진되었습니다.

|어휘| boring 圈 지루한　sold out (표가) 매진된

18 ③

M　Welcome to the aquarium. If you look to your left, you'll see some dolphins. Dolphins are very interesting animals. They're very smart. Their IQ is around eighty, which is the same level as a seven or eight-year-old child. Dolphins live in warm, tropical oceans throughout the world. They mainly eat fish and squid. The average dolphin lives for about thirty to forty years.

남　수족관에 오신 것을 환영합니다. 왼쪽을 보시면, 돌고래가 보이실 텐데요. 돌고래는 매우 흥미로운 동물입니다. 아주 영리하죠. IQ가 80 정도인데, 이는 7~8살 아이와 같은 수준입니다. 돌고래는 전 세계의 따뜻한 열대 대양에서 서식합니다. 주로 물고기와 오징어를 먹죠. 일반적인 돌고래는 약 30년에서 40년 동안 삽니다.

|어휘| aquarium 圐 수족관　dolphin 圐 돌고래　tropical 圈 열대의　mainly 囝 주로　squid 圐 오징어　average 圈 보통의, 일반적인

19 ⑤

W　Excuse me. Can you please take this pasta back to the kitchen?
M　Of course. May I ask what's wrong?
W　The noodles are overcooked, and the cheese is too salty.
M　I'm so sorry. I'll ask the chef to make it again.
W　That's not necessary. I'd just like the check, please.
M　You don't need to pay for your meal tonight.

① It's more expensive than I expected.
② Sure. I'll get a dessert menu for you.
③ No, thank you.
④ I'd like you to make it again.

여　실례합니다. 이 파스타 좀 다시 주방으로 가져가 주실래요?

남	알겠습니다. 무엇이 잘못됐는지 여쭤봐도 될까요?
여	면은 너무 익었고, 치즈가 너무 짜네요.
남	정말 죄송합니다. 주방장에게 다시 만들어 달라고 요청할게요.
여	그러실 필요 없습니다. 그냥 계산서 주세요.
남	오늘 저녁 식사비는 내지 않으셔도 됩니다.

① 생각보다 더 비싸네요.
② 물론입니다. 후식 메뉴를 가져다드리겠습니다.
③ 아니요, 괜찮습니다.
④ 그것을 다시 만들어주시면 좋겠어요.

|어휘| noodle 圐 국수, 면　overcooked 圈 너무 익힌　salty 圈 짠　chef 圐 주방장　necessary 圈 필요한　check 圐 계산서
[문제] dessert 圐 후식, 디저트　pay for ~에 대한 값을 지불하다　meal 圐 식사

20 ①

W　What are you listening to?
M　It's my favorite band. What do you think of this song?
W　I like it. It doesn't sound like anything I've ever heard before.
M　They will have a concert tomorrow, and I have an extra ticket.
W　Oh, really?
M　Do you want to go with me? It will be lots of fun.
W　Okay, I'd love to. When does it start?
M　It starts at 6:00 p.m.

② It's a brand-new song.
③ We met at 5:00 p.m.
④ It will be held at City Stadium.
⑤ I've liked them for a long time.

여	뭐 듣고 있니?
남	내가 가장 좋아하는 밴드야. 이 곡 어때?
여	마음에 들어. 이전에 내가 들었던 어떤 곡과도 다르게 들린다.
남	그들이 내일 콘서트를 하는데, 나한테 여분 표가 한 장 있어.
여	아, 정말?
남	나랑 같이 가고 싶니? 엄청 재미있을 거야.
여	좋아, 가고 싶어. 언제 시작하는데?
남	오후 6시에 시작해.

② 그건 신곡이야.
③ 우리는 오후 5시에 만났어.
④ City 경기장에서 개최될 거야.
⑤ 나는 그들을 오랫동안 좋아했어.

|어휘| extra 圈 여분의　**[문제]** brand-new 圈 아주 새로운

시험 직전 모의고사 2회

pp. 174-175

01 ②	02 ⑤	03 ③	04 ③	05 ②
06 ②	07 ④	08 ④	09 ⑤	10 ①
11 ②	12 ③	13 ⑤	14 ③	15 ④
16 ④	17 ①	18 ⑤	19 ②	20 ②

01 ②

M Good morning, Baltimore! This is Steve Gray with the weekly weather report. From Monday to Tuesday, there will be rain showers, so you will need your umbrellas for the next few days. It will warm up slightly on Wednesday, but it will be cloudy all day. It will be cooler on Thursday, and there is a 50 percent chance of snow. On Friday and Saturday, it will snow.

남 좋은 아침입니다, 볼티모어 주민 여러분! 저는 주간 일기 예보를 전해드릴 Steve Gray입니다. 월요일부터 화요일까지는 소나기가 예상되니, 다음 며칠 동안은 우산을 챙기셔야겠습니다. 수요일에는 약간 따뜻해지겠지만, 종일 흐리겠습니다. 목요일에는 더 선선해지겠으며, 눈이 내릴 가능성이 50%입니다. 금요일과 토요일에는 눈이 오겠습니다.

|해설| 수요일에는 종일 흐린 날씨가 예상된다고 말하고 있다.

|어휘| weekly [형] 매주의, 주간의 rain shower 소나기 slightly [부] 약간 cool [형] 시원한, 선선한 chance [명] 가능성

02 ⑤

M Hi, Martha. What are you working on?

W I'm designing the cover for my new knitting book. What do you think?

M It looks great! I really like the picture of a scarf at the top.

W Thanks! I put the title, *Everyone Can Knit*, in the center.

M Oh, there is a picture of two knitting needles under the title! How cute!

W I'm glad you like it.

남 안녕, Martha. 무슨 일 하고 있어?

여 나의 새로운 뜨개질 책을 위한 표지를 디자인하고 있어. 어때?

남 멋져 보여! 맨 위에 있는 목도리 그림이 정말 마음에 드네.

여 고마워! 가운데에는 'Everyone Can Knit(누구나 뜨개질을 할 수 있다)'라는 제목을 넣었어.

남 아, 제목 아래에 두 개의 뜨개질바늘 그림이 있구나! 정말 귀여워!

여 맘에 든다니 다행이다.

|어휘| knitting [명] 뜨개질 scarf [명] 목도리, 스카프 knit [동] 뜨개질하다 needle [명] 바늘

03 ③

W Are you excited about your field trip to the zoo tomorrow?

M Not really. Will there be any snakes?

W Of course! The Snake House is the most popular part of the zoo.

M Oh, no! I had a nightmare about a snake last night. It almost ate me.

W Don't worry, Trevor. They won't be able to hurt you.

M I know... But I can't get it out of my mind.

여 내일 동물원으로 현장 학습 가게 돼서 신나니?

남 그다지. 뱀이 있을까?

여 당연하지! Snake House는 동물원에서 제일 인기 있는 곳이야.

남 아, 안 돼! 나 어젯밤에 뱀이 나오는 악몽을 꿨거든. 뱀이 하마터면 나를 잡아먹을 뻔 했어.

여 걱정하지 마, Trevor. 뱀은 너를 해치지 않을 거야.

남 알아… 하지만 뱀 생각이 머릿속을 떠나지 않아.

|어휘| excited [형] 신이 난 field trip 현장 학습 popular [형] 인기 있는 nightmare [명] 악몽 almost [부] 거의, 하마터면 hurt [동] 해치다 get ~ out of mind ~가 머릿속을 떠나다

04 ③

M Sorry I'm late.

W It's okay. Thanks for picking me up, Dad.

M You're welcome. Did you have fun at your friend's house?

W I did! Tracy and I made something special for her mom's birthday.

M That was very thoughtful of you. What did you make?

W A candle. We put it in an old glass jar.

M That's very creative! How did you know how to make it?

W She read about it on the internet.

남 늦어서 미안하다.

여 괜찮아요. 데리러 와주셔서 고마워요, 아빠.

남 천만에. 친구 집에서 재미있게 놀았니?

여 네! Tracy랑 저는 그 애 엄마 생신을 위해서 특별한 걸 만들었어요.

남 정말 사려 깊구나. 뭘 만들었는데?

여 양초요. 그걸 오래된 유리병에 넣었어요.

남 그거 아주 창의적인데! 양초 만드는 법을 어떻게 알았니?
여 Tracy가 인터넷에서 그것에 관해 읽었어요.

|해설| 여자는 친구 어머니의 생일을 위해 친구와 함께 양초를 만들었다고 했다.

|어휘| thoughtful [형] 사려 깊은, 친절한 candle [명] 양초 jar [명] 병 creative [형] 창의적인

05 ②

M Hello. I'm here for my checkup.
W Okay. The doctor will be with you in ten minutes. He's seeing another patient right now.
M I understand. How long will this take? I'm planning to see a magic show at 2:00 p.m.
W About an hour. Have you eaten anything in the last twelve hours?
M No, I haven't.
W Good. We'll be able to do all the tests then.

남 안녕하세요. 건강검진 받으러 왔는데요.
여 네. 의사 선생님이 10분 뒤에 봐주실 겁니다. 지금 다른 환자분을 보고 계시거든요.
남 알겠습니다. 검진받는 데 얼마나 걸릴까요? 제가 오후 2시에 마술 공연을 보러 갈 거라서요.
여 한 시간 정도요. 지난 12시간 동안 뭔가 드셨나요?
남 아니요, 안 먹었습니다.
여 좋습니다. 그럼 모든 검사를 할 수 있겠군요.

|어휘| checkup [명] 건강검진 patient [명] 환자

06 ②

W Hi, Mr. Baker. I'm calling to let you know that my son Paul is staying home today.
M Oh, really? That's too bad. Our school is having a career fair today.
W I know. Paul was planning to talk to the firefighters, but he has a high fever.
M I see. I will stop by their booth and pick up an information sheet for Paul.
W I really appreciate it. Paul is sad about missing the fair, but I think that will cheer him up.

여 안녕하세요, Baker 선생님. 제 아들 Paul이 오늘 집에 있을 거라고 말씀드리려고 전화 드렸습니다.
남 아, 정말이요? 너무 아쉽네요. 오늘 학교에서 직업 박람회를 하거든요.
여 알고 있습니다. Paul은 소방관분들과 대화를 나눌 계획이었는데, 고열이 있네요.
남 그렇군요. 제가 그 부스에 들러서 Paul에게 줄 정보지를 가져오겠습니다.
여 정말 고맙습니다. Paul이 박람회에 참석하지 못해서 슬퍼하지만, 그게 아이를 기운 나게 할 것 같아요.

|해설| 직업 박람회에 참석하지 못하게 된 아들에게 교사가 정보지를 구해주겠다고 하자 여자가 감사의 뜻을 표하고 있다.

|어휘| career fair 직업 박람회 firefighter [명] 소방관 high fever 고열 stop by ~에 들르다 information [명] 정보 sheet [명] 시트, (종이) 한 장 appreciate [동] 고마워하다 miss [동] ~에 참가[출석]하지 못하다 cheer ~ up ~을 기운 나게 하다

07 ④

W Gary, have you decided what to buy for our niece?
M Not yet. Do you have something in mind?
W What about a cute doll?
M We gave her a doll for Christmas. How about some balloons?
W That's a good idea, but I want to give her something practical.
M I just remembered that she needs new pajamas.
W Oh, really? Then let's get her some. We can go shopping this afternoon.

여 Gary, 우리 조카를 위해서 뭘 살지 결정했어?
남 아직. 뭐 생각하는 것 있어?
여 귀여운 인형은 어때?
남 크리스마스에 인형을 줬잖아. 풍선은 어떨까?
여 좋은 생각이지만, 뭔가 실용적인 것을 주고 싶어.
남 그 애한테 새 잠옷이 필요하다는 게 막 기억났어.
여 아, 정말? 그러면 그걸 사 주자. 오늘 오후에 쇼핑하러 가면 되겠다.

|어휘| niece [명] (여자) 조카 practical [형] 실용적인 pajama [명] 잠옷, 파자마

08 ④

M Wow, the kitchen smells so good.
W I'm making a flower bouquet for your brother's graduation. It's tomorrow.
M I know. I already told my coach that I would miss baseball practice.
W Oh, good. Can I ask you to do me a favor?
M Sure. What do you need?
W When I was at the flower shop, I forgot to get some ribbon. I need it to tie the bouquet.
M Okay. I can get some for you now.

남 와, 부엌에서 정말 좋은 향기가 나요.
여 네 형의 졸업식을 위한 꽃다발을 만들고 있어. 내일이잖니.
남 알아요. 저 이미 코치님께 야구 연습을 빠질 거라고 말씀드렸어요.
여 아, 잘했다. 내가 부탁을 해도 될까?
남 물론이죠. 뭐가 필요하세요?
여 내가 꽃 가게에 있을 때, 리본 사는 것을 깜박했어. 꽃다발을 묶으려면 그게 필요하거든.
남 알겠어요. 제가 지금 사 오면 되죠.

|어휘| bouquet [명] 꽃다발 graduation [명] 졸업식 do ~ a favor ~에게 호의를 베풀다 tie [동] 묶다

09 ⑤

M Lisa, are you still working on your art project?
W Yeah, but I'm almost done with it. We're having an exhibition of our work from tomorrow through March 10th.
M Cool! Where will the exhibition be held?
W At Rockwell Gallery. There will be more than 100 works by student artists.
M Wow. How many students are a part of the show?
W Twelve, including me.
M I really want to see the exhibition. Can I come?
W Of course. It is open to everyone.

남 Lisa, 너 지금도 미술 프로젝트 작업 중이니?
여 응, 하지만 거의 다했어. 우린 내일부터 3월 10일까지 작품 전시회를 열어.
남 멋지다! 전시회는 어디서 열려?
여 Rockwell Gallery에서. 학생 예술가들의 작품 백 점 이상이 있을 거야.
남 와. 전시회에 학생 몇 명이 참여한 거니?
여 나를 포함해서 열두 명.
남 그 전시회 정말 보고 싶다. 내가 가도 돼?
여 물론이지. 누구나 와도 돼.

|어휘| exhibition [명] 전시(회) artist [명] 예술가 including [전] ~을 포함하여

10 ①

M Attention, Wondermart shoppers. One of the cars in the parking garage is parked in a disabled parking spot. The car is a dark blue SUV. The license plate is 4287. If this is your car, please come to the customer service counter. If you don't come to the counter within fifteen minutes, you will have to pay a fine.

남 Wondermart를 찾아주신 쇼핑객 여러분께 알려드립니다. 주차장에 있는 차량 한 대가 장애인 전용 주차 공간에 주차되어 있습니다. 짙은 파란색 SUV 차량입니다. 차량 번호판은 4287입니다. 이 차량의 소유자는 고객 서비스 카운터로 와주시기 바랍니다. 15분 이내에 카운터로 오지 않으시면, 벌금을 내셔야 합니다.

|어휘| attention [감] 주목하세요, 알립니다 parking garage 주차장 park [동] 주차하다 disabled parking spot 장애인 전용 주차 공간 license plate 번호판 customer [명] 고객 fine [명] 벌금

11 ②

W Adam! It's been a long time since I saw you! How was your winter vacation?
M Hey! I just came back from Vietnam. It was hot and humid the whole time.
W Oh, really? It's been cold in Korea lately. How long were you there?
M Six days.
W What did you do there?
M I went to Hanoi to visit some of my relatives.
W Oh, wow. How was it?
M It was a lot of fun. My aunt taught me how to make Vietnamese noodle soup.

여 Adam! 오랜만에 보네! 겨울 방학 어떻게 보냈니?
남 안녕! 나 막 베트남에서 돌아왔어. 내내 덥고 습하더라.
여 아, 정말? 한국은 요즘 추웠는데. 그곳에서 얼마나 오래 있었어?
남 6일.
여 거기서 뭘 했니?
남 친척들 몇 분을 찾아 뵈러 하노이에 갔었어.
여 우와. 어땠니?
남 정말 재미있었어. 우리 이모가 베트남 국수 만드는 법을 가르쳐 주셨어.

|어휘| humid [형] 습한 lately [부] 최근에

12 ③

M Hey, Jessica! Where are you going?
W I'm going to the Museum of Science and Technology.
M Oh, there is an interesting exhibit on electricity there. Are you going to see it?
W I've seen it already, and it was very good.
M So you're going to see it again?
W No. I'm planning to see the newly built space center.
M Oh! I heard that a world-famous architect designed it. Tell me all about it later.

남 안녕, Jessica! 어디 가는 중이니?
여 과학기술 박물관에 가고 있어.

남 아, 그곳에 전기에 관한 흥미로운 전시가 있지. 그거 보러 가니?
여 그건 이미 봤는데, 정말 좋더라.
남 그래서 다시 보려고?
여 아니. 새로 지은 우주 센터를 관람할 계획이야.
남 아! 세계적으로 유명한 건축가가 그 건물을 설계했다고 들었어. 나중에 그것에 대해 모두 말해줘.

|어휘| electricity [명] 전기 newly [부] 새로 space [명] 우주 world-famous [형] 세계적으로 유명한 architect [명] 건축가 later [부] 나중에

13 ⑤

W Hello. How can I help you?
M Hi. I'd like to buy tickets for the city tour bus.
W Okay. There's a bus that leaves at 2:30.
M Great! I need tickets for two adults and one child.
W Do you want one-way or round-trip tickets?
M One-way tickets, please.
W All right. The tickets for adults are $15 each, and for children, $10 each.
M Okay. Here you are.

여 안녕하세요. 무엇을 도와드릴까요?
남 안녕하세요. 도시 관광버스 표를 사고 싶은데요.
여 네. 2시 30분에 출발하는 버스가 있습니다.
남 잘됐네요! 성인 두 명과 아이 한 명 표가 필요해요.
여 편도 표를 원하세요, 아니면 왕복 표를 원하세요?
남 편도 표로 주세요.
여 알겠습니다. 성인은 한 장에 15달러이고, 아이는 한 장에 10달러입니다.
남 네. 여기 있어요.

|해설| 편도 버스표가 성인은 한 장에 15달러이고 아이는 10달러인데 성인 두 명과 아이 한 명이라고 했으므로, 남자가 지불해야 할 금액은 40달러이다.

|어휘| leave [동] 떠나다, 출발하다 adult [명] 성인, 어른 one-way [형] 편도의 round-trip [형] 왕복의

14 ③

[Cell phone rings.]
W Hello?
M Hello, Mrs. Martin. This is Mr. West from Brooklyn Middle School.
W Good morning, Mr. West.
M I'm calling to let you know that your son Brian won first place in the science fair!
W That's great! He worked so hard on his volcano project.
M Yes, he did a fantastic job. There will be a couple of interviews after school today, so he is going to leave school around six.
W Okay. Thanks for calling.

[휴대전화벨이 울린다.]
여 여보세요?
남 안녕하세요, Martin 씨. 저는 Brooklyn 중학교의 West 교사입니다.
여 안녕하세요, West 선생님.
남 아드님 Brian이 과학 박람회에서 1등을 했다는 소식을 알려드리려고 전화 드렸습니다!
여 잘됐네요! 그 애가 화산 프로젝트를 정말 열심히 했거든요.
남 네, Brian이 정말 훌륭히 해냈죠. 오늘 방과 후에 인터뷰 몇 건이 있을 예정이라서, Brian은 6시쯤 하교하게 될 겁니다.
여 알겠습니다. 전화해 주셔서 감사합니다.

|어휘| win first place 1등을 하다 volcano [명] 화산 a couple of 두서너 개의

15 ④

M Oh no! What's the matter, Molly? You don't look well.
W I have a runny nose and a sore throat.
M I'm sorry to hear that. Would you like me to make you some tea?
W No, thanks. But I do need some medicine. Could you pick some up for me at the pharmacy?
M Sure. I can get you some after I drop my bike off at the repair shop.
W Thank you!

남 아, 저런! 무슨 일이야, Molly? 안색이 안 좋아 보여.
여 콧물이 나고 목도 아파.
남 저런. 내가 차 좀 끓여줄까?
여 아니, 괜찮아. 그런데 나 약이 좀 필요해. 약국에서 좀 사다 줄 수 있어?
남 물론이지. 수리점에 자전거를 맡기고 나서 사 올 수 있겠다.
여 고마워!

|어휘| have a runny nose 콧물이 나다 have a sore throat 목이 아프다 tea [명] 차 medicine [명] 약 pharmacy [명] 약국 repair shop 수리점

16 ④

M Hi, Emily! Why are you up so early? It's Saturday.
W Hi, Dad. I'm going to school to watch the soccer

game. It starts at nine o'clock.

M Oh, that sounds fun. Are any of your friends playing?

W My friend Tina is the goalkeeper. She's the best player on the team.

M That's great! Will you be back for lunch? I'm making spaghetti.

W No. I'm going to see a movie with Sam after the game.

남 안녕, Emily! 왜 이렇게 일찍 깼니? 오늘 토요일인데.

여 아, 아빠. 오늘 축구 시합 보러 학교에 갈 거거든요. 9시에 시작해요.

남 아, 재미있겠구나. 네 친구 중에 경기하는 애가 있니?

여 제 친구 Tina가 골키퍼예요. 그 애는 팀에서 최고의 선수죠.

남 대단하구나! 점심 먹으러 돌아올 거니? 스파게티 만들 건데.

여 아니요. 경기 끝나고 Sam이랑 영화 보러 갈 거예요.

|어휘| be up 잠이 깨어 있다 goalkeeper [명] 골키퍼

17 ①

① **W** Excuse me? How much is this book?
M It's $20, but it's on sale today.

② **W** I would like to check out this book on dolphins.
M Okay. It's due back in seven days.

③ **W** Where is the library? I can't find it.
M It's between the bank and the post office.

④ **W** What are your favorite hobbies?
M My favorite hobbies are reading and camping.

⑤ **W** What will the weather be like tomorrow?
M It's going to be cold and windy.

① **여** 실례합니다. 이 책 얼마인가요?
남 20달러인데, 오늘은 할인 판매하고 있습니다.

② **여** 돌고래에 관한 이 책을 대출하고 싶어요.
남 알겠습니다. 7일 안에 반납하셔야 합니다.

③ **여** 도서관이 어디 있나요? 못 찾겠네요.
남 은행과 우체국 사이에 있어요.

④ **여** 제일 좋아하는 취미가 뭐니?
남 내가 제일 좋아하는 취미는 독서와 캠핑이야.

⑤ **여** 내일 날씨가 어떨까요?
남 춥고 바람이 불 거예요.

|어휘| check out (책 등을) 대출하다 due [형] (언제) ~하기로 되어 있는

18 ⑤

W Hello, Pineland Middle School students. This is an announcement about the school talent show. It will take place in the concert hall on June 2 from 7:00 to 9:00 p.m. The auditions will be held on May 23. If you're interested in participating, please write your name on the sign-up sheet. You can find the sheet in the teachers' office.

여 안녕하세요, Pineland 중학교 학생 여러분. 교내 장기자랑에 관한 발표입니다. 장기자랑은 6월 2일 저녁 7시부터 9시까지 공연장에서 개최될 예정입니다. 오디션은 5월 23일에 열릴 것입니다. 참가하는 데 관심이 있으시다면, 참가 신청서에 이름을 적어 주세요. 신청서는 교무실에서 찾으실 수 있습니다.

|어휘| announcement [명] 발표 take place 개최되다 audition [명] 오디션 participate [동] 참가하다 sign-up sheet 참가 신청서 teachers' office 교무실

19 ②

M Hi, Stacy. Can you still come over to my house tomorrow afternoon?

W Of course I can! I'm really looking forward to meeting your family.

M My parents are going to teach you how to play Yunnori. It's a traditional Korean board game.

W That's sweet of them. Do they need me to bring anything?

M Why don't you bring a game you like to play?

W No problem! I would be happy to.

① I wish I could go, but I have other plans.
③ I don't like Korean food.
④ Do you need some help?
⑤ Thank you for inviting me.

남 안녕, Stacy. 내일 오후에 우리 집에 올 수 있는 것 맞지?

여 당연히 갈 수 있지! 너희 가족 만나는 것을 정말 기대하고 있어.

남 우리 부모님이 너에게 윷놀이하는 법을 가르쳐 주실 거야. 윷놀이는 전통적인 한국의 보드게임이야.

여 정말 친절하시다. 너희 부모님이 내가 뭔가 가져가기를 원하시니?

남 네가 하고 싶은 게임을 가져오는 건 어때?

여 문제없어! 기꺼이 가져갈게.

① 가고 싶지만, 다른 계획이 있어.
③ 나는 한국 음식을 좋아하지 않아.
④ 도움이 필요하니?
⑤ 나를 초대해줘서 고마워.

|어휘| traditional [형] 전통적인

20 ②

W Dad, are you busy tonight?

M No. Why do you ask?

W I want to ask you a favor.

M Sure. What is it?

W Jill and I are going to see a movie tonight. Would you give us a ride to the theater?

M No problem. What time is the movie?

W It starts at 7:00.

M Okay. Tell Jill that we'll pick her up at 6:20.

W <u>That sounds good. Thanks a lot.</u>

① Jill can't go with us tonight.

③ Yes. I'll call you after the movie ends.

④ I'm sure you will really like the movie.

⑤ I'm too busy to join you guys tonight.

여 아빠, 오늘 밤에 바쁘세요?

남 아니. 왜 그러니?

여 부탁 하나 드리고 싶어서요.

남 그래. 뭐니?

여 오늘 밤에 Jill과 제가 영화를 보러 갈 건데요. 극장까지 저희를 좀 태워 주시겠어요?

남 그래. 영화는 몇 시니?

여 7시에 시작해요.

남 알겠다. Jill에게 6시 20분에 우리가 태우러 가겠다고 전해주렴.

여 <u>좋아요. 정말 감사해요.</u>

① Jill은 오늘 밤에 우리와 함께 갈 수 없어요.

③ 네. 영화가 끝난 후에 전화할게요.

④ 아빠는 분명 그 영화를 정말 좋아하실 거예요.

⑤ 나는 너무 바빠서 오늘 밤에 너희와 함께 할 수 없어.

|어휘| ask ~ a favor ~에게 부탁하다 give ~ a ride ~을 태워 주다

MEMO

MEMO

기초부터 실전까지 중학 듣기 완성

1316
LISTENING LEVEL 2

10분 만에 끝내는 영어 수업 준비!

NETutor

NE Tutor는 NE능률이 만든 대한민국 대표 **영어 티칭 플랫폼**으로
영어 수업에 필요한 모든 콘텐츠와 서비스를 제공합니다.

www.netutor.co.kr

· 전국 영어 학원 선생님들이 뽑은 NE Tutor 서비스 TOP 4! ·

교재 수업자료 ELT부터 초중고까지 수백여 종 교재의 부가자료, E-Book,
어휘 문제 마법사 등 믿을 수 있는 영어 수업 자료 제공

커리큘럼 대상별/영역별/수준별 교재 커리큘럼 & 영어 실력에 맞는
교재를 추천하는 레벨테스트 제공

한국 교육과정 기반의 IBT 영어 테스트 어휘+문법+듣기+독해 영역별
실력을 정확히 측정하여, 전국 단위 객관적 지표 제공 & 학습 처방

문법 문제뱅크 NE능률이 엄선한 3만 개 문항 기반의 문법 문제 출제 서비스,
최대 50문항까지 간편하게 객관식&주관식 문제 출제

NE_Tutor

NE 능률

www.nebooks.co.kr

필수 개념부터 서술형 문제까지 한 권에 多 담았다!

with **workbook**

GRAMMAR
Inside

LEVEL 2

A 4-level grammar course
with abundant writing practice

NE_ Neungyule

A Best-Selling
Grammar
Book

전국 **온오프 서점** 판매중

중학 영어에 필요한 모든 것 Inside 시리즈

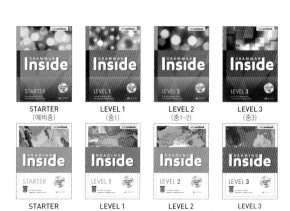

STARTER
(예비중)

LEVEL 1
(중1)

LEVEL 2
(중1-2)

LEVEL 3
(중3)

STARTER
(중1)

LEVEL 1
(중1-2)

LEVEL 2
(중2-3)

LEVEL 3
(중3)

GRAMMAR Inside

· 꼭 알아야 할 중학 영문법 필수 개념만 담아 4단계로 구성
· 많은 양의 문제 풀이로 충분히 연습하여 완벽히 이해
· 서술형 문제를 대폭 수록하여 학교 내신에 철저히 대비
· 풍부한 양의 추가 문제를 수록한 워크북으로 복습 완성

READING Inside

· 문·이과 통합, 타교과 연계 지문이 수록된 원서형 독해서
· 다양한 유형의 질 높은 문제로 내신 및 서술형 시험 대비
· 필수 문법, 어휘, 지문 분석 연습을 위한 코너 수록
· 워크북 추가 문제 풀이로 학습 효과 극대화